Albert Fleischmann

Distributed Systems
Software Design
and Implementation

With Contributions by
J. Tischer and R. Bell

With 250 Figures

Springer-Verlag

Berlin Heidelberg New York
London Paris Tokyo
Hong Kong Barcelona
Budapest

Albert Fleischmann
Burgfriedenstraße 16
D-85276 Pfaffenhofen

ISBN-13: 978-3-642-78614-3   e-ISBN-13: 978-3-642-78612-9
DOI: 10.1007/978-3-642-78612-9

CIP data applied for

© Springer-Verlag Berlin Heidelberg 1994

Softcover reprint of the hardcover 1st edition 1994

Cover Design: Design & Concept, Heidelberg
Typesetting: Data conversion by Springer-Verlag
SPIN 10092300   33/3140 – 5 4 3 2 1 0 – Printed on acid-free paper

Dedicated to
my wife, my children,
and my parents

Preface

The purpose of this book is to make the reader famliar with software engineering for distributed systems. Software engineering is a valuable discipline in the development of software. The reader has surely heard of software systems completed months or years later than scheduled with huge cost overruns, systems which on completion did not provide the performance promised, and systems so catastrophic that they had to be abandoned without ever doing any useful work. Software engineering is the discipline of creating and maintaining software; when used in conjunction with more general methods for effective management its use does reduce the incidence of horrors mentioned above.

The book gives a good impression of software engineering particularly for distributed systems. It emphasises the relationship between software life cycles, methods, tools and project management, and how these constitute the framework of an open software engineering environment, especially in the development of distributed software systems.

There is no closed software engineering environment which can encompass the full range of software missions, just as no single flight plan, airplane or pilot can perform all aviation missions. There are some common activities in software engineering which must be addressed independent of the applied life cycle or methodology. Different life cycles, methods, related tools and project management approaches should fit in such a software engineering framework.

Different software life cycles, development methods, tools and project management methods are described. These can be used as components to be introduced into the open software engineering framework.

As the price of computer systems (especially smaller desktop computers) declines, the attractiveness of connecting computers of varying performance from personal computers to supercomputers increases. It will soon be the case that networked computers will be more common than freestanding computers, and all types of computers will be found in networks. Networks of computers are already used in many applications. Their major advantages over freestanding computers are increased performance and reliability, graceful degradation of performance and simple system growth by the addition of nodes. Users are finding that considerable cost savings can be made by replacing centralized mainframe systems with distributed systems. However the implementation of each distributed system involves different design problems; the purpose of this book is to provide managers and specialists with detailed information about methods for implementing applications on such systems.

In distributed computer systems, application programs are based on several interconnected computers. A distributed program is implemented as a set of processes running on various computer systems which comprise a network. These processes cooperate closely to achieve some common goal like members of a football team. The different processes which constitute the program are executed concurrently by the various computer systems. In order to achieve a common goal the processes must exchange information and synchonise their execution like members of a football team. Thus a software engineering environment for the development of distributed programs must support processes, their distribution among the computers, and the communication and synchronisation of the processes.

In so-called client/server systems parallelism as described above is hidden from the user; clients request support from servers. Client and server computers are connected by a network. The clients run a comfortable user interface (e.g. X-windows) and the main program of an application. The application program uses services offered by servers e.g. database services. Services are used and invoked like procedures in sequential programs. Because these procedures are executed on remote systems this type of procedure invocation is called remote procedure call (RPC). During the execution of a service, the execution of the application program on the client is stopped. Programs for client server systems can be implemented like sequential programs. For a software developer there is no essential difference between normal procedure calls and remote procedure calls. Hiding concurrency allows the use of software development environments as in the case of conventional sequential programs.

Still there are some reasons not to hide concurrency. Some problems can be structured more clearly as a set of concurrent processes even in centralised systems. This type of program is what is known as cooperative program. For more than twenty years operating systems, process control systems for power plants, communication systems, etc., have been structured as cooperative programs. . Additionally, visible concurrency allows the use of the complete power of networked computers. This book considers client/server and concurrent programs and enables the reader to develop such programs.

In the past software engineering research and application had been influenced by the desire to possess or develop a software engineering environment which is suitable for all aspects of software development and for all types of programs and programmers. There are major differences in the development of database and accounting applications, process control systems for controlling power plants, flexible manufacturing and automation systems and telecommunication switching systems. The nature of the application, the type of system to be used, the capabilities of the staff to be employed, and the available budget, all influence the choice of the software engineering environment of a project.

In order to create a software engineering environment which takes into account these aspects, it is necessary to know as much as possible about available software development methods and tools, project management techniques and their suitability to the various types of projects etc.

Before software engineering is considered in detail, the reader is introduced to distributed systems in the first chapter of the book. There is no precise and generally accepted definition which covers all aspects of distributed systems. However the various aspects of distributed systems are explained using a number of examples, mainly process control and communication systems.

Then general aspects of software engineering and the major activities of software development are explained. Next the structure of an open software engineering environment based on these activities is defined. Particular life cycles, methods, tools, and project management techniques can be introduced in this framework for a software engineering environment.

Different types of programs need different software engineering environments. Particular life cycles, methods, tools, and project management techniques are suitable, depending on certain basic properties of the problem to be solved and the intended solution. A classification scheme is explained which allows the major properties of a program such as domain dependent, fault tolerant, time critical, distributed or centralised, to be identified. These influence the selection of the correct software engineering environment. Those aspects which are important in distributed applications are discussed in detail.

Next the different types of software life cycles, methods, tools, and project managements are discussed in detail. The advantages and disadvantages of different life cycles and the basic types of software development methods are explained. These basic concepts are illustrated by several existing software engineering environments: functional decomposition, Michael Jackson´s method, Warrier/Orr method, structured analysis, object oriented development etc. The extent to which each basic concept can be used in the development of distributed systems is discussed.

After discussing software engineering methods mainly used to develop sequential programs, concepts are introduced which are important in the development of distributed software systems. These concepts are processes, process behaviour, interprocess communication and process synchronisation. Various ways of describing process behaviour such as state transition systems, behaviour expressions and communication and synchronisation concepts such as messages, remote procedure calls, semaphores and monitores are described in detail. The integration of these concepts into particular software engineering environments such as LOTOS, Estelle, SDL, REVS is described.

General problems of tool support and project management are described. Tools are strongly to be recommended for the practical use of development methods and they are essential for efficient software development.

Project management must integrate life cycles, methods, tools and particularly the people who will do the work. These different aspects of project mangement are discussed in more detail.

Next a particular software engineering environment for distributed programs is described. This environment is based on the framework of an open software engineering environment but is more detailed; processes, process behaviour, interprocess communication and synchronisation are added. This framework of a software engineering environment for distributed software systems is called SAPP/ PASS (SAPP stands for Structured Analysis of Parallel Programs and PASS stands for Parallel Activities Specification Scheme). SAPP is a particular method for, decomposing a system into subsystems and finally into processes which communicate with each other via messages or shared data. PASS is a structure for specifying each process in detail. It allows to use different message concepts, behaviour description methods and various programming concepts also used for sequential programs especially object oriented programming. *In PASS processes can be considered as subjects which communicate with each other and use objects by invoking methods. Therefore we also use the term subject oriented programming. In the last chapter a more detailed justification is given for the use of that term.*

Tools and project management concepts have been developed based on SAPP and PASS tool concepts. How they enable the efficient use of SAPP/PASS is demonstrated with several examples. However SAPP/PASS is not proposed as a closed software engineering environment rather the user is encouraged to adapt it to his special requirements and environemnt.

Most people understand complex problems better if they are presented graphically. For this reason the concepts introduced in the book are presented graphically and each concept is illustrated by examples.

At the end of each chapter control questions are also provided which allow the reader to check whether he can remember the salient points, and to allow him to apply what he has learnt to specific problems.

Books and papers for further reading are listed at the end of each chapter. These are normally easy to obtain contain more detailed explanation of the contents of the chapter. In addition specialised publications are included in the literature list at the end of the book; these are not always easily acccessible.

The book can be used as a textbook or a reference book. It is not necessary to read it from beginning to end. If the reader is only interested in the software engineering system SAPP/PASS he need only read chapters 10 to 19. Each chapter from 1 to 8 are largely self contained so that reading need not follow any order.

The contents of the book are based on lectures on software engineering for graduate students. Some knowledge of programming is required. The book is recommended for senior undergraduate or graduate students and software developers and managers who intend to develop distributed software.

Acknowlegements:
A book is not created only by its authors. Teachers, friends, and colleagues helped a lot both consciously and unconsciously.

My teachers at the University of Erlangen, Professor *F. Hofmann* and Professor *H. J. Schneider*, provided the foundations of my understanding of asynchronous parallel processes and software engineering.

My friend *P. Holleczek* strongly supported the work on PASS over many years. He facilitated the start of the work as a master thesis together with *J. M. M. Koch*. My colleague R. Besold had the courage to use the first version of PASS in his doctorate and as a consequence made valuable proposals for its practical applications.

W. Effelsberg and *G. Müller* supported me in trying out several ideas for the development of distributed programs and encouraged me to begin this book.

M. Bever contributed significantly through his critical and constructive suggestions to the clarifications of the presentation.

Professor *J. Nehmer* made it possible to adapt the material presented in this book
better to the needs of students in the course of lectures given at the University of
Kaiserslautern.

Professor H. Krumm made valuable suggestions at the very start and the completion of the writing of this book.

*M. Trautner, C. Andres, R. Kummer, W. Mühlbauer, G. Klebes, G. Kragl, C. Feder-
Andres, F. Leugner, S. Pape, K. Urbschad, T. Kunze, G. Lieberknecht, M. Siegmund,*
and many others contributed with their work as colleagues or students to this work.

Finally we are particullary grateful to *Mr. Rossbachs team* at Springer Verlag for
their support and patience.

Pfaffenhofen/Ilm, March 1994   Albert Fleischmann
                                                       Jörg Tischer
                                                       Robert Bell

Contents

Part I

In part I the major properties of distributed systems are described and the basic concepts of software engineering are introduced. The various aspects of a software engineering environment are described in detail. The extend to which each basic concept can be used in the development of distributed systems is discussed.

Part 1

1 Introduction to Distributed Systems and Distributed Software

We describe the main characteristics of distributed systems, their classification and programming techniques. Examples demonstrate the application areas of distributed systems.

1.1 Changes in Computing Technology

During the last two decades the principal application of the information processing and computing technology has been to central computers. Up to several thousand terminals have been connected to such centralised systems. Users sitting in front of their terminals have shared the central processor, the attached equipment for data storage, and the available programs. Each user is granted time slices of the central processor, so that the computer is shared between the various users. The execution of the users' programs is interleaved with several users sharing the execution time of the central processor. This type of system is called a **time sharing system**; it can be regarded as the parallel or concurrent execution of several programs i.e. their execution on several processors. If the same program is executed by several users each execution is in a different state, i.e. each user has his own set of data and the program instruction to be executed next is specific to the user. The execution of a program for a particular user is called a process (A more detailed discussion of the term process is given in section 1.3). Each process is given individual time slices of the central processor.

Several processes can have access to the same data base concurrently. This can lead to a situation in which the database is in an inconsistent state. This happens if for example one process wants to write to the database but access to the central processor is given to another process so that only parts of the new data have been written to the data base. As such other processes can have altered the data base before the first process can again access the central processor.

To keep the data in a consistent state, access to shared data must be synchronised. In order to do this several synchronisation concepts have been developed. Synchronisation allows the execution of processes to be controlled, e.g. a process is stopped until another process has reached a certain state.

Most programs have involved access to data bases. The major task of data base applications has been the retrieval, processing, updating, and replacing of data in data bases. The programs process one or more data bases. The aim has been to develop a data model which covers all data aspects of an organisation in order to avoid that the same data is contained in more than one data base. This has been done by designing a single closed data base or by merging several existing data bases.

The application programs try to meet the requirements of organisational units but they cannot cover the requirements of small groups or individuals. The computer has to be used for the most important tasks of as many users as possible in order to recoup its high cost. There has been no room for individual wishes and requirements. Before starting the development of a new program or changing an existing program the requirements of all the users have to be ascertained. This is a complicated and cumbersome process. The development or alteration of a program has taken a long time, especially if new data which is not available in the existing data bases or was not even foreseen in the data model has been required.

Since the eightes a new trend emerged, personal computers or PC's. These allow the environment of each user to be individually configured. All the computing capability, storage capacity, data, and programs belong to the owner of the PC. This has made it possible to implement programs which meet the reqirements of a single user much better. The exclusive ownership of computer capability has allowed the development of very convenient user interfaces and individually tailored solutions. This has been supported by window oriented operating systems, text processing systems, table calculation programs, graphics programs, etc. PC's have provided a very individual and convenient form of computer access.

In order to provide access to data which is shared by several users PC's have been connected to host computers. PC's, workstations (which can be considered as more powerful PC's) and host computers have been combined in client server systems. The PC's are considered as clients which can use the services provided by specialised servers. The main part of the application program runs on the client but some parts run on specialised servers. For example a data base application together with a convenient user interface runs on a PC separate and apart from the database system which runs on a server. Via special communication services, clients can access the facilities provided by the servers.

Another technique has been to connect computers with each other directly. These loosely coupled computer systems can exchange data directly instead of sharing data stored on a connected server. Instead of shared data, messages are used. These different types of computer networks support different types of applications and programs.

1.2 Characteristics of Distributed Systems

A precise and general definition of a distributed system is not very easy and as far as we know, a definition does not exist which has been generally accepted. Therefore we do what nearly all authors who have written books about different aspects of distributed systems do: we try to give the reader a good understanding of the nature of distributed systems by describing their major characteristics. Experience has shown that this is an adequate substitute for a definition.

Distributed computer environments are based on distributed computer systems which consist of a set of processing components connected by a communication network. The software systems running on the various processing components exchange data through the communication network. This type of system is also called loosely coupled distributed system.

Processing nodes can be composed of several processors which share memory. This shared memory is used to exchange information by the software executed on such a node. This type of system is called a tightly coupled distributed system. The advantages of distributed systems are outlined in nearly all books and papers related to the topic e.g. /SHWA89/, /CODO88/. Below we mention the most important ones /SHWA89/:

- Increased Performance
  Performance is generally defined in terms of average response time and throughput. If processing capability can be located where it is required the response time can be highly reduced. Data can be processed locally before it is sent to other nodes for further processing. This increases throughput.

- Increased reliability
  Normally nodes in a distributed system can take over the tasks of other nodes which are currently out of order. This means that a distributed system continues its work with reduced performance but with little or no reduction of functionality

- Increased flexibility
  Additional functionality can be added to a distributed system or the number of users can be permanently increased. A distributed system allows this system growth by simply adding more processing nodes.

1.3 Parallel or Concurrent Programs

Before we consider the characteristics of distributed software in more detail, we have to consider the concepts of parallel processes and programs.

Parallel or concurrent programs are characterised by a set of statements interrelated by multiple control threads. Each sequence of statements executed by one or more control threads is called a process object /NEHM88a/ /ZOHO88/ (The term 'process' shall be used instead of 'process object' when it is clear from the context that we mean a process object).

The relationship between processes or threads and process objects is shown in the following figure.

processes or threads executing the
statements of the process object

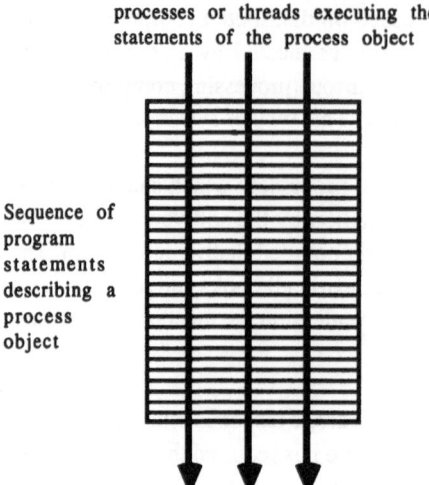

Sequence of
program
statements
describing a
process
object

Figure 1.1: Processes/Threads
and Process Objects

The statements (operations) of the individual processes are executed overlapped or interleaved or both. If a single processor is multiplexed among several concurrent processes, the machine instructions of these processes can only be interleaved in time. For a certain time slice, the processor is assigned to a process in order to execute the statements of a process object. Assigning a processor to another process is called context switching. This type of concurrency is also called multitasking. The following figure shows an example of how a processor is shared between several processes.

processes or threads executing the
statements of the process object

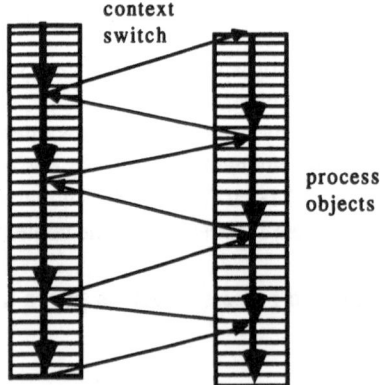

context
switch

process
objects

Figure 1.2: Multitasking

Machine instructions of processes running on different processors can be overlapped at each node at which a processor is available. These are distributed programs.

Concurrent or parallel programs are either interleaved, distributed, or both. For a programmer it is not necessary to know whether multitasking or a distributed system is used to run his program.

Normally the processes of a concurrent program share the resources such as processor, memory, disk, and databases, and if they cooperate in order to reach a common goal they exchange information and synchronise their activities.

Their are two reasons to structure a program in parallel executable process objects:

1. Fine grain parallelism is mainly used to accelerate large numerical computations. This type of parallism is often achieved by using vector processors and the pipelining of operations. It is mainly implemented by hardware.

2. Structural parallelism is used if the structure of the task to be performed is fundamentally parallel. The process objects are a very important concept for structuring programs in certain application areas, e.g. operating systems, real time systems, and communication systems. Especially in real time systems which must react to external events, processes (objects) are used to achieve separation of the tasks /FAPA88/. Each process handles a related set of events and cooperates with other processes to achieve a common purpose. In order to cooperate, processes exchange information either via shared data or via messages.

When considering the software running on a distributed system we can distinguish between networked computing systems and cooperative computing systems /SHWA89/. In the following sections the major aspects and applications of these two distributed software types are discussed.

1.4 Networked Computing

1.4.1 Network Structure and the Remote Procedure Call Concept

Networked computing is characterized by several sequences of jobs which arrive independently at various nodes. The jobs are designed and implemented more or less independently of each other and are only loosely coupled. The distributed system serves primarily as a resource sharing network.

A very common example of resource sharing is the file server. All files are located on a dedicated node in a distributed system. Software components running on other nodes send their file access requests to the file server software. The file server executes these requests and returns the results (to the clients).

In addition to file servers many other kinds of servers such as print servers, compute servers, data base servers, and mail servers have been implemented As with the file server, clients send their requests to the appropriate server and receive the results for further processing. Servers process the requests from the various clients more or less independently of each other. The programs running on the clients can be viewed as being designed and developed independently of each other.

The following figure shows the concept of client/server systems.

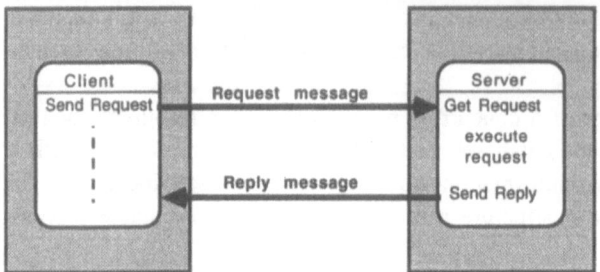

Figure 1.3: The Concept of Client/Server Systems

In client server systems, the clients represent the users of a distributed system and servers represent different operating system functions *or a commonly used application.*

The following figure shows a simple example of a client server system.

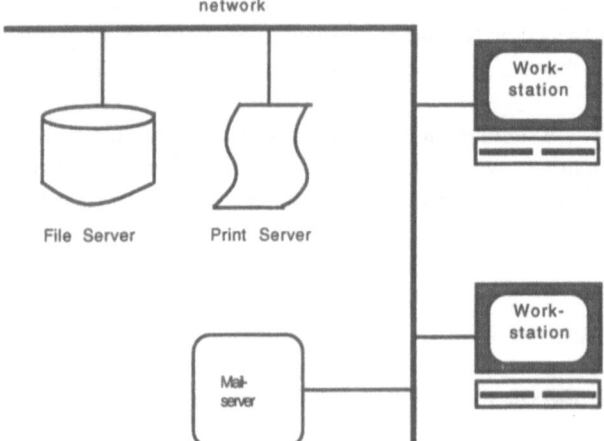

Figure 1.4: A small Client/Server System

This system has a print server, a file server, and the clients (users) which run on workstations (WS) and personal computers (PC). The server software and the client software can run on the same type of computer. The different nodes are connected by a local area network.

From a user's point of view a client/server system can hardly be distinguished from a central system, e.g. a user cannot see whether a file is located on his local system or on a remote file server node. For the user the client/server system appears to be a very convenient and flexible central computing system. Mostly the user does not know whether a file is stored on his PC or on a file server. To the user, the storage capacity of the server appears to be a part of the PC storage capacity. Client/server systems are also very flexible. For a new application a specialised new server can be added e.g. data base systems run on specialised data base servers which have short access times. Data base applications are primarily controlled by the local client; all the data is stored at the data base server and special computations are executed by a compute server (also called number cruncher). The application program running on the client, calls the required functions provided by the servers. This is done mainly by way of remote procedure calls (RPC). An RPC resembles a procedure call except that it is used in distributed systems. The follwing is a description of how the RPC works. The program running on the client looks like a normal sequential program. The services of a particular server are invoked via a remote procedure call. The caller of a remote procedure is stopped until the invoked remote procedure is finished and the server has provided the results to the calling client in the same way that parameters are returned by a procedure. The servers are used in the same way that library procedures are used. This means that remote procedure calls hide the distribution of the functions of the system even at the program level. The programmer does not need to concern himself with the system distribution.

The figure below shows the basic structure of a client/server system.

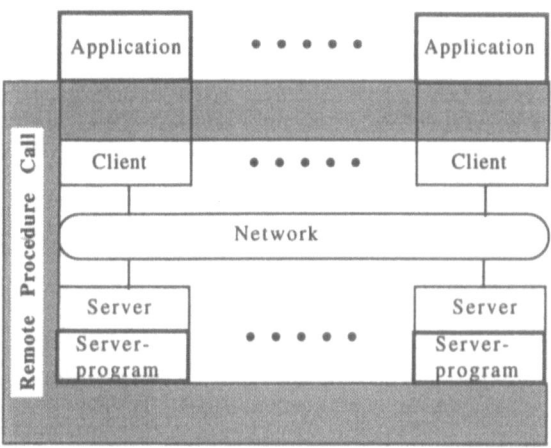

Figure 1.5: Remote
Procedure Call Concept

1.4.2 Distributed Computing Environment (DCE)

The Distributed Computing Environment is a comprehensive integrated set of tools which supports network computing in a heterogenous computing environment. This set of technologies has been selected by the Open Systems Foundation (OSF) to support the development of distributed applications for heterogenous computer networks. The following figure shows the OSF DCE architecture.

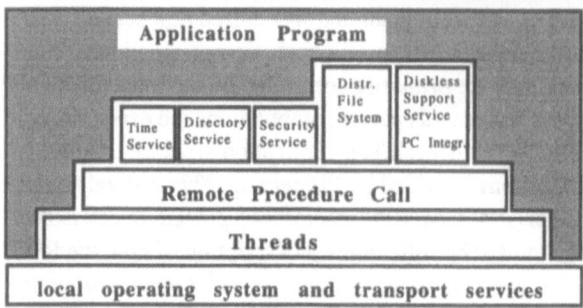

Figure 1.6: Architecture of OSF DCE

In the DCE client and server programs are executed by threads i.e. processes. Threads use an RPC in order to communicate with each other and binary semaphores and conditional variables (described in chapter 7) for synchronisation. In the DCE remote procedure calls are supported by directory services (DCE Call Directory Service) and security services (DCE Security Service). Directory services map logical names to physical addresses. If a client calls a particular service provided by a server, the directory service is used to find the appropriate server. The DCE security service provides features for secure communication and controlled access to resources. Distribute Time Service provides precise clock synchronisation in a distributed system. This is required for event logging, error recovery, etc. The distributed file service allows the sharing of files across the whole system. Finally the diskless support service allows workstations to use background disk files on file servers as if they were local disks /SCHILL93/, /OSF92/.

1.5 Cooperative Computing

In cooperative computing a set of processes runs on several processing nodes. These processes cooperate to reach a common goal and together they form a distributed program. This is different from the client/server systems described above. In cooperative systems the processes which comprise the distributed program are coupled very closely. This means that the closely coupled processes are executed on a loosely coupled system.

In cooperative systems, the distribution of computing capability is not hidden behind prgramming concepts. The different program sections running on different computers comprise a single program; but it can be seen at the programming level that the program sections are executed concurrently. These different program sections are also processes. Processes form a very important concept for central systems, client server systems and cooperative systems. If processes have to work together to perform their task, they must exchange data and synchronise their execution. Programming systems for concurrent systems contain communication and synchronisation concepts. Cooperative programming resembles a human organisation which works together to achieve a common goal. Its members must communicate with each other and must synchronise their activities. The following figure shows the basic structure of cooperative systems.

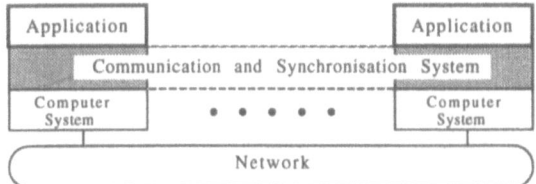

Figure 1.7: Structure of Cooperative Systems

Cooperative systems are mainly used for the automation of technical processes and the implementation of communication software, etc. Technical processes in the mostly part consist of several parallel activities, for example checking the level of a tank has to be done in parallel with controlling the rate of flow of a pump. Therefore the structure of technical process control software is very similar to the structure of the technical process to be controlled. For the automation of technical processes such as manufacturing control systems, the environment of the program, the technical process, is considered as a set of processes which interact with software processes. This means that several processes which can be implemented in different ways work together to perform their task.

1.5.1 Communication Software Systems

A communication system consists of a communication network and the communication software which runs on the various processing nodes (refered to as host systems). The communication software provides a more or less convenient communication service for the application software. The application software on each node uses the communication service to exchange messages with the application software running on other nodes. The communication service is based on the underlying network (A network is usually made up of lines and several switching nodes although most local area networks do not contain switching nodes).

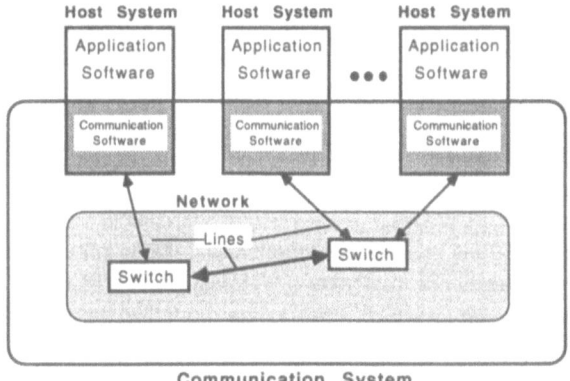

Figure 1.8: Structure of Communication Systems

In order to provide a convenient communication service the communication software systems also exchange messages. This message exchange is based on the simpler communication mechanism provided directly by the network. For example the network provides a communication service which only allows the transfer of a single byte. The communication service provided by the communication software allows byte strings of a fixed or even an unlimited length to be sent or received. This can be implemented in the following way:

The application software of a host system A wants to send a sequence of bytes to the application software of a host system B. The sequence of bytes is given to the communication system by the application system. The communication system on host system A sends a byte with the length of the byte string (the number of bytes) to the communication system on host system B. The communication system on host system B sends back an acknowledgement. This is a byte with a certain value. After the communication software on host system A has received the acknowledgement it starts to transfer the bytes of the byte string. When system B has received the number of bytes indicated in the first byte it again sends an acknowledgement. After sending the acknowledgement, the communication software on host system B gives the received byte string to the application software.

This communication sequence which implements the transfer of a byte string is just a simplistic illustration of what communication software can do.

As the example above shows, the communication between the communication software systems follows well defined rules. These rules are called protocols. The need to provide convenient communication services for the application software leads to software communication protocols which can be extremely complex and must be organised in layers. Each layer offers an improved communication service to the layer above. The widely used reference model for Open Systems Interconnection (OSI) defined by the International Standard Organisation (ISO) proposes seven protocol layers /ISO7498/. Each layer provides a certain service to the layer above. The service provided by a layer is implemented by the protocol specific to its layer and by the services of the layer below. In a host system the services specific to the layer are realized by protocol entities. The layer protocol is defined between protocol entities of the same layer. These exchange information by using the service of the layer below. In each host system there must be at least one entity per layer. The set of entities of different layers in a host system is called a protocol stack. The implementation of these protocol stacks is called communication software. Communication software has the following execution properties /DROB86/:

- interleaved execution of several entities on the same system
- distributed execution of entities of the same layer on different systems.

Interleaved and distributed computations are usually modelled as systems of parallel processes. Processes executing in parallel normally have to exchange information if they are to cooperate in solving a common task. Entities are modelled by one or more processes. Using or providing a service means exchanging infomation with processes representing entities of the layer below or above. The figure above shows

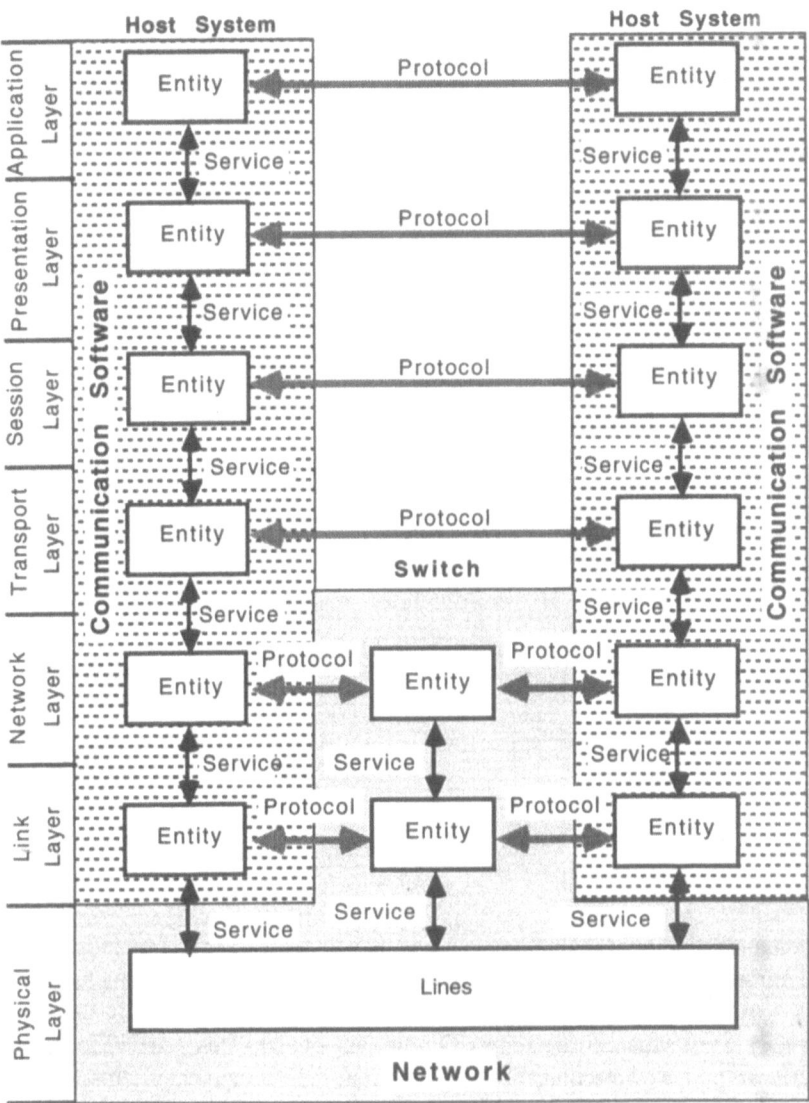

Figure 1.9: Structure of Communication Software

the structure of communication software systems based on the ISO/OSI reference model. Protocol stacks in the different host systems are implemented independently of each other and are embedded in the communication systems. This means that the implementation of a communication system to support communication in a distributed program is itself a distributed program.

1.5.2 Technical Process Control Software Systems

Another important example of cooperative computing is a distributed technical process control system.

The basic structure of technical systems controlled by computer systems is shown in the following figure /NEHM84/.

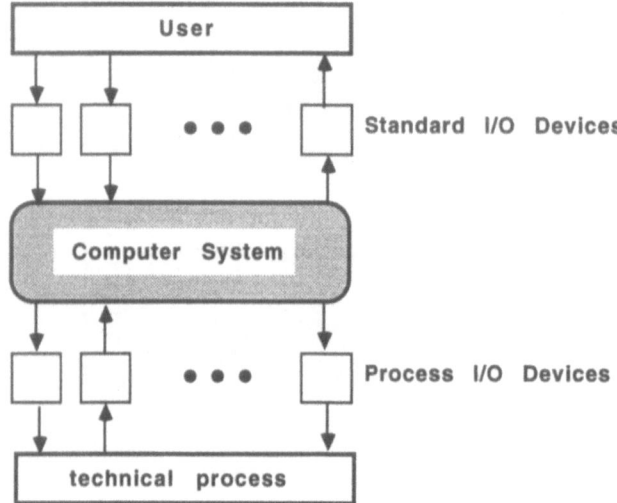

Figure 1.10: Structure of Process Control Systems

The communication between computer systems and technical systems must meet hard realtime requirements, whereas the communication with the user is more or less dialogue-oriented with less emphasis on time conditions (except in the case emergency signals such as fire alarms). For the sake of simplicity, we will focus on the relationship between technical systems and real-time computer systems.

A technical system consists of several mutually independent functional units which communicate via appropriate interfaces with the computer system. Therefore the real time program must react to several simultanous inputs. This implies the structuring of a process control software system that takes into account a number of processes. Each process handles a certain group of signals.

The basic requirement for a process control software system is the capability to follow the changes of the technical system as fast as possible. The infomation in the process control software must be as close as possible to the state of the technical system. The easiest way to achieve this is to design a process for each interface element. This leads to the software system structure shown in the following figure /NEHM84/.

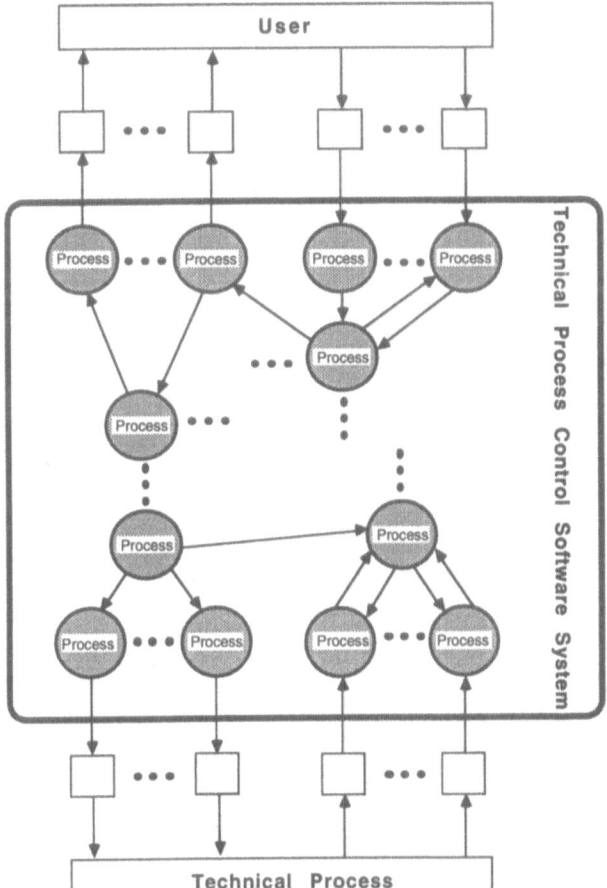

Figure 1.11: Structure of
Process Control Software

Software system processes can run on a single centralized system or can be distributed over several computer systems. In the latter case it is possible to locate the computers close to the device or the plant being controlled. The main advantages of distributed solutions are:
- reduction of wiring costs
- faster response
- easier development and maintenance
- a higher degree of fault tolerance

1.5.3 Electronic Data Interchange (EDI)

Electronic Data Interchange (EDI) is the computer-to-computer exchange of inter- and intracompany technical and business data, based on the use of standards /DIGIT90/ (see figure below of the EDI business model).

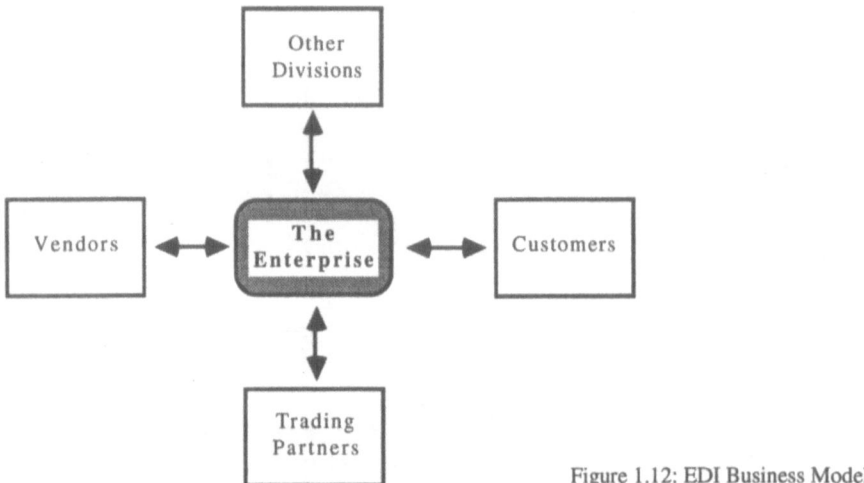

Figure 1.12: EDI Business Model

These data can be structured or unstructured. Exchanging unstructured data follows specific communication standards although the data content is not in a structured format. More important is the exchange of structured data. Examples of structured data exchange are:

– *Trade Data Interchange*
  This type of EDI document exchange is mainly used to automate business processes. Examples of trade data interchanges include a request for quotation (RfQ), purchase orders, purchase order acknowledgements, etc. Each company and industry has its own requirements for the structure and contents of these documents. A number of specific industry and national bodies have been formed with the intention of standardising the format and content of messages. For the chemical industry CEFIC is the EDI standard and for the auto industry the related EDI standard is called ODETTE. The standard defined by CCITT is called EDIFACT. In order to exchange EDIFACT documents very often the CCITT E-Mail standard X.400 is recommended /HILL90/.

– *Electronic Funds Transfer*
  Payment against invoices, electronic point of sale (EPOS) and clearing systems are examples of electronic funds transfer.

- *Technical Data Interchange*
  Improvement in technical communication can play a key role in determining the success of a project. There is a growing demand from traders for communication between their CAD (computer aided design) workstation and the workstations of important vendors.

The following example shows how the different types of EDI interactions are used to handle a business process.

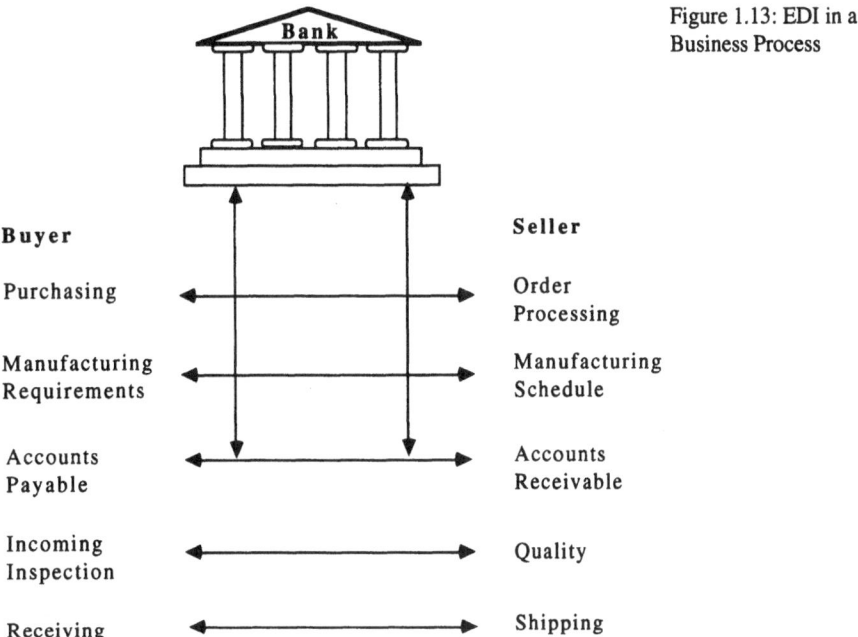

Figure 1.13: EDI in a Business Process

1.5.4 Groupware

In organisations people work together to reach a common goal. The formal interaction between members of an organisation is described by structures and procedures. Additionally there exist informal interactions which are very important. Both types of interactions can and should be supported by computers. Computer Supported Cooperative Work (CSCW) deals with the study and development of computer systems called groupware, which purpose it is to facilitate these formal and informal interactions /ENGLEH88/.
CSCW projects can be classified into four types /ENGLEH88/ namely:
1. Groups which are not geographically distributed and require common access in realtime Examples: presentation software, group decision systems
2. Groups which are geographically distributed and require common access in realtime Examples: video conferencing, screen sharing

3. Asynchronous collaboration among people who are geographically distributed. Examples: notes conferences, joint editing
4. Asynchronous collaboration among people who are not geographically distributed – Examples: project management, personal time schedule management

Groupware requires computers connected by a network. Thus groupware systems are distributed systems. Members of a group share data and exchange messages. Therefore groupware software systems are combinations of network and cooperative computing.

1.6 Combination of Network Computing and Cooperative Computing

Cooperative computing can be combined with client server systems. Processes in a distributed system can have access to servers. From the standpoint of a client server system the processes of a cooperative system can be considered as client processes. In a technical process control software system a process can collect data from the technical process. This data is stored in a file located on a file server node. The following figure shows an example of a combination of a cooperative and a client/ server system. Process A, Process B and Process C form a cooperative software system. Process B and Process C use the file server. This means that process B and process C are clients of the file server.

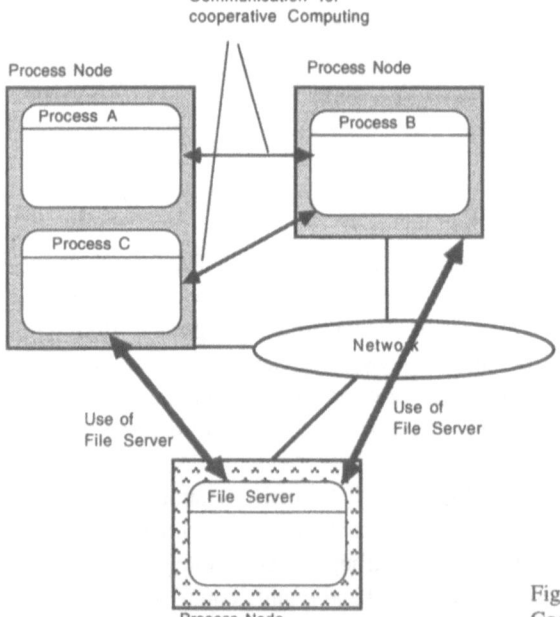

Figure 1.14: Combination of Cooperative and Client Server System

Recommended Reading:

/CODO88/   Couloris G. F., Dollimore J.
            Distributed Systems, Concepts and Design
            Addison-Wesley, Workingham, England 1988
            This book covers only network computing topics. All major aspects
            of network computing are discussed and illustrated with examples.

/SHATZ89/   Shatz S. M., Wang J.-P.
            Distributed Software Engineering
            IEEE Computer Society Press, New York 1989
            This book contains a collection of articles about software engineering
            for distributed systems. In the introduction the characteristics of dis-
            tributed systems are discussed.

Control Questions:

1. Describe the major evolutionary steps in computer systems?
2. What are the characteristics of a distributed system ?
3. What are the characteristics of concurrent/parallel programs?
4. What are threads or processes ?
5. What are the characteristics of network computing?
6. What is the difference between procedure calls and remote procedure calls?
7. What are the major components of DCE?
8. What are the characteristics of cooperative computing?
9. What are the major application areas of distributed computing?

Exercises:

1. Where do distributed systems occur in your professional environment?
2. What are the components of these distributed systems?
3. Are these distributed systems used for network computing or for cooperative
    computing?

2 Software Engineering

This chapter provides a general introduction to software engineering. It describes the major activities in software development and the structure of a software engineering environment .

At the beginning of the computer age, software was developed by hiring a group of programmers to write a program. The style of a program depended on the personal taste and experience of the programmers. A program had the flavour of a work of art, and the programmer was a kind of artist. This method of programming did not cause severe problems at the time the programs that were written were small and not very complex. Then new memory technology based on integrated circuits enormously extended the amount of memory available for programs. This allowed more complex programs to be written for more complex applications; but the methods of producing programs were not appropriate for large programs. They resulted in delays in development schedules, and also produced programs which were very difficult to maintain. The cost of developing software increased enormously. In order to limit the cost explosion, systematic ways of producing software had to be found; these had to be analogous to the paradigms used by engineers to solve problems. Thus software engineering was born. An early definition of software engineering was given by F.L. Bauer at the first major conference /NAUR69/ dedicated to the subject: Software engineering is "the establishment and use of sound engineering principles in order to obtain economically, software that is reliable and works efficiently on real machines."

First the focus of software engineering research was on technical aspects. There was a strong belief that high level programming languages, abstract description languages, program verification techniques, etc. would solve the major problems. However it has gradually been discovered that program development is not only a technical problem. There are many factors which influence the success or failure of a software development project, e.g. the human element which had often been ignored in computing /WEIN71/, /SMITH91/. Social aspects such as the interpersonal relationships between the implementors; the experience of the implementors; relationships with the customer and the nature of the task, e.g. specified or unspecified, are at least as important as the technological factors. The problem is that neither do we know all factors which influence software development nor the extent of the influence of the known factors. In /JON86/ C. Jones investigates the factors which can influence software development. and their importance. According to /JON86/

the extent of the influence of 20 factors is known but unknown for some 25 others (We are sure that there are still more factors which influence software development). It is impossible to find a recipe which optimizes the effect of all known factors. Depending on the experience of a development manager and a development team, different combinations of these factors will be optimal. During the last decades, the focus has been on different factors or combinations of factors. The following section gives a summary of the different aspects of software engineering research in the last decades.

2.1 Milestones in Software Evolution

High Level Programming Languages:
In the last decades the main focus of research was on the technological aspects like improvements in programming languages. High level programming languages such as FORTRAN, Algol60, PL/I were developed and have replaced assembler languages continously since 1960.

Structured Programming:
In 1968 GOTO statements were considered harmful /DIJK68b/. Dijkstra suggested that only conditional clauses (if A then B) , alternative clauses (if A then B1 else B2), choice clauses (case(i) of (B1......Bn)), and repetition clauses (while A repeat B, repeat B until A) and recursive procedures should be used. The programming style based on these clauses has been called structured programming.

Stepwise Refinement:
Program development by stepwise refinement was introduced by Wirth /WIRTH71/ in order to improve the development process. Based on structured programming, a program is developed in a sequence of refinement steps. In each of these steps, one or several instructions of the program is broken down into a sequence of more detailed instructions. This is repeated until an executable version of the program is reached. Stepwise refinement can also be successfully used in programming-in-the-small. However it does not offer much support in defining the structure of large programs.

Abstract Data Types:
Parnas suggested criteria to be used in decomposing systems into modules /PARN72/ Each module should hide design decisions from the other modules of the program.

Software Life Cycle:
In the years 1972 and 1973 there was increased awareness of total software life /OMLE90/. The various activities in software development – requirement engineering, design, coding, testing, and maintenance – were combined to the conventional life cycle /ROYCE70/.

Chief Programmers Team:
During this time, management aids for the development process were also proposed. In order to organize the cooperation of program developers during the different phases of the development process, the chief programers team was suggested /BRO75/. Programmer teams are structured hierarchically like surgical teams. A chief programmer is responsible for all the work but he is supported by several assistants for documentation, administration, etc.

Requirement Specification Techniques:
From 1974 to 1977 research concentrated on requirement specification and design techniques in order to improve program reliability . Research activities were based on the assumption that a complete understanding and precise description of the task to be performed would reduce the total development effort. The first formal or semi-formal techniques for requirement and design specification were developed /WAR74/, /WAR81/, /JACK75/, /CHEN76/, /ROSS77/, /DEMAR79/, /ALF77/. A classification of the major techniques of software specification and design can be found in /ZAVE90/. Chapter 4 in /THDO90/ contains a collection of papers about software specification and design.

Software Development Tools:
Since then, many attempts have been made to develop tools which support a number of the specification and design techniques described above. These tools help to auto-mate the software development process. A collection of papers describing software engineering tools is contained in chapter 5 of /THDO90/.

Computer Aided Software Engineering (CASE):
A set of integrated tools which supports many or all software development activities is called a CASE environment /MCCLU89a/. CASE environments often run on per-sonal computers (PC) or workstations (WS).

Object Oriented Programming:
During the last years, object oriented programming has become a major aspect of software development. There are promising signs that object oriented pro-grammingm will make a major contribution to efficient program development and its reuse /PETE87/.

Methods for developing concurrent and distributed software systems have arisen within this general evolutionary path of software enginering. In the sixties, during the construction of large operating systems, new methods for implementing concur-rent systems were proposed /HANS73/.

In 1965 Dijkstra /DIJK65/ /DIJK68a/ lay the foundation for concurrent systems. He analyzed communication and synchronisation problems in concurrent pro-grams. Subsequently, many communication and synchronisation concepts for con-current systems were published /DIJK65/, /HOARE74/, /CAHA74/, /HANS78/, /HOARE78/. Parallel to the development of these concepts, which are more related to programming languages, several attempts were made to describe concurrent systems at a more abstract level /PETRI62/, /KERA82/, /PETE81/, /REIS82/, /ALF77/, /ALF85a/, /MILN80/, /SDL/, /ESTELLE/, /LOTOS/. The concepts have been used to define the requirements of concurrent systems and are important for implementing operating systems, process control systems, communication systems, and online information systems.

2.2 Software Engineering Activities

The major software engineering activities are requirement specification, design, and implementation. A specification defines the requirements of a system to be developed; the design describes the components of a system and their purpose; and the program is produced in the implementation.

Specification, design, and implementation are intimately interconnected /SWBA82/. It is not possible to separate these activities exactly. A lot depends on the circumstances; whether for example the requirement that the final software system must run on a Unix system is considered to be part of the requirement specification or is an implementation issue. If a company follows the strategy that all applications must be developed on a Unix platform then it is part of the requirement specification.

Every specification is a design and implementation of some other high level specification. *This means that each definition of what is specification, design or implementation is arbitrary.* Despite this, the result of all these activities must be a running system: the implementation. The major activities performed in the software development process are described in more detail in this section. The sequence in which these activities are described does not imply that they are executed in that order. They have to be performed whatever the type of program to be developed. They can be based on different development philosophies or concepts and can be supported by a particular tool set.

2.2.1 Software Requirement Engineering

In general, requirement engineering is a combination of the analysis of the functions of a special system and their documentation in a requirement specification. Software requirement engineering is concerned with analyzing and documenting the requirements of a software system. The analysis of the needs of a software system involves deciding on the task domain, which tasks have to be performed, which subset of the tasks are to be performed by the system to be developed (the objective). Included in the task domain is the environment of the system to be implemented. After that the requirements of the system to be implemented must be analysed. We can distinguish between functional and non- functional requirements /GRCA85/.

The functional requirements describe a model of the solution system. This involves modelling the relevant internal states and the behaviour of the solution system and its environment /GRCA85/. The solution model serves as a vehicle for communication between customers and developers as well as between developers.

Non-functional requirements describe the technical, political, and commercial framework into which the solution system must fit. Examples include the use of a certain database system, hardware system, operating system or programming language. A very important non-functional requirement is that the system to be developed must cooperate with existing software systems. Other non-functional technical requirements might take into consideration portability, interface, performance, and availability constraints.

Examples of political non-functional requirements are the use of components from only a certain vendor or the exclusion of components from certain countries, i.e. embargos.

The best known commercial non-functional requirement is that the solution must be developed within a given maximum cost.

The various requirements are documented in a requirement specification. Different approaches can be applied to the documentation of the results of the requirement analysis in a requirement specification. In /ZAVE90/ three principal approaches are distinguished:

- *Natural language specifications*
  These types of specifications are well known and used the most. The requirements are described in natural language.

- *Operational Specifications*
  An operational model of software requirements can be executed. The description language used in the requirements specification has semantics defined in terms of an execution model.

- *Mathematical Specifications*
  The semantics of a mathematical specification language is based on a proof system. Proofs are used to validate a requirements specification in order to discover inconsistencies, check completeness, and derive consequences of the specification.

In practise requirement specification languages are mostly mixtures of these basic types. Non-functional requirements are usually expressed in natural language. Operational and mathematical requirement specification techniques are mainly restricted to functional requirements. Performance and time constraints can be expressed in some of these requirement specification languages, especially in languages developed to describe communication and process control software systems.

2.2.2 Software Design

As already mentioned, the difference between specification and design is not very clear. Different authors consider the same technology either as a requirement specification technology or as a design technology. Sometimes structured analysis (see chapter 6) is either considered as a specification technology /PRESS87/, /FAIR85/ or a design technology /JON79/, /YATS86/.

In this book we follow /FAIR85/ when defining the different steps of software design, irrespective of the design technology used.

During the software design process a software solution which meets the software requirements definitions is developed. Designing a software system involves identifying the components (subsystems) and describing the functions of these components. According to /FAIR85/, /YATS86/ there are three distinct types of design activities:

- *External design*

  In the external design the observable characteristics of a software system are described. Examples of these characteristics are external behaviour, interfaces, report layouts, data sinks, and data sources. The external design can be considered as the bridge between the requirement analysis and the design activities. This also means that the boundary between specification and external design is very fuzzy. Depending on one's point of view, an activity can be considered as specification or design.

- *Architectural design*

  In the architectural design, the software system is decomposed into functional parts and internal data objects. These components can be further decomposed into subcomponents. In the archtectural design a hierarchy of component levels is built.

- *Detailed design*

  In the detailed design the internal structure of the components developed during the archtectural design are specified in detail. The detailed design includes the data structure and the operations for manipulating the data, and can even include the algorithms which implement the operations.

Three principal approaches to the architectural and detailed design can be distinguished /JON79/,/YATS86/:

- *Functional/Data analysis*

  The traditional view of software is that it is composed of a collection of data that represents some information and a set of functions that manipulate the data. A function always produces the same set of output, results, and global updates from a given set of inputs, arguments, and global data. A system design with the functional/data approach can start with either the functions or the data.

  In the functional analysis approach, the functions which build up a system are identified and described. One way to identify the functions is the top-down approach. The design starts with the global function of the system to be designed and is broken down into levels of functions. Each function level is based on the function of the level below. The process of decomposition ends when a function level is mapped on to the functions of an existing system, i.e. programming language or operating system.

In the data analysis approach, the starting points are the data objects of a system and their structure. The structure of the data defines the structure of the program. After the definition of the data structures, the functions which manipulate the data are defined.

- *Object-oriented analysis*
  Objects are a combination of data and functions. An object describes the possible values and structure of a data object together with the operations which can be executed on it. The operations define what can be done to a data object. There is no other way to manipulate the data object except with these operations. Data types represent objects found in the solution space. Many objects can be described by the same general description. A description of one or more similar objects is called an object class. Each single object can be considered as an instance of an object class.
  A class can be modified to construct another class. The new class inherits every property of the class from which it is derived. A class which is derived from another class is called a subclass. The class from which the subclass is derived is called a superclass.
  Objects use the operations of other objects to implement their own operations. In order to invoke the operations of another object, the invoking object sends a message to the invoked object. A message consists of a selector which identifies the operations to be invoked and a set of parameters. The semantics of an operation invocation and a procedure invocation are the same.
  There have been many attempts to extend object-oriented programming in the direction of concurrency /YOTO87/. There is a widespread opinion that there is no contradiction between concurrency and object-oriented programming. In order to avoid confusion we will discuss both programming paradigms separately. In later sections we will discuss concurrent object oriented programming in more detail.
  An object-oriented design follows five major steps /BOOCH86/.
  1. Objects and object classes which are used to construct the software solution are identified.
  2. The operations for each object and object class are defined.
  3. The visibility of each object to other objects is defined.
  4. The interface of each object is defined.
  5. Each object is implemented.

- *Process oriented design*
  As discussed in the previous chapter, the process concept is used when the system requirements demand that several tasks be carried out simultanously /AXFO89/. Concurrent programming is important in real-time computing (structural parallelism) and as well as parallel computing (fine grain parallelism). The decomposition of the software system into processes is the most important design step, particularly for real-time systems. Real-time systems communicate with their environment i.e. the technical process which is controlled; or

another node in a distributed system; and processes represent components of the environment in a software system (see section 2.2).

Normally process-oriented designs are completed by data/function or object-oriented design components. Processes use functions to transform data and perform operations on an object.

The concept of a module is very closely related to program design. Modules are elements which are individually named and addressed i./PRESS87/. These elements are normally identical to components defined during the architectural design. A good design is characterised by a strong cohesion between the parts of a module and weak coupling between parts of different modules. In data/function-oriented designs, modules are composed of functions which are similar or manipulate the same set of global data space. In data-oriented design, a module consists of a data object and the functions which manipulate it. In object-oriented design an object is identical to a module. One or more processes can comprise a module.

A detailed dicussion of the module concepts can be found in many books on software engineering: e.g. /FAIR85/, /PRESS87/.

2.2.3 Implementation and Testing

As requirement specification and design activities can overlap, so it is with design and implementation these activities also cannot be exactly separated. Implementation involves the transformation of the software design into a representation which can be executed on a computer system. This means that the modules defined during the design phase must be described in a high level programming language. One style of design involves the use of a high level programming language with detailed comments. The comments ensure that the structure of the design can be seen.

The starting point of the implementation is the software design. The most suitable prgramming language for the particular design technique must be chosen. If a data/function oriented design technique is used, standard programming languages such as C or Cobol can be used. The situation is different if an object-oriented or process-oriented design technique is being used. Here the programming language should support the particular features of these design techniques. A programming language which supports concepts such as objects, object classes, and inheritance, makes it easy to transform an object-oriented design into a computer program. Examples of such languages are Smalltalk-80, Ada, and C++. Fortran and Cobol have also been supplemented by language features which support object-oriented programming.

The implementation of each module must be tested to determine whether it satisfies the definition of the module: this is the module test. In the integration test the whole system is tested to determine whether it fulfils the requirements.

At module level, white box tests are executed. Here the test cases are derived from the internal structure of the program. Such a test should execute all the statements and branches in the program to check whether the modules behave as defined in the design.

Black box test cases are derived from the requirement specification of the system to be tested. Therefore black box testing is only used in the acceptance tests of the final implementation. In a black box test the implementation of the system is not checked. Methods for black box testing include random testing, testing at boundary values, and putting the system under stress by inducing errors.

2.2.4 Project Management

Projects are activities which are carried out to meet established goals given certain budget, time, and quality objectives (these are known as the parameters of the project). In our special case, these activities are the development of software systems. Project management must optimize the project parameters. A successfully managed project is one that is completed with the specified level of quality, within budget, and on or before the deadline.

A project moves through three different phases:

Definition and planning of a project:
When the nucleus of the project team has been assembled the goals of the project has to be clarified. All members of this team and the customer must have a common understanding of the project goals. In the definition phase the goals of the project are discussed and analysed. The project definition and the final objectives of the project are written down. The objectives can be separated into those that are mandatory and those that are optional. Different solution strategies are developed and evaluated and a course of actions based on the chosen solution strategy is defined.

In the subsequent planning steps the solution strategy is refined to a detailed project plan /CORI85/. The work to be done is broken down into subunits or work packages. These are collectively known as the Work Breakdown Structure /TAUS80/. The requirements of each subunit or work package are defined. Then the time dimension can be planned. This has to take into account the limited resources (manpower, skills, etc.) that are available. For each subunit the required development time and resources are defined. Next the sequence in which the subunits must be completed is decided in order to document the time schedule of the project. Several techniques have been developed for controlling the time schedule of a project e.g. PERT, CPM, GANTT. An overview of these techniques and references to further literature can be found in /CORI85/.

The budget plan is derived from the time schedule. It contains the cost components of each work package. The cost components are for example labour, overhead, equipment, administration, offices and profit (if applicable).

Implemention of a project plan:
The implemention of a project plan involves the execution of the following four tasks:

Organization:
The organization of a software project involves the identification of tasks, the grouping of these tasks and the design of a formal structure and authority relationships between these tasks /THAY88/. In /THAY88/ several examples of organisational structures, e.g. project, matrix, functional, are described. In addition to this overall organisational structure a software project is organized around software teams usually between three and seven teams. Each team is assigned a certain task in accordance with the breakdown of the work. An important example of such teams, is the chief programmer team /BRO75/. This team consists of between three and five permanently assigned team members. A chief programmer is supported by a deputy chief programmer, back-up programmers, a program librarian, and other auxilary programmers and administrative personnel. The chief programmer is responsible for all the technical and managerial aspects of the projects which are assigned to his team. The backup programmer must be able to replace the chief programmer during any period of absence. The librarian maintains all documents, files, code versions, etc., and does all the administrative work.

Staffing:
The staffing of a software engineering project consists of filling and keeping filled the positions that were established by the project organisational structure /THAY88/. This includes selecting candidates for certain positions and training staff in particular skills. It is important that consideration be given not only to the technical matters but also to the social aspects in a team. If there is a good social relationship between the members of the team, then the technical, scheduling, financial planning, and other problems etc. can be solved much easier.

Direction:
The direction of a software project involves the motivation and coordination of the development team towards the attainment of the common goal: a project completed on time, with the desired quality, within the budget. Direction also includes keeping in touch with the customer in order to check whether the implementation satisfies his requirements.

Controlling:
Controlling a software project involves all the management activities which ensure that a project follows the time schedule and the financial plan. Controlling involves checking whether milestones are met and, if they can not be met, the initiation of remedial action. If a project is exceeding the budget a suitable response is also needed. Controlling also includes the adaptation of existing plans to reality.

Completing a project:
The goal of the project is to obtain acceptance by the client. This means that the final result must satisfy the requirements of the client. In the final but usually very cumbersome step, the documentation of a software engineering project must be

completed. The project documentation must be prepared for the maintenance phase. This might involve transferring the documentation of the project to the maintenance department. In this case the maintenance personnel must be trained in using the software and must know the internal structure of the software.

2.3 Software Engineering Environments

The purpose of a software engineering environment is to support a developer or a development team in performing all the activities previously described and to overcome all the various problems which influence the evolution of the project.

Software engineering encompasses three elements /CHAR86/; /PRESS87/:

Procedures:
These describe the chain of activities - requirement specification, design, implementation and testing - which produces a particular software product. These activities can be executed in different orders. In the extreme case, the software development activities are executed exactly in the order: specification, design, implementation and testing. This sequence follows the conventional life cycle (see chapter 5). At the other extreme, the different activities follows no particular order: little specification is followed by a little design, a lot of programming, much more testing, a little design, and so on. Between these extremes several variations can be defined. These procedures are often referred to as software engineering paradigms or software life cycles.

Methods:
These provide the techniques which are used to define, describe, abstract, modify, refine, and document the software product. In order to collect and document requirements, several methods are suggested (this also applies to the design and programming activities). In the sections above, we gave an outline of these techniques. The methods are based on the procedures. Different methods are more suited to different development procedures. If a certain method forces one to finish a requirement specification before one can move on to the design activities, a software system can only be developed according to the conventional life cycle mentioned above.

Tools:
These provide automated or semi-automated support for methods.

Software development management maintains harmony between procedures, methods, tools and people in order to reach the goal.

The procedures, methods, tools and management techniques required to produce a software system are known collectively as a software engineering environment. The following figure shows the relationship of all aspects of a software engineering environment.

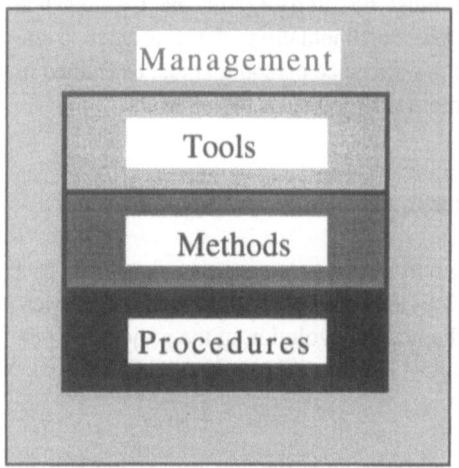

Figure 2.1: Aspects of a Software
Engineering Environment

If a complex software system is to be developed it is sensible to use procedures, methods, management techniques, and tools which are appropriate for the type of software being produced. Techniques used by programmers to implement an accounting system are different from those used to implement a process control system. For the development of a distributed application such as communication software, other technologies and paradigms must be used than those for the implementation of a computer game.

The main properties of the final software system which influence the choice of a software engineering environment are discussed in chapter 3.

Recommended Reading

/OMLE90/   Oman P. W., Lewis T. G. (Ed)
            Milestones in Software Engineering
            IEEE Press, Washington 1990
            This tutorial contains a collection of important articles about different
            aspects of software engineering. It gives a good overview of the evo-
            lution of software development.

/CHAR86/   Charette R. N.
            Software Engineering Environments
            McGraw Hill, New York 1986
            In this book software development activities and their relationship to
            software engineering environments are discussed in detail.

/MABU87/   Marco A. , Buxton J.
            The Craft of Software Engineering
            Addison Wesley, International Computer Science Series, Working-
            ham, England 1987
            This book contains a very practical discussion of various aspects of
            software development.

Control Questions:

1. What are the milestones in software engineering? Explain them.
2. What are the major software engineering activities? Explain them.
3. What are the most important aspects of a software engineering environment ?
4. Explain the relationship between the different components of a software engineering environment?

Exercises:

1. What milestones of software engineering are known in your professional environment?
2. Identify in the software development process of your professional environment
   the different software development activities.
3. Compare the structure of your software engineering environment with the structure of the software engineering environment described in this book.

3 Classification of Software System Types

In this chapter a classification scheme for programs is presented and the different types of software are described. These need different versions of the software environments described in chapter 2.

In this chapter the different aspects of software engineering environments are discussed. Just as there is no one programming language which is suitable for all types of applications, so there is no software engineering environment which is correct for all types of projects. Where it is necessary to implement programs embedded in a more complex environment, methods must be used to specify the interaction of the program with its environment.

If there are time requirements, then specification, design and implementation methods must be used that allow the description of these requirements. There are special requirements in a software engineering environment for the development of fault tolerant programs. Designing a concurrent or distributed program is different from designing a sequential program. Even the hardware architecture influences the choice of the right software engineering environment. In order to use the special features of a particular hardware architecture, special techniques are required.

In summary the type of software system depends on the following major characteristics:

- The *relationship to the environment,* e.g. interactive, non-interactive
- The *general system behaviour,* e.g. time constraints, fault tolerance
- The *expected program type,* e.g. sequential or concurrent
- The *system architecture* on which the software will run, e.g. distributed or not distributed

These characteristics are covered by different aspects of a software engineering environment. The relationship of a software system to the environment requires certain software life cycles and methods. In order to describe time constraints for example a specification method must have corresponding language features. The system architecure can be hidden by tools. A compiler can translate a program into code which is executed concurrently.

In the following sections, the characteristics of software systems and their relationship to different aspects of software engineering environments are described.

3.1 Relationship to the Environment

Software systems can be classified how the tasks to be performed and the software system interact /GIDD84/, /LEH80/, /MABU87/.

3.1.1 Domain Independent Software

Domain independent software is characterized by the independence of the task to be performed and the class of tasks which can be performed. The task does not change with respect to time. Domain independent software can by divided into two subclasses /LEH80/, /MABU87/:
- Programmable systems (P-type).
- Specifiable systems (S-type) and

In P-type systems the requirements can be exactly specified and an implementation can be achieved which exactly satisfies the requirements. The development process is the selection of one of many good solutions. Examples of P-type systems include numerical and sorting algorithmns.

In the case of S-type systems a precise definition of the task can be given but only an approximate implementation is possible. In the development process a solution has to be found which is as close as possible to the original requirements. Examples of S-type systems include game playing systems and some mathematical problems. Chess programs have a precise specification: "Win each game". However we know that no such program exists. All chess programs try to come as close as possible to the "Always win" requirement.

In order to develop domain independent software, the specification, design, and implementation of a program can be executed in that order. The specification can be completed before the design activities start. The specification methods allow only complete specifications. Specification tools can check the completeness of a specification.

Domain independent tasks are not common in ordinary program development. Normally requirements change or requirements are not completely known. A software system can change its own requirements. After the development of a software system is the task to be performed is better understood. New requirements are discovered or the importance of the requirements is changed. This leads to domain dependent software systems.

3.1.2 Domain Dependent Software

The main characteristic of domain dependent (DD) software is the change of requirements with time. This happens either because the class of tasks to be performed changes or because the existence of the system affects the real world environment in some way /MABU87/. In /MABU87/ and /LEH80/ domain dependent software systems are called evolutionary systems. According to /GIDD84/ DD-systems can be divided into DD-software experimental (DDEX) and DD-software embedded (DDEM) systems. The development process of DDEX systems is characterized by an inherent uncertainty about the range of tasks to be performed. Examples of this type of software include the investigation of economics or physical phenomena. The use of DDEX software can lead to the specification of software with different areas or applications, e.g. an economic model which can be used in a management information system.

DDEM software is characterized by the interdependence between the class of tasks to be performed and the software. The software can change the area of application and hence the statement of the task to be performed. Examples of DDEM software include office automation systems, software engineering systems, successive generations of large scale operating systems, and production control systems. The following figure shows the dependency of a software system on its environment and how a software system changes its environment.

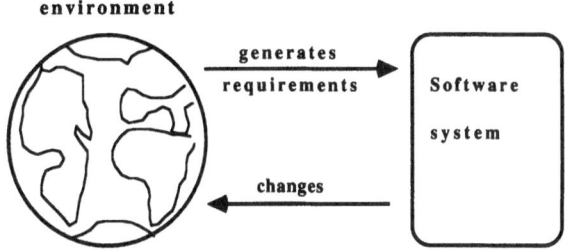

Figure 3.1: Domain dependent Software Systems

In order to develop domain dependent software systems, appropriate life cycles and methods must be applied. Life cycles should be used which start with incomplete requirements and continue with the design and implementation of an incomplete system. After this the development process continues with a requirement specification phase. Then this second stage is designed and implemented, and so on. This method of software development also implies that the specification method must allow the expression of incomplete requirements. The design and the design method must be flexible in order to survive the many changes.

3.2 General Behaviour

There are two major aspects to software which can increase the complexity of a system enormously:
- time constraints
- fault tolerance requirements

Specific methods have to be used to design a system that take these aspects into consideration, since they can influence the choice of software engineering environment and methods.

3.2.1 Time constraints

Software systems must respond in a time dictated by the nature of the task. The following system classes which relate to increasing time requirements can be distinguished:

- *Non real-time requirements.*

Examples of software systems without time restrictions are batch systems. A batch system obtains the input, computes the results, and provides the output when the job is done.

- *Weak real-time requirements.*

Examples of software systems with weak time requirements are dialogue systems. Here humans represent the environment. Queries are typed in and the system has to answer in a reasonable time. A long response time is inconvenient for the user but is normally not disastrous.

- *Hard real-time requirements.*

A system which must meet time requirements in order to work correctly is called a hard real-time system. Examples of hard real-time systems are communication and process control systems.

Communication systems

Several computers can be interconnected to form a network which is used to exchange packets of information. The environment of a computer consists of all the other computers to which it is connected. A computer can communicate with its environment by sending information packages to other computers in the network. In order to confirm that an information packet has arrived at its destination, the communication rules (also called communication protocols) may require that the receiver send back an acknowledgement packet. If the response packet does not arrive within a certain period of time, the sender of the data package assumes that the receiver is not working or the packet was lost in the network. Time-outs are very important in communication protocols. This is the only means of telling that a computer in a network is down. A computer must reply within a finite period of time; otherwise the sender assumes that the receiver is down. This example shows how important time constraints are in communication systems.

Process control systems

When a technical process such as an assembly line is controlled by a computer system, the software in the computer interacts with the technical system. This interaction leads to two major real-time requirements /LAUB84/:

- The control system has to perform actions at a certain point in time.
- The control system has to react to stochastically occurring events within the technical process.

For both requirements, the system must guarantee a certain reaction time; otherwise the results could be disastrous .

A specification method must allow the expression of time requirements. Tools can help to simulate which provide a first impression as to whether a system will perform as required. Specification methods which are very effective when specifying editors, can be completely inappropriate for communication systems.

3.2.2 System Reliability

According to /RALETR78/ system reliability is related to the success with which a system provides the service specified. There are two approaches to constructing highly reliable systems: there is the **fault intolerance approach** and the **fault tolerance** approach /AVIZ76/. Fault intolerance encompasses all the known techniques such as requirements definitions, walkthroughs, proving and testing, which ensure that software contains no faults. Experience has shown however that these techniques can help only to reduce faults but never guarantee their elimination. Fault intolerance is the method normally used in software engineering. Fault tolerance incorporates techniques which ensure an acceptable service in spite of faults that remain after the use of fault intolerant methods. Redundant elements are introduced into a system in order to replace faulty components. In the absence of faults these elements are not necessary to provide the specified service. If a software system is to be fault tolerant, the neccessary design decisions have to be made and appropriate methods used. The requirement of fault tolerance in developing a software system can increase its complexity enormously. In order to develop fault tolerant systems it is necessary to use appropriate methods to specify the type and degree of fault tolerance. These methods must be incorporated into the software engineering environment.

3.3 Program Types

Whether a sequential or parallel program is to be developed it depends on the type of application, the computer system to be used, and finally the personal taste of the programmer . The methods for developing sequential and parallel programs are very different so therefore a choice must be made before the beginning of program development and the software engineering environment suitable to the type of programming used.

Sequential Programs are characterized by a set of statements interrelated by a single thread of control /NEHM88a/. From the point of view of the user, a sequential program is executed by one single process, although there may be hidden parallelism such as vector or array computation (which is not considered here). In sequential programs, one is only concerned with the input/output behaviour. The input/output behaviour is the relation between the starting and termination state of a program /ALF85a/. A lot of business and engineering software has been developed as sequential programs. Compilers and editors for PCs are typical examples.

In chapter 2 the characteristics of parallel or concurrent programs were already discussed. **Parallel or concurrent Programs** are characterised by a set of statements interrelated by multiple threads of control. Whether a concurrent or sequential program is to be implemented depends on the computer system and the requirements

Fine grain parallelism is normally hidden by compilers or by the hardware system. A sequential program is split into several concurrent processes by the compiler. These processes are executed in parallel by a multiprocessor system (see next section). Processor pipelines can execute one statement while the next statement is being transferred from the memory to the processor. Because fine grain parallism is hidden by compilers or by the hardware architecture it has almost no influence on the software engineering methods.

This is different from structural parallelism. Structural parallelism is of fundamental importance in some applications. As described in chapter 2, process control and communication software systems especially are modelled as systems of concurrent processes. In order to implement systems of this type, special description and programming techniques have to be used. These programming techniques are the main topic of this book. We describe these techniques in considerable detail in the next chapters.

3.4 Computer Architecture

The main components of a computer are the processors and the memory. Different types of computer systems can be distinginshed /NEHM88b/ according to the relationships between these components.

- Centralized computer systems

In these systems there is exactly one processor which has access to the memory (see figure below).

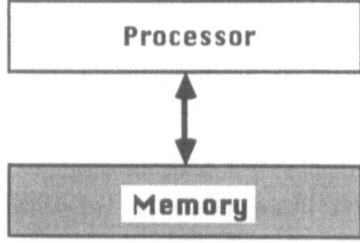

Figure 3.2: Structure of
Centralized Computer System

- Multiprocessor systems

Multiple processors share a single memory (see figure).

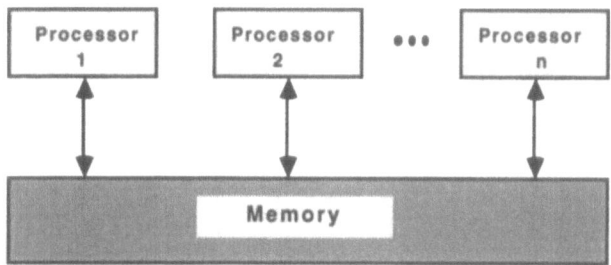

Figure 3.3: Structure of
a Multiprocessor System

- Distributed systems

Defining a distributed system is very difficult. Many controversial definitions are to be found e.g. in /NEHM88b/, /ENSL78/, /SLKR87/. In this book we follow the definition contained in /BSTA88/: A physically distributed system consists of multiple autonomous processors, each of which has its own primary memory. In a distributed system all communication is done by messages which are exchanged via a message transport system (see figure).

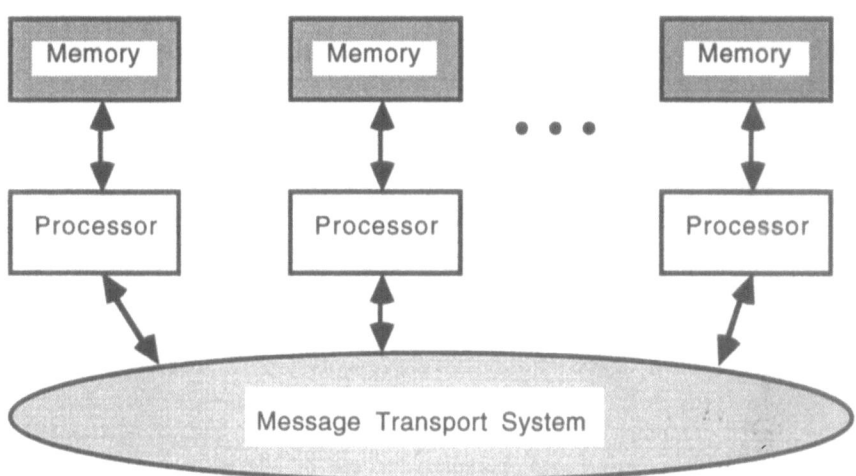

Figure 3.4: Structure of a distributed System

- Distributed Multiprocessor Systems

A distributed multiprocessor system consists of multiple multiprocessor systems connected by a message transport system (see figure).

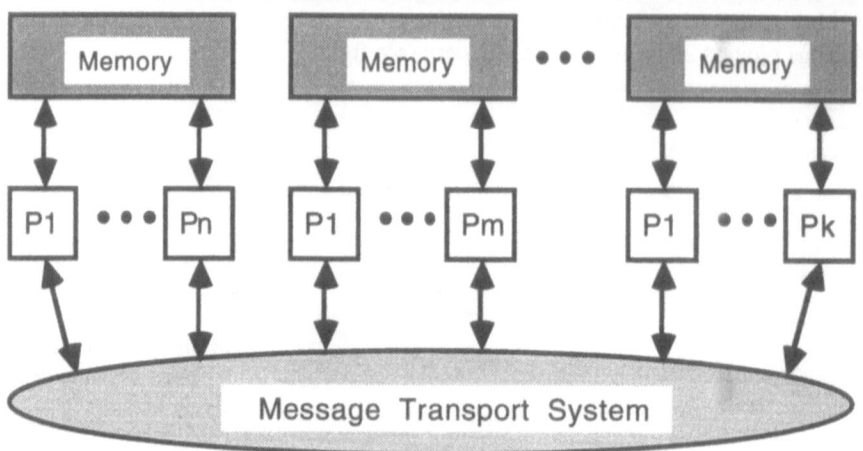

Figure 3.5: Structure of distributed Multiprocessor System

As well as the program type, the system architecture can be hidden by tools such as precompilers or compilers. Only if the special architecture of a system is to be used explicitly, is it necessary to take it into account in the software development. As already described the development of a distributed system that runs on a distributed system architecure requires special methods. In this book we assume that a developer knows that he has to implement a distributed software system (see chapter 2). This way he can use the advantages of distributed systems, explicitly.

3.5 Examples

Several software systems are considered in order to illustrate the classifications introduced in the previous sections. In the table below the properties of an editor, a compiler, a fast Fourier transformation, a chess program, a flight reservation system, a physical model, and a flight control system are described. There are certain characteristics which a program can have but must not necessarily have. In the table optional properties are indicated by a question mark, e.g. an editor can be but must not necessarily be fault tolerant.Some characteristics can be alternatives, e.g. a flight reservation system can run on a centralized or distributed system such as a distributed data base system.

Properties / Program	Relationship to the Environment — Domain independent: S-Type	P-Type	Domain Dependent: Emb.	Exp.	General Behavior — fault tol.	Time Constraints: no	weak	hard	Program Type: seq.	par.	System Architecture: cent.	cent.Mult.	dist.	dist. Mult.
Fasst Fourier	x					x			x		x			
physical model				x		x			x		x			
Chess		x				x			x		x			
Editor			x		x?		x		x		x			
Compiler	x					x			x		x			
Flight Reservation			x				x			x	x		x	
Flight Control System			x		x			x		x		x	x	x

3.6 Discussion

We are aware that the classification introduced in the previous sections may not be sufficient, but they cover a wide spectrum of software systems. One area which is not fully covered is artificial intelligence (AI). AI requires knowledge /RICH83/. but because knowledge is voluminous, hard to characterize accurately, and is constantly changing, special techniques are requested to represent it. It is possible to solve AI problems, e.g. theorem proving and natural language understanding, without using AI techniques, although these solutions are not likely to be very good. Currently, AI systems are implemented in LISP or PROLOG. These languages can be characterised as sequential but this does not say much about the specific tasks. This shows that our software taxonomy is only a first step in describing the complexity of a software system; nevertheless we think it can help in the traditional areas of software.

Recommended Reading:

/MABU87/   Marco A., Buxton J.
              The Craft of Software Engineering
              Addison Wesley, International Computer Science Series, Working-
              ham, England 1987
              The method used for classifying software is not the same as in this
              book.

/GIDD84/   Giddings V. R.
              Accomodating Incertainty in Software Design
              Communications of the ACM, May 1984
              In this article various aspects of program classification are discussed
              in detail.

Control Questions:

1. What are major the characteristics of program classification? Explain them?
2. Give some examples of programs and classify them according to the schema given in this book?

Exercises:

1. Classify the programs in your professional environment.
2. Compare your software engineering environment with your program classification.

4 Software Life Cycles

The different software life cycles and their advantages and disadvantages are explained. It is discussed which life cycles are apropriate for the different types of programms as described in chapter 3.

Implementing computer systems involves certain basic tasks /WEKE89/: task identification, solution definition i.e. requirements analysis, logical and physical design, programming and implementation, program testing and maintenance (see also chapter 2). All these tasks have to be performed but they do not have to be done in a specific order. There are also different approaches to defining the boundaries between the requirements analysis, design, implementation, and testing. These depend on the methods used in a particular phase.

The sequence in which these different tasks are performed and which technologies are used reflect different methods for software development.

In the following sections some of the main methods for software development are described and their suitability for the implementation of communication and process control software systems is discussed. The following basic methods for software development can be distinguished /WEG84/, /AGRES86b/, /BACC83/:

- the conventional life cycle and its variants /ROYCE70/, /BOEHM76/, /AGRES86a/, /PETE78/, /KEFR81/,
- prototyping /LANTZ/, /AGRES86b/, /TAST82/, /CAMA83/, /SCHA83/,
- the operational life cycle /AGRES86b/, /ZAVE84/,
- the transformational paradigm /AGRES86b/, /BAUER82/, /PAST83/
- the knowledge based life cycle /BACC83/.

4.1 The Conventional Life Cycle

There are several variations of the conventional life cycle, also known as the waterfall model, but essentially in this method software is developed by a sequence of general activities as shown in the following figure.

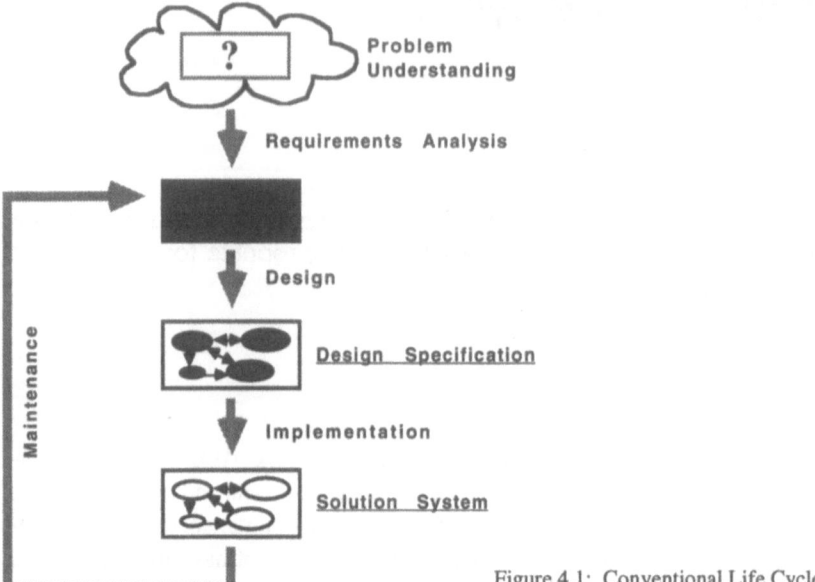

Figure 4.1: Conventional Life Cycle

In the requirements analysis phase the needs of the user are analysed and defined.

The result of the requirements analysis is the requirements specification. This document plays a central role in the early phases of system development /ZAVE81/, /PETE78/, /LIBE86/. It contains an agreement between customer and developer of the function which the system is supposed to perform. The requirements are task oriented.

At the requirements specification stage of the conventional approach, the system is treated as a "black box". All the required characteristics of its external behaviour ('what'), but no characteristics of the internal structure generating that behaviour ('how') /ZAVE84/ are defined. A prototype can be developed in order to determine the requirements of the system. After this the user can experiment with the prototype to find out whether or not it concurs with his ideas. Prototypes are mostly slow, too big and awkward to use, and therefore should not be used for implementing the final system /BRO75/. This type of prototyping is called "throw away" prototyping. A more general discussion of prototyping follows in the next section.

In the design phase the internal structure of the program, i.e. the module structure is defined. The requirement specification is concerned only with the task but the design specification takes into account the specific features of the run-time environment such as resource configuration and resource allocation strategies.

In the design phase, the internal structure of the system is usually determined by breaking down into modules. The design specification contains a description of the relationships between modules, the module interfaces, and the function of each module. A more detailed description of a module would include the resources required, the plan for testing, the performance requirements, and the formal specifications of module behaviour.

In the implementation phase, the components identified in the design stage are implemented using a particular programming system. The implementation also includes the testing of the system and its integration into a particular production environment. Different techniques have been developed to support designers through the software life cycle. An overview of different software engineering techniques is given in /RAMA86/.

In the conventional approach maintenance involves changing the source code /BACC83/.

Ideally, maintenance involves passage through all the stages (see figure). However, by going through all the development phases, the addition of new requirements is normally considered as to expensive.

4.2 Prototyping

In /HEIN88/ prototyping is divided into the following main categories, based on the relationship between the prototype and the final system:
- Throw away prototyping
- Evolutionary prototyping
- Incremental prototyping

Throw away prototyping is often used for the requirements identification in the requirements analysis phase of the conventional life cycle. Therefore it is not a type of life cycle but rather a method used in the conventional life cycle. In contrast evolutionary and incremental prototyping are ways of organizing development activities. These types of life cycles are therefore discussed in more detail.

4.2.1 Evolutionary Life Cycle

The evolutionary approach tries to overcome some of the disadvantages of the conventional life cycle. In the evolutionary approach /BATU75/ a skeletal implementation, sometimes known as the system core, is used as the starting point. The system core is a sample of the most important aspects of the task. It is simple enough to understand and to implement and gives the user a first impression of what the final system will do. Because this skeleton is the core of the whole system, its design is very important. It should allow all subsequent changes to the functionality to the system under development. Therefore the design of the skeleton of a system is the crucial activity in the evolutionary approach /BRO87/.

New features are then added one at a time until the system is completed /CHAR86/, /WEG84/. Thus the system is not completed at particular time, rather it grows with the passing of time /BRO87/.

The following figure shows the phases of the evolutionary life cycle.

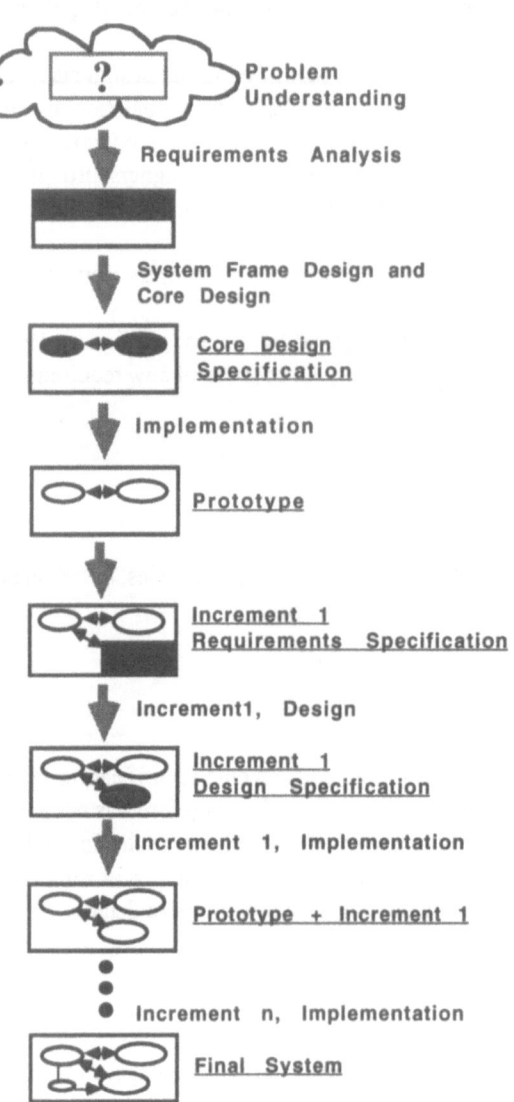

A project control list contains all the tasks that have to be performed in order to achieve the desired final implementation. At any given time the project control list shows the distance from the current state to final implementation. Tasks are removed one by one from the list until there are no more. At this point the system is completed.

For each development step requirement, design, and implementation activities are performed. After each increment has been implemented, the new system is available to the user; it is the old system with some additional features.

Enhancement means adding some additional steps. The spiral model introduced in /BOEHM88/ is a special example of evolutionary development.

4.2.2 Incremental Life Cycle

In the incremental life cycle a complete requirement specification and a complete design is started and then modules are designed, implemented and added in sequence. This means that the difference between the conventional and incremental life cycle is only in the implementation phase. As with the evolutionary life cycle the system grows gradually but in a less dynamic way. The incremental life cycle, lies between the evolutionary and the conventional life cycle. The following picture shows the different phases of the incremental life cycle.

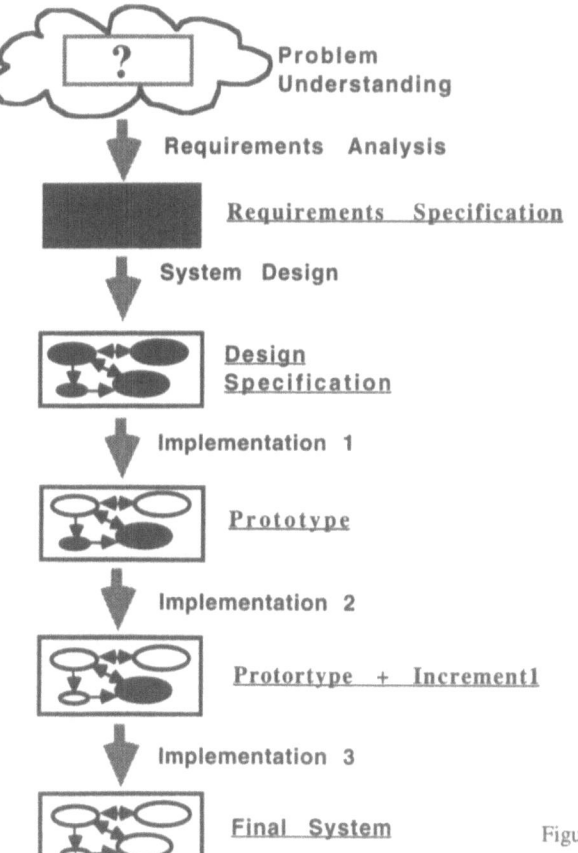

Figure 4.3: Incremental Life Cycle

4.3 Operational Life Cycle

For the requirement specification of the operational approach, a system is specified which performs the required task. This system is specified in terms of structures which are independent of the implementation. The structures generate the behaviour of the specified system as an operational abstraction. An operational specification is as formal as a behavioural specification. An executable specification only defines the behaviour of a system implicitly by its set of internal computations /WEG84/.

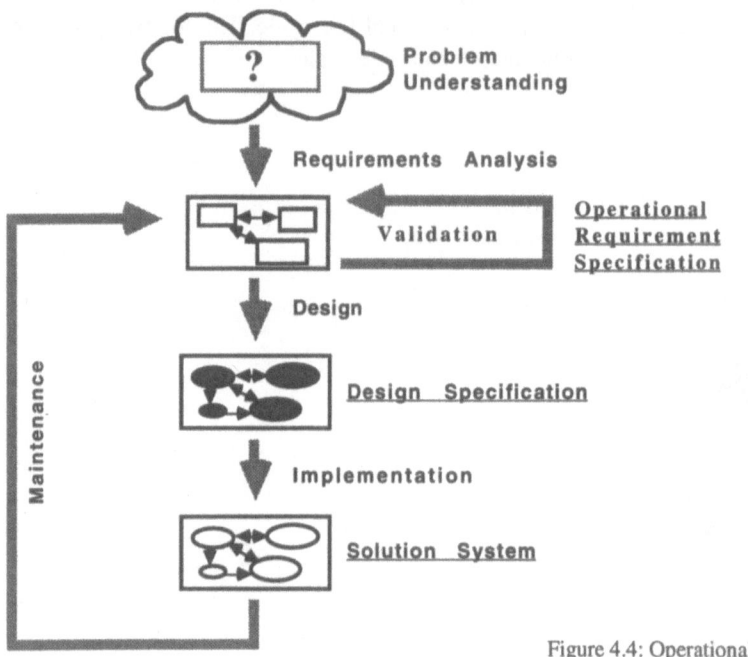

Figure 4.4: Operational Life Cycle

The structure of an operational specification is task oriented and the structures provided by an operational specification language are independent of specific run-time environments (a design however refers to specific run-time environments). An operational requirements specification can be used by the final user of the system to determine whether it meets his requirements.

During the design phase, the operational specification is transformed into a design specification. This transformation must preserve the external behaviour of a requirement specification. In design specifications, the special features of resource configurations or resource allocation strategies are taken into account. In the implementation phase, a design is implemented, i.e. coded in a particular programming language and for a particular computer system.

An overview of the operational approach is given in Figure 4.4 /ZAVE84/.

The operational approach allows the requirements specifications to be tested if an appropriate execution system exists. This means that at a very early stage the properties of the system can be validated by the customer.

Maintenance requires that the whole life cycle be repeated. But the operational approach can be combined with the evolutionary approach. From this perspective tools for the operational software life cycle can be considered as tools for rapid prototyping.

4.4 The Transformational Life Cycle

In the transformational approach to software developement a series of transformations is effected. These tranformations change a specification into an actual software system.

The figure below shows a scheme of the transformational approach.

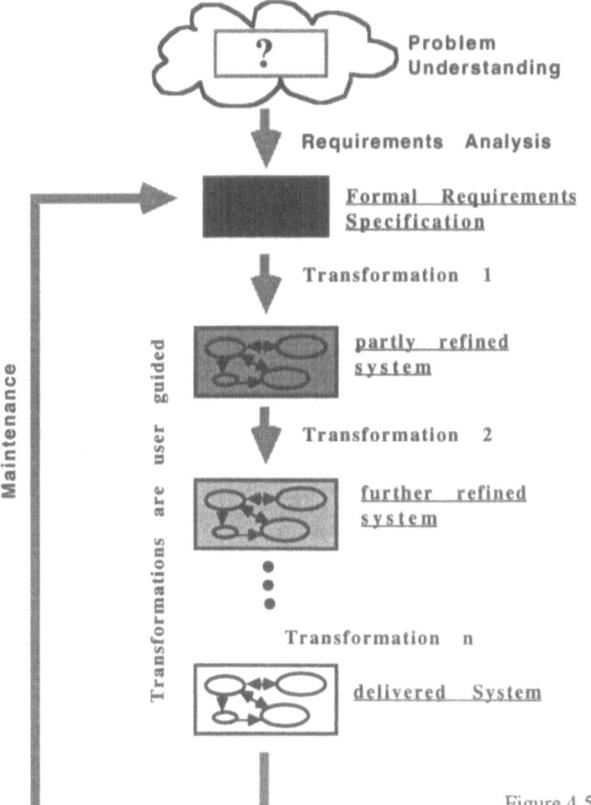

Figure 4.5: Transformational Life Cycle

The transformational approach is based on the formal specification /AGRES86b/. The specification is

- the object that is validated against the user requirements
- the starting point for the transformation phase
- the object on which maintenance is performed

It is assumed that the specification expresses what the program is to do without expressing how it is to be accomplished. The 'what' specification is transformed step by step into a 'how' implementation /BALZ81/. Each transformation step adds a new property to the target system (programming language, operating system etc.).

4.5 Knowledge Based Life Cycle

The knowledge based life cycle can be considered as a combination of the operational and transformational methods. The operational approach is enhanced by tools which allow a more or less automatic derivation of a program from a specification. Additionally, the decisions made during the software development process are supported and documented by knowledge-based systems /BACC83/. The software engineering knowledge domain is separated from the application knowledge domain. During the specification phase application knowledge is especially important. This also includes the validation of the specification. In the later phases, software engineering knowledge becomes more important /BARS87/. The following figure shows the structure of a knowledge based software development method. It is expected that software development support systems of this type -without the drawbacks of the other methods- will be available in about 10 years /BACC83/ *(which is today but have not seen it yet)*.

A survey of program design and constructions tools related to this program development method is contained in /GOLD86/.

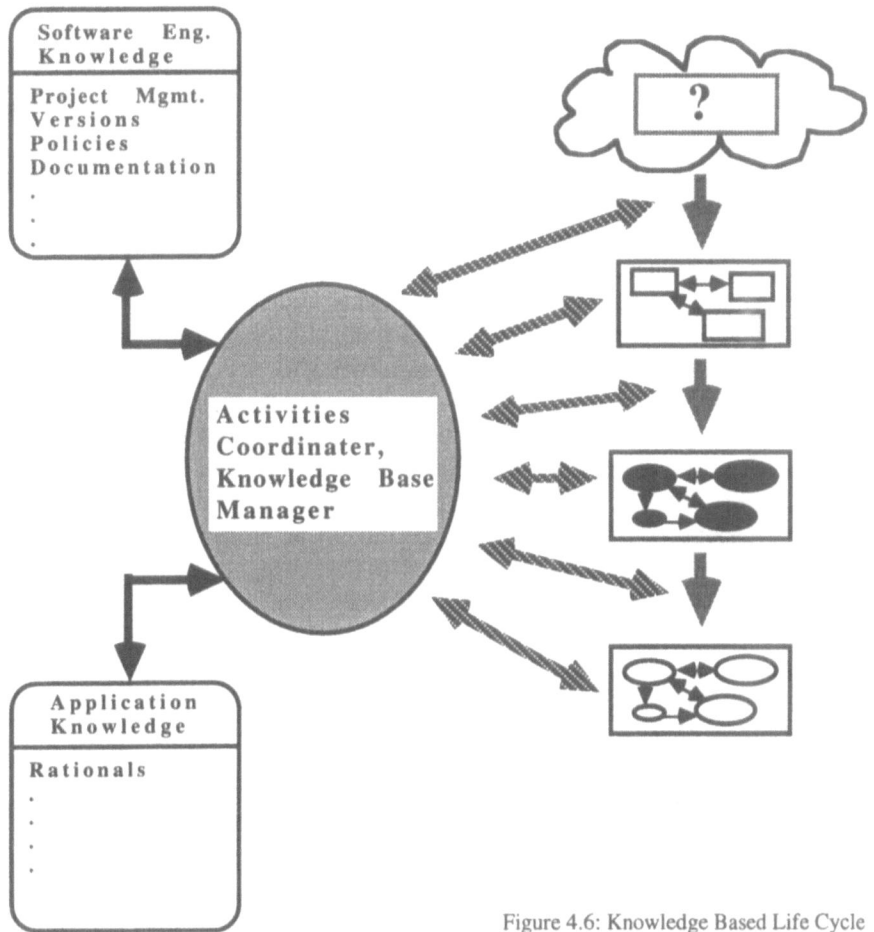

Figure 4.6: Knowledge Based Life Cycle

4.6 Evaluation

The basic software development methods introduced in previous sections are not adequate for all types of software systems.

The conventional software life cycle presumes a complete requirements specification. According to the classification schema introduced in chapter three, the conventional life cycle would be adequate for domain independent software systems. The conventional life cycle would be very weak however for domain dependent software, where the system requirements must be developed with interaction from the user who represents the environment /AGRES86c/, /MCJA80/, /WEG84/, /PACL85/. If the complete system is implemented then it is possible to determine whether the system satisfies the wishes of the customer. However this could not be done in the case of domain dependent systems because the inevitable changes would be expensive.

The evolutionary software development paradigm tries to produce an executable system kernel very early. This kernel is the foundation for further requirements which are added to the system step by step. A permanent system with which compare the wishes of the user, makes the evolutionary approach adequate for domain dependent software.

The major drawback of the evolutionary method is that it is not possible to automate the development process to a greater extent. The evolutionary life cycle has to be executed manually. Furthermore if the evolutionary approach is used, the design is a central issue. The original design of the kernel must be very flexible because the features to be added are more or less unknown /BRO87/.

The operational software life cycle allows a wide use of support tools. The specification is executable and can be transformed into a program or program frame automatically. The executable specification can be used to check whether the intentions of the user are satisfied. It seems that this method would also be good for developing domain dependent software such as communication and process control software systems.

Like the conventional life cycle, the transformational method also assumes a complete requirement specification. In addition, this approach requires a formal specification. It is therefore more appropriate for domain independent software systems. Currently this development method has only been applied to small tasks /AGRES86b/, /PAMO86/.

The knowledge based method is still a research topic. It is expected that by 1995 some practical experiences with it will have been gained. Some aspects of software development are currently supported by expert systems /GOLD86/.

The operational method seems to be a good choice if we want to have a software engineering environment which allows wide tool support . It is applicable to domain dependent software systems and allows the development of tools with reasonable effort. In addition, the operational approach can be combined with the evolutionary life cycle. Starting from a kernel which is specified in an operational manner, a system can be developed step by step. Thus the combination of the operational and the evolutionary life cycles provides an executable system as early as possible, provided suitable tools are available.

Recommended Readings

/AGRES86a/ Agresti W. W. (Ed.)
New Paradigms for Software Development
IEEE Computer Society Press, 1986
This book contains a broad collection of articles about different types of software engineering.

/ARTH91/   Arthur L. J.
Rapid Evolutionary Development
John Wiley, New York, 1991
This book discusses many aspects of evolutionary software development including management.

Control Questions:

1. What are the major types of software life cycles?
2. What are their characteristics?
3. Which problems are best suited to each type of life cycle?

Exercises:

1. What type of life cycle is used in your professional environment?
2. Does this life cycle always fit with the type of software you develop?

5 Methods: Concepts

The basic concepts of software engineering and the different methods of software development are explained. All software engineering methods contain elements of several basic concepts.

In software engineering environments, methods are required to define, describe, abstract, modify, refine, and document a software product. Methods define the detailed steps and techniques in every phase of the underlying life cycle. For each phase of a life cycle, dedicated methods can be used. For requirements engineering other techniques are used than for design or test activities. Methods used in one phase of a certain life cycle must allow a smooth transition to the methods used in the succeeding phase. A chain of such methods is called a methodology. It is based on a certain life cycle or possibly several different types of life cycles. In the following discussion no great distinction is made between the terms methods and methodology; however we consider mainly methodologies.

If an incremental life cycle is preferred, the methodology used must allow the transition between an incomplete requirements specification and the design activities.

In conventional and transformational life cycles, complete requirement specifications are assumed before the design phase is started. This means that requirement specification methods which support completeness checks are preferred to those which do not.

If an operational life cycle is used a method has to produce executable requirement and/or design specifications.

Different methods are used in different program development activities. For requirement specification activities abstract and-user oriented methods are preferred. The requirements are defined in cooperation with the final user of the system to be developed.

In design activities, more computer-oriented methods are applied. The design is the first step towards a computer based solution of the problem defined in the requirements. During coding and testing, methods are applied which depend on the programming language and computer system used.

Methods are based on concepts and languages derived from these concepts. A method is based on certain fundamental concepts which comprise the philosophy behind the method. Languages are defined on the basis of these concepts. These languages allow the expression of facts or requirements. Finally, a method defines a set of procedures suggesting the direction and order by which the required results can be obtained. The following figure shows the internal structure of methods.

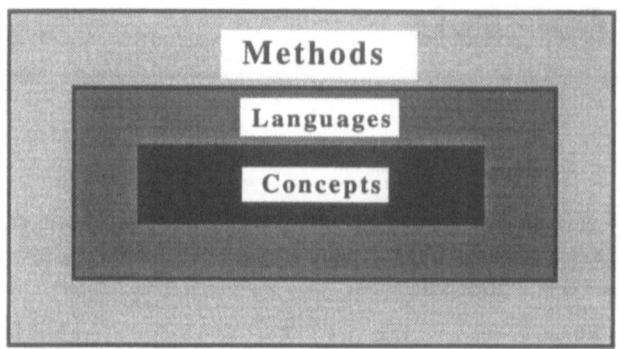

Figure 5.1:
Structure of Methods

Appropriate methods have been developed for each major activity in software development i.e. requirements specification, implementation, integration, and testing. The basic concepts, especially for requirements specification and design methods, are /JON79/,/BERG81/, /ZAVE82/, /BALZ89/:
- function oriented
- data structure oriented
- data flow oriented
- control flow oriented
- object oriented

As already stated, the boundary between requirement specification and design activities is not very precise. Very often it depends on the personal taste and experience of an author or developer whether a language or method is considered a specification or a design method. Therefore we do not make a clear distinguish distinction between specification and design techniques. The techniques described in the following sections are sometimes considered as specification and sometimes as design techniques. This concurs with other authors who consider specification and design methods together /ZAVE90/, /SWBA82/.

In addition to the concept oriented distinction, methods can also be classified according, to their language properties. In formal languages mathematical notations are used. Structured languages allow in addition informal components but the description components and their relationships are clearly defined. In these languages graphical notations are combined with natural or formal language oriented notations. Finally there are less organized methods which are well known: one has to simply start coding.

In the following sections some examples of different types of methods are described. The examples given do not claim to be a complete collection of suggested analysis and design methods. They are only intended to illustrate the methods mentioned above and to provide an understanding of our development method for distributed software described in part II.

The following figure shows to which class the examples described belong and in which section they are outlined.

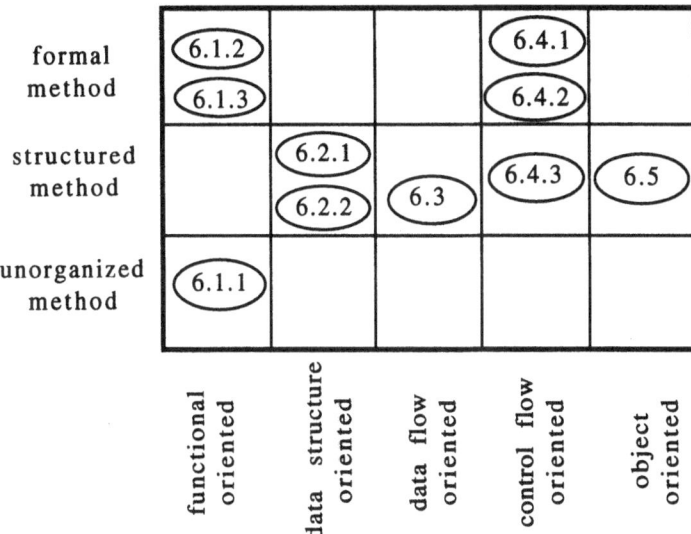

Figure 5.2: Method Classification Scheme

In order to develop software all or at least several of the basic concepts have to be combined in a method or methodology. But the various methods or methodologies emphasise one of the concepts mentioned above. In the following sections we describe the basic concepts and some development methods or methodologies which emphasis this aspect.

5.1 Function Oriented

Function-oriented development methods are the oldest ways of specifying and implementing programs. The focus of function-oriented methods are the functions to be executed. Function-oriented description techniques seam natural for defining system requirements. A simple example is illustrated in the statement: 'We need a system which prints a price list of all the wines we have'.

A program is considered as a set of functions. High level functions are decomposed into low level functions; these are further simplyfied and so on. "Divide and conquer" is the principle behind this kind of program development. At each decomposition step more details of the final program are described. This method of developing programs can be characterized as a top-down approach to problem description and solution.

The following figure illustrates this principle.

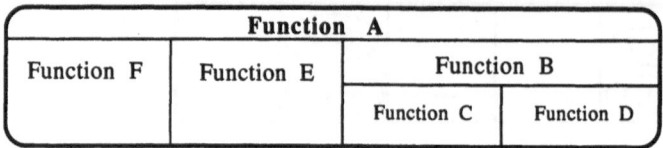

Figure 5.3:
Divide and Conquer

In function oriented specification methods two types of abstraction can be distinguished/LIBE86/:

Procedural abstraction:
In procedural specifications, input data are mapped to output data. Procedural abstractions are implemented as procedures or subroutines. Input and output data can be global variables which are read or changed by a procedure, or certain parameters. The description of a procedural abstraction consists of an interface specification and a behavioural specification. The interface information consists of the procedure names, the module name, and the name and type of the sources and destinations of the inputs and outputs.

There are two main ways with which to describe the behaviour of a procedural abstraction: input/output specifications and operational specifications. Both ways describe the relationship between the input and output of a procedural abstraction.

Input/output specifications describe the behaviour of a procedural abstraction implicitly. They describe the values of the input and output data before and after the execution of the procedure. An example of a formal input/output specification method is discussed in section 5.1.2.

Operational specifications define the behaviour of a procedure explicitly. The transformation of the input and output data is specified by a program which computes the desired function. The operational specification languages should be simpler and easier to use than programming languages.

The behaviour of procedural abstractions can be described informally and formally. Natural languages and diagrams can be used for informal descriptions, but formal specification methods use mathematical logic.

Data abstraction:
A data abstraction consists of an abstract data type or a family of related data types. An abstract data type is a set of objects and a related finite set of operations which are allowed on these objects. An abstract data type is completely characterized by the behaviour of the operations. Objects of a certain type can only be manipulated or read by the operations belonging to this type No other access is allowed.

Two basic formal specification methods for data abstractions are the axiomatic specification and the abstract model methods. Axiomatic specifications define the behaviour of an abstract data type by a set of axioms. The axioms describe the relationship between the operations of an abstract data type. In the abstract model approach, the objects of a data type are represented by other data types. These simpler data types are specified in advance. Finally all abstract data types are derived from well known data types such as set, integer, real, boolean, etc.

5.1.1 Informal Functional Specification

A very old but still popular way to represent functional decomposition is the use of hierarchical graphs. One possible decomposition of our wine price list requirement mentioned above is shown in the following figure.

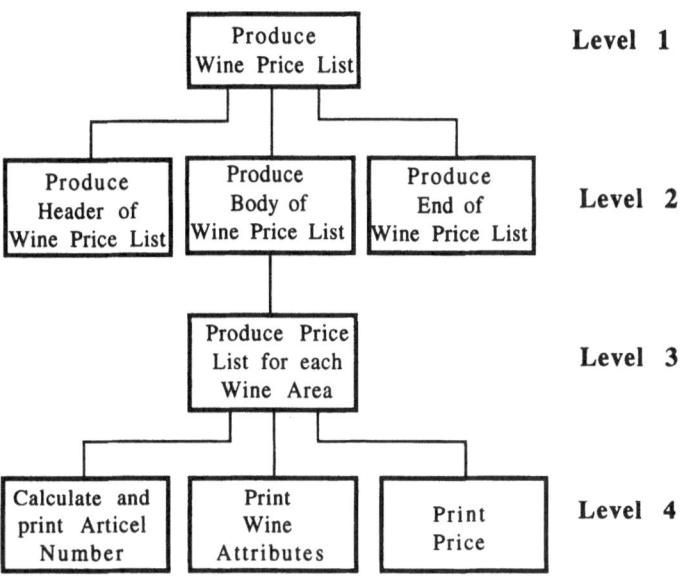

Figure 5.4: Functional Decomposition of 'Printing a Wine Price List'

The nodes in the diagram above represent different procedural abstractions. Their behaviour is normally described using an informal operation oriented specification technique. One operation oriented language for describing procedural abstractions is called program design language (PDL) or structured English. Structured English incorporates basic procedural constructs such as sequence, selection, and iteration combined with English language phrases. Two examples of PDL specifications are shown below.

Procedure: Produce price list for all wine areas (wine_file)
    repeat until end of wine file is reached
        Read wine entry in wine file (Order_no, attributes, price);
        Calculate_and_print_article_number (Order_no)
        Print attributes
        Print price
    endrepeat
  endprocedure

Procedure: Calculate_and_print_article_number (Order_no):
    Order_No := article_no mod 1000
    Print Order_No
  endprocedure

The steps of a related method for developing a software system specification are /BERG81/:

1. Clearly state the required function
2. Break down the required function into subfunctions. Each subfunction represents a part of the required function. The subfunctions together return the same result as the required function. Describe the subfunctions and their relations.
3. Repeat step 2 until no further decomposition of the subfunctions seems necessary.

Discussion:

The methods for deriving subfunctions from given or previously derived subfunctions are not very clear. Different people will obtain different results from the application of these methods. There are no decomposition criteria. A function can be broken down with respect to temporal order (as in our example), data flow, the structure of the input/output data, or logical groupings. There is no clear measurement system to determine whether a particular decomposition is good or bad.

Informal functional decomposition can be based on each life cycle because this method is not described very precisely. If the conventional life cycle is used, each decomposition path must be completed before detailed design and coding is started. This method can also be used for incremental development. Several decomposition paths can be considered later in the development cycle, but this has implications for the decomposition process. The decomposition paths implemented later must be independent of the earlier components implemented.

Functional decomposition can also be used to develop concurrent programs. The decomposition criterion can be that different subfunctions can be executed on different computers or can be implemented as processes.

Informal functional decomposition allows for nearly everything but does not offer support for the production of specifications and designs.

5.1.2 Predicate Transformation

Predicate transformations belong to the input/output-oriented specification class.

The essence of predicate transformation is that the semantics of a statement are defined by state transformations. A statement transforms a program from one state to another. A state associates the identifiers of a program with values. The set of states to which a statement can be applied is defined by preconditions. The execution of a statement requires that the precondition is true. The possible states after the execution of the statement are described by postconditions - after execution of the statement the postcondition is true. The semantics of a statement is defined by the corresponding precondition and postcondition. If P is the precondition, S the statement, and R the resulting postcondition, then this relationship is written formally in the form:

$$\{P\} \; S \; \{R\}$$

The termination of a statement S which begins in a state satisfying P is guaranteed in a finite amount of time. The resulting state will satisfy predicate R. When P is the weakest precondition i.e. P describes the largest set of states satisfying P, this is expressed in the form

$$P = wp(R,S)$$

The weakest preconditions of the most important programming statements are as follows /GRIES81/,/BERG81/:

Skip, composition:
The skip statement is the empty statement and does not change anything. This is formally expressed in the form

$$\text{skip:} \quad wp(skip,R) = R.$$

Sequential decomposition is one way to break down larger programs into smaller parts. S1 and S2 are two commands. Then S1,S2 is a new command. It is executed by first executing S1 and then executing S2. Its formal definition is

$$\text{composition}: \; wp(\,'S1,S2'\,, R) = wp\,(S1, wp\,(S2,R))$$

Assignment:
The command X:= e can only be properly executed in a state in which e can be evaluated. Execution consists of evaluating the value of the expression e and identifying each occurrence of the identifier X with that value. Its formal definition is

$$\text{assignment:} \quad wp('X:=e', R) = R^x_e$$

Selection:
The selection statement has the form

$$\begin{aligned}
\text{IF} == \quad &\text{if } B_1 -> S_1 \\
&\pi \; B_2 -> S_2 \\
&\cdots\cdots \\
&\pi \; B_n -> S_n \\
&\text{fi;}
\end{aligned}$$

This is valid where n > 0 and B_i are Boolean expressions called guards and the S_i are statements. Each B_i -> S_i is a guarded command. The symbol ¬ serves to separate unordered alternatives. The command IF can be executed if at least one guard is true. One guarded command B_i -> S_i with true guard B_i is chosen and S_i is executed. Its formal definition is

Selection: wp(IF, R) = BB and B_1 -> wp(S_1,R) and .... and B_n ->wp(S_n, R) where BB denotes the disjunction B_1 or B_2 or ...... or B_n

The disjunction BB indicates that at least one guard must be true. The rest indicates that execution of each statement S_i with a true guard B_i terminates with R true.

Iteration:

The iteration statement takes the form:

$$DO == do \ B_1 -> S_1$$
$$\pi \quad B_2 -> S_2$$
$$........$$
$$\pi \quad B_n -> S_n$$
$$od;$$

where n>= 0 and each B -> S is a guarded command. Iteration statements are executed as follows: repeat until no longer possible: choose a guard B_i which is true (if more than one guard is true then an arbitrary choice is made) and execute the corresponding command S_i. Upon termination all guards are false. Its formal definition has the form:

$$\text{Iteration: } wp(DO,R) = (E \ k : 0 <= k : H_k(R))$$

where $H_k(R)$ for k <= 0 is the weakest precondition such that the execution of DO terminates in k or fewer iterations in a state satisfying R.

The formal definition of the DO statement is not easy to use and gives no insight into program development. Therefore a theorem has to be developed that allows the use of a precondition- which is not the weakest precondition- of a loop. This condition is true just before and after each iteration, so that it is also true after termination. Such a predicate P is called an invariant relation, or simply an invariant. An invariant P allows us to argue that the loops perform as desired:

1. P is initially true.
2. Each iteration of the loop leaves P true.
3. Then P is true before and after each iteration and upon termination.
4. Show that the loop terminates using a bounded variable t which is decreased after each loop iteration. After termination t = 0.
5. Then P together with the falsity of all guards after termination implies R.

There is no straightforward method of finding an invariant. Normally invariants are developed by weakening the result assertion R. Some heuristics which do this are described in /GRIES81/.

The development method centers around a formal proof based on weakest preconditions and some theorems /GRIES81/. The initial design task consists of formally specifying the required result of a program. Assertions stated in the predicate calculus are used to define the required postcondition. The appropriate preconditions are derived while working back through the program to be developed. This way of working back is based on the weakest preconditions for program statements which are described above. The program statements and the corresponding assertions showing the predicate transformations are developed in parallel. This is a top down method. The program and the corresponding predicates can be created in stages by a sequence of stepwise refinement. In /GRIES81/ a set of principles and heuristics are presented which support the development strategy described. These principles help to develop loops from invariants and bounds and particular they provide some heuristics to find invariants.

Discussion:
The development of programs following the method outlined above requires the developer (and even the user) to have a thorough mathematical education. A developer cannot expect that a user of the system has the mathematical skills to validate the assertions made especially during the requirements analysis .

Proofs showing that the precondition is derived according to the appropriate weakest precondition are lengthy, difficult, and therefore prone to error. Proofs can be much longer than the program itself. These may be the reasons that this method is hardly used in industrial program development.

The development process follows the conventional life cycle. Transformations can be applied in order to derive a program from a specification program

The normal predicates are not powerful enough in order to develop concurrent programs. For concurrent programs the logic for describing assertions and the transformations must be extended. Many proposals for such extensions have been made. Examples which formally describe parallel programs are state variable oriented and event oriented concepts. A collection of papers related to the formal aspects of the development of concurrent programs can be found in /BAKK86/, /RATT90/, /ZILLI87/.

5.1.3 Algebraic Specification

In algebraic specifications /GUTT79/ abstract data types are considered as algebraic structures. An algebraic structure consists of a set of objects with a corresponding set of operations for which a set of rules is defined. This set of rules from the axioms of an abstract data type.

The axiomatic specification of an abstract data type consists of an interface specification and a behaviour specification. The interface specification provides the syntactic and type checking information: names, domains, and ranges of the operations associated with this type. The behaviour of the operations is defined by axioms which specify the relationships of the operations of an abstract data type to each other and to the state of the abstract data type. All objects of the defined type must be produced by constructor operations of the specified type. Other operations of the particular type provide the only way to extract information from an object of that type or to manipulate its values. These operations are called inquiry operations. A "stack" is an abstract data type which is very frequently used as an example of algebraic specification. A limited "stack" can only store a limited number of items. With an operation commonly called "push" an item can be stored in a stack. The operation "pop" removes the data item stored with the last push operation (last in first out). In addition to these basic operations, the abstract data type stack has the operations "top", "depth", and "limit". The operation "top" returns the value of the most recently stored data item. The number of stored data items is returned by the operation "depth" and the operation "limit" returns the number of free slots. The following figure shows the formal definition of the data type "stack". In addition to the inquiry operations "push", "pop", "depth", and "limit" there is one constructor operation called "c_stack". The operation "c_stack" creates an object of the abstract data type STACK. A parameter of type integer defines how many items can be stored in the object created. The abstract data type definition itself has a parameter called ITEM. This parameter defines the data types which can be stored in the stack.

abstract_data_type: STACK(ITEM)

interface	:c_stack	:NAT->	STACK
push	:STACK x ITEM->		STACK
pop	:STACK->		STACK
top	:STACK->		ITEM
depth	:STACK->		NAT
limit	:STACK->		NAT

axioms for: k elem NAT, i elem ITEM, s elem STACK

(1)	pop(push (s,i))	=	s
(2)	top (push (s,i))	=	i
(3)	depth(stack(k))	=	0
(4)	depth(push(s,i))	=	depth(s) + 1
(5)	limit(stack(k))	=	k
(6)	limit(push(s,i))	=	limit(s) - 1

Figure 5.5: Example of an Algebraic Specification

The interface definition describes the domain and ranges of the operations. The axioms specify the relations between the different operations.

Axiom (1):
The operation pop removes item i from the stack. Item i was put on the stack s by the last push operation.

Axiom (2):
The operation top returns the value of the data item which was put on the stack by the last push operation. The operation top does not change the stack.

Axiom (3):
The operation depth returns the value 0 when it is executed immediately after a c_stack operation. After a c_stack operation the created stack is empty.

Axiom (4):
After a push operation the number of items stored in the stack is increased by one.

Axiom (5):
The operation limit returns the value k when it is executed immediately after a c_stack operation. After a c_stack operation the number of empty slots is equal to the size of the stack.

Axiom (6):
After a push operation the number of free slots in the stack is decreased by one.

Axiomatic specifications can be hierarchical. The specification of an abstract data type can be based on other previously defined abstract data types. In our example the specification assumes the existence of a data type NAT (natural numbers).

Discussion:
It is difficult to find the set of axioms to describe an abstract data type. There can be contradictions in the set of axioms or it can be incomplete. In order to find the right set of axioms a thorough education in mathematics is required.

Algebraic specifications are based on the conventional life cycle. A system must be completly specified before the next phase can be started. In order to use axiomatic specifications for concurrent software systems, substantial extensions are necessary. These problems are very similar to the issues described in the previous section.

5.2 Data Structure Oriented

The structure of input and output data form the basis of data structure oriented methods. A program is considered as that which transforms input data into output data. Input and output data have different structures and different representations. The following figure shows the basic philosophy of programming based on data structures.

Input data   Output data

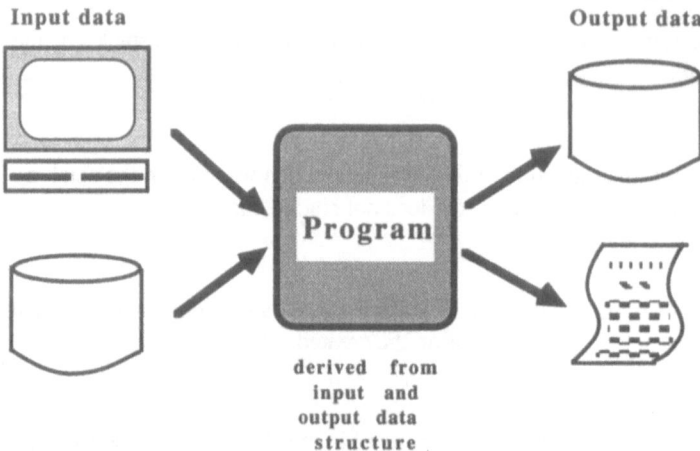

derived   from
input   and
output   data
structure

Figure 5.6: Programming based on Data Structure

The program which transforms the input data into the required output data is derived
from their structures. Therefore methods based on data structure start by defining
the structure of the input and output data. Normally the focus is on the structure of
the output data because this is the data that the user is interseted in generating. A
simplified requirements specification which implies methods based on data structure always has the following form:

'We have to produce a report containing the following information and with the
following structure: ....'!

Different languages and methods have been developed in order to describe the
structure, attributes, use and relationships of data objects. Examples are Jackson
Structured Programming (JSP) /CAM89/, Warrier/Orr /WAR74/, /ORR77/,
/ORR81/ and the Entity Relationship technique /CHEN76/. These methods are
described in more detail in the following sections.

5.2.1 Jackson Structured Programming (JSP)

JSP is based on a graphical language which allows the description of data and control structures. It is simple and easy to learn, consisting of only three basic elements:
- sequence
- choice
- iteration.

The following figure shows the corresponding graphical representations and a short
description of their interpretation.

Sequence:

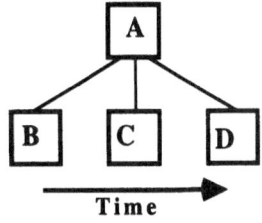

A consists of
one B followed by
one C followed by
one D

Time

Choice:

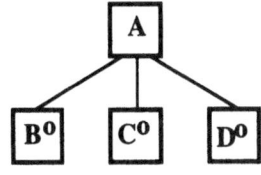

A consists either
of one B,
or one C,
or one D.

Iteration:

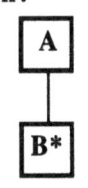

A consists of zero
or more Bs.

Figure 5.7: Graphical Symbols of JSP

Using the language outlined above the JSP method has four major steps /CAM89/:
1. Analysis of output and input data structures and their representation as data diagrams.
2. Merging these data diagrams into a single structure diagram, the program structure diagram.
3. Making a suitable list of executable operations and the definition of the algorithm structure. If a problem arises during this step then the program structure is not correct.
4. Converting the algorithm structure to a particular programming language.

The details of JSP are illustrated below by a simplified version of an example from /BALZ82/.

A wine shop distributes every three months a price list of all the wines they offer to their customers. The database containing a description of all articles they offer is used to produce the price list.

Step 1: Analyzing input and output data structure
Structure of the data base of the articles, i.e. the input data:

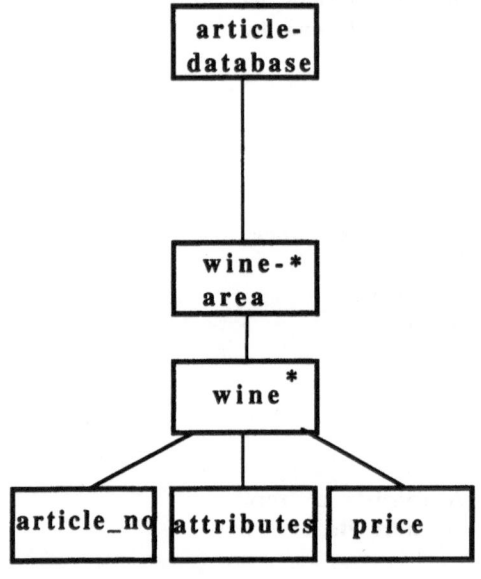

Figure 5.8: Structure of the Input Data

Content and layout of the price list, i.e. the output data:

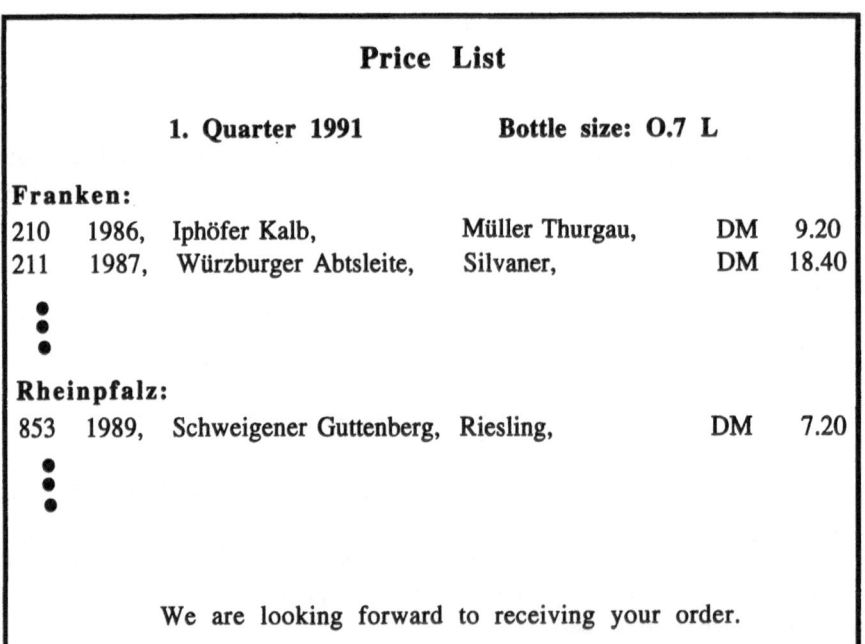

Figure 5.9: Layout of the Price List

Structure of the price list (output data):

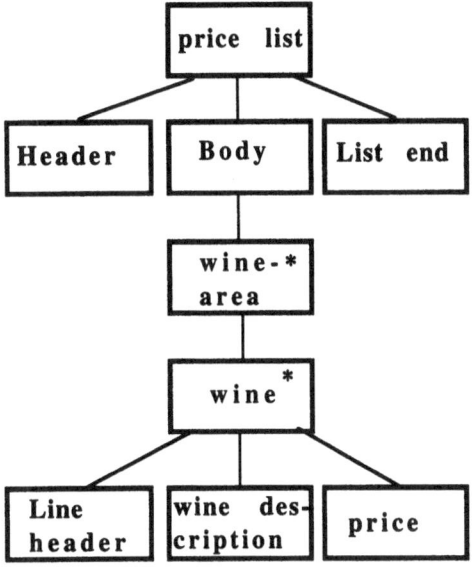

Figure 5.10 : Structure of the Output Data

Step 2: Deriving program structure from input and output data structure

In step 2 the input and output data structures found in step 1 are merged. This means that corresponding components in the output and input data structures must be identified. The corresponding components form a single component in the program structure. The following figure shows how the input and output data structure of our example are merged to a program structure.

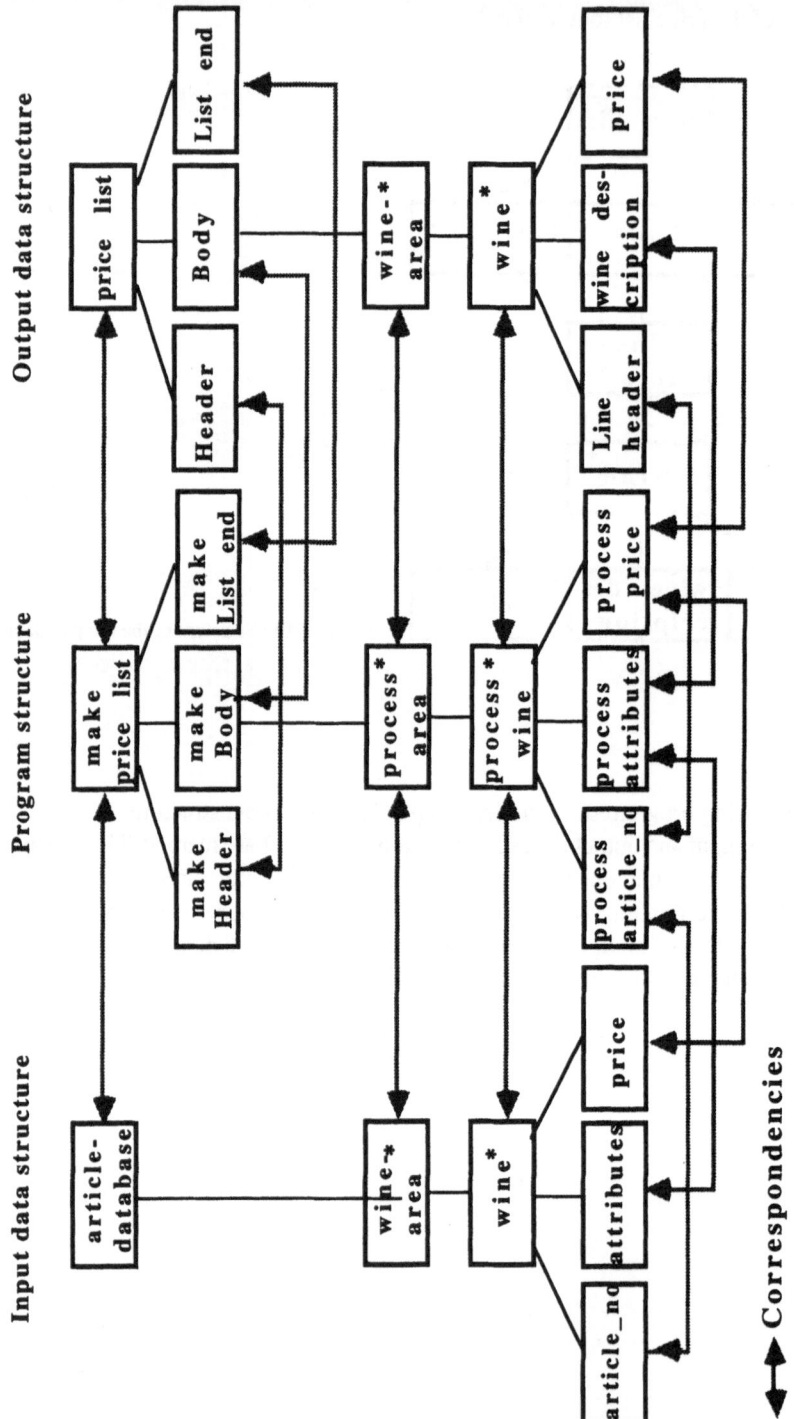

Figure 5.11: Program Structure derived from Input and Output Data Structures

Step 3: Identifying and allocating operations

The operations to be identified are executable statements of the programming language to be used. The executable statements are assignment statements, procedure calls and I/O operations. The following figure shows the program structure derived in step 2 with the executable operations inserted.

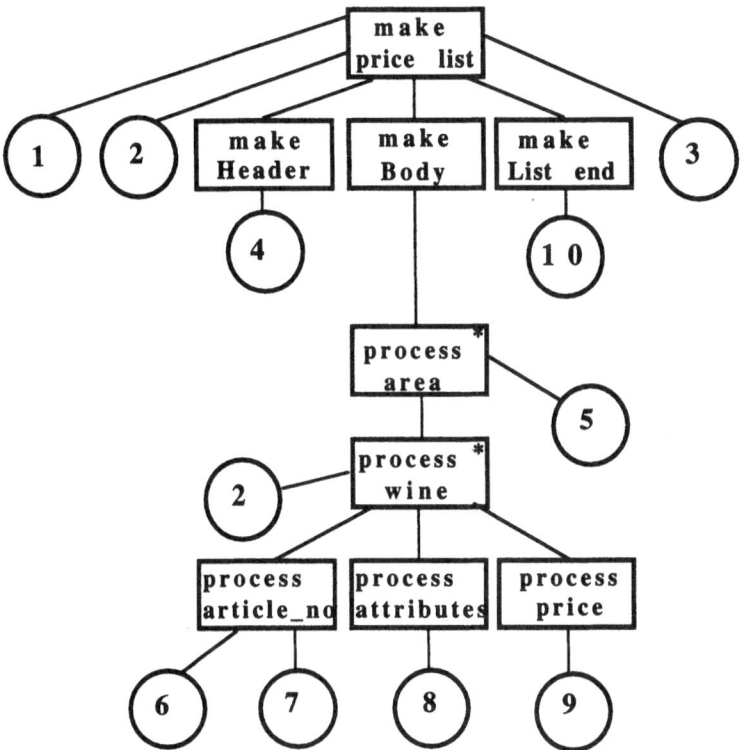

Figure 5.12: Program Structure with executable Operations

List of executable operations:
1 Open article database
2 Read entry from article database
3 Close article data base
4 Print header: Quarter: , Bottle size:
5 Print area
6 Order_No := article_no mod 1000
7 Print Order_No
8 Print attributes
9 Print price
10 Print Tailor

Step 4: Conditions and program text

In this step the program is written in text form for the first time. Several intermediate steps such as structured text, pseudocode, or Nassi/Schneiderman diagrams can be inserted before achieving the final program. The figure below shows the Nassi Schneiderman diagram for our example. This is finally transformed into program code.

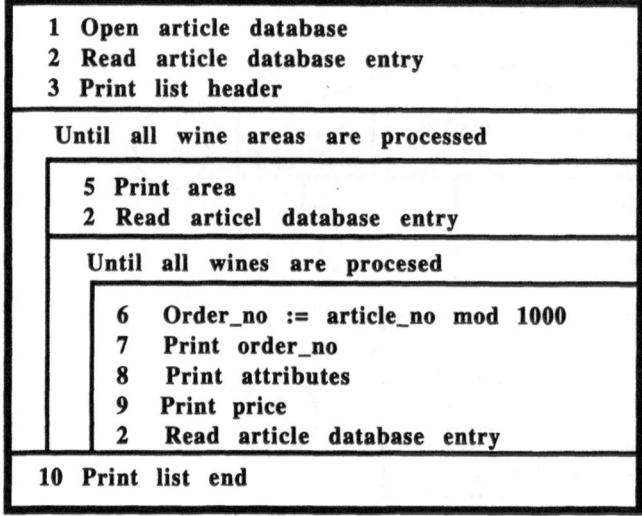

```
1  Open  article  database
2  Read  article  database  entry
3  Print  list  header

Until  all  wine  areas  are  processed

    5  Print  area
    2  Read  articel  database  entry

    Until  all  wines  are  procesed

        6    Order_no  :=  article_no  mod  1000
        7    Print  order_no
        8    Print  attributes
        9    Print  price
        2    Read  article  database  entry

10  Print  list  end
```

Figure 5.13: Nassi/Schneiderman Diagram for Printing the Price List

Discussion:

JSP is based on the conventional life cycle. First the complete program requirements must be stated. This is the structure and layout of the output data. The program design is based on the structure of the available input data and the required program output. Step by step the executable code is derived. JSP allows the user to go from one phase of the conventional life cycle to another without great difficulty. This means that JSP also supports some aspects of the transfomational life cycle.

It is difficult to apply JSP to life cycles other than the conventional and the transformational ones. Evolutionary development with JSP would mean that the output data would be modified at each step. At each step new data components would be added to the output data. Hence additional input data could be neccessary. The different structure of the input and output data could result in different program structure (Step 2).

JSP is not the right method for developing programs that must react to events in their environment such as communication or process control programs. JSP does not support concurrent or distributed programming. It contains no features to separate programs into concurrent processes or to distribute program components over several processing nodes. In general the programs developed with JSP are sequential. JSD Jackson System Development (JSD) has been developed in order to overcome these disadvantages /CAM86/, /CAM89/. (It is described in section 5.4 because it contains data and control flow concepts).

5.2.2 Warrier/Orr Program Design and Construction Method

The Warrier/Orr method is based on Warrier diagrams /WAR74/ which allow a hierarchical description of data structures. In the following figure a Warrier diagram is used to describe the structure of a letter.

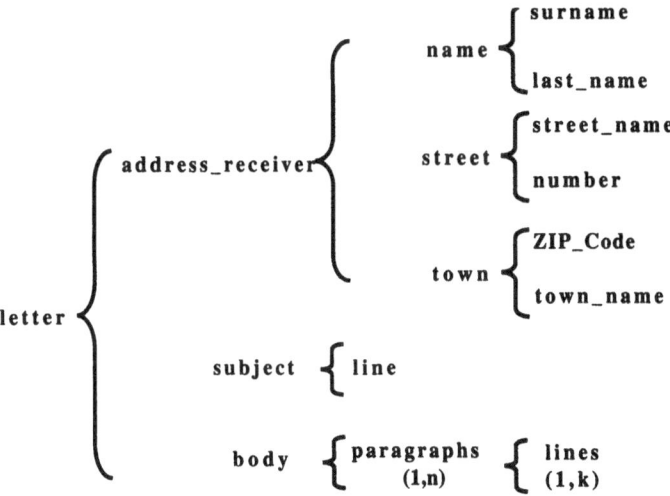

Figure 5.14: Warrier/Orr Diagram Showing the Structure of a Letter

Braces are used to separate levels of the information hierarchy. All names on the right side of a brace represent a sequence of information items. In our example a letter consists of 'destination', 'subject', and 'body'. The body of a letter consists of 1 to n paragraphs and each paragraph contains 1 to k lines. Brackets below the names represent repetitions. Warrier/Orr diagrams also allow the description of selections and negations but for simplicity these features are not used in our examples (For details see /HIG79/).

The Warrier/Orr method for program design and construction consists of six steps /HIG79/, /WAR74/, /ORR77/:

1. Define the program outputs
2. Define the logical database
3. Define events
4. Design the physical database
5. Design the logical program
6. Design the physical program

The details are explained using the same example as for JSP. We want to develop a program which prints a wine price list. The wine price list should have the same structure and layout as in the JSP example (see section above).

Step 1: Define the program outputs
Based on the layout of the wine price list, the logical structure of the contents can be derived and described by a Warrier/Orr diagram. The result is shown in the following figure.

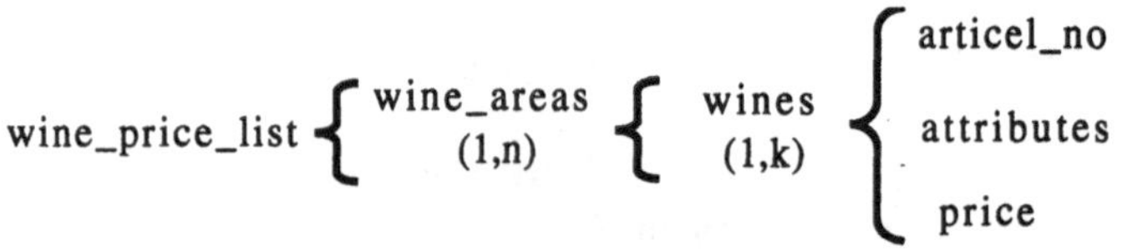

$$\text{wine\_price\_list} \left\{ \begin{array}{c} \text{wine\_areas} \\ \text{(1,n)} \end{array} \right. \left\{ \begin{array}{c} \text{wines} \\ \text{(1,k)} \end{array} \right. \left\{ \begin{array}{l} \text{articel\_no} \\ \text{attributes} \\ \text{price} \end{array} \right.$$

Figure 5.15: Warrier/Orr Description of the Price List Structure

Step 2: Define the logical database
The logical database (LDB) contains all the data needed to produce the output required. In a first intermediate step, a list is made of all elements appearing in the output. The following conventions are used to describe information items in the list:
1. Names of variables are written in small letters.
2. Terms that are constant are written in capital letters and enclosed in quotes.
   The following figure shows the list of data elements in the wine price list.

'PRICE LIST:'
quarter
'QUARTER'
year
'BOTTLE SIZE: 0.7 LITRE'
area
articel_no
attributes
price
'WE ARE LOOKING FORWARD TO RECEIVING YOUR ORDER'

Figure 5.16: List of Data Elements in the Wine Price List

After defining the data elements they are mapped to the data structrure of the output produced in step 1. The following figure shows the result of that mapping.

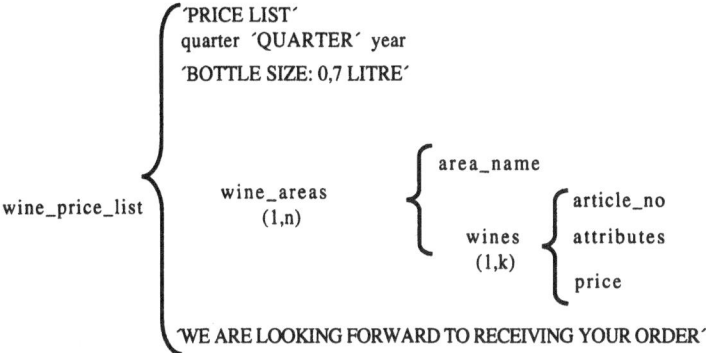

Figure 5.17: Data Structure and Data Elements

The logical output structure (LOS) shown in the figure above, charts the relationship between all the data elements contained in the wine list. The LOS is the starting point for designing the LDB. In order to derive the LDB from the LOS the following three steps have to be performed :

1. Develop the logical structure of the input by eliminating all constant terms in the LOS.
2 Eliminate data items which can be computed using other elements.
3. Eliminate redundant data elements.

For our simple example steps two and three are unnecessary. The result of applying step 1 is shown in the following figure.

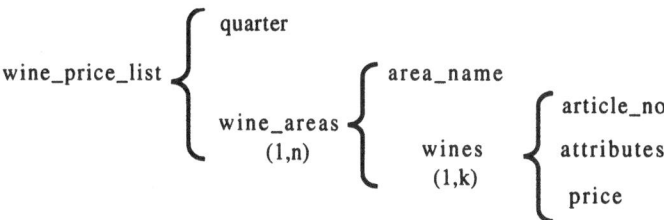

Figure 5.18: Structure of the LDB

Step 3: Define Events
In this step the LDB is examined for possible exceptions. The basic idea behind event analysis is the preparation of a program for possible data changes which might be needed during the use of the program.

The LDB is decomposed into entities with their attributes. Entities of an LDB are names of hierarchical braces. When all data entities have been collected, the attributes are the data elements that are left on the LDB. The following figure shows the entity/attribute list from our example.

entities	attributes
wine_price_list wine_areas wines	quarter area_name article_no, attributes, price

Figure 5.19: Entity/Attribute List

Now for each of the entities all events which can affect the associated attributes are defined. For each entity it is necessary to determine:
1. Which of their attributes may change?
2. Which events cause the attributes to change?
   The following figure shows the event analysis from our example.

wine_price_list
'quarter' can have the values 1, 2, 3 or 4

wine_areas
wines of a new area can become part of our 'portfolio'

wines
a new wine will be offered; this implies a new article number

Figure 5.20: Event Analysis

These events can be taken into account in the program design (step 5 and step 6)

Step 4: Define Physical Database
The physical database is the physical implementation of the LDB. In this step it is defined whether the LDB is to be mapped to a flat file, hierarchical file, hierarchical database, relational database, or some other structure. This is the first step towards an implementation. A lot depends on which storage system is to be used. Therefore we do not consider it here in detail (see /HIG79/).

Step 5: Define the Physical Process
In step 4, we developed the system to store the required input data. In step 5 we start

to develop the program which transforms the input data in the physical database into the required output format.

The starting point for developing the logical program (in this method also called process) is the structure of the output data defined in step 1. The development of the logical process (LP) is based on the assumption that large programs can at least be broken into a beginning, a middle, and an end. This is done by adding the words '.Begin' and '.End' at each level of the hierarchy segments except the lowest level which will be considered below. The preceeding dot indicates that the name of that particular level (e.g. wine_price_list.Begin) is to be used. The result of this step is shown in the next figure from our example.

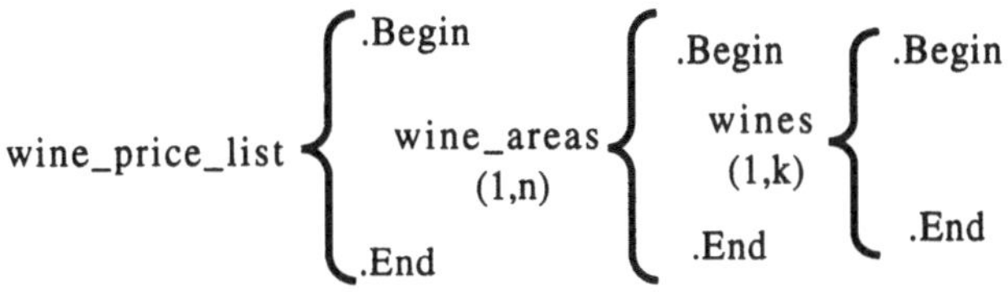

$$
\text{wine\_price\_list} \left\{ \begin{array}{l} \text{.Begin} \\[1em] \text{wine\_areas} \\ \text{(1,n)} \\[1em] \text{.End} \end{array} \right. \left\{ \begin{array}{l} \text{.Begin} \\[1em] \text{wines} \\ \text{(1,k)} \\[1em] \text{.End} \end{array} \right. \left\{ \begin{array}{l} \text{.Begin} \\[2em] \text{.End} \end{array} \right.
$$

Figure 5.21: Structure of the LP

The details of each level are added to the basic structure of the LP, starting at '.End' of the highest level and finishing at '.Begin' of the same level. See the following figure.

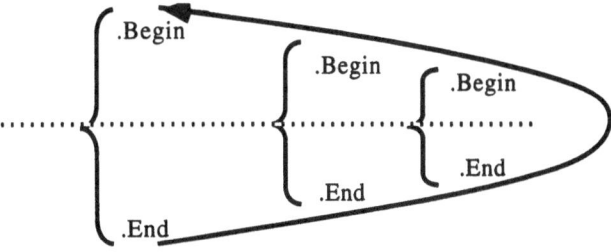

Figure 5.22: Direction of Process Completion

The final result of the step is shown below.

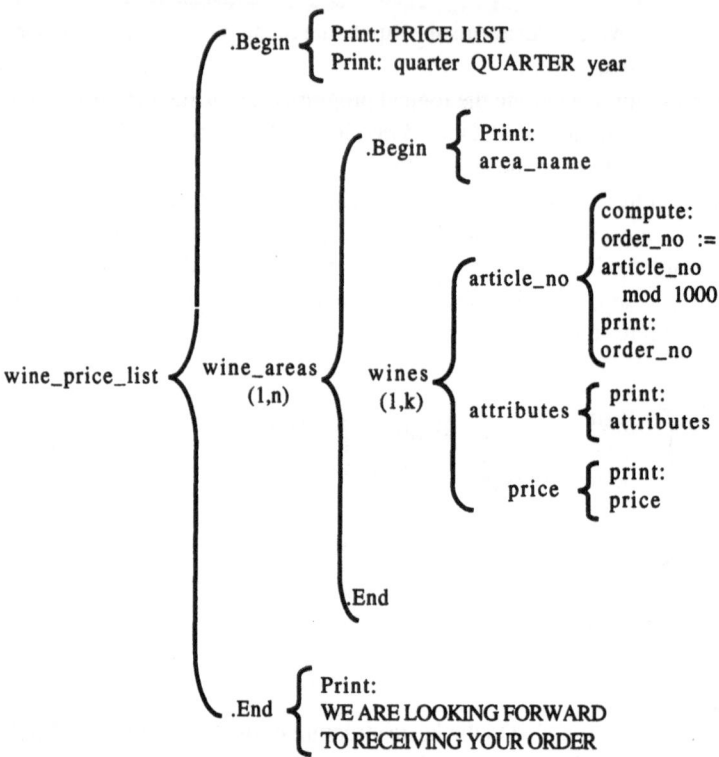

Figure 5.23: Complete Logical Process

Step 6: Design the physical process
In the last step the designer adds the control logic of the program. In order to emphasise the separation between the logical and the physical design, the control logic is
not included in the Warrier/Orr diagram of the logical process. Instead it is placed in
footnotes. Each bracket is considered as a DO UNTIL structure. In the footnotes the
corresponding termination conditions are described. The LP has to be completed
with statements for setting the termination conditions and for closing and opening
files.

The translation of the physical process into a programming language is very
simular to transforming a Nassi/Schneidermann diagram into program code. Hence
we will not discuss it in detail.

Discussion:
The Warrier/Orr method described above can only be based on the conventional life
cycle. The complete content and layout of the required output must be available
before the development process can be started. Later changes of the output require a
complete development cycle.

The development process described above cannot be extended to concurrent or distributed programs. In /HIG79/ some ideas are outlined for supporting concurrency but these ideas are rudimentary and not ready for immediate use. At the time writing more recent literature on this aspect of the Warrier/Orr method could not be found.

5.2.3 Entity Relationship Diagrams

The software development methods described in the sections above start from the required result and derive the necessary input data and program structure. Several programs which produce different output data may require the same common input data. This case is shown in the figure below.

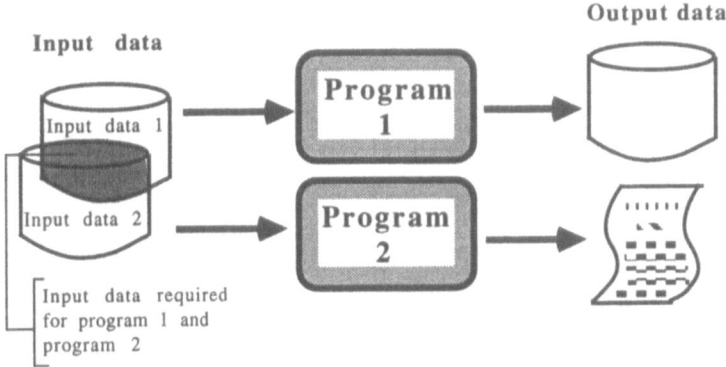

Figure 5.24: Input Data for two Different Programs

The same data can be stored several times for use by different programs. This consumes additional data storage and consistency problems may arise. If a data item required in several programs (and therefore stored several times) has to be changed, it must be updated in the input data storage of all the programs. In order to avoid this kind of problem, all the input data for all the programs is stored in a central database. The programs have access to the relevant parts of the central database.

The structure of such a central database can be very complicated. The entity-relationship diagram is a method for describing the structure of the database used by several different programs.

The basic notation for entity-relationship diagrams is shown in the next figure. Each box represents a data object. The connecting lines indicate associations between different data objects. The different associations are also explained in the figure.

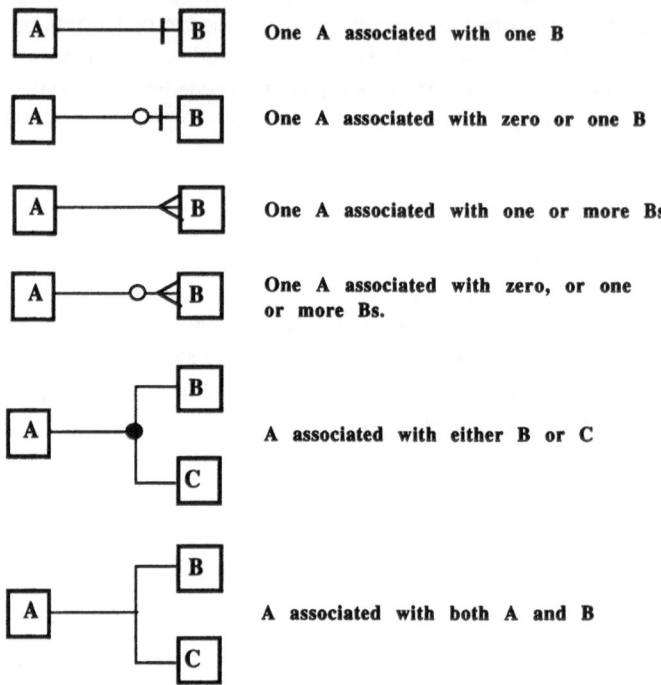

Figure 5.25: Symbols for Entity-Relationship Diagrams

A simple example of an entity relationship diagram is shown below. It describes the structure of a customer article database for our wine store example.

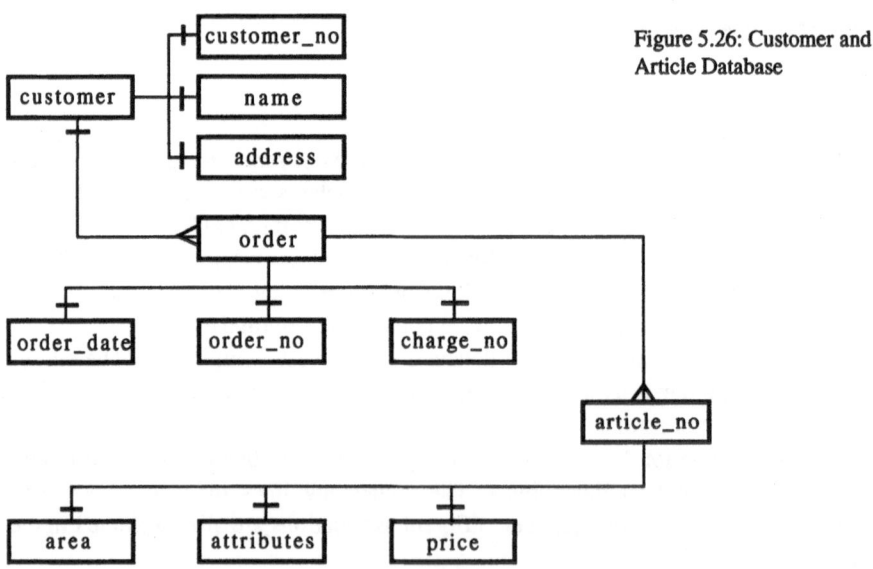

Figure 5.26: Customer and Article Database

The diagram shows that there is only one customer number, one name, and one address. Each customer can have one or more open orders. Orders can be identified by exactly one order date, one order number and one charge number. Orders are associated with one article_no and each article_no is defined by one area, one attribute list and one price.

The data structure described by the entity-relationship diagram shown above allows an article list, a customer list with each customers order, and a price list be printed.

Discussion:
As far as the authors of this book know there is no method which describes different steps for developing a program where the input data structure is defined by an entity-relationship diagram. In this sense entity-relationship diagrams are not like JSP and Warrier/Orr but are very important and powerful for describing data models of organisations, including all the data they need now or later.

5.3 Data Flow Oriented

The most important data flow oriented analysis and design methods currently are described in /DEMAR79/ and /GASA79/. Both methods are based on the following idea: a data flow description shows the flow of information through a system. The system accepts input data from its environment, transforms the information received and produces output data. The environment of a software system is also called its context. The following figure shows a data flow oriented description of our 'wine price list' example (the description languages described in /DEMAR79/ is used in the examples below).

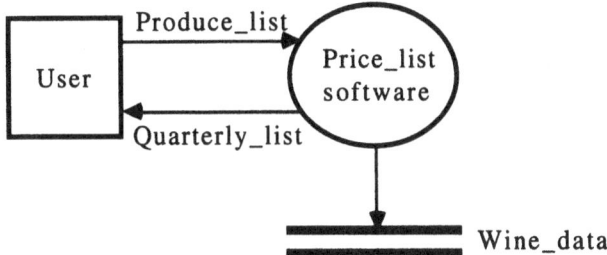

Figure 5.27: Data Flow Diagram of the 'Wine Price List' System

The 'user' requires that the software system 'Price_list_software' produces the quarterly price list. He gives the data 'Produce_list' to the transformation entity and gets the data 'quarterly_list' back. The information required for producing the price list is contained in a data store called 'wine data´.

A software system can be considered as carrying out transformations. It obtains input from the context and one or several data stores and transforms that input in order to produce the required output which is given to the context. The example above already contains all the symbols necessary to describe data flow diagrams (DFD). Entities belonging to the context are represented as rectangles; transformations (sometimes called functions or processes) of a software system are represented as circles; and data stores as double lines. The arrows define the data flow and are marked with the identification of the data item transferred.

In order to describe more complex software systems, a system may consist of several function entities which obtain their input from and provide their output to other function entities. The following figure shows a more complex example of a data flow diagram.

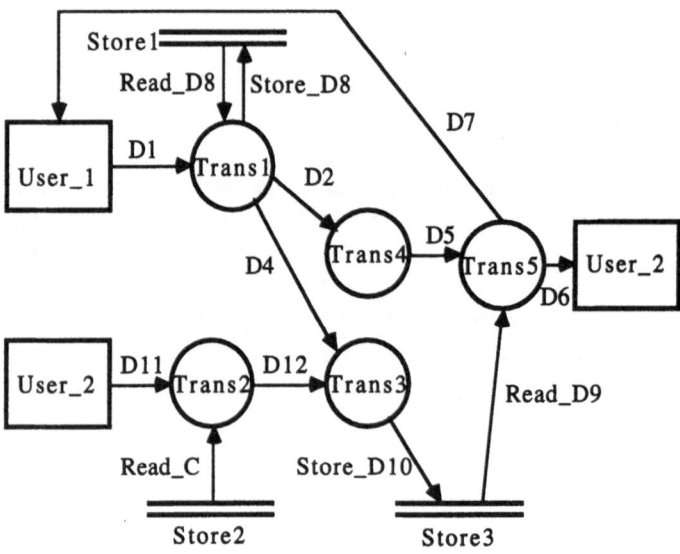

Figure 5.28: Example of a DFD

A transformation entity itself can be described by a DFD and the functional entities of that DFD can also be described by DFDs. A succeeding DFD is a refinement of a transformation node. This means that a DFD will allow a system to be described hierarchically. The following figure shows an example of a hierarchical DFD.

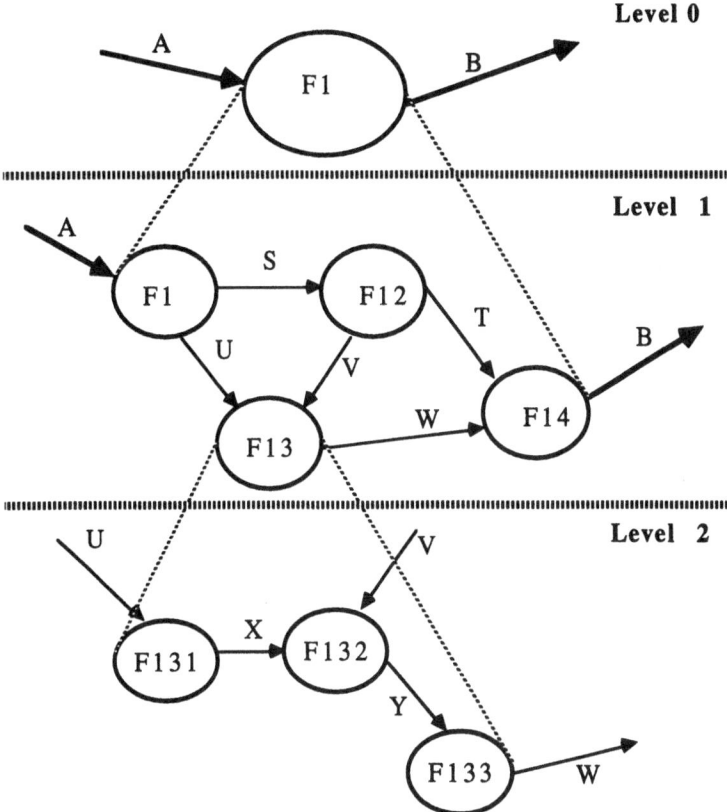

Figure 5.29: Hierarchical DFD

The specification is still incomplete. In addition to data flow, the structure of each information item associated with the arrows has to be defined. The data items associated with each arrows can consist of several smaller information items which can themselves consist of more primitive data items and so on. For this part of the specification, data structure oriented languages are appropriate. The data dictionary has been proposed as a quasi-formal method for describing the structure of the information items associated with arrows. The data dictionary notation allows sequences, selections, and repeated groups of data items. An example of an information item is shown in the example below. It shows that the information item 'address' consists of the name, street and town. The information item name consists either of the items first name or first name followed by middle name and surname. Street and town can be refined in a similar way.

Example:
address = name + street + town
name   = [first name I first name + middle name] + surname

The last aspect which has to be described in more detail is the functionality of the transformation entity. For the specification of the transformation entity, structured English as described in section 5.1.1. is normally used.

Detailed methods have been developed based on the data flow concept and the associated language described above. The best known are described in /DEMAR79/, /GASA79/, /WARD84/. The major steps of all methods are:
1. Describe the environment or context of the system to be developed
2. Refine the specification step by step using hierarchical description.
3. Specify the structure of the information exchanged
4. Specify the functionality of the transformational entities.

These steps must not necessarily be executed in this order. Step 2, 3 and 4 can interleave each other. These steps can be completed for each description layer before the next refinement step is started.

After the DFD is completed functionally oriented specifications can be derived from the data flow diagram. The DFD is transformed into a hierarchical system of functions, when is considered the design phase. This transformation is executed in several steps and is supported by a set of so called design heuristics /PRESS87/.

Discussion:
DFD oriented methods are currently widely accepted, because they are easy to learn and are well supported by tools. DFD oriented methods support the complete development process including project management /DEMAR82/. This means that for structured analysis, a nearly complete software engineering environment is available.

Structured analysis supports all program development activities and allows the use of several life cycles. In addition to the conventional life cycle the evolutionary and incremental life cycles can also be used. The possibility of describing a software system hierarchically allows the use of incremental and evolutionary life cycles. Parts of a system can be described in detail later.

Extensions allow the development of real-time systems. In /WAME85/ and /HAPI87/ data flow based methods which support the development of distributed systems are described. They contain methods for the definition of the control flow of such systems. These are described in the next section.

5.4 Control Flow Oriented

The control flow specification describes the order in which different actions inside a system are executed and how it reacts to stimuli from its environment.

Single and multiple control flow systems can be distinguished. Single control flow system are described by sequential programs and multiple control flow systems are described by parallel programs.

Examples of single control flow description techniques are finite state machines and some derived description techniques such as state transition matrices. Other low level flow control oriented description techniques are Nassi/Shneiderman diagrams and control flow diagrams; these are mainly used as implementation techniques. They are well known and therefore are not further described here. See, for example, /PRESS87/, /MABU87/

Examples of multiple control flow specification techniques are communicating asynchronous processes and Petri nets /REIS82/.

Essentially a control flow oriented specification defines all allowed action sequences of a program. Each action changes the state of a program, i.e. the values of its variables. In each state a set of successor actions is allowed.

A finite state machine (abbreviated to FSM) is a very old and commonly used tool to describe the external behavior of a software system. There are hundreds of papers dealing with various aspects of FSM's. /MOR82/ contains a good introduction, especially about program development.

A finite state machine is a hypothetical machine. It can be in only one of a given number of states at any given time. An FSM reacts to its input. This causes the FSM to change its state and generate an output. The new state and the output are functions of the input and the current state, only. The changes of states are called transitions. Each FSM has a defined starting state. It is also possible to have one or more end states. No further transitions are possible from end states, i.e. end states do not have successor states. There are several ways to describe FSMs. The following example shows an FSM described by a state transition diagram. In state transition diagrams, states are shown as circles and transitions as arrows leading from a state to a possible successor state. The circles are marked with the name of a state. The arrows are marked with the name of the input which causes the transition and the name of the output generated during the transition.

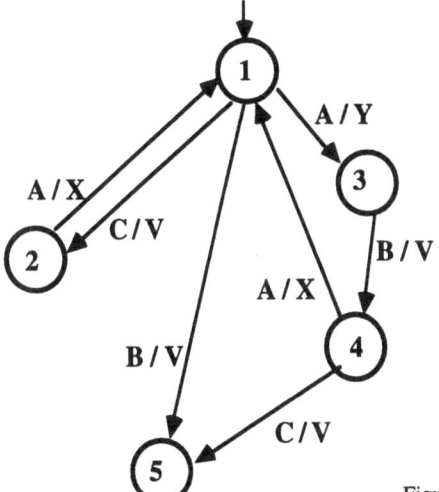

Figure 5.30: Example of a State Transition Diagram

The example above shows an FSM consisting of 5 states. The state names are numbers from 1 to 5. State 1 is the start state. If in state 1 the event A occurs the FSM generates the output Y and enters state 3. In state 3 the transition to state 4 is performed if event B occurs. This generates output V. The rest of the FSM can be interpreted in the same way. State 5 is a final state because no transitions are possible from that state.

The example above also shows that state transition diagrams are an appropriate way to describe the interaction with an external entity. The external entity produces the inputs and receives the appropriate outputs. The following example shows the interaction of a telephone with its user.

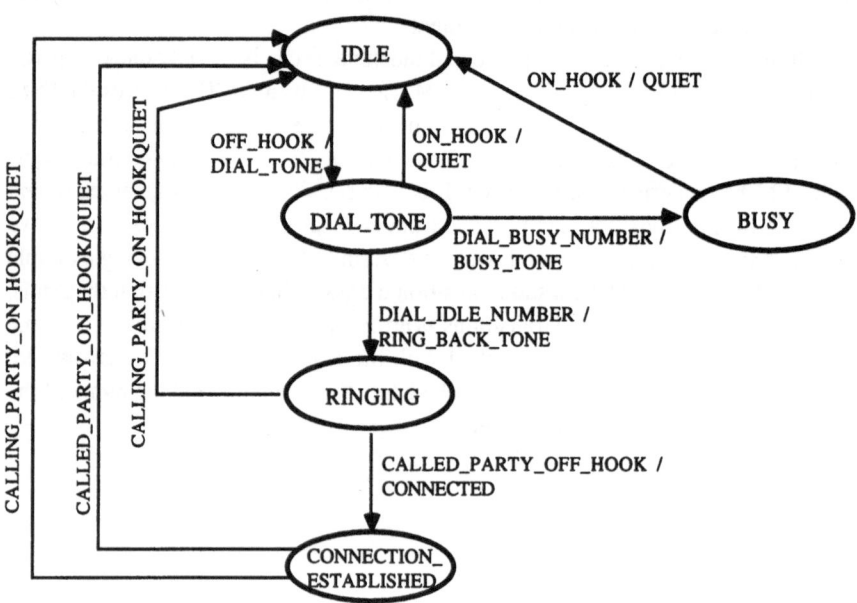

Figure 5.31: State Transition Diagram of the Use of a Telephone

The telephone system starts in the state IDLE. If the system receives the input OFF_HOOK it executes the transition to the state DIAL_TONE and the output DIAL_TONE is generated. If an idle number is dialled (input: DIAL_IDLE_NUMBER) the output RING_BACK_TONE is generated and the system enters the state RINGING. If the party that is called takes the telephone off the hook (input: CALLED_PARTY_OFF_HOOK) the output CONNECTED is generated and the transition to the state CONNECTION_ESTABLISHED is executed. In the state RINGING the calling party can put the telephone on the hook (input: ON_HOOK). In this case the system enters the IDLE state and the output QUIET is generated. In the state CONNECTION_ESTABLISHED both parties can put their telephones on the hooks (input CALLED_PARTY_ON_HOOK or input

CALLING_PARTY_ON_HOOK). In both cases the system returns to the state IDLE and generates the output QUIET. In addition to the main path described, some side paths are posible. These can also be seen in the figure.

State transition matrices, STMs, are often used instead of state transition diagrams. STMs are tools for translating conditions and actions into tabular form. A decision table is a matrix. The columns are labelled with all possible states and the rows are labelled with all possible inputs. The matrix elements consist of two components. One element describe the output generated and the other element defines the successor state. The following figure shows our telephone system as described in STM notation.

States \ Input	IDLE	DIAL_TONE	RINGING	CONNECTION_ ESTABLISHED	BUSY
OFF_HOOK	DIAL_TONE DIAL_TONE				
ON_HOOK	QUIET IDLE	QUIET IDLE	QUIET IDLE	QUIET IDLE	QUIET IDLE
DIAL_IDLE_ NUMBER		RING_BACK_ TONE RINGING			
CALLED_PARTY_ OFF_HOOK			CONNECTED CONNECTION_ ESTABLISHED		
CALLED_PARTY_ ON_HOOK				QUIET IDLE	
DIAL_BUSY_ NUMBER		BUSY_TONE BUSY			

Figure 5.32: STM of a Telephone System

FSMs and STMs are difficult to misinterpret and can even be used as machine readable specifications in order to produce table driven code.

Many specification and design methods are based on FSMs, especially where the interaction of a program or other program components with the environment has to be defined. The environment of a system specified as an FSM can be also defined by another FSM. The output of one system is the input of the other. A concurrent system can be considered as a set of cooperating FSMs.

Hence the FSM concept is very often used as a basis for languages and methods for developing concurrent systems. The languages and methods described in chapter 7 - SDL, Estelle, LOTOS, REVS, etc.- are all based on the FSM concept.

Discussion:

As already mentioned, FSMs form a basic concept for specifying concurrent systems. Depending on the specific notation, FSM based specification languages and methods allow the application of different types of software cycles. FSM based techniques will be discussed in greater detail, beginning in chapter 7.

5.5 Object Oriented

Since the early eigthies, object oriented programming has become a very promising approach to the production of better and more reusable software.

In the following sections the basic concepts of object oriented programming are introduced and the extension of the object oriented development approach to concurrent and distributed systems is discussed.

5.5.1 Principles of Object Oriented Software System Development

In object oriented development the programmer maps the real world domain to abstractions called objects /BOOCH86/. Objects with the same charateristics belong to an object class. My American Heritage Dictionary is an object of the class "books". Conversely objects are instances of classes.

Object oriented development supports analysis, design and programming activities. When object oriented programming is used, the analysis and design activities are coupled with implementation activities. Object classes identified in the analysis phase can be found in the implementation. The system structure developed in the design stage is nearly identical to the final program structure. Entities of the design can immediately be mapped to entities of an object-oriented programming language. An object-oriented design specification can be considered as a blueprint for the complete implementation.

Object oriented program development is centered around the following four basic concept:
1. abstraction,
2. encapsulation,
3. inheritance,
4. polymorphism.

Abstraction and Encapsulation:

In general, an abstraction is a concise and condensed representation of a more complicated object or idea. Details, or what are considered as details, are not considered further. Instead only those characteristics of an object that distinguish it from other kinds of objects in its environment are emphasised. An abstraction focuses on the exterior view of an object, i.e. how its behaviour is seen from other objects and not how it is implemented. The implementation details are encapsulated in the object.

The concept of abstract data types as described in section from the core of object oriented system development because it supports abstraction and encapsulation. An object is a package of information and the description of its manipulation /ROBS81/. Each object consists of a data structure (local state) and a set of operations defined on that data structure. These operations are the only way to change or to read the local state of an object. The following figure shows the basic structure of an object /BOOCH86/, /BOOCH91/.

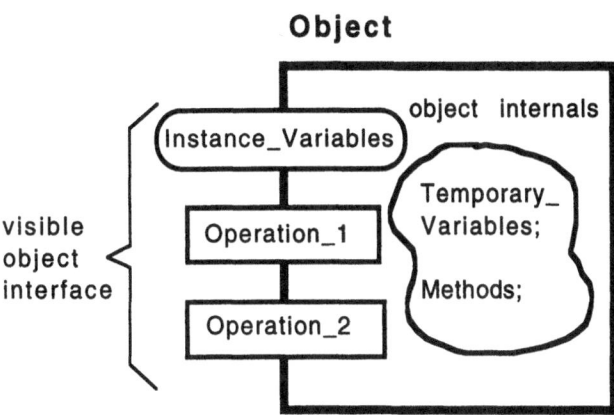

Object

Figure 5.33: Structure of Objects

An object can invoke the operations of other objects in order to implement its own operations. The initiator of an operation invocation will be notified that an operation has been finished, e.g. by a return of the value of the operation. The invoking object always waits until an invoked operation is finished. A standard object based program has only one thread of control.

Operations of an object are invoked by messages sent by other objects.

Note: The term 'messages' used in conjunction with object-oriented programming has another meaning to that used in communicating processes. This was explained earlier. It is more like a procedure call.

Each message consists of the name of the destination object, a selector which identifies the operation to be invoked, and a set of operation arguments. The set of messages that can be handled by an object is called the protocol of an object.

Note: The term 'protocol' used in conjunction with object oriented programming has another meaning to that used in communication systems (see chapter 1).

The following figure shows a system consisting of three objects.

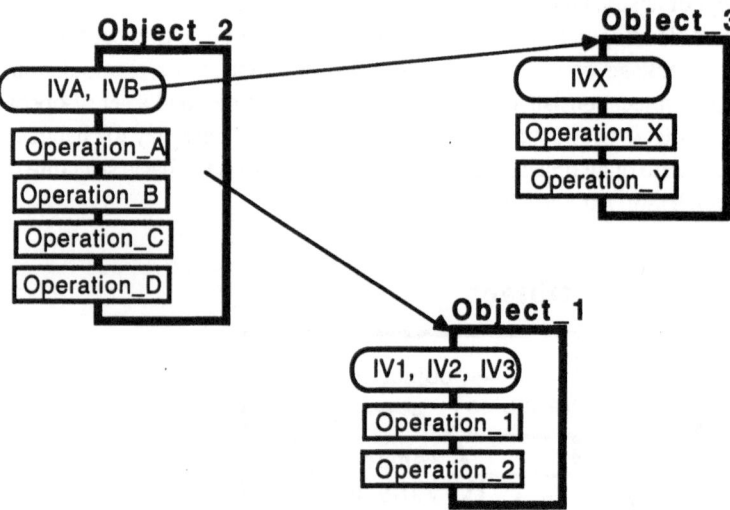

Figure 5.34: An example of an Object Oriented System

Object_2 has the instance variables IVA and IVB. The value of the instance variable IVB is Object_3. The value of the variable IVB can be manipulated by executing the appropriate operations. Operations of Object_1, are invoked in the implementation of the methods of Object_2. Object_2 uses Object_1, i.e. Object_2 invokes operations of Object_1 internally to implement its methods. This means that in the methods of Object_2 operations of Object_1 are invoked. The example above shows two major ways that objects know other objects. Objects can be values of instance variables of other objects and operations of objects can be used to implement methods of other objects. A third relationship is the parameter relationship. An object can be a parameter of an operation invocation.

Objects with the same characteristics belong to an object class. Each individual object is considered as an instance of a class. Classes are templates for creating simelar objects. Each object derived from a class has the local data structure and the corresponding operations of the class. An object of a certain class can be created by sending messages to the corresponding class. The class reacts by creating a new object of the related class type.

Inheritance:
Inheritance is a way of constructing different levels of abstraction.

Hierarchies of classes can be constructed in object-oriented development systems. Classes that are lower in the hierarchy are subclasses of higher level classes i.e. superclasses. Subclasses inherit the data structures and operations of their superclasses but can change the inherited operations or add new data structures and operations. Inheritance is a property of classes and not between of objects.

The following example shows the class 'BOOKS', the derived subclasses 'REPORT' and 'DICTIONARY', and the objects 'MONTHLY_REPORT' and 'MY_DICTIONARY'. In this example the same symbols for classes and objects are used as in /BOOCH91/.

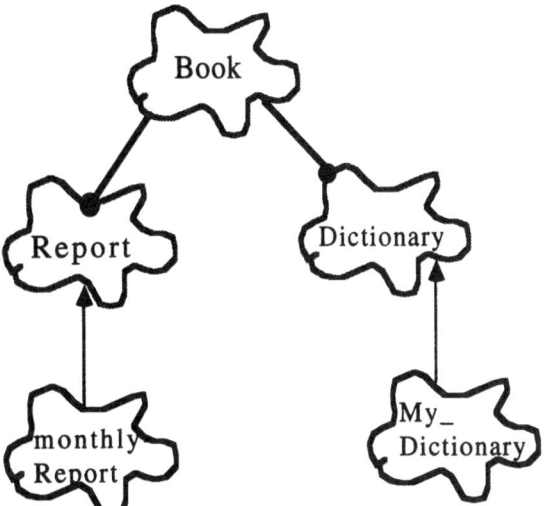

Figure 5.35: Example of Inheritance

Polymorphism:

Polymorphism is the ability of different objects to respond appropriately to the same selector name. Whole families of classes can be treated as if they were a single parent class; they are infact subclasses of the parent class. Instead of invoking an operation in an object of a subclass, the corresponding operation in the parent class is invoked. A particular operation on an object of a derived subclass is invoked using the selector and the parameter type.

We will use the simple example that follows to illustrate polymorphism. There is a class called 'SHAPE' with an operation 'DRAW ()'. Derived from SHAPE we have the subclasses RECTANGLE and CIRCLE. The operation DRAW is defined differently for each of these subclasses i.e. rectangles and circles are drawn differently. Therefore the class SHAPE does not contain a method for the operation DRAW. SHAPE contains only a pointer to the different subclasses which contain methods for the operation DRAW. In our program we have the variables my_rectangle of type RECTANGLE and my_circle of type CIRCLE. Given a pointer P, of type SHAPE, how is a call P->DRAW(my_rectangle) handled? The relevant table of method names is first found by examining the class to which P points. Now there are several pointers to subclasses containing methods for operation DRAW (RECTANGLE and CIRCLE). The decision that operation DRAW is to be chosen depends on the parameter type. In our case the parameter is of type REC-TANGLE and the operation DRAW in class RECTANGLE is chosen.

Several variations of polymorphism exist. There are slightly different ways of implementing polymorphism in different object-oriented programming languages. A short discussion is given in /BOOCH91/.

5.5.2 Object Oriented Concurrent Systems

The term 'message' can imply that objects are concurrent entities. Concurrency is not a major property of object oriented programming. Normally the invocation of an operation by a message has semantics similar to a procedure call. The initiator of an operation invocation waits until the associated method has returned an answer. All the computations are sequential. However the structure of object-oriented programms implies the introduction of concurrency.

Two types of method can be used to introduce concurrency /BAWE88/, /WEG87/.

1. In general objects are sequential entities. Concurrency is introduced by a special class called 'process'. Each object of the class process is executed by just one thread of control. It is possible that several processes invoke operations or even the operation of an object concurrently. This type of concurrency is already used in Smalltalk /GORO83/.

2. In general, objects can be executed in parallel. Each object is associated with a process. Such a object is very often called an actor /HEW77/. Everything including procedures and data is uniformly represented as actors. In Act 1 /LIEB87/ this type of concurrency is used.

3. More than one thread of control can be executed on one object at the same time. Each operation invocation can result in the creation of a new thread of control which performs the invoked operation. In addition to these dynamically created processes there can be processes executing background tasks.

In concurrent object oriented programs, processes must cooperate as in standard concurrent systems. This is also done by using appropriate communication and synchronisation methods. The basic concept behind these methods is the same as for 'normal' concurrent programs. These methods are discussed in chapter 7.

/YOTO87/ contains an overview of object oriented concurrent programming systems.

5.5.3 Object Oriented Distributed Systems

The object oriented programming approach can also be extended to distributed systems /SHM89/, /SCHN88/. As mentioned in previous sections, each process in a distributed system has its own separate address space. Therefore a process cannot have direct access to resources outside its address space /WEG87/. As in object-oriented concurrent programming only objects of a class process can be executed in parallel. Parallel objects have the same communication and synchronisation concepts as concurrent objects. However the distribution of objects brings new problems.

In purely object oriented systems, parameters of messages are also objects. If the operation of an object which is located on another physical system is invoked the objects and the relevant class definitions have to be moved from one system to the other.

Moving an object with its class definition means that its context changes. On the new host there can be a parent class with the same name but a different protocol. This can mean that some operations are no longer defined in the parent class or if they are defined they can have a totally different meaning.

Distribution makes it expensive to share non-local resources. In /WEG87/ it is even stated that inheritance which is normally considered typical for object oriented programming is inconsistent with distribution.

The difficulties described above do not allow efficient implementations of object oriented distributed programming systems. Therefore /SCHILL90/ recommends that parallel processes which exchange messages are used for realtime applications such as communication and process control software. *This means that object oriented paradigms are mixed with 'classical' concurrent programming concepts.*

An overview of object oriented distributed programming can be found in /SCHILL90/ and /SHM89/. Several object oriented distributed programming systems are described in /SGHM90/, /BHJL86/, /BHJLC87/, /MAKRSL89/, /BENN87/, /NIERS87/, /MSKFH89/, /LISKOV85/, /YOTO87/ and /NHMWR87/.

5.5.4 Example of an Object Oriented Development Method

In /BOOCH91/ a language and method for developing programs in an object-oriented way is described. This language and the related method is explained below, using some examples.

The object oriented design method is based on four diagrams which provide answers to the major issues which must be considered in object oriented design:
- Class diagrams
  What classes exist and how are those related? /BOOCH91/
- Object diagrams
  What mechanisms are used to regulate how objects collaborate?
  /BOOCH91/
- Module diagrams
  Where should each class and object be declared? /BOOCH91/
- Process diagrams

To which processor should a process be allocated and how should the multiple processes of a particular processor be scheduled? /BOOCH91/

The four diagrams mentioned above describe mainly the static aspects of a program design; but an object oriented program has also important dynamic aspects. The time ordering of external events influences the state of each instance of a class. Objects can be created and destroyed during execution. In order to describe these dynamic aspects, each class in the class diagrams may be supplemented by a state transition diagram. Object diagrams are only snapshots of a current configuration. There can exist a timing diagram for each object diagram which shows the temporal ordering of messages as they are sent and processed.

Class Diagrams and State Transition Diagrams:
    'A class diagram is used to show the existence of classes and their relationship in the logical design of a system' /BOOCH91/. In a class diagram each class is represented by a cloud. The relationship between classes are shown by lines connecting related classes i.e. clouds. The following figure shows a simple example of a class diagram.

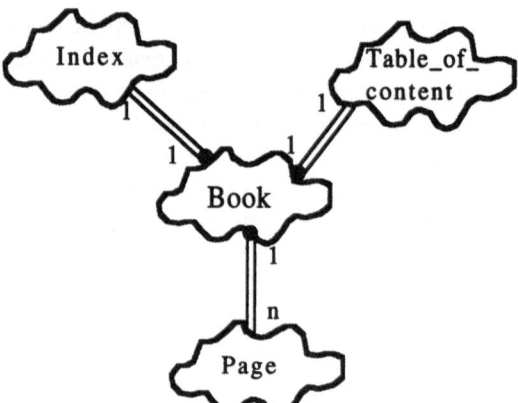

Figure 5.36: Class Diagram

In the above example the class BOOK uses one instance of the TABLE_OF_CONTENT class and one instance of the INDEX class but several instances of the PAGE class. A dot indicates the class that is using the resources of another. The integers indicate the number of classes that are being used. In our example the '1' at class BOOK and the 'n' at class PAGE shows that one instance uses several instances of class PAGE.

    An arrow pointing from the subclass to the parent class shows the inheritance relation. Our example in figure 5.33 shows that dictionary is a subclass of class BOOK.

    Our example shows only the symbols for the two most important relationships between classes. In /BOOCH91/ it is also possible to describe other types of relationships like metaclass or instantiation.

For each class shown in the class diagram there is a class template. The class template describes in natural language some details of a class e.g. name, documentation, visibility, list of operations etc. Operation templates specify details of the operation of a class e.g. parameters, results, etc.

In order to support the design of large program systems /BOOCH91/ proposes hierarchies of class categories. A class category is a collection of logically related classes.

State transition diagrams as described in section 5.4 are used to describe the dynamic behaviour of a class. The actions indicated in a state transition diagram can point to another object diagram.

Object Diagrams and Timing Diagrams:

Object diagrams are used to show the existence and the relationship between objects in the logical design of a system. The relationships between objects are defined by the way they know each other. They are made visible to each other when:
1. Objects belong to the same lexical scope,
2. an object is passed as a parameter to another object,
3. an object is the value of an instance variable.

Objects can be created and destroyed. Therefore object diagrams are not static like class diagrams. There are several object diagrams which show the key constellations of a system.

The following figure shows an example of an object diagram.

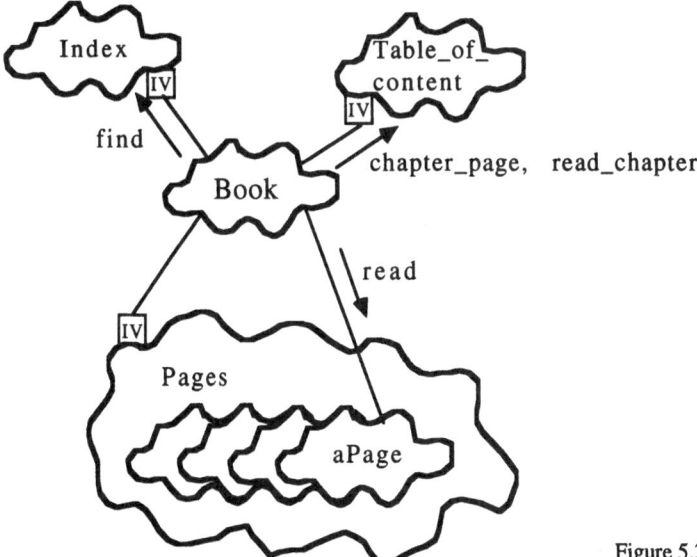

Figure 5.37: Object Diagram

The above example shows the object diagram of a Book which is based on its class diagram. Objects of the classes Index and Pages are used as instance variables. This is shown by lines ending with rectangles with the letters 'IV' in it. Normally a book has several pages. Therefore an array of page objects is used in the object Book. Different arrows marked with names show the operations and how they are invoked. The arrows in our example show simple operation invocations. These are similar to procedure calls. Other types of operation invocations would be asynchronous and synchronous messages (see chapter 7).

There is a relationship between class diagrams and object diagrams. Methods used in object diagrams must also be described in the relevant class diagram and vice versa. If a method is removed from a class, all object diagrams derived from it must also be changed.

Object diagrams show neither the flow of control, nor the order of events. In /BOOCH91/ one of the suggested methods for describing the sequence of events, is the use of timing diagrams which are already used in hardware design. The following figure shows an example of a simple timing diagram.

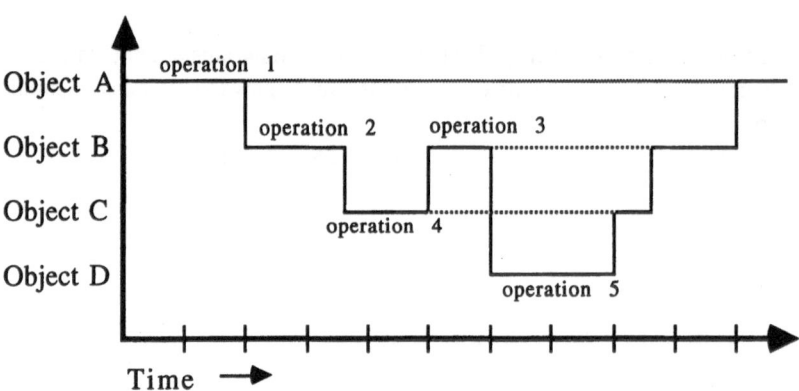

Figure 5.38: Example of a Timing Diagram

In a timing diagram time moves from left to right. First operation 1 in object A is invoked. The execution of operation 1 invokes operation 2 of object B. Operation 2 passes operation 4 messages to object C. Operation 4 invokes operation 3 and so on. The dotted lines indicate a dynamic nesting of messages. The operations are continued when control returns.

Module Diagrams:
Class and object diagrams show the logical design of a system. Module diagrams are used to show the allocation of classes and objects to modules in the physical design. This is necessary because several programming languages support the module concept in addition to the class and object concept. A module can contain one or more

classes and objects. The designer must decide which classes and objects will be allocated to which modules. For languages which do not support an additional module concept a module diagram is not necessary.

The following figure shows an example of a module diagram.

one_book

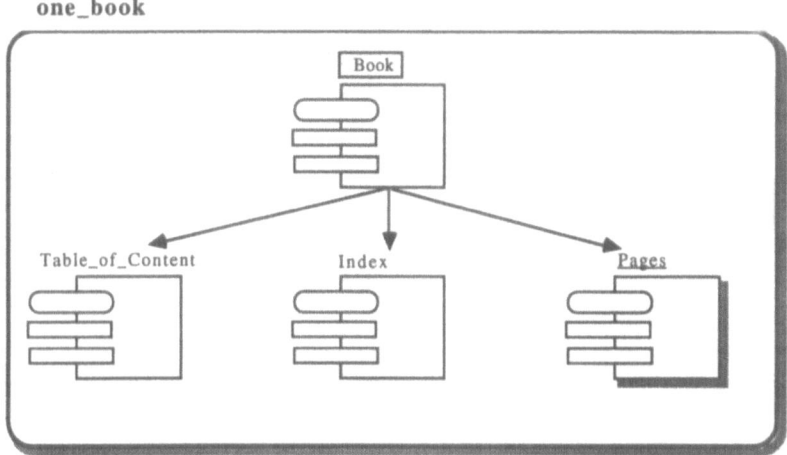

Figure 5.39: Example of a Module Diagram

The module diagram above shows the subsystem 'one_book'. It consists of four modules. The interface of the module Book is exported to other subsystems; this is shown by the rectangle around the name. The module Pages is imported from another subsystem; this is shown by the underlining of the name. The modules Table_of_Content and Index are part of the subsystem one_book.

Process Diagram:
Process diagrams shows which processes are allocated to which processors. This means according to /BOOCH91/ that distributed systems are supported, i.e. that a programming language is available which supports distributed object-oriented programming. /BOOCH91/ does not consider distribution until the programming phase. The problems mentioned in section 5.5.3 must be solved now.

The following figure shows an example of a process diagram.

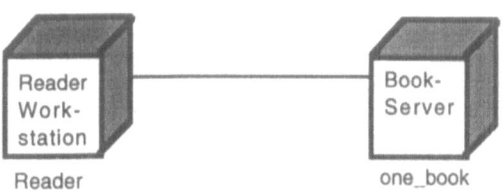

Figure 5.40: Example of a Process Diagram

The example above shows two computer systems. One computer system is a workstation on which the subsystem Reader runs. The other computer system is a server which runs the subsystem one_book.

Method:
In /BOOCH91/ an incremental and iterative development process is suggested for object oriented analysis and design. It emphazises that an iterative development is best, especially for new software applications. Transitions between implementation and design and analysis activities are necessary because a new problem is not completely understood. During the development process the understanding of the problem increases. Data abstraction, encapsulation, inheritance, and particularly polymorphism all support incremental development. Parts of a program can be changed and the effects limited to only a few objects and classes.

For object oriented design four major activities are suggested /BOOCH91/:
–   Identifying classes and objects
    Here objects and object classes of the problem domain are identified. The results are lists of classes, objects or object attributes. Objects or classes which are sufficiently understood can be completly specified using the class template mentioned above. During the development process the list is changed. Some classes and objects are added, removed, or described in more detail.

–   Identifying the semantics of classes and objects
    In this step the meaning of the classes and objects is defined. Particular the interfaces and protocols of the different classes and objects are specified. Here the developer has to view classes and objects from the perspective of an outsider.

–   Identification of the relationships between classes and objects
    Here the relationships between classes and objects are identified. For classes, the using, inheritance, instance, and metaclass relations are specified. For objects the object diagrams which describe the relationships between objects are drawn.

–   Implementing classes and objects
    Here a representation of classes and objects has to be chosen. If a programming language with a module concept is used, the classes and objects are allocated to different modules.

The steps described above do not have to be executed completely in this strong order. The developer can switch between these steps as required.

Recommended Reading:

There are numerous very detailed books about software development engineering. The following two were more or less randomly chosen.

/FAIR85/   Fairly R.
            Software Engineering Concepts
            McGraw-Hill, New York 1985

/PRESS87/   Pressman R. S.
            Software Engineering, A Practitioner's Approach
            McGraw-Hill Book Company, New York 1987

Control Questions:

1. What is the difference between a method and a methodology?
2. What is the internal structure of all software methods?
3. What types of concepts for software methods do you know?
4. Explain one example of each concept?
5. Which software life cycle is assumed in each of the method described?
6. Which concepts can be used for distributed programming?

Exercises:

1. What methods are used in your software engineering environment?
2. On which concepts are these methods based?
3. Which aspects are mainly covered by the methods used in your professional environment?
4. Is it possible to extend the methods you use?

6 Methods for
Concurrent Software System Development

The various features of software development for distributed systems are described. It is shown how these are integrated into different software development methods.

In order to describe distributed software, the basic concepts presented in the previous chapter have to be combined to give a specification technique. Descriptions of control flow are very important, especially for real-time applications /ZAVE82/.

Many languages have been developed to describe systems of parallel processes. An overview can be found in /ANSC83/, /BSTA88/, and /NEHM88b/.

Concurrent specification or programming languages can be classified according to various aspects /JORA78/, /LISKOV79/, /STOTT82/, /NEHM88b/, /SLKR87/ and /MUEHL86/ The following classification scheme is a combination of those described in the afore-mentioned literature. The most important features for classifying concurrent programming or specification languages are thus:

- System decomposition and process structure
- communication features
- synchronisation features
- description of process behaviour
- task allocation
- methods.

In the following sections the different features and the concepts which can be used to specify the different aspects of a concurrent program are described.

The languages SREM, SDL, Estelle, and Lotos are used to illustrate the different aspects of concurrent program specification methods in detail. Other specification methods are described briefly.

Software Requirements Engineering Methodology (SREM) was first published in 1976/1977 /ALF77/. It was designed for the development of real-time systems. Since its first presentation, SREM has been extended to address the problems of specifying system level requirements and defining a distributed design /ALF85a/.

SDL, Estelle, and LOTOS are specification languages supported by the standardisation organisation Association of Postal and Telecommunication Authorities (CCITT) and the International Standard Organisation (ISO). These languages are mainly used to specify communication protocols.

Further in the section five other specification languages are briefly summarised. We have chosen those because literature about them is easily accessible, there are many other important specification languages, possibly hundreds.

6.1 System Decomposition and Process Structure

A major feature of all specification and programming languages is the possibility of breaking down a system into a set of smaller systems. This includes ways of specifying the relationship and interaction of the different subsystems. In chapter 5 several methods for decomposing systems were described. Decomposition concepts in standard programming are functions, data types, and objects. In addition, several related functions, data types and objects can be combined into modules.

In cooperative programs, the major decomposition concept is the process. Processes cooperate to achieve their common goal. In a program the number of parallel processes can be static or dynamic.

In a static process structure the maximum possible number of processes as well as their type and identification are known at compile time. This does not exclude that those processes are created or deleted at run time. This is desirable for saving memory as the maximum number of processes defined during compile time can not exceeded however it increases the administrative overhead costs.

In a dynamic process structure the number and identification of processes are not known at compile time. Processes are created during runtime. These processes are defined by various process objects. The number of possible processes is only restricted by the available resources, especially memory.

6.1.1 Decomposition Concepts in SREM

SREM has been extended to address the problem of defining system requirements and allocating them to the data processing units. This extension is known as System Requirements Engineering Methodology, SYSREM.

In SYSREM a system is considered to be a transformation of inputs into outputs. The transformation takes place over an interval of time and ends when the criteria for completion are satisfied. During the transformation a sequence of input items is transformed into a sequence of output items. An input or output item can contain several concurrent sequences of lower level items, and so on. A completion criterion is a boolean condition on the input.

Functional decomposition is supported in SYSREM. A system is considered as a hierarchy of functions. Each function transforms input to output over a certain period of time. Some low level functions operate concurrently and some operate in a particular sequence. The following figure shows the system decomposition of a burglar alarm system based SYSREM. When the house owner is at home he can switch the alarm on and off. In controlled houses the noise level is measured. The results are sent to the control center where the results of the measurements are stored and evaluated.

The SYSREM description shows that the burglar alarm system consists of several components which monitor a house. These components run in parallel as shown by the symbol '&'. The component 'control_a_house' consists of the components 'switch_on_control', 'control', and 'switch_off_control'. These components are executed sequentially. The component 'control' is divided into two components running in parallel. These components are called 'collect_control_inf' and 'evaluate_control_info'. The solid lines in SYSREM show the control of the system. Dotted lines show the input and output of the different functions. In addition to functional decomposition, input and output can also be further refined refined in SYSREM.

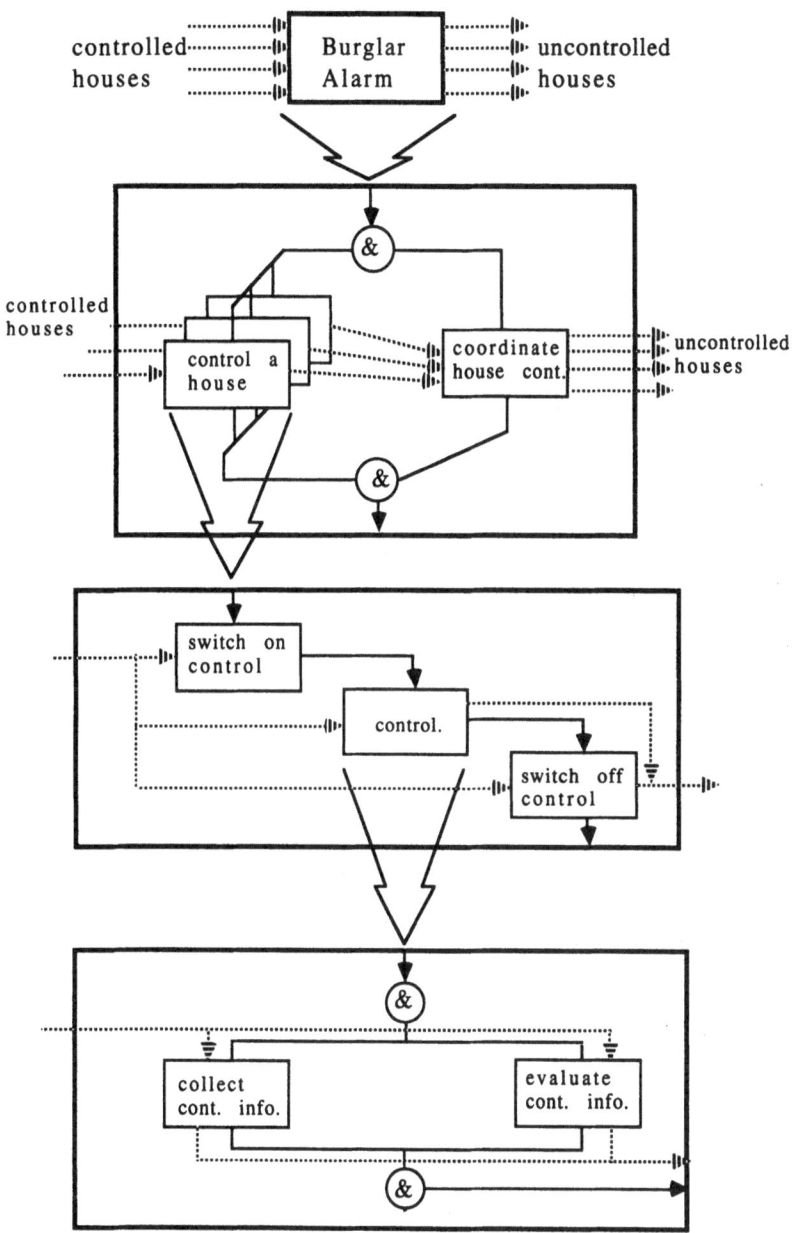

Figure 6.1: Decomposition of a Burglar Alarm System in SYSREM

6.1.2 Decomposition Concepts in SDL

In SDL /SDL/ a system may be considered from a static or dynamic point of view. Blocks represent the static structure of a system, while processes represent the system behaviour. Each block can contain one or more processes.

A system is composed of a number of blocks connected by channels. A channel is a unidirectional transport route for signals. A channel definition contains a list of all signals that can be conveyed on it.

A block can be divided further into subblocks and channels. The hierarchy of blocks defines the static structure of a system, i.e. the block tree.

In parallel with the subdivision of blocks is the subdivision of channels. If a block contains several sub-blocks these are also connected by channels. The channels arriving at the block can be separated into sub-channels inside it. The sub-channels are connected by sub-blocks. The signal list of all sub-channels derived from the same channel must be disjointed and the union of all the sub-channels must be identical with the signal list of the channel from which they are derived.

Each block can contain sub-blocks or one or more processes. Sub-block definitions must include at least the sub-process definitions resulting from the division of the processes in the block to which they belong.

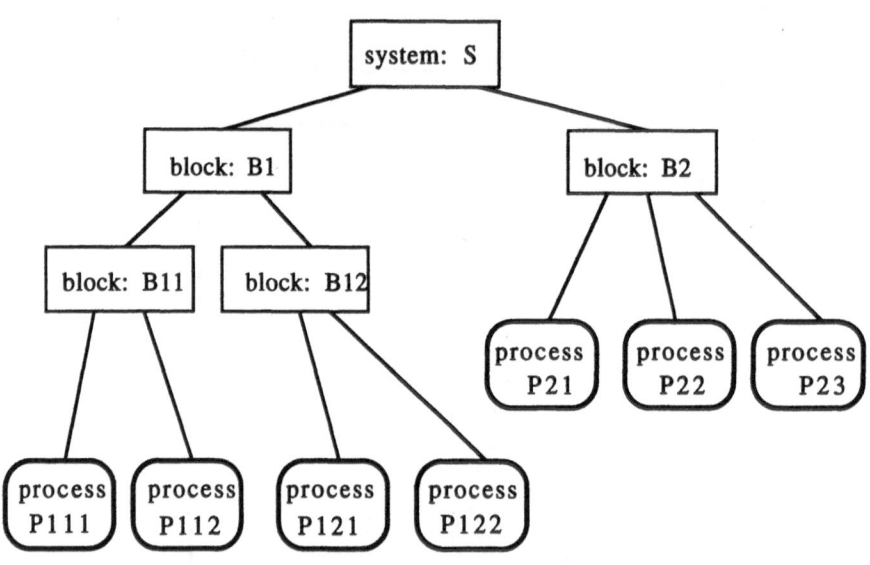

Figure 6.2: Structure of SDL Specifications

Processes can be created and terminated dynamically. A process can be created by another process or it can already exist at system initialization time. Processes run in parallel without special restrictions unlike in Estelle where a child process can only run when its parent process is blocked.

6.1.3 Decomposition Concepts in Estelle

In Estelle /ESTELLE/, /LINN86/ a specification can be a complete self-contained module or be broken down into a set of nested modules. A module defined within the scope of another module is only visible within the scope of the embodying or parent module. A module nested within another module is called a child module. In Estelle there are two types of modules: processes and activities.

Processes can run in parallel with other processes at the same level of the hierarchy. The execution of activities at the same level must be interleaved. No module can run in parallel with its parent module and a parent module is given preference over its children. This means that when a module executes transitions all its children modules are blocked. Scheduling of modules at the same level is nondeterministic.

6.1.4 Decomposition Concepts in LOTOS

In LOTOS /LOTOS/ a single process can be decomposed into interacting subprocesses. These subprocesses can be further refined into subprocesses. A LOTOS specification is a hierarchy of process definitions.

LOTOS subprocesses are refinements of the embodying process and therefore a process cannot run in parallel with its subprocesses. Processes can run in parallel; this means that in LOTOS the actions of different processes interleave with each other. Real parallelism is not possible.

A process A can enable another process B, but A must be successfully completed before process B can start. The symbol 'exit' is used to mark the place of successful termination in a process. Values can be passed from an enabling process to an enabled process.

Processes create instances of subprocesses when the name of a subprocess appears in the behaviour description of the creating process. When a process is created from another values can be passed from the creating process to that which is created.

A process can disable another process. Process A can be interrupted by the start of process B. Process A does not resume after the interruption; only process B is continued.

6.1.5 Decomposition Concepts in Other SEE's or Programming Languages

Modular Approach to Software Construction, Operation, Test (Mascot)
Mascot has been developed by the British Ministry of Defense; It is intended to provide support during all phases of a variation of the conventional life cycle (specific to Mascot). An outline of Mascot can be found in /AXFO89/. For external requirements specification, Mascot does not prescribe any specific language or method. In this stage any suitable method is allowed. A language which is specific to Mascot is introduced for the design specification.

In Mascot a system design is considered a network of concurrent processes called activities. Processes interact with each other via intercommunication data areas (IDA). Communicating processes always share an IDA.

Mascot allows the hierarchical specification of a system. A system can consist of several subsystems, which can themselves consist of further subsystems, and so on. The subsystems of the lowest levels consist of one or more processes called activities. An activity can be broken down into modules called roots or subroots. Each activity has one root which corresponds to a main program and several links to subroots which may themselves have links to other subroots, and so on. These links only specify the calling hierarchy. They do not show the control flow of the activity, i.e. the process behaviour.

Structured Development of Real-Time Systems (SDRTS)

/WAME85/ describes an extension of data flow specifications. This extension allows the specification of real-time systems and is called Structured Development of real-time systems (SDRTS).

In SDRTS a system is decomposed into transformations and these are connected by data flows as in structured analysis; (see section 6.3). In addition to data flow and data store transformations, Ward and Mellor have introduced control transformations: control flow and control store. The control flow of a system specifies events which initiate transformations (see communication and synchronisation in sections 6.2, 6.3). The control flow can also be also hierarchically, similarly to the data flow.

Strategies for Real-Time Development (SRTD)

SRTD is an extension of data flow diagrams, similar to SDRTS. It was proposed by Hatley and Pirbhai in /HAPI87/. A system is considered to be a set of transformations connected by data flows. The specification of the data flow is also extended by a specification method for control flow.

Design Approach for Real-Time Systems (DARTS)

Data flow diagrams are also the basis of the requirement analysis in DARTS /GOMA84/, /GOMA89/. First transformations are grouped into tasks. Tasks are processes and can be executed concurrently. Task identification requires the determination of which transformations must be executed sequentially and which can be executed concurrently. The data flow between transformations is mapped onto the corresponding communication mechanisms.

Process-oriented, Application, and Interpretable Specification Language (PAISLey)

In PAISLey /ZAVE81/, /ZAVE82/, /ZAVE84/ a system is simply considered a set of cooperating processes as the name suggests. There is no decomposition concept beyond the highest level.

6.2 Communication

Concurrent processes belonging to the same program have to exchange information in order to coordinate their activities. Processes can exchange information directly or indirectly.

6.2.1 Indirect Information Exchange

Indirect information exchange means that processes use objects. Here objects are data structures and the necessary operations. Operations defined on a shared object can be executed by several processes.

Simple examples of shared objects are variables of predefined type which can be assigned to or read by different processes e.g. variables of type boolean which can be assigned to or read by cooperating processes.

More sophisticated shared objects are user defined abstract data types. Data abstraction allows a programmer to specify a data object in the context of those operations or procedures that can be applied to it. In parallel programs, different processes can execute operations on the same object simultaneously. Some processes can use operations which change the state of a shared object and other processes perform operations which read the state of this shared object. Parallel processes exchange infomation via shared objects. Following the terminology introduced in /BSTA88/, this type of system would logically non-distributed.

The following figure shows an example of a shared object. It contains the operations Op 1, Op 2 and Op 3, where Op 1 is called by process A and B, Op 2 is executed by process B and Op 3 is executed by process C.

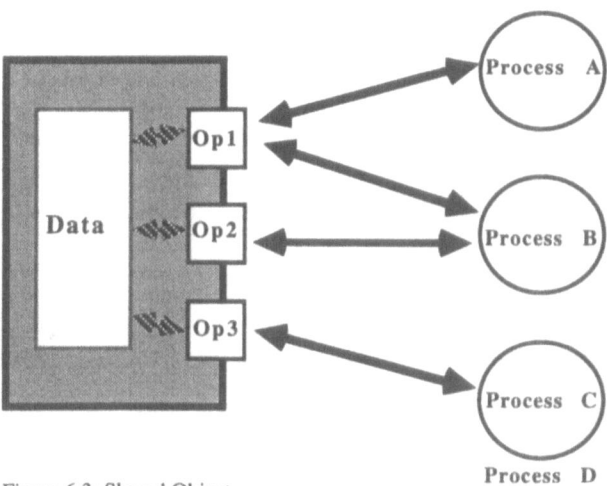

Figure 6.3: Shared Object

The invocation of operations is normally implemented using procedure calls. Therefore shared objects can be easily implemented on systems with common memory. In a distributed system other communication methods must be used. Shared objects on distributed systems can be implemented by remote procedure calls (RPC).

6.2.2 Remote Procedure Call

Remote procedure calls are the standard communication mechanism in client/server networks (see section 2.3). The user interacts with application programs which may be clients of services offered on several server nodes of a computer network. Clients can invoke certain services by remote procedure calls. These are similar to normal procedure calls but the calling process is executed on another processor other than that of the called procedure. The procedure call is sent to the appropriate server node as a request message. On the server node the request message is accepted by a corresponding server process. The server process executes the invoked procedure and sends back the results as a reply message.

Server and client are not in the same address space. This has some implications for parameter passing. An RPC only allows call by value. This means that the values of input parameters are copied into the execution environment of the procedure by the request message. Output parameters are also copied to the execution environment of the calling process by the reply message. Standard procedures also allow call by reference. The execution environment of the called procedure obtains the addresses of the parameters. This is faster than copying values. However the separated memory spaces do not allow parameter passing by address. For the same reason pointers are not allowed as parameters.

Except for the restrictions on parameter passing, a user does not normally see that an RPC is implemented by messages. The following figure shows the basic concept of RPC.

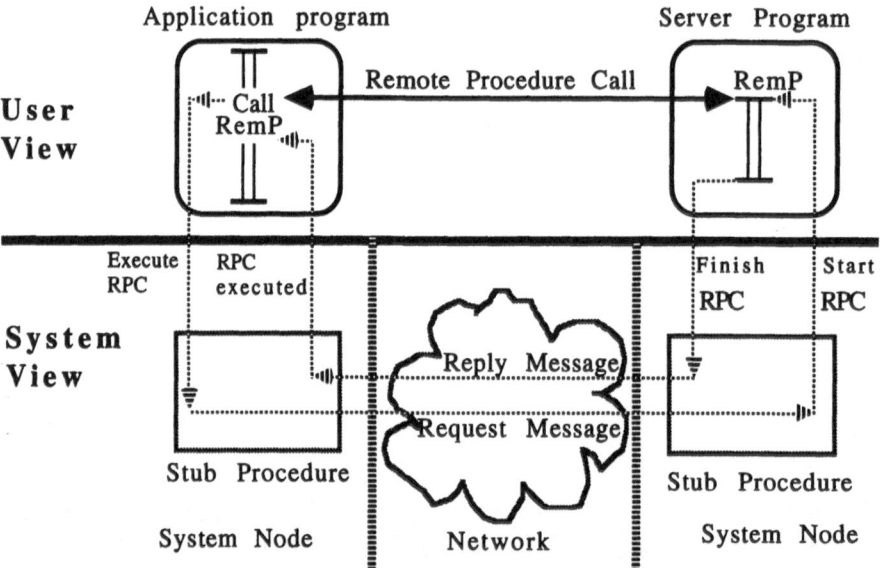

Figure: 6.4 Remote Procedure Call

A compiler replaces an RPC in a client by the code of the so-called stub procedure. This prepares the input data for the transfer via a network and initiates the transfer of the request message. The stub procedure of the server receives the request message and prepares the parameters for the procedure invocation. The stub procedure executes the called procedure on behalf of the calling program on the client system. After the procedure is completed the stub procedure of the server prepares the output parameter and sends the reply message via the network to the stub procedure of the client process. The stub procedure of the client prepares the output data and returns control to the calling application program. A very detailed discussion of RPC can be found in /CODO88/, .i./MUSC92/.

The decision whether to use RPC can be considered a design decision. This is true for most applications but not for time critical and fault tolerant systems. An RPC takes much more time than a normal procedure call and as such request and reply messages can be lost. Therefore it could be necessary in the requirements specification to define which functions are provided by servers and which functions are implemented by clients. Additionally it could become necessary to specify the reactions of clients and servers if they discover that messages have been lost i.e. because of an interrupted communication line and a remote procedure call can not be completed.

The DCE initiative of the Open Systems Foundation (OSF) is based on RPC. DCE provides standardised services and tools that support the creation, use and maintenance of distributed programs.

6.2.3 Direct Communication

Direct information exchange means that processes exchange information without using intermediate objects. Software processes communicate by explicit message passing. These systems are called logically distributed systems /BSTA88/. In order to discuss the different aspects of direct communication we shall use the basic model shown in the following figure /NEHM85/.

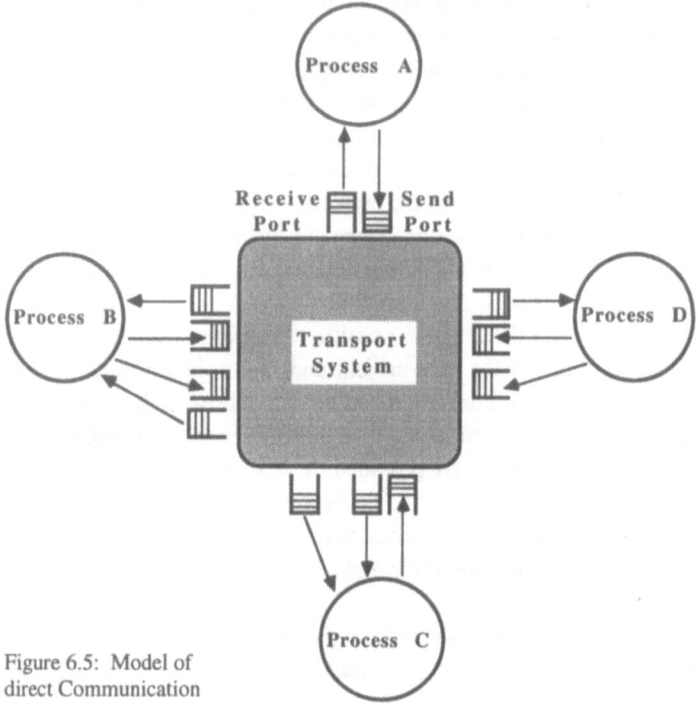

Figure 6.5: Model of
direct Communication

Ports are access points to the transport system. Two types of ports can be distinguished: receive ports and send ports. Processes receive messages via receive ports and send messages via send ports. Processes can be connected to several send and receive ports.

The different types of communication methods are variations of this basic model. Models vary only in the following main aspects:
- direction
- naming and connection patterns
- transaction patterns

Direction:
Two types of information exchange can be distinguished in the information flow:

- Unidirectional:
If the information can only be transferred in one direction, the type of information exchange is called unidirectional.

A message transaction consists of the transfer of a message from a source to one or more destinations

- Bidirectional
If it is possible to exchange information in both directions during one interaction,

the communication concept is called bidirectional. The rendezvous in Ada is an example of this.

Naming and Connection patterns:
Naming is used to identify the senders and receivers involved in an interaction. Naming can be either direct or indirect as well as symmetric or asymmetric /SLKR87/.

In order to identify the recipients and sources of messages either port or process identifiers can be used. If port identifiers are used then the naming is indirect.

A message is sent by a local send port and is received by the corresponding receive port. The binding of send ports to receive ports is done separately. The association between send and receive ports can be detrmined during system generation or at run time. If connections are set up during system generation, the connections are called static; otherwise they are called dynamic. Dynamic connections are established at run time and can also be modified or deleted at run time.

Mailboxes are a special case of indirect naming where the connected send and receive ports have the same name.

If the ports are not visible to processes and therefore process identifiers must be used, then the naming is indirect. This is shown in the figure below.

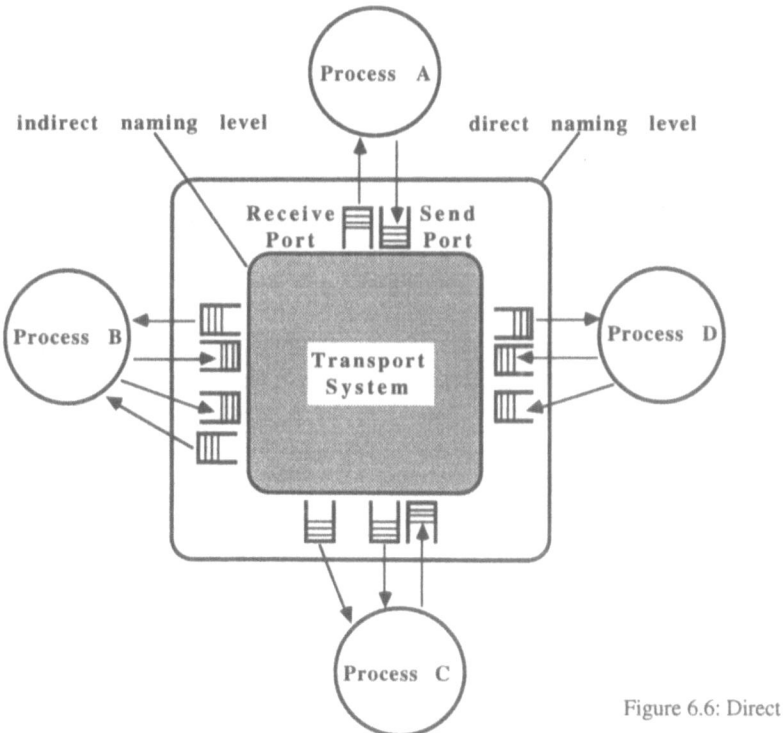

Figure 6.6: Direct Naming

When direct naming is used, it is assumed that the required connections exist between the communicating processes. It does not matter whether they are established during the start-up phase of a system or dynamically when a message is sent.

Direct and indirect naming can be either symmetric or asymmetric.

Symmetric naming means that the sender has to identify the recipient and the recipient has to identify the sender.

When asymmetric naming is used three possibilities exist:

- The sender identifies the recipient but the recipient does not identify the sender.
- The sender does not identify the recipient but the recipient identifies the sender.
- Neither the senders identify the recipients nor the recipients identify the senders.

Senders and recipients are identified by process or port names depending on whether direct or indirect naming is used .

Naming variables can be introduced independent of whether direct or indirect naming is used. If indirect naming is used, ports can be either be identified as constants or port identifiers which are contained in port variables. If direct naming is used process variables can be introduced instead of port variables.

Port and process variables allow a process to compute its communication partners dynamically by assigning new values to themselves.

Transaction Patterns:

A transaction pattern describes the number of processes involved in a single communication interaction using one communication primitive. For unidirectional communication a single communication interaction involves the use of a single SEND of an application message and a single RECEIVE.

For bidirectional communication the response is included.

The following list shows the different transaction patterns /SLKR87/:

1-1: One sender and one receiver participate in one interaction. This is the most simple and most commonly used form of communication.

1-n: Many receivers are involved in this type of communication; it is commonly known as multidestination communication. It can be used to distribute status and alarm information. This transaction pattern is not usually provided for bidirectional communication since the meaning of multiple replies is unclear.

n-1: Many senders and only one receiver. This can be used to provide redundant information for fault tolerant systems, i.e. collecting information from different sources at the same time. This transaction pattern is difficult to implement.

m-n: Many sources and many receivers. This is similar to n-1 but more difficult to implement.

6.2.4 Relationship between Communication Type and System Architecture

Parallel programs which are logically distributed or not distributed can run on a distributed or non-distributed system architecture. Thus according to /BSTA88/ the following four categories of physical and logical distribution can be distinguished:

1. Logically distributed software running on physically distributed architecture
2. Logically distributed software running on non-distributed hardware
3. Logically non-distributed software running on physically distributed architecture.
4. Logically non-distributed software running on a non-distributed system.

A typical example of the first type is a collection of processes running on several workstations which communicate with each other by sending messages over a local area network. Other examples are process control and communication software systems.

The second class uses shared memory to simulate message communication. The third type tries to hide the physical distribution by making the system look like a system with shared memory. The fourth type also uses shared memory for communication, but the implementation of shared objects is much easier on systems with shared memory than on distributed systems.

A program can be a mixture of type 1 and type 4. Several shared memory systems comprise a physically distributed system.

Similarly several logically non-distributed systems comprise a logically distributed system. Processes which communicate via shared data are located on a system with shared memory. Processes on a particular system communicate with processes on another system via messages, as shown in the figure below.

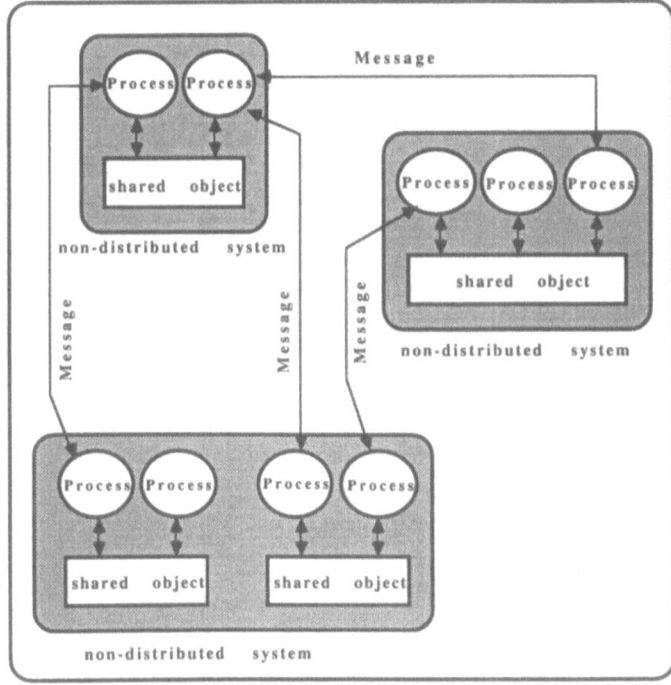

Figure 6.7: A Distributed System which Comprises several Non-distributed Systems

6.3 Synchronisation

In order to cooperate processes must not only communicate but must also synchronize with each other. To communicate, one process must send information and the other processes detect the send actions. This means that the two events 'perform a send action' and 'detect a send action' are constrained to happen in this order. Synchronisation can be viewed as a set of constraints on the order of events /ANSC83/, where events are operations on shared objects or message operations.

Synchronisation concepts can be classified according to whether communication is direct or indirect:
- Direct process control
- Synchronisation concepts for indirect communication
- Synchronsation concepts for direct communication

6.3.1 Direct Process Control

Direct process control is a mixture of decomposing a system into processes as described above and the coordination of process cooperation. In order to synchronize their activities, processes can create, destroy, stop and restart each other directly.

An early mechanism for direct process control was the use of fork and join statements /DEHO66/. A process activates another process by a fork statement and both processes continue in parallel. The invoking process can execute a join statement to synchronise the invoking and the invoked process. Executing a join statement delays the invoking process until the invoked process has terminated. The fork/join statements allow the invocation of several processes executed on the same process declaration. Fork/join statements allow the transfer of parameter values from the invoking process to the invoked process and vice versa. Processes cannot communicate between the fork and the join statement. This shows that the fork/join statements are a combination of system structuring with a dynamic number of processes and the synchronisation of processes. The following figure shows an example of a program with fork/join statements. The execution of process B is initiated when process A executes the fork statement. After the execution of the join B statement process A is delayed until process B is terminated. Then process A is continued.

invoking process A

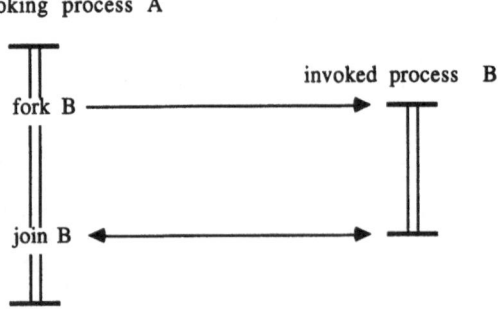

Figure 6.8: Processes
with Fork/Join Statements

It can be very difficult to understand the structure of a programm using fork/join statements since they can be executed in conditionals and loops

6.3.2 Synchronisation Concepts for Indirect Communication

As already mentioned indirect communication implies that communicating processes use shared objects. Operations defined on such objects can be executed simultanously by several processes. In order to keep such an object in a consistent state it is necessary to constrain the simultaneous execution of operations on a shared object. For example if a process executes an operation which changes the state of a shared object other processes are not allowed to access this object at the same time. A straightforward way to avoid simultaneous access to shared objects is to restrict the degree of parallelism of processes sharing objects. Processes sharing objects are not allowed to run in parallel.

Synchronisation concepts for indirect communication provide more flexibility in describing constraints on parallelism. See, for example, /ANSC83/. These synchronisation concepts are called process- oriented when the constraints are part of the definition of process objects. Constraints on the use of the operations of an object can also be part of the specification of the object. This type of synchronisation concept is said to be resource-oriented /GOEHN81/.

Restriction in Parallelism:
Processes sharing objects cannot run in parallel. This means that if one process is allowed to execute operations the others blocked. When the executable process is blocked or terminated another process can run. In most cases this type of synchronisation is used together with other synchronisation concepts and direct communication.

Process-oriented synchronisation:
If process oriented synchronisation is used, the operations for synchronizing the access to shared objects are contained in the specification of the corresponding process object. The following figure shows the basic structure of process oriented synchronisation.

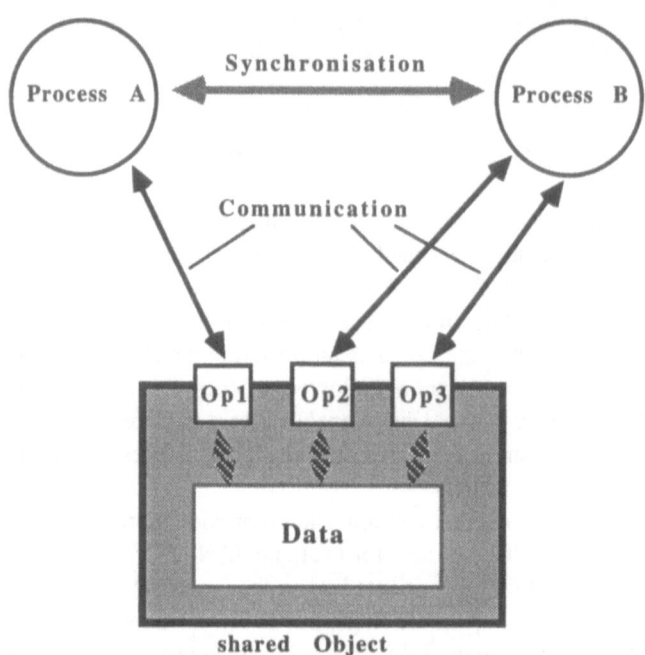

Figure 6.9: Indirect Communication and Process Oriented Synchronisation

Semaphores are an example of a process oriented synchronisation concept /DIJK68a/. A semaphore is a non-negative integer valued variable on which two operations are defined: P and V.

Given a semaphore s the operation P(s) decrements the value of s by one
s : = s - 1, if s > 0.
If s = 0 the process executing P(s) is delayed until s > 0.

The operation V(s) increments s by one (s := s + 1). The P and V operations are indivisible.

The following example shows the use of semaphores to restrict the access to shared objects. Process A executes the operation Op 1 and process B the operation Op 2 on the shared object SO. The operations Op 1 and Op 2 are mutually exclusive. This means that if a process X executes Op 1 then another process Y calling Op 2 is delayed until X has finished Op 1 and vice versa.

The figure below shows the structure of the example. The initial value of semaphor s is one. Assume A executes P(s) first and process B is delayed if it also executes P(s) because the value of s = 1. When A has finished operation Op 1 it executes V (s) which increments s (s = 1). Now B can execute P(s).

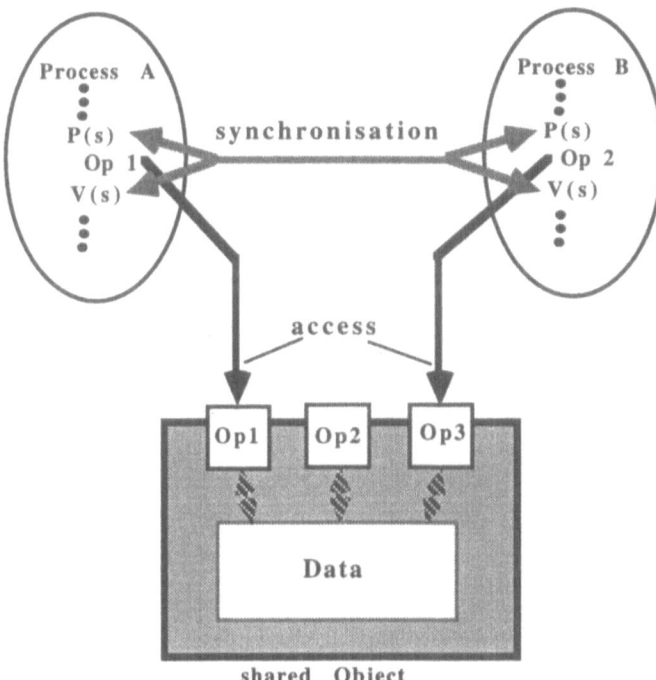

Figure 6.10: Semaphores

If several processes try to execute P(s) simultaneously only one process will be successful. This process is chosen randomly.

Resource oriented synchronisation concepts:
If resource-oriented synchronisation concepts are used the synchronisation operations are contained in a shared object. The following figure shows the basic structure of resource-oriented synchronisation. The shared object manages its own access constraints.

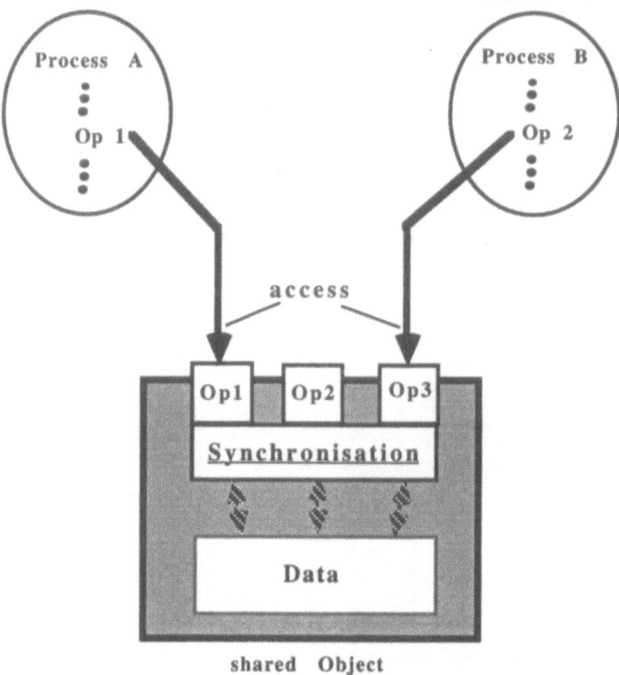

Figure 6.11: Resource Oriented Synchronisation

Examples of resource oriented synchronisation concepts are path expressions /CAHA74/ and monitors /HOARE74/. The monitor concept will be discussed in more detail in order to illustrate this type of synchronisation.

A monitor consists of a set of permanent variables which are used to store the state of the monitor and a set of procedures or operations which operate on these variables. For each monitor there exists an initialization code sequence which is executed before any other procedure can be performed. The values of the permanent variables are retained between activations of monitor procedures. The permanent variables form the memory of the monitor. They are not visible from outside the monitor. They can only be accessed by the monitor procedures. The activation of a monitor procedure has the usual semantics associated with a procedure call. In addition it is guaranteed that the execution of monitor procedures is mutually exclusive. This ensures that the permanent variables are never accessed concurrently. Some constructs have been introduced to allow condition synchronisation. This is needed if the state of the monitor enforces a delay in the execution of a monitor procedure, i.e. a wait operation is performed. If a monitor procedure is delayed by condition synchronisation, other processes can enter the monitor. These processes can execute monitor procedures where signal operations are executed, thereby allowing delayed processes to continue.

The following figure shows the structure of the above example using a monitor.

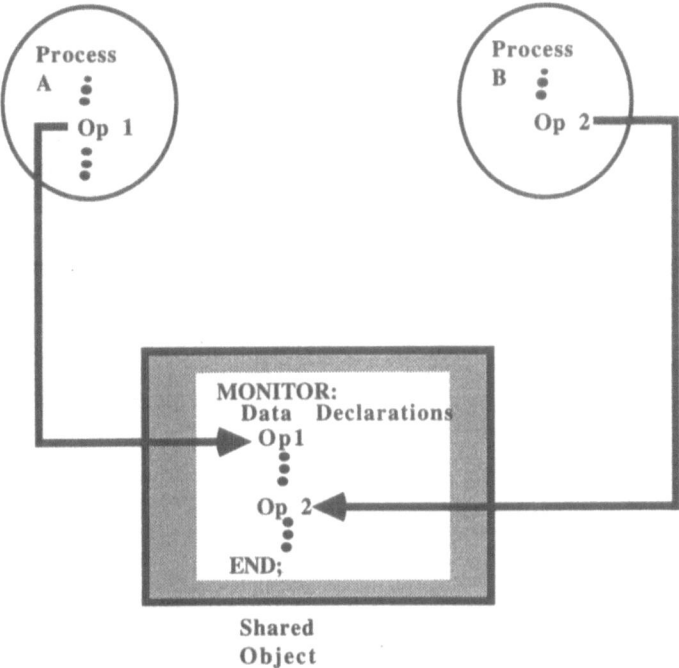

Figure 6.12: The Monitor Concept

6.3.3 Synchronisation Methods for Direct Communication, Message Passing

Three different forms of message passing can be distinguished, according to the type of synchronization used in the communication event:
1. asynchronous message passing
2. restricted asynchronous message passing and
3. synchronous message passing.

Asynchronous message passing means that a sending process is never blocked. The messages are stored in an unbounded queue located between the communicating processes. A sending process adds its message to the queue and continues execution. A receiving process checks whether one of the expected messages is on top of the queue. If so the message is removed.

Several variations of this basic technique exist. For example, several different queues are allowed between processes or several processes can add or remove messages from the same queue.

All these asynchronous techniques have disadvantages. The implementation of an unbounded queue is impossible. What happens if, in a real system, there is no free memory available is not defined. It does not matter here whether the memory is virtual or physical. This is similar to the problem of representing numbers in computers. The data type integer represents only a limited range of the natural numbers because of the number of bits used to represent numbers.

A restricted form of asynchronous message passing analogous to the data type integer is introduced. If restricted asynchronous message passing is used, a process which attempts to send a message is suspended until space is available in the receiving port /NEHM87/.

When using synchronous message passing, sending and receiving processes wait for each other. A sending process waits until the receiving process accepts the message and vice versa. A major disadvantage of this kind of message passing is the strong relationship between the communicating processes.

Asynchronous message passing requires an additional process to be employed as a buffer which has to be specified explicitly.

6.3.4 Examples: Communication and Synchronisation

6.3.4.1 Communication and Synchronisation Concepts in SREM

Communication in SREM is based on a combination of direct process control and message exchange. As already outlined in section 6.1.1 the '&' operator is comparable to the fork and join operations. Direct process control is closely related to system structuring. Hence in SREM the system decomposition already shows process synchronisation. Functions in SREM, i.e. processes, receive their input from the environment or other functions and produce output. Input can also invoke functions but current publications do not explain the synchronisation method used. Therefore we cannot explain it here in more detail.

6.3.4.2 Communication and Synchronisation Concepts in SDL

In SDL processes communicate with one another by signals, i.e. messages. Signals in SDL have names, i.e. the signal identifier, and can contain parameters, i.e. the signal parameters.

When a process outputs a signal, the values of the signal parameters are identified with the values of local variables and the signal is transported to the destination process. A process executing a send action is never blocked. The signals are stored in a FIFO queue outside the process to which they are directed until the process is ready to receive the signal, i.e. asynchronous communication is used. A signal is consumed when the destination process receives the signal. When a signal is received the values of the message parameters are copied into local variables in the receiving process.

Signals are not persistent in the SDL model. If a signal is not expected in a particular state it is eliminated. Signals in the input queue of a process which are not expected but will be received in another state can be kept in the input queue by a special operation.

In SDL there are other ways in which two processes can exchange data other than by signals. A process can read the data of another process if this process belongs to the same block and if the data has been declared as a "shared value". The "shared value" which another process sees has always the same value as that seen by the owner process.

A process can only access data from a process in another block when the data has been declared as an 'exportable' value, i.e. global. All other processes with a corresponding importable data definition are allowed to obtain a copy of the value of the data. The value of the data given to an importing process remains constant even if the actual value of the data is changed. A process must copy the current value explicitly. Access to shared values and exportable values cannot be synchronized.

6.3.4.3 Communication and Synchronisation Concepts in Estelle

In Estelle, modules communicate with each other via messages, called interactions. Messages can be directly exchanged between a parent module and its children and between processes on the same hierarchical level which have the same parent module.

Processes which want to interact with each other must be connected explicitly. To establish these connections, Estelle provides several operations, e.g. 'connect' and 'disconnect' which can be used by a module to connect itself to one or several of its children or to connect its children with each other. By executing these operations in hierarchically ordered modules, a module can be connected to its grandchildren and other descendents.

The following figure shows an example of an Estelle specification structure and a possible communication relation.

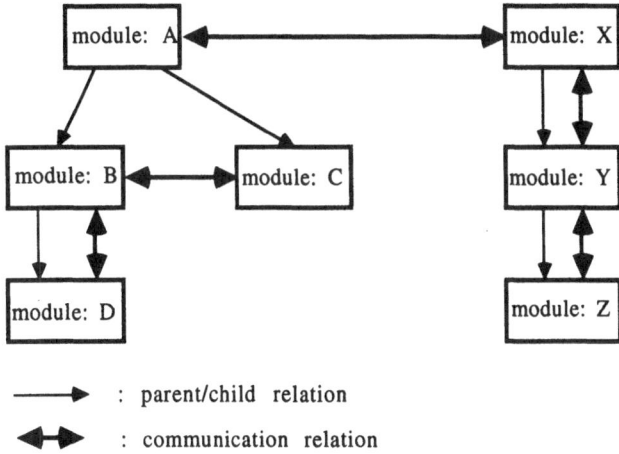

    ⟶   : parent/child relation

    ◀▶   : communication relation

Figure 6.13: Structure of an Estelle Specification

The communication relation can be changed dynamically subject to certain restrictions e.g. module A cannot communicate with module Z directly. Modules can work as relays. In our example all messages from module Z are transferred to module X. Module Y does not realise that a message is being transferred to module X or to module Z. Module Y can disconnect this communication relation.

In Estelle, shared variables are allowed between processes with a parent/child relationship and activity modules with the same parent module. Because of the priority of a parent process over its children and the mutual exclusion of activities, the access to shared variables must not be synchronized.

Estelle only allows asynchronous message exchange. A conceptionally infinite FIFO queue is used for transferring messages between modules.

6.3.4.4 Communication and Synchronisation Concepts in LOTOS

In LOTOS a process communicates with its environment by means of interactions. The atomic form of an interaction is an event. It is a unit of synchronized communication which can exist between two processes that can both perform this event. LOTOS events can be structured. A structured event consists of a gate name identifying the point of interaction and a finite list of attributes. Two types of attributes are possible: value declarations and variable declarations. A value declaration is an expression describing a data value preceded by an exclamation mark. The expression of a value declaration can contain variables. Examples of value declarations are:

$$! (3+5) \qquad ! \max (a,b).$$

If a value declaration attribute is combined with a label name g, and the expression e has the value v, then the event after g! e describes the potential event g<v>. If a value expression contains variables then an event is described for each set of actual values of these variables.

A variable declaration has the form ?x: t, where x is the name of the declared variable and t its type identifier. Examples of variable declarations are:

$$? d: integer, \qquad ? text: string$$

If a variable declaration ?x:t is associated with a gate g, then g?x:t describes the set of all events g<v> for all values v in the value domain of the type t.

Different kinds of interactions between processes can be described with these two types of attributes. Interactions between processes can take place if all participating processes execute identical events.

The different types of interactions are shown in the table below:

process A	process B	sync. condition	interaction	effect
g!E	g!E	value(E) = value(E)	value matching	synchronisation
g!E	g?x:t	value(E) ∈ domain(t)	value passing	after synchronisation x = value(E)
g?x:t	g?y:u	t = u	value generation	after synchronisation x=y=v for v ∈ domain(t)

Figure 6.14: Interaction Types in LOTOS

When a process creates a subprocess, values can be passed from the process to the subprocess created; similarly values can be passed from an enabling process to an enabled process. The values passed can be contained in variables. These variables can be considered shared variables i.e. shared between a creating and a created process or an enabling and an enabled process. Processes having a create or enable relation do not run in parallel; therefore the access to these variables need not be synchronized.

6.3.4.5 Communication and Synchronisation in Other SEE's and Programming Languages

Modular Approach to Software Construction, Operation, Test (Mascot)
As already described in section 6.1.5 processes in Mascot use Intercommunication Data Areas (IDA) for exchanging information. An IDA is a shared object, i.e. data plus the appropriate access operations. The following figure shows a simple example of two activities – Producer and Consumer – which communicate via an IDA called Store.

Figure 6.15: Communication in Mascot

The paths to and from an IDA are marked with the name of an access interface. This defines a set of procedure names. In our example we have the access interfaces insert and remove. In order to synchronise the access an IDA is regarded as a monitor (see section 6.2.1).

Structured Development of Real-Time Systems (SDRTS)

In SDRTS data flow and control flow are specified between data transformations and control transformations. A data flow can be continuous or discrete. Control flow is implemented by events exchanged between transformations. A transformation is invoked, i.e. output is generated, if the required discrete input is available; in this case the transformation is synchronous. Events can also invoke the execution of a transformation. The event controlled execution of transformation is controlled by the control transformations.

Data transformations can have access to the same data store. This means that they use shared data for communication.

To summarise, communication and synchronisation in SDRTS are implemented by message exchange, shared data, and direct process control.

Strategies for Real-Time Development (SRTD)

As in SDRTS, data flows between data transformations. A data transformation is activated when all required input data are available, i.e. the transformation is data triggered. Additional transformations are activated by control signals. The possible control sequences and the corresponding sequences of process activations are defined in the control specification. SRTD supports message exchange, shared data and direct process control similarly to SDRTS.

Design Approach for Real-Time Systems (DARTS)

DARTS is based on data flow diagrams. There can be a direct data flow between transformations or several transformations can have access to the same data store. This means that the interfaces between tasks are either data flow interfaces or shared data interfaces.

In DARTS task interfaces are handled by Task Communication Modules (TCM) or Task Synchronisation Modules (TSM). A TCM contains a data structure and defines the access procedures to the data structure. There are two types of TCMs: MCMs that allow either synchronous or asynchronous message exchange. Information Hiding Modules (IHM) implement shared data accesible to two or more tasks. The IHM defines the data structure of a shared data object as well as the procedures for accessing it.

Tasks can exchange events via a TSM. Events are only used for synchronisation purposes and do not allow information transfer.

Process-oriented, Application, and Interpretable Specification Language (PAISLey)

In PAISLey interaction, i.e. communication and synchronisation, takes place through exchange functions. These perform bidirectional, point to point, and mutually synchronised communication. Exchange functions are exchanged via a channel;

they have one parameter and a type. Two exchange functions exchange their parameters if they match. Exchange functions can only match if they are on the same channel and if they are of the correct type. Exchange functions can be of the type x, xm or xr. An x function matches with any exchange function on the same channel. If there is no other exchange function pending, an x type exchange function waits until there is another exchange function available on the same channel.

xm exchange functions match only with x type and xr type exchange functions. They do not match with other xm exchange functions. Xm functions restrict the number of functions that an exchange function can match.

Exchange functions of type xr do not wait if no other suitable exchange function is pending. xr exchange functions can only match with x and xm exchange functions.

To summarise, PAISLey supports bidirectional asynchronous message exchange with a non-waiting variant, the xr type.

6.4 Specification of Process Behaviour

6.4.1 General Remarks

Each process has a set of local and possibly shared objects, i.e. variables. The values of these objects define the state of a process. The statements of a sequential program defining the process can be likened to atomic actions (also called transitions), which change the state of the process. The history of the process can be considered as a sequence,

$$S_1 \xrightarrow{T_1} S_2 \xrightarrow{T_2} S_3 \xrightarrow{T_3} \bullet\bullet\bullet\bullet S_i \xrightarrow{T_i} S_{i+1} \xrightarrow{T_{i+1}} \bullet\bullet\bullet$$

where the S denotes a state and T a transition.

The execution of a parallel program can be considered as the interleaving of the sequences of atomic action of each component process. If two actions which do not influence one another are executed concurrently, then they can be executed in either order. The possible order is restricted by the definitions of the different processes and the constraints defined by the synchronisation methods used, e. g. a receive operation cannot be executed before a send operation.

Several techniques have been suggested for describing the permissible sequences of a process, i.e. the definition of a process object (see /BARR86/). According to /SCAN86/, a variety of specification approaches can be based on
- the permissible state sequences or
- the initial state and the permissible atomic action sequences.

Given a state sequence the corresponding (atomic) action sequence can be constructed and vice versa. In addition the permissible state or action sequence can be described explicitly or implicitly /KRUMM89/.

Explicit behaviour specification
- State sequences:

If the permissible state sequences are described explicitly the only description of sequence allowed is the set of possible successor states of a given state. State machine specifications, net specifications, graphic models of computations, and programming languages are examples of the explicit description of permissible sequences of states /SCME82/, /ALF85a/.

- Action sequences:

The permissible transition sequence can be specified explicitly by expressions. These expressions are constructive definitions of permissible action sequences. An example of such a description technique is the Calculus of Communicating Systems CCS, developed by Milner /MILN80/.

Implicit behaviour specification
The state sequences can be specified implicitly by requirements which must be fulfilled by the history of the states or transitions. Temporal logic has been developed for expressing properties of execution sequences /ALF85a/, /HAIL82/.

In the following three sections an example of each type of process behaviour specification is described in more detail.

6.4.2 State Oriented Explicit Specification of Process Behaviour

A transition like that illustrated in the sequence above (S_i -> T_i -> S_{i+1}) can be labelled by an operation symbol /KELL76/ which in this case would be written (S_i -> T_i (Ok) -> S_{i+1}). Any operation can be represented by a pair P0 , F0, where P0(S) is an enabling predicate defined on the state space and F0(S) is an action function such that F0(S) is defined when P(S) is true. Thus operations have the following general structure /KELL76/:

$$O: \textbf{when} \quad P(S) \quad \textbf{do} \quad S <- F(S)$$

This is to be read as follows: when the predicate P is true for a certain state S , the action function F(S) is executed, where S denotes the state space of the system, i.e. the cross product of the state spaces of all processes belonging to the system.

If the enabling predicate and the action function depend only on the values of the local variables, the transition is called local or spontaneous. The transition does not depend on or affect directly the state of any other process.

Depending on the communication and synchronsation method used, enabling predicates can depend on the values of shared variables, i.e. objects, or on messages which a process wants to send or receive.

A semaphore is a well-known synchronization concept based on shared variables (refer to previous sections). The P-operation on a semaphore sem is characterized by the following enabling predicate /BOCH83/:

$$PP(sem)(sem) := (sem > 0)$$

and the transition function

$$FP(sem)(sem) := sem - 1$$

Similarly, the V-operation is characterized by

$$PV(sem)(sem) := true$$

and

$$FV(sem)(sem) := sem + 1.$$

If a process tries to perform a P-operation when the value of sem is equal to zero it will be blocked until another process executes a V-operation.

If message passing is used, the enabling predicate of an operation can contain the receipt of a message. If the message is available, the enabling condition is true.

Depending on whether synchronous or asynchronous message passing is used, the transmission of messages is expressed by the enabling condition or the action function.

If synchronous message passing is used, the send request of a process is part of the enabling predicate. A process is blocked until the receiver accepts the message. If asynchronous message passing is used, a message can always be sent; a process is never blocked if it wants to send a message. Thus the sending of a message is part of an action function.

The description of the permissible sequences of states can be excessively long. To reduce the length, only the important states are considered. These important states are known as the main or major states. The introduction of main states means that the number of variables spanning the state space is broken down. Very often a main state variable is introduced /ESTELLE/. This variable contains the current main state. The remaining variables are known as context variables, shortened to 'context'. State models using this distinction are called extended state models.

In extended state models the possible transitions are characterized by /BOCH83/:

from	< present major state >
when	< interaction >
provided	< condition >
to	< next major state >
begin	< statement list > **end**

A transition is possible when the enabling predicate is true. This is the conjunction of the 'from', 'when', and 'provided' clauses. The 'from' clause identifies the major state. The 'when' clause contains necessary interactions with other processes. The 'provided' clause is a predicate on the context variables. If the transition occurs the transition function defined by the 'to' and 'begin/end' clauses is executed. The 'to' clause assigns a new value to the major state variable and the statement list of the 'begin/end' clause can update the other state variables, i.e. the context variables.

The specification techniques based on an extended state model differ in the restrictions they impose on the different clauses. For example the sending of a message is not allowed in the 'when' clause if asynchronous message passing is used. If message passing is used and the corresponding transition cannot be executed because the 'provided' clause is false then messages to be sent are stored in a queue if the message passing is asynchronous; if it is synchronous then the offering process is blocked.

6.4.3 Transition-Oriented Explicit Specification of Process Behaviour

The permissible transition sequences can be specified explicitly by expressions defining the possible sequences or by requirements which must be fulfilled by a history of transitions /SCME82/. A theoretically very important technique for describing the behaviour of processes explicitly is the Calculus of Communicating Systems (CCS) /MILN80/. CCS therefore is described in more detail as an example of the explicit definition of behaviour sequences.

CCS and its theoretical framework provide a means of specifying and verifying cooperating processes (also called agents). In CCS the behaviour of a process, i.e. an agent, is described as a rooted, unordered, finite branching tree where each of the branches is labelled by a member of a label set. The root of the tree represents the initial state of a process. The labels on the outgoing edges of each node represent possible next steps of a process, also called actions or transitions.

In CCS observable and unobservable actions are distinguished. An observable action can be seen from the outside of a process, e.g. by other processes. An unobservable action, called T, is not visible from outside a process. An unobservable action can be executed silently at any time by a process.

In order to express infinite behaviour, recursive equations are used. Within behaviour expressions, variables can be used which refer to behaviour expressions. An elementary algebra is defined for these behaviour trees. The operations are:

NIL	empty operator (nullary operation): NIL is the tree: ●
+	alternative operator (binary operation): 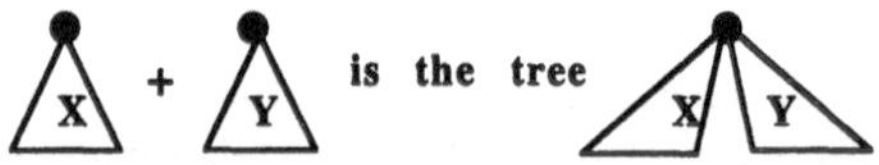
*	sequence operator (unary action for each a ∈ Label set) 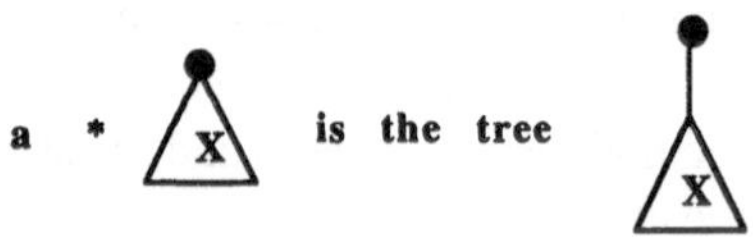

Figure 6.16: Basic Operations of CCs

They obey the following laws:

Associativity:	(X+Y)+Z = X+(Y+Z)
Commutativity:	X+Y = Y+X
Nullity:	X+NIL = X

Figure 6.17 : Basic Laws in CCS

The trees describing the behaviour of processes, called behaviour trees, can be represented as expressions:

Behaviour Tree   **Behaviour Expression**

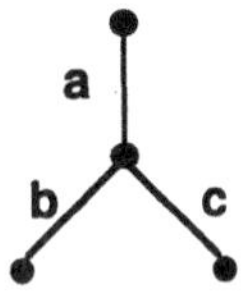

a * (b * NIL + c * NIL)

Figure 6.18: Example of Behaviour Expressions and Trees

After step a in the above example either step b or step c can be executed.

Behaviour Tree   **Behaviour Expression**

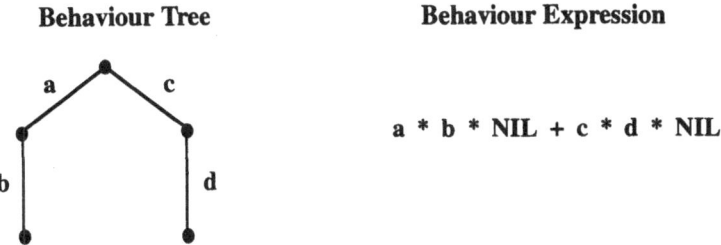

a * b * NIL + c * d * NIL

Figure 6.19: Another Example of Behaviour Expressions and Trees

In this example either step a or step c is executed. If step a is executed as the first step then step b follows, otherwise step d.

The next figure shows the behaviour trees and the corresponding behaviour expressions specifying the three infinite agents X,Y and Z. X and Y can have both finite and infinite behaviour, since they contain terminating branches, whereas Z exhibits infinite behaviour. The behaviour of Z proceeds by recursively activating Z.

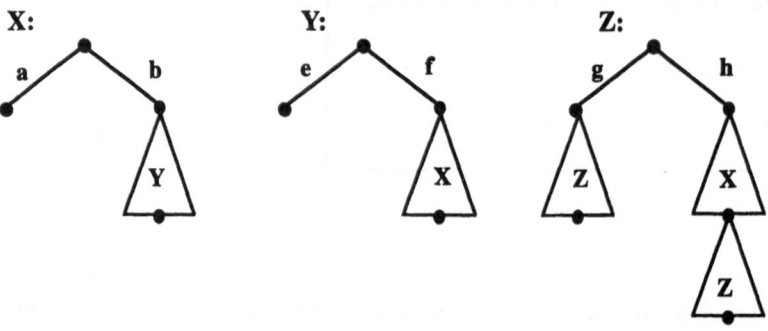

X = (a * NIL) + (b * Y * NIL)

Y = (e * NIL) + (f * X * NIL)

Z = (g * Z * NIL) + (f* X * Z * NIL)

Figure 6.20: Infinite Process Behaviour

The next problem is how processes interact in CCS. For each observable action, there exist a complementary observable action, e.g. '-a' is the complementary action to 'a' and vice versa. If complementary actions appear in two different process trees then these processes can interact with each other. These interactions are equivalent to synchronous message exchanges. Here '-a' would denote the sending of a message and 'a' the receipt of a message.

Processes which communicate with each other must be linked with each other by the composite operator. The dyadic operator 'I' merges the behaviour of two agents, i.e. they are executed concurrently. The resulting behaviour is the sum of all possible interleavings of the two arguments. An interaction results in the unobservable event T.

The following figure shows the application of the composite operator.

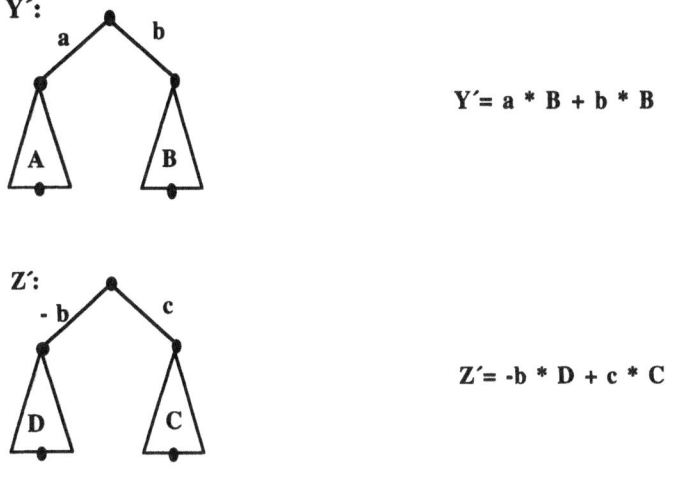

$$Y' = a * B + b * B$$

$$Z' = -b * D + c * C$$

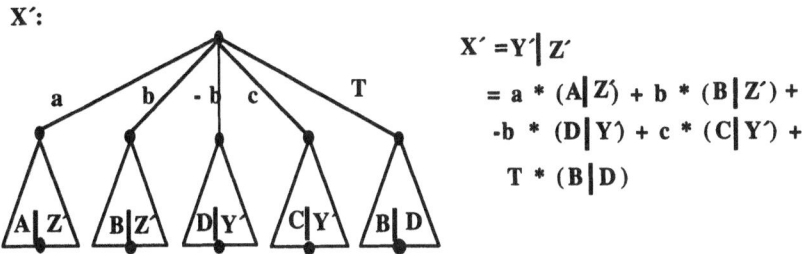

$$X' = Y' | Z'$$
$$= a * (A | Z') + b * (B | Z') +$$
$$-b * (D | Y') + c * (C | Y') +$$
$$T * (B | D)$$

Figure 6.21: The Application of the Composite Operator

The definition of the composite operator does not allow true concurrency. In the example above, a transition in Y' cannot be performed simultaneously with a transition in Z'. The behaviour defined by Y'|Z' specifies only that the transitions in Y' and Z' can be performed in any order. In CCS parallelism is modelled by the interleaving of all processes.

The restriction and relabelling operators, / = Restriction, () = Relabelling, support the definition of combined systems. The restriction operator allows labels to be encapsulated within a system. They are not visible from outside the system. The next figure shows an example of the use of the restriction operator.

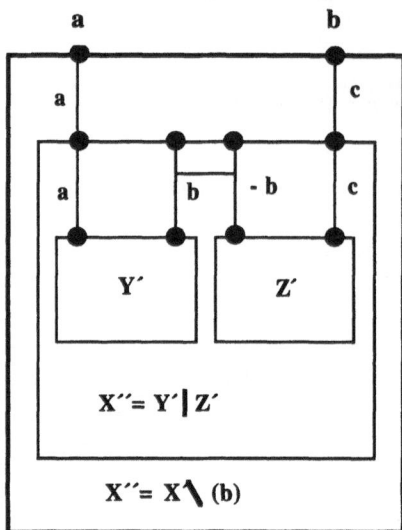

$$X'' = a * (A \mid Z'') \diagdown (b) +$$
$$c * (C \mid Y') \diagdown (b) +$$
$$T * (B \mid D) \diagdown (b)$$

Figure 6.22: The Use
of the Restriction Operator

Different processes can use the same labels or the complements of labels used in other processes. If such processes are to be combined and interaction is not desired for particular labels, the relabelling operator must be applied in one process. With the relabeling operator no conflicting label identifiers can be introduced.

6.4.4 Implicit Behaviour Process Specifications

Predicates can be used instead of describing the permissible sequences of states or transitions explicitly . Predicates define the properties of sequences of transitions or states. Formulae of predicate or temporal logic can be used to represent such properties /KRUMM89/. A program is implicitly specified if all execution sequences satisfy all these predicates.

Predicate Logic:
In /HOARE85/ properties described in predicate logic are used to specify the intended behaviour of a process. These predicates define the properties of the trace of a process. A trace of a process shows the observable events of the process up to a given moment in time.

Example /HOARE85/:
In this example the behaviour of a vending machine is considered. After the insertion of a coin in the slot of the vending machine (event: coin), a chocolate bar can be extracted from the dispenser of the machine (event: choc). A trace of the process that takes place after the first three customers is:

< coin, choc, coin, choc,coin, choc >

This trace can easily be continued for further customers. Now several properties of these traces can be specified. The most important are the 'FAIRNESS' and 'MONEY_MAKING' properties. The 'FAIRNESS' property specifies that a customer gets a chocolate bar if he or she has inserted a coin and that no further coins can be inserted until the vending machine has dispensed a chocolate bar. Expressed in a formal way this property is /HOARE85/:

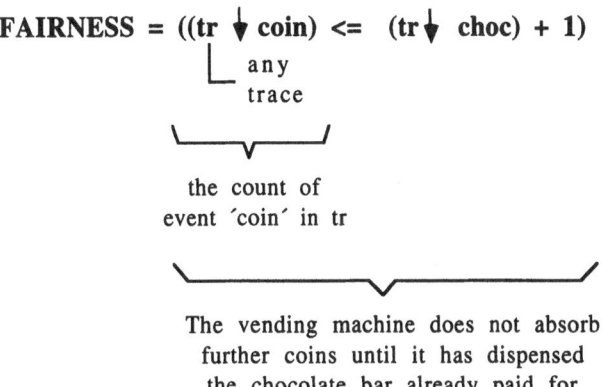

Figure 6.23: The FAIRNESS Property of the Vending Machine

In contrast to the 'FAIRNESS' property the 'MONEY_MAKING' property defines that the owner of the vending machine earns money. This property specifies that the number of dispensed chocolate bars never exceeds the number of coins inserted. This is expressed formally as /HOARE85/:

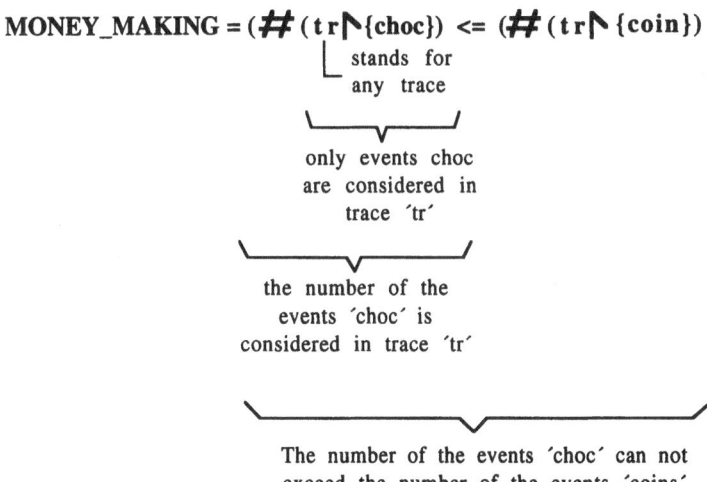

Figure 6.24: The 'MONEY_MAKING' Property of the Vending Machine

All the desired properties of the vending machine can be specified in a similar way.

Temporal Logic:
Several specification methods based on temporal logic have been suggested e.g. /LAMP83/, /MAWO84/. Whereas /LAMP83/ is based on sequences of states, /MAWO84/ is based on sequences of events. In addition they use slightly different types of temporal logic (see the conclusion in /LAMP83/). In our opinion the specification technique used in /LAMP83/ is more relevant from a practical point of view /HAIL82/. and therefore it is considered in more detail.

The temporal logic system used in /LAMP83/ uses four types of assertions. These assertions are defined as follows:

P_i :   true at time i if and only if it is true on state s_i

$\Box P_i$:   true at time i if and only if P is true at all times j>= i
spoken: henceforth

$\Diamond P_i$:   true at time i if and only if P is true at some time j >= i
spoken: eventually

$\Box \Diamond P_i$:   true at time i if and only if P is true at infinitely many times j >= i
spoken: infinitely often

Figure 6.25: Types of Assertions in Temporal Logic

Examples:
1. P is not always true if and only if it is eventually false

$$\text{not } \Delta P == \Diamond \text{ not P}$$

2. Program termination

$$at\_P \longrightarrow \Diamond \ after\_P$$

where at_P is true in the control state at the beginning of the program and after_P is true in the control state at the end of the program /HAIL82/.

6.4.5 Examples

6.4.5.1 Behaviour Description in SREM

In SYSREM as part of SREM a system is decomposed into functions. These functions are further broken down to the level at which they can accept discrete messages. Now these functions can still be further broken down into a stimulus and response level. Functions accept messages and perform the appropriate state transition. This means that in SREM function specifications are based on a state machine model. In order to overcome the problem of representing huge state spaces in one diagram a special notation called R-Net is used in SREM. A function can be specified by several R-Nets. Each R-Net specifies the transformation of a single input message and the corresponding state into output messages and an updated state. At one time only one R-Net is active in one function.

The following figure shows an example of an R-Net. The example contains only the most important symbols and possibilities of R-Nets.

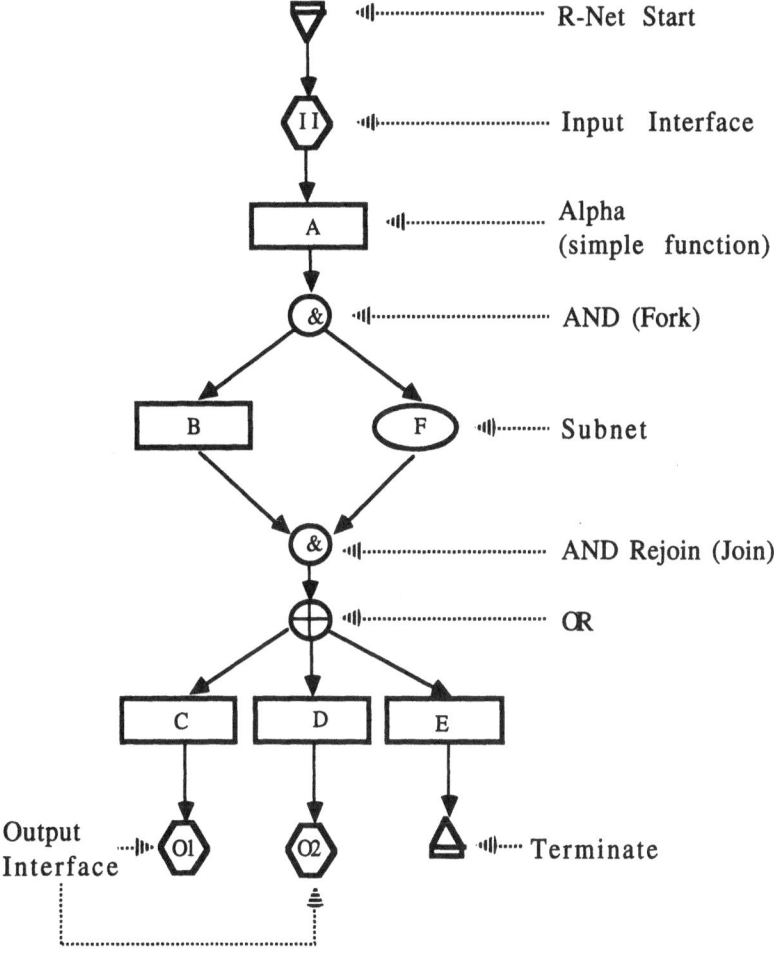

Figure 6.26: Example of an R-net

6.4.5.2 Behaviour Description in SDL

In SDL the behaviour of a process can be represented graphically or in text form. Since the graphical representation as a process graph is easier to understand, this representation is explained in more detail. The following figure shows the SDL symbols for describing process behaviour.

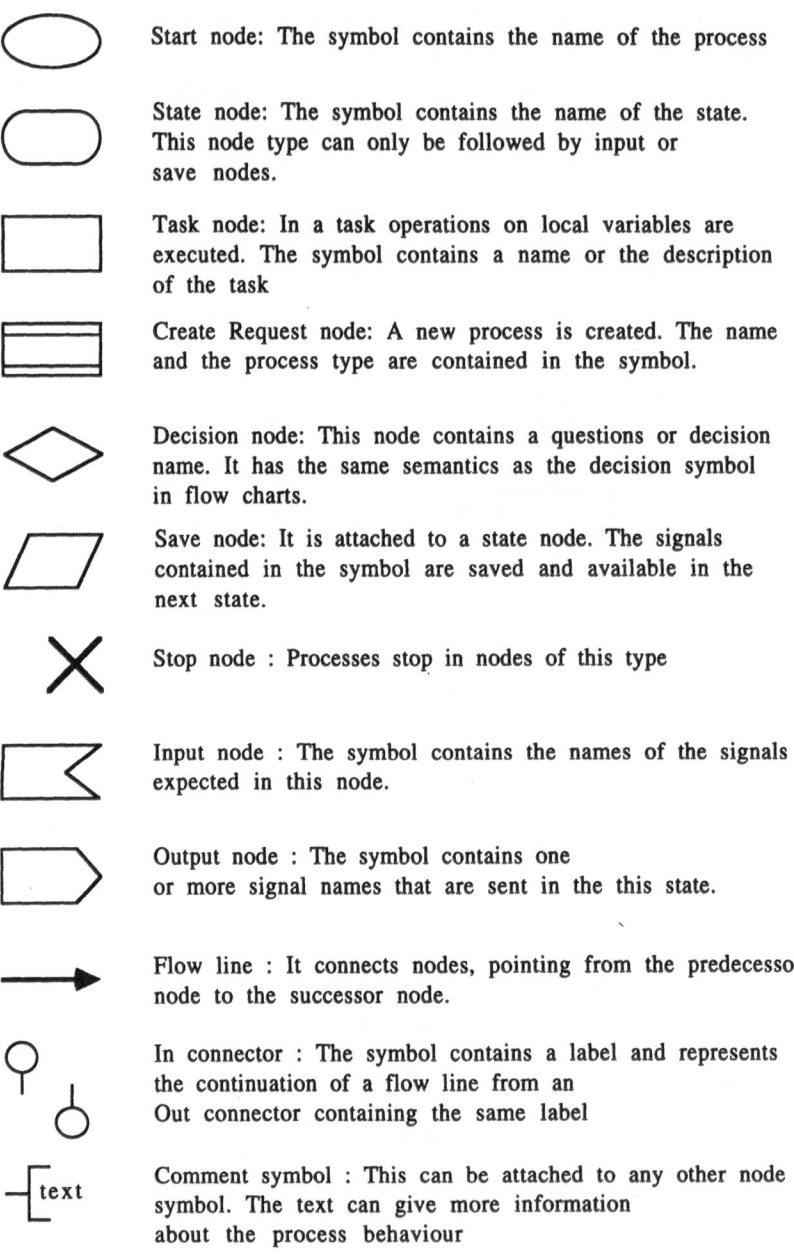

Start node: The symbol contains the name of the process

State node: The symbol contains the name of the state. This node type can only be followed by input or save nodes.

Task node: In a task operations on local variables are executed. The symbol contains a name or the description of the task

Create Request node: A new process is created. The name and the process type are contained in the symbol.

Decision node: This node contains a questions or decision name. It has the same semantics as the decision symbol in flow charts.

Save node: It is attached to a state node. The signals contained in the symbol are saved and available in the next state.

Stop node : Processes stop in nodes of this type

Input node : The symbol contains the names of the signals expected in this node.

Output node : The symbol contains one or more signal names that are sent in the this state.

Flow line : It connects nodes, pointing from the predecessor node to the successor node.

In connector : The symbol contains a label and represents the continuation of a flow line from an Out connector containing the same label

Comment symbol : This can be attached to any other node symbol. The text can give more information about the process behaviour

Figure 6.27: SDL Symbols for Describing Process Behaviour

The symbols shown in the figure above can be connected by arcs, i.e. the 'next' symbol but with some restrictions, e.g. a save symbol can only be connected to a state symbol (see /SDL/ for details) The formal parameters of signals, variable definitions, etc., are not contained in a process graph. These are described using a separate language called SDL/P. Details of this language are given in /SDL/.

6.4.5.3 Behaviour Description in Estelle

Estelle uses a finite state transition model to model the dependency of outputs on inputs. Starting from a defined initial state, modules execute transitions from one state to another state. As mentioned in chapter 2, a transition is defined by its effect on the values of the module variables. One of these variables in Estelle is the major state variable called STATE.

Each transition is defined by:
- the present major state ("from" clause)
- the input interaction ("when" clause)
- the enabling predicate ("provided" clause)
- the delay condition ("delay" clause)
- the priority ("priority" clause)
- a list of actions to be performed including generation of output interaction, the "Begin/End" clause
- the next major state, the "to" clause

All these clauses are optional. Syntactically, a transition or a set of transitions is introduced by the keyword trans. The clauses defining the enabling conditions and the transitions themselves, i.e. the changes of the variables, are described syntactically as follows:

trans
priority	expression
from	current_major_state
to	next_major_state
provided	predicate
when	received message
begin code	**end**

If several transitions in the same module can occur, the transition with the highest priority is chosen.

Transitions with a 'when' clause are called input transitions and transitions without this clause are called spontaneous transitions. Spontaneous transitions can have a 'delay' clause; this is not possible for input transitions. A transition with a 'delay' clause, i.e. 'delay (d1, d2)', can be enabled when its enabling condition has been continuously satisfied for d1 time units and must be enabled with in the following d2 time units.

6.4.5.4 Behaviour Description in LOTOS

A process in LOTOS can be imagined to be like a black box that communicates with its environment. The observable behaviour is expressed by behaviour expressions. These expressions formally define the order in which events can occur. Behaviour expressions are contained in the process definition.

The format of a process definition is:

> **process**   <process_identifier> <parameter_list> :=
>   <behaviour_expression>
> **endproc**

The process identifier is the name by which a process is referred in the behaviour expression of another process.

If a process name A is contained in a behaviour expression of another process B, then an instance of process A can be created by process B. The type of values that can be passed to a process that is created are contained in the parameter list.

The parameter list consists of two parts. One part contains a list of gate names and the other part a list of 'normal' variable names.

When a process is created, the formal gate names are also replaced by actual gate names. This means that different instances of the same process can communicate via different gates.

Infinite behaviour can be defined in LOTOS by the recursive occurrence of process identifiers in behaviour expressions.

The completely inactive process is represented by 'stop'; it cannot perform any action. An action prefix produces a new behaviour expression from an existing behaviour expression. For example if B is an existing expression and a!(3+5) an event, the result is written as a!(3+5);B. The process behaviour a!(3+5);B is interpreted: first the event a!(3+5) occurs. Then this has taken place the behaviour B occurs.

Alternative behaviour expressions can be defined for a process using the choice operator. For example if B1 and B2 are existing behaviour expressions then (B1 () B2) denotes a process that behaves like either B1 or B2. Which behaviour is chosen is determined by the behaviour of the environment. If the environment provides the event which is the initial event of B1, then B1 is selected. If the environment provides an initial event of B2, then B2 is selected. If B1 and B2 have the same initial event the outcome is not determined.

LOTOS also has an operator, the parallel operator, which reflects the parallel composition of subprocesses. If two subprocesses are denoted by A and B, the expression A /(e1,....en)/ B describes a parallel composition of A and B communicating via the events e1......en. Another operator closely related to the parallel operator is the hiding operator. If A is a behaviour expression containing several parallel processes and e1,.....en are event names, then 'hide e1,...en, in A' represents a behaviour similar to A in which e1,....en, have become internal events. They are not observable and occur without the participation of the environment.

In LOTOS any behaviour expression can be proceeded by a predicate. If the predicate is true the behaviour described by the behaviour expression is possible. If the predicate does not hold, the whole expression is equivalent to a 'stop'. Usually a choice between several guarded expressions is given.

6.4.5.5 Behaviour Description in Other SEE's and Programming Languages

Modular Approach to Software Construction, Operation, Test (Mascot)
It is not explicitly defined in Mascot which specification technique should be applied to describe the behaviour of activities. Program Description Language (PDL) described in section 6.2.1 or a state transition oriented technique can be used.

Structured Development of Real-Time Systems (SDRTS)
and Strategies of Real-Time Development (SRTD)
Techniques similar to those used in structured analysis are used to describe the data flow. For the specification of the control transformations a state transition technique as described in section 6.4 is used.

Design Approach for Real-Time Systems (DARTS)
The usual techniques, i.e. PDL, is used to describe the behaviour of the transformations.

Process-oriented, Application, and Interpretable Specification Language (PAISLey)
In PAISLey the behaviour of a process is specified by supplying a set of all possible states, i.e. the state space of a process, and a successor function on that state space. The successor functions specify the successor state of each state in the state space.

6.5 Task Allocation

During system analysis and design a task is decomposed, i.e. is broken down into smaller parts. Task allocation means the assignment of processes -which have been identified during the analysis and design activities- to the processing nodes of a distributed system, or even the design of the distributed system.

The communication between processes causes communication costs in processor and network capacity. The communication between processes on the same processor, i.e. intra-processor communication is cheaper than communication between processes on different processors, i.e. interprocessor communication. Two goals of task allocation are the minimization of the communication costs and the optimisation of the load balance, i.e. the assignment of approximately the same load to each processor. However these are conflicting goals. Minimizing the communication costs would require all processes to be assigned to the same processor. But this would result in a totally unbalanced system. One processor would do everything while the others would be completely idle. On the other hand a good load balance can cause enormous inter-processor communication costs.

In order to solve the allocation problem we can enumerate all process/processor combinations. This would mean that for n tasks and m processors we have n•m different combinations. It is easy to see that even a relatively small number of tasks and processors produce a huge number of different combinations. Therefore task allocation techniques which determine an optimal solution can only be used on small distributed programs. For an overview see /WESE80/, /HERG89/. Examples of optimisation strategies are the graph theoretic method and the integer programming (0/1) method /WESE80/.

Heuristic methods have been used to reduce the amount of computation required to find a good task allocation. In heuristic methods some assumptions are made which reduce the amount of computing time used to allocate processes. Examples of such assumptions are that processors in the system are homogeneous and that they are fully connected /WESE80/.

Depending on the period of time an allocation is valid we can distinguish static and dynamic task allocation. Static allocation means that a task allocation is valid during the whole execution time.

Task allocation is only valid for a certain period of time if dynamic task allocation is used. Tasks can be transferred from a highly loaded node to a lightly loaded node according to the current load balance of the system.

Task allocation is influenced by several factors e.g. the communication and synchronisation methods used or whether the number of proceses is static or dynamic.

It is clear that process allocation becomes very complicated if the number of processes is variable. Creating a new process means that a decision is required as to which processor the new process should be allocated. This requires that the current and future load balance as well as the current and future inter-process communication costs be known.

Inter-process communication costs are influenced by the communication method used. Communication mechanisms based on shared memory can be implemented efficiently. They are suitable communication methods for communication within a single processor. Communication methods based on shared objects can be very expensive for inter-processor communication. This is shown in the following example.

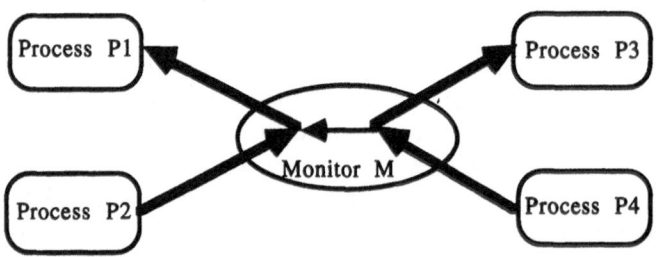

Figure 6.28: Interprocessor Communication with Shared Objects

Process P2 sends a large amount of data to process P1 and process P4 sends most of the data to process P3. Only some of the data sent by process P4 is directed to process P1. The system has to be allocated to the nodes, i.e. processors N_1 and N_2.

The problem is to assign the monitor to a node. If P1, P2 and M are placed on node N1 the data sent from P4 to P3 are first transferred from N2 to N1 and then transferred back. In addition to the process allocation there is always the problem of the monitor. This example shows the impact of the communication and synchronisation mechanism and the related design decisions on the task allocation problem.

Task allocation is a very difficult problem. Up to now a good solution depends on the experience of the designer. Normally only trial and error helps to find a more or less optimal task allocation.

Only few specification and design languages allow task allocations to be described. In the following sections we give an overview of the extent to which SREM, ESTELLE, SDL, LOTOS, and other languages support the specification of task allocations.

6.5.1 SREM

As already mentioned SYSREM is an extension of SREM (see section 6.1.1.) SYSREM allows the decomposition of complex systems to be described. It also supports the allocation of tasks. Functions identified during system decomposition activities are assigned to processors. This means that in SYSREM task allocation is done at a very early stage of system development.

The following figure shows an example.

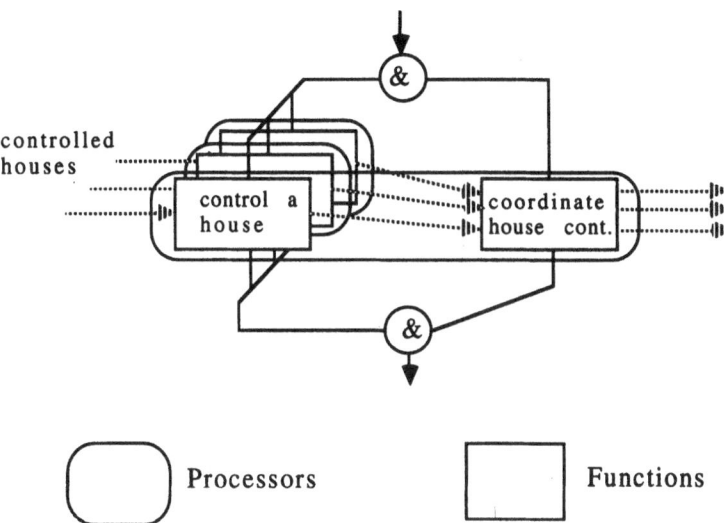

Figure 6.29: Task Allocation in SREM

The figure shows a possible task allocation for the burglar alarm system described in section 6.1.1.

6.5.2 Others

At the time of writing Estelle, SDL, Lotos, Mascot, SARTS and PAISLey do not support task allocation.

DARTS support messages and shared objects. This allows task allocation to be taken into account. Processes which run on the same processor can use shared objects for their interactions.

Shared objects and messages allow tuning but no direct support

Strategies for Real Time Design:
SRTD provides a very thorough support for system design. The architecture flow diagram (AFD) allows the physical partitioning of a system into its component parts or physical modules and the data flow between them to be described. The main purpose of the AFD is to allocate the transformations identified during systems analysis to the physical units of the system. An AFD looks very similar to a data flow diagram. Bubbles represent physical components instead of transformations. In order to specify how the information flows from one architectural module to another, the architecture interconnect diagram, AID, is used.

In order to avoid the problems described above in SRTD, it is recommended that the requirements and the system are specified in parallel. The following figure shows the requirements to architecture template.

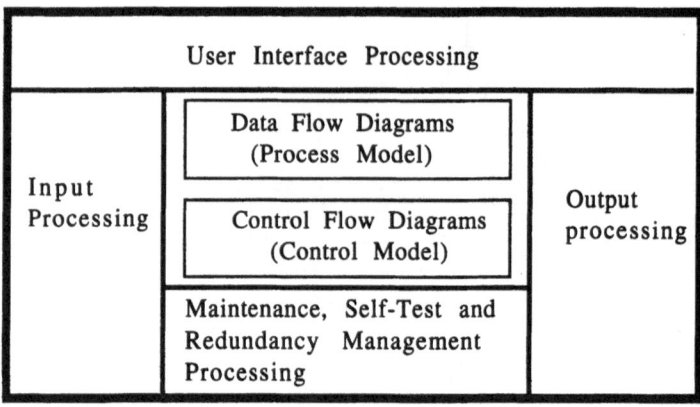

Figure 6.30: SRTD Requirements to Architecture Model

The different aspects contained in this template can be refined step by step. Each layer consists of one or several specifications based on the template shown above.

6.6 Methods/Methodologies

Some methods support only requirements analysis activities. They do not offer any support for design or even task allocation, implementation, or testing.

6.6.1 SREM

One of the most important factors of SREM is that there is a very detailed methodology which covers many aspects of distributed system development.

As already mentioned, SYSREM is used to specify the system requirements; this includes the design of the system architecure. This means that task allocation is part of SYSREM. The SYSREM methodology has nine phases /ALF85b/. These are namely:

1. Define System
   In this phase the system inputs, outputs, performance requirements, constraints, etc. are defined.
2. Identify Components
   In phase 2 the potential component classes or subsystems, i.e. sensors, controllers, communication components, etc. are identified.
3. Decompose to System Logic
   In phase 3 the structure of the system function down to the system logic is identified. The system logic defines the time sequences of function executions, input, and output.
4. Decompose and Allocate
   In this phase the different functions are allocated to the different components and subsystems of the system.
5. Estimate Feasibility and Cost
   Each subsystem allocation is analysed for feasibility and cost. This phase is executed in seven subphases. In the subphases the different feasibility and cost aspects, i.e. interfaces, system load, etc. are analysed.
6. Identify Critical Issues and Resources
   In this step the results of phase 5 are used to identify the critical issues and resources of the system to be developed.
7. Add Resource Management and Fault Tolerance
   In this phase additional functions and system components are identified to support system level failure and system reconfiguration, and to meet system performance requirements.
8. Plan Integration and Test
   The foundations of the system development are defined. The steps for developing subsystems and their testing and integration into the complete system are defined.
9. Optimize the Design
   The design is evaluated and the possibility of finding a better solution is investigated and evaluated.

After the specification of the system requirements SREM is used to define the software requirements. This is done in seven steps /ALF85a/:

1. Define Kernel
   In this phase all I/O messages, R-Nets, and Alphas are identified. This phase ends when all inputs have been processed and all outputs generated.
2. Establish Baseline
   The development database is tidied up and all R-Nets are plotted. This is continued until the naming is consistent.
3. Define Data
   In this step all input and ouput data of each alpha are identified. It ends when no data is used before it has been assigned a value.
4. Establish Tracability
   The specification is traced to establish whether all requirements are satisfied.
5. Simulate Functionality
   The subfunctions are simulated.
6. Identify Performance Requirements
   Response time and accuracy are rechecked.
7. Demonstrate Feasibility
   A rapid prototype is developed for critical algorithms.

In the design phase, the processing is allocated to modules and tasks. A module is defined in two phases: preliminary design and detailed design. The preliminary design is accomplished by partitioning an R-Net into modules. Required data is also partitioned into logical units. The mapping of required data and processing onto modules is expressed in the Module Definition Language MDL. This is a special form of a PDL.

The transformation of MDL into a programming language is a straightforward job. SREM can also be used to express test specifications.

Thus SREM covers nearly all aspects of system development, at least to a great extent.

6.6.2 Estelle, SDL, LOTOS

Estelle, SDL, and LOTOS are languages developed by ISO or CCITT. SDL is intended for the specification of telecommunication systems and Estelle and Lotos for the specification of communication protocols. They contain some features - module hierarchies - which support top-down development but none of the languages has a dedicated method or methodology known to the authors of this book.

6.6.3 Others

Mascot:
The Mascot method recommends six main steps of software development /AXFO89/:

1. External Requirements and Constraints
   In this phase a complete software and hardware requirement definition is developed. Mascot does not prescribe a special method for this step.
2. Design proposal
   In this stage a top level design is developed based on the requirements found in step 1.
3. Network Decomposition
   A more detailed design is developed. Here the data flow specification language specific to Mascot is used.
4. Element Decomposition
   The processes identified in stage 3 are specified in more detail.
5. Program definition
   In this stage the templates developed in stage 4 are implemented using a suitable programming language.
6. Test System Definition
   The complete software is integrated and tested

Darts:
In DARTS the following major development steps are defined:

1. Data Flow Analysis
   In this stage a system, considered as a set of transformations between data flow diagrams is defined. Normal data flow methods are applied.
2. Decomposition into Tasks
   In this stage concurrency is identified. The transformations in the logical processes of the data flow diagrams are analysed to identify which can run concurrently and which are sequential.
3. Definition of Task Interfaces
   In this stage the type of communication and synchronisation is identified.
4. Task design
   In this stage the tasks are designed using structured design techniques /YOCO79/.

SARTS:
In structured analysis of real-time systems, the development process is considered as the definition of a sequence of models. Each model is derived from the predecessor by adding some additional aspects. In SARTS 3, major models are defined:

1. Essential model
   First the focus is on the components of the environment which interact with the system to be developed. Then a model is developed which describes the behaviour of the system in the same way as in SARTS.

2. Implementation model
   In this stage processors, tasks, and modules are introduced and defined. This includes the specification of the interfaces.
3. Implementation of the system

SRTD:
SRTD is based on an iterative life cycle. It allows the production of a layered set of specifications. The system requirements and the system architecture are developed in parallel and in the same way. The life cycle on which SRTD is based is shown in the following figure /HAPI87/.

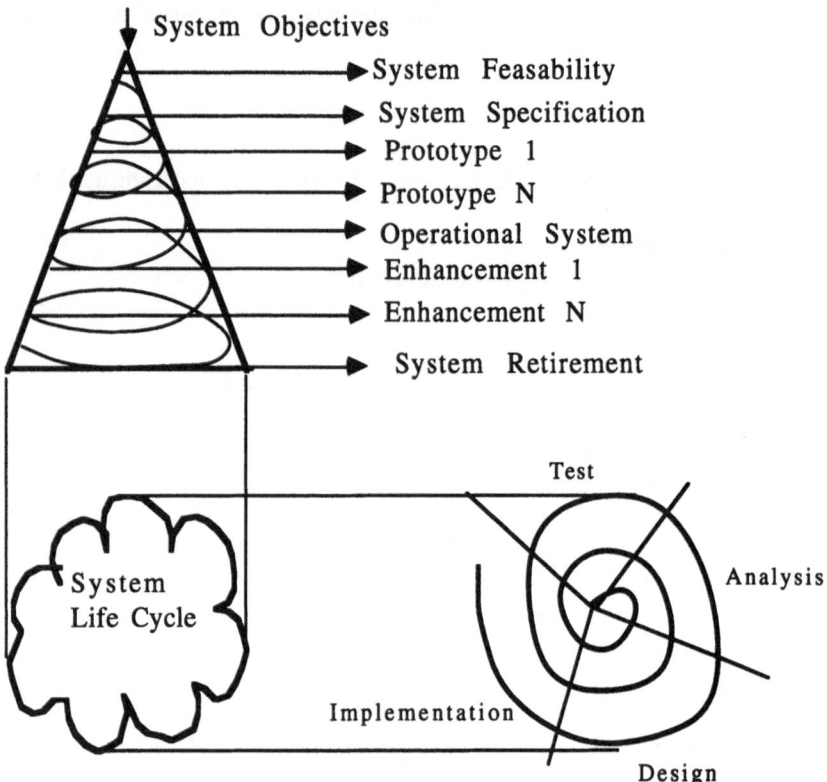

Figure 6.31: SRTD Development Life Cycle

Following the life cycle shown above the data flow specification, control flow specification, and the system architecture is developed. For each of these main activities SRTD offers some heuristics in order to support the developer (see /HAPI87/.

PAISLey:
PAISLey allows the hierarchical description of a system. It supports top-down development but there is no explicit methodology as in SREM.

Recommended Reading:

/ANSC83/   Andrews G. R., Schneider F. B.
Concepts and Notations for Concurrent Programming
ACM Computing Surveys, March 1983
This article gives a short and comprehensive introduction to concurrent programming.

/SLKR87/   Sloman M., Kramer J.
Distributed Systems and Computer Networks
Prentice Hall International, Englewood Cliffs 1987
This book contains an in-depth discussion of different aspects of distributed software systems. The focus is on process control and communication software.

/ALF85b/   Alford M. W. et. al (Ed.)
Distributed Systems, Methods and Tools for Specification
Lecture Notes in Computer Science 190,
Springer Verlag, Heidelberg 1985
This book covers many aspects of distributed software development. It covers theoretical aspects and it contains as an example a detailed description of SREM.

/AXFO89/   Axford T.
Concurrent Programming
Wiley, Series in Parallel Computing, Chichester 1989
In this book mainly the programming aspects of concurrent programs are described. It is an easily readable introduction.

/HAPI87/   Hatley D. J. , Pirbhai I. A.
Strategies for Real-Time System Specification
Dorset House Publishing, New York 1987
This book described a complete software engineering environment for distributed software. It is shown how the various basic concepts for software development can be combined to create a software engineering environment which covers many aspects of distributed software systems development.

/MUSC92/   Mühlhäuser M., Schill A.
Software Engineering für verteilte Anwendungen
Springer Verlag, Heidelberg, 1992
This book is written in German and covers remote procedure calls.

Control Questions:

1. What are the major aspects of the classification of concurrent programming environments?
2. Describe some ways to decompose software systems?
3. Describe the basic communication concepts for concurrent programs and how they are used in SEEs.
4. Explain various synchronisation concepts and their relationship to different types of communication concepts.
5. Explain the different concepts for the specification of process behaviour.
6. How is task allocation described in different SEEs?
7. Which methodologies are used in the various SEEs?

Exercises:

1. What types of decomposition, communication, synchronisation and behaviour description concepts do you need for your distributed programs?
2. What are your criteria for task allocation?
3. How do the various aspects of software development for distributed systems fit into your standard software development environment?

7 The Management of Software Development

Various aspects of project management, especially those which influence the success or failure of a software project, are described.

The management of software development involves the supervision and coordination of activities related to software development in order to produce software that satisfies the requirements of the user (with an acceptable error rate) and that does not cost more the available funds. Project management is the development and execution of a plan to complete a project on time, with satisfactory quality, and within the given budget. These major objectives of project management imply three different planning activities:
- Project scheduling
- Resources and budget
- Quality assurance activities

The planning activities start after a project has been initiated. A project is initiated when somebody recognises a situation which needs to be improved and possibly has some idea as to how this can be done. After establishing a project by installing the core of a project team the project is planned and will be implemented according to this plan. The different activities described in the project plan are executed and their execution is controlled by the project manager. The project manager maintain control to ensure that the project follows the established time schedule, budget plan and quality guidelines.

After completion of the project the results are reviewed and the experience gained is documented. It must also be checked to see how far or to what extent the project goal has been reached.

The following figure shows the different phases of a project and their relation to software life cycles.

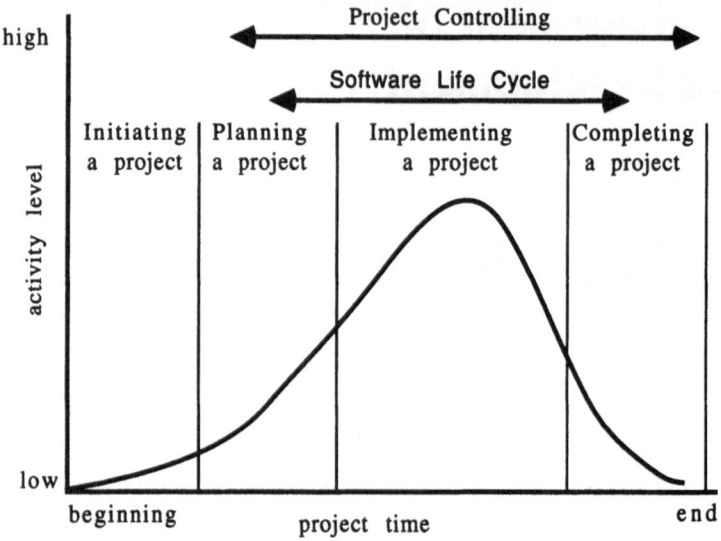

Figure 7.1: Project Life Cycle

7.1 Defining a Project

Projects are normally initiated by higher mangement, clients or staff members. A project is started when somebody reacts to a problem in his environment or when somebody sees a new or better business opportunity.

The initiators of a project usually have unclear and vague ideas on the different aspects of a problem or opportunity recognised. Therefore after the nucleus of a project team has been established, the goals of the project have to be more clearly defined and the different expectations of the initiators of the project have to be clarified as far as possible. It is neccessary to investigate how similar projects have been structured in the past and what experience has been gained with this structure. Much discussion is necessary to define the goals of the project more precisely. The definition of the goals of a project can be regarded as the specification of the system requirements at a very abstract level. During the system analysis the requirements are described in great detail, where possible.

The project implementation strategy is defined based on the project goals and their exactness and stability. Several development strategies, i.e. software life cycles, should be considered and evaluated.

The definition of the project is always subject to change because the the problems to be solved are better understood project proceeds. It happens very often that only vague project goals can be defined especially in advanced research and development projects. In such cases the development strategy should follow an evolutionary or incremental life cycle during the implementation of the project.

The development strategy also includes the decisions about project organisation, resources, time frames, partners, cooperation, etc.

At the latest a project is reviewed after project definition. It is decided whether the goals defined can be reached within a reasonable time frame and budget. Based on the results of this review, top mangement must decide whether to assign funds to the project or not. Their final decision can include major project milestones, which can be used reviewing the project in order to decide whether it should be continued or cancelled.

Depending on the project size an escalation procedure is defined in the case that the project runs over time or into problems of financing.

Detailed planning of the project can start when the definition of the project is complete.

7.2 Planning a Project

The planning of a project produces a master project schedule. This is the basis for the organisation, direction and control of the project /THAY88/. The planning of a project involves the following steps /CORI85/:

1. Define the project objectives
    A statement of the project objectives defines the results to be achieved. The objectives are the basis for the whole planning process.
2. Break down the work to be done
    After defining the objectives of the project the work is divided into activities to be performed. The result is a work break down structure (WBS) /TAUS80/. The WBS is a list of activities to be performed in order to meet the objectives of the project. The WBS also defines which persons or departments are responsible for which part of the project.
3. Sequence the project activities
    There are interrelations between the different work packages identified in the WBS. This influences the sequence in which the different activities are to be performed. Methods such as PERT and CPM can be used to describe sequences of activities identified in a WBS. A discussion of the advantages and disadvantages of these different techniques can be found in /CORI85/.
4. Estimate the required effort, i.e. time, cost, and manpower for each activity
    In this planning phase the effort required for each activity is estimated. The result is the start and completion time for each activity. Different techniques have been suggested for estimating the effort required for an activity. A review of these different techniques can be found in /BOEHM84/.
5. Reconcile the project master schedule with the project constraints.
    In this phase the anticipated duration, the critical path, and the amount of float of the non-critical activities are determined. The different planning techniques mentioned in step 3 can be used to reconcile the project plan.
6. Reconcile the master schedule of the project with the resource constraints.
    In this phase the project master plan is adapted to the available resources.

7. Review the schedule.

   The project master schedule must be repeatedly adapted to the actual situation. Planning a project is an evolutionary process. As the project progresses the master project schedule must be adjusted to the actual situation. All steps except step 2 are more or less independent of the different life cycles and software development methods.

7.2.1 Work Breakdown Structure

A WBS shows the structure of a project as a hierarchy; its highest level depends on the life cycle used /LIHO89/. The figure below shows a WBS based on a conventional life cycle.

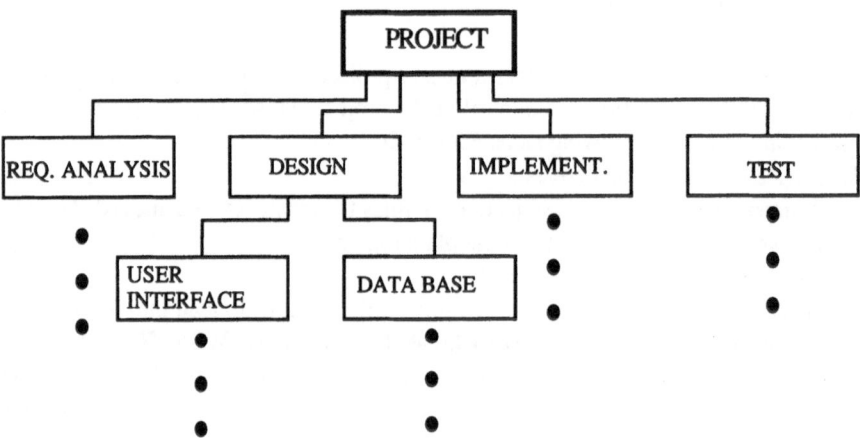

Figure 7.2: WBS based on a Conventional Life Cycle

The first level of the WBS shows the different phases of the conventional life cycle. The figure below shows a WBS based on an incremental life cycle.

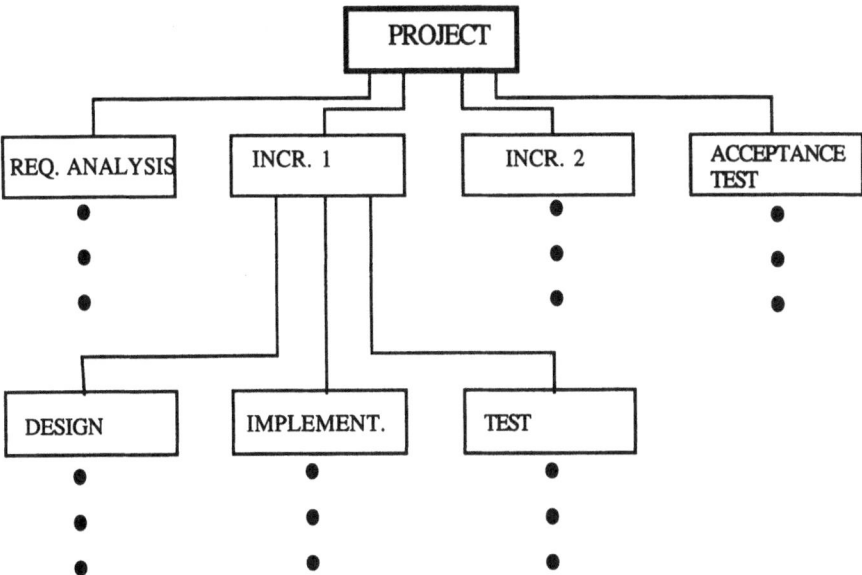

Figure 7.3: WBS based on an Incremental Life Cycle

In a similar way, the first level of a WBS can be identified for all other development methods.

The work packages are identified and described, based on the initial structure of the WBS which depends on the life cycle used.

7.2.2 Project Schedule

For each work package defined in the WBS, the three project parameters - time, budget, and quality - are defined. The activities identified in the WBS are entered in a time sequence and the duration of each activity in the WBS is estimated whether effort estimation or the definition of the time schedule is done first depends on personal taste and other factors such as the available manpower or the latest completion date. Several methods can be used to estimate development effort and describe time schedules.

Effort estimation:
The estimation of development effort is a very difficult task but also one of the most important. Wrong estimates can drive a company into bankruptcy. Despite its importance there are no estimation methods available which can guarantee a defined and acceptable error rate. Estimation becomes much more difficult if the requirements of the system to be developed are not accurately known; this is frequently and perhaps mostly the case. As the project progresses the effort can be estimated more precisely. In /BOEHM84/ the following methods for effort estimation are identified:

1. Algorithmic models

An algorithm computes the required development effort using several parameters. For instance, these parameters can be the number of source instructions, the complexity, the programming language used, the nature of the storage to be used and the time requirements. Some estimation methods have about a hundred input parameters. The major drawback of these estimation methods is that the values of the input parameters are estimated subjectively.

A very detailed analysis of how different parameters influence programming productivity can be found in /JON86/. In /BOEHM84/ several of these algorithmic estimation methods are described and compared.

In /DEMAR82/ an estimation method is described which is based on data flow specification techniques i.e. based on the number of data flows, transformations, specification levels, etc. It also allows these estimates to be revised according to the progress of the project, using data from the project control as described later in this chapter.

2. Expert Judgment, Analogy, Parkinson's Law and the Price of Winning

These estimates are made independently by several specialists. The values to be used in planning, e.g. the average estimates, can be derived from these estimates. The effort required to complete a work package is not regarded as the sum of the effort associated with the sub-work packages because some management and integration efforts have to be added.

We suppose that this is the estimation technique mostly used because it is cheap at least at the beginning of the project. However it can become very expensive later. Project efforts can overrun expert estimations by as much as 300 percent.

In order to achieve estimates which are realistic as possible, they are usually made by experts who have already worked on similar projects. An estimate is made based on the resemblence to these other projects.

The estimates of experts is also influenced by their personal attitude towards the project. If they are eager to develop a system they mostly underestimate the effort. Conversely if they do not like the project or if they think that there are enough development resources they tend to overestimate the effort required. Especially if there is enough staff available, management will want to provide work for everybody. The cost estimate is made on the basis of the available staff.

Conversely salesmen who want to win an order make cost estimates based on their customer´s budget. They expect subsequent projects and are eager to win the initial project at any price.

To summarise, estimates of effort are heavily influenced by the personal background and attitudes of the estimators.

3. Top Down and Bottom Up

In top down estimation an overall estimate for the complete project is made. The complete effort is divided into the effort required for the individual work packages identified in the WBS. Top down estimates are based on the general properties of the system to be developed rather than on software details.

The other approach is bottom-up estimation. The effort required for each individual work package is estimated. The effort required for integration is added to the estimates for the individual packages. Bottom up estimates are precise but can be very expensive because they require almost a complete software design.

Scheduling Techniques:
The relations between different work packages influence the sequence in which the different activities are performed. Several techniques have been developed to describe these sequences. Three of the methods most used are discussed below. For a more detailed discussion of the various other methods see, for example, /CORI85/, /PRESS87/, /MABU87/. A comparison of five scheduling techniques can be found in /CORI85/.

Milestone Chart:
This is the simplest method of preparing development schedules. It shows only the completion dates of the various tasks; the starting dates are not shown. This method can be best applied to small projects developed by small teams.

The milestone chart can express interrelationships between tasks only in a very restricted way and therefore it should not be used for projects with complicated structures. Milestone charts are very often used to give a summary of the time schedule of very large and complicated projects.

GANTT Charts
Gantt charts can be used to express the time sequence and the interrelationships of a project. They show the starting and completion time of each activity. The duration of each activity is shown by a bar. A shaded bar implies slack time and diamonds indicates milestones. A second small bar below an unshaded bar shows the time already used. That part of the time which has been already used is shaded. The following figure shows an example of a Gantt chart.

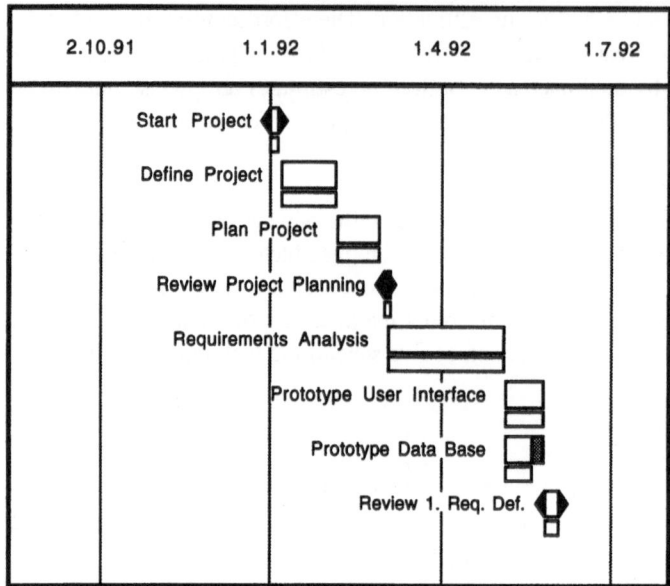

Figure 7.4: Gantt Chart

Precedence Networks:

A precedence network shows the relations between various activities in a project. The most popular forms of precedence networks are the Critical Path method (CPM), the Program Evaluation and Review Technique (PERT), and their variants.

The differences between CPM and PERT are not fundamental. CPM emphasises activities while PERT is event-oriented. On a CPM chart, nodes shown by circles represent events. Activities are represented by arrows connecting events. Shadow activities are represented by dotted lines. These represent relations between events for which no work is required. The following figure shows an example of a CPM.

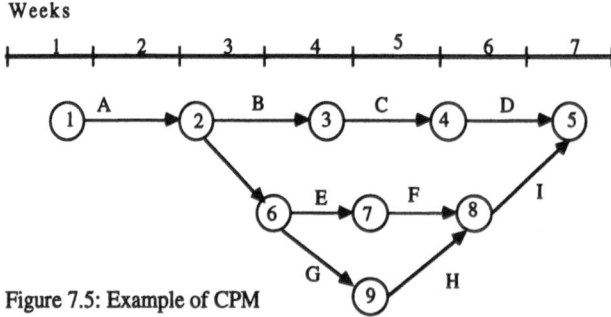

Figure 7.5: Example of CPM

The numbers represent events and the letters beside the arrows describe activities.

A PERT chart is shown in figure 7.6. In a PERT chart activities are represented by boxes. The boxes are marked with the names of the activities. In addition the boxes can be marked with the starting and completion date of the activity, the names of those responsible or the project leader, etc.. The lines which connect the boxes have no special meaning. The following figure shows an example of a PERT chart. The oval boxes represent milestones. The boxes and the broad lines show the critical path of the project. The critical path is the longest path through the network and as such identifies essential steps that must be completed on time to avoid delay in completing the project.

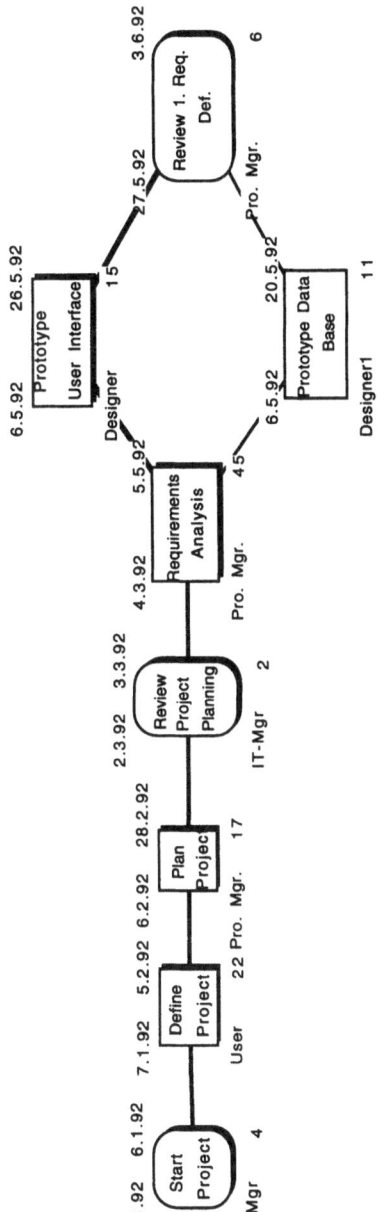

Figure 7.6 : Example of a PERT Chart

The type of precedence network to be used depends on the personal taste and experience of the project manager responsible and also on some of the characteristics of the project. A precedence network should include at least 20 activities; otherwise it is better to use a GANTT chart. PERT allows the explicit treatment of probabilities associated with the earliest and latest start and completion dates; This is not possible in CPM. Hence PERT is mostly used in research and advanced development projects. CPM is used in construction and similar industries where the project is well understood and has a low level of uncertainty.

7.2.3 Resources and Budget

The time schedule of a project describes the time frame in which the project has to be executed. After defining the time frame, the budget and resources required have to be planned in detail. The resources assigned to each work package are based on the estimates of the effort required for each work package and the intended implementation schedule of the project. Resources include developers, i.g. personnel, office space, computing power, terminals, travel expenses, training and cost of communication by telephone and mail. Resources cost money and therefore they are considered as cost components. A project costing worksheet can be used in order to document the budget for each working item and its cost component . This is a matrix where each row represents a work package and each coloumn represents a cost component. The following figure shows a project costing worksheet related to the previous example (see figure 7.6).

Cost Comp. / Work Pack.	Labor	Comp. Power	Travel Exp.	Office	Com. exp.	•••
1. Requirements Analysis	130	15	10	5	7	•••
2. Prototype User Interface	50	15	2	3	2	•••
3. Prototype Data Base	40	15	2	3	3	•••
⋮	⋮	⋮	⋮	⋮	⋮	⋮

Figure 7.7: Costing Worksheet

The total cost of the various work packages, cost components, or the complete project can be spread over the planned development time. The following example shows how the planned budget would be used. At the beginning of the project the costs increase slowly because less resources are required. During project execution the costs grow much faster whereas at the end of the project the costs should decrease.

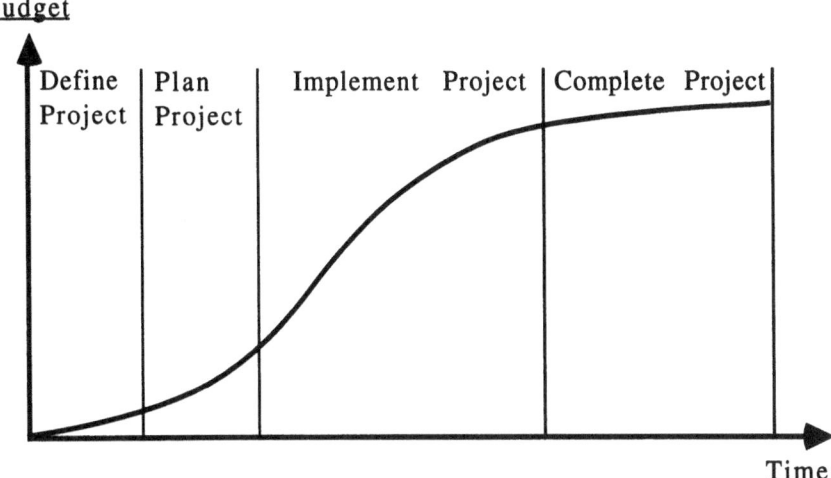

Figure 7.8: Typical Cumulated Costs of a Project

Manpower is normally the most expensive resource. Therefore it is very important to plan the use of manpower thouroghly. It may be necessary to adapt the time schedule to the manpower available. This can lead to an increase or decrease in the length of the project. The figure below shows the manpower assigned to our project. The shaded bars indicate that this resource is not required full time in this activity. The part of the bar which is not shaded corresponds to the time in which the resource is fully assigned to the project.

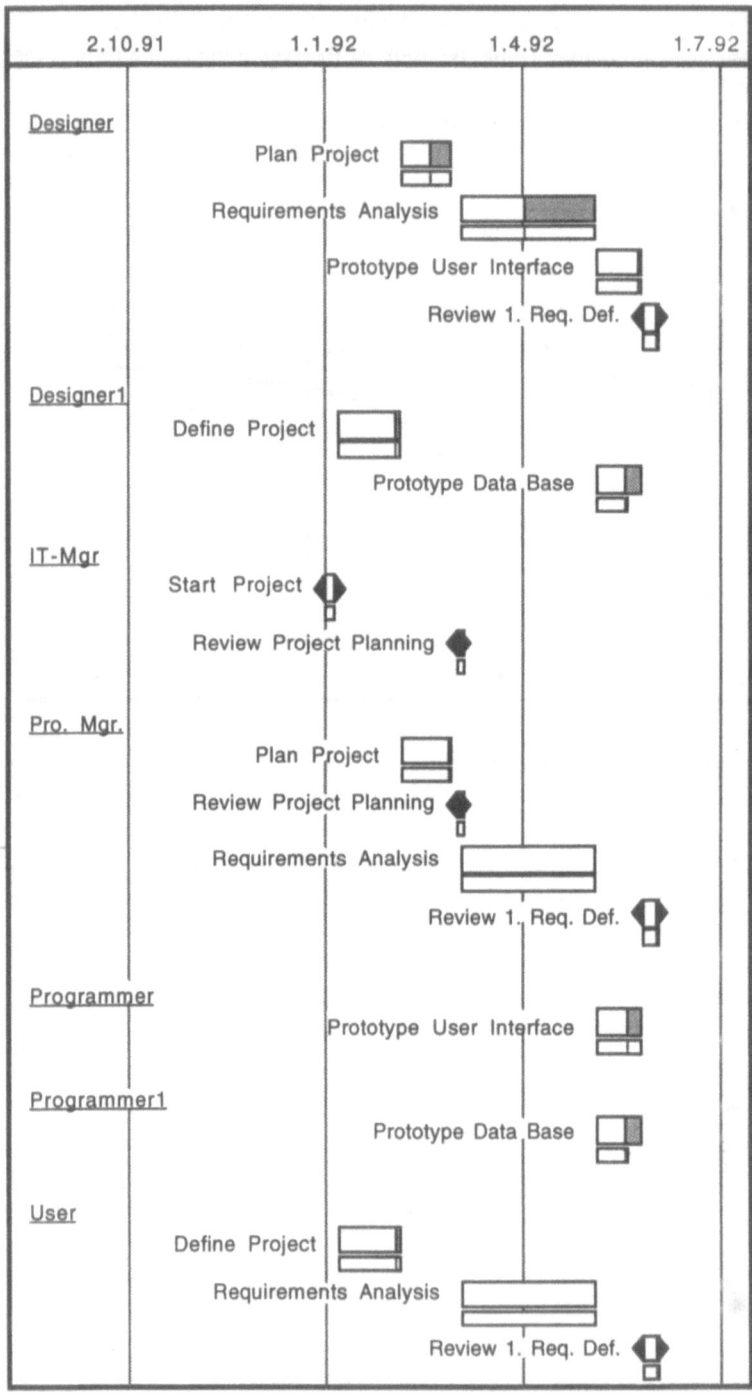

Figure 7.9: Resource Plan

7.2.4 Software Quality

Software quality assurance (SQA) activities are intended to assure the quality of software systems and products. However this raises the question of the measurement of software quality. The range of possible definitions starts with the number of errors discovered per unit of time or per 1000 lines of code /JON78/ and ends with very detailed lists of quality factors. The importance of quality depends on the end user of the software, i.e. the organisation which uses or maintains the software system, not the organisation which produces or buys the software.

There exist several lists of quality factors from the point of view of the user, e.g. in /CAMC78/ /DEUT88/. These lists overlap. The union of these lists is shown below:

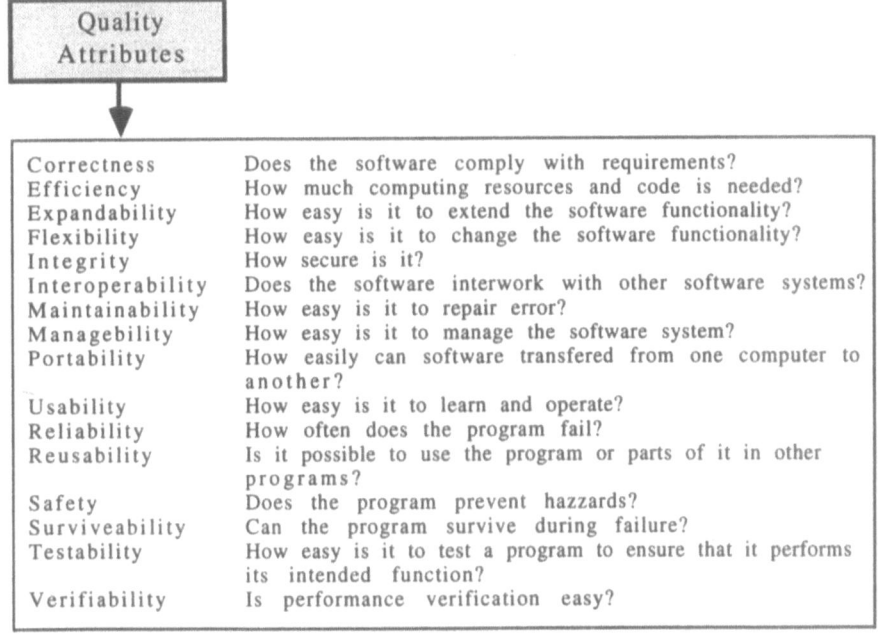

Correctness	Does the software comply with requirements?
Efficiency	How much computing resources and code is needed?
Expandability	How easy is it to extend the software functionality?
Flexibility	How easy is it to change the software functionality?
Integrity	How secure is it?
Interoperability	Does the software interwork with other software systems?
Maintainability	How easy is it to repair error?
Managebility	How easy is it to manage the software system?
Portability	How easily can software transfered from one computer to another?
Usability	How easy is it to learn and operate?
Reliability	How often does the program fail?
Reusability	Is it possible to use the program or parts of it in other programs?
Safety	Does the program prevent hazzards?
Surviveability	Can the program survive during failure?
Testability	How easy is it to test a program to ensure that it performs its intended function?
Verifiability	Is performance verification easy?

Figure 7.10: Quality Attributes for the User

These quality attributes for the user have not been identified directly. They are based on quality engineering /DEUT88/, i.e. the engineering of quality into software. In /DEUT88/ 27 types of engineering attributes which developers can build into software during the development process are listed.

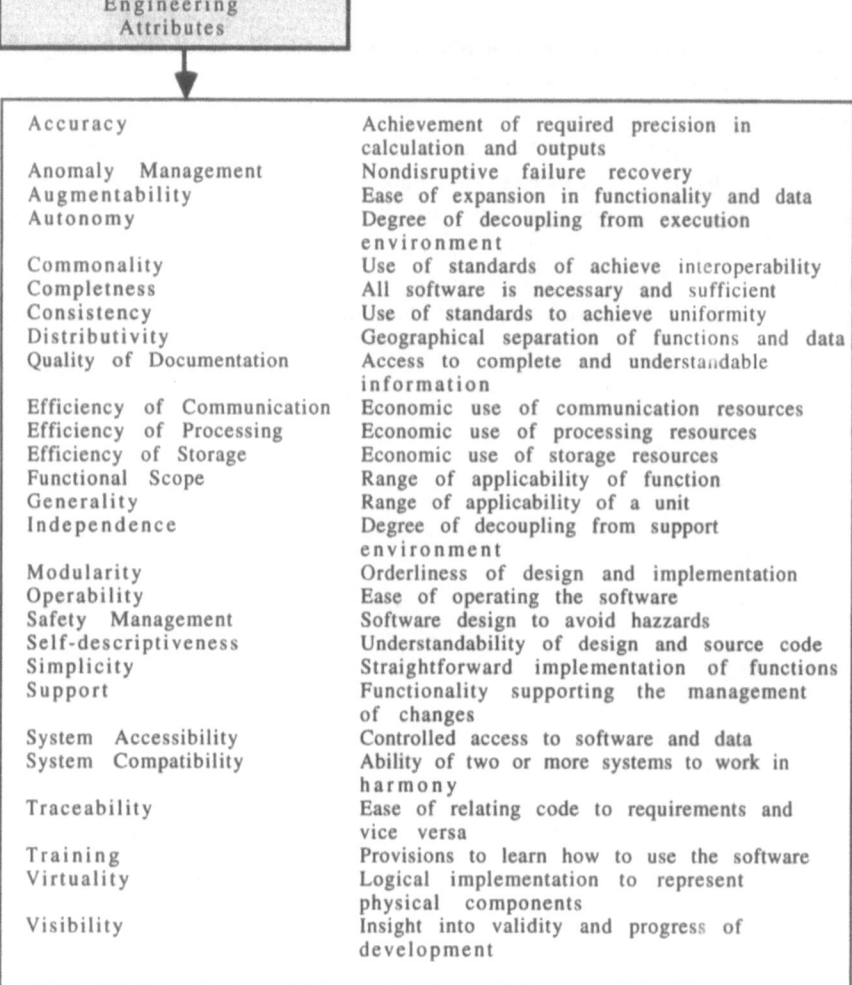

Engineering Attributes	
Accuracy	Achievement of required precision in calculation and outputs
Anomaly Management	Nondisruptive failure recovery
Augmentability	Ease of expansion in functionality and data
Autonomy	Degree of decoupling from execution environment
Commonality	Use of standards of achieve interoperability
Completness	All software is necessary and sufficient
Consistency	Use of standards to achieve uniformity
Distributivity	Geographical separation of functions and data
Quality of Documentation	Access to complete and understandable information
Efficiency of Communication	Economic use of communication resources
Efficiency of Processing	Economic use of processing resources
Efficiency of Storage	Economic use of storage resources
Functional Scope	Range of applicability of function
Generality	Range of applicability of a unit
Independence	Degree of decoupling from support environment
Modularity	Orderliness of design and implementation
Operability	Ease of operating the software
Safety Management	Software design to avoid hazzards
Self-descriptiveness	Understandability of design and source code
Simplicity	Straightforward implementation of functions
Support	Functionality supporting the management of changes
System Accessibility	Controlled access to software and data
System Compatibility	Ability of two or more systems to work in harmony
Traceability	Ease of relating code to requirements and vice versa
Training	Provisions to learn how to use the software
Virtuality	Logical implementation to represent physical components
Visibility	Insight into validity and progress of development

Figure 7.11: Software Engineering Attributes

Each quality attribute for the user is related to one or more engineering attributes. The following table shows the relations /DEUT88/.

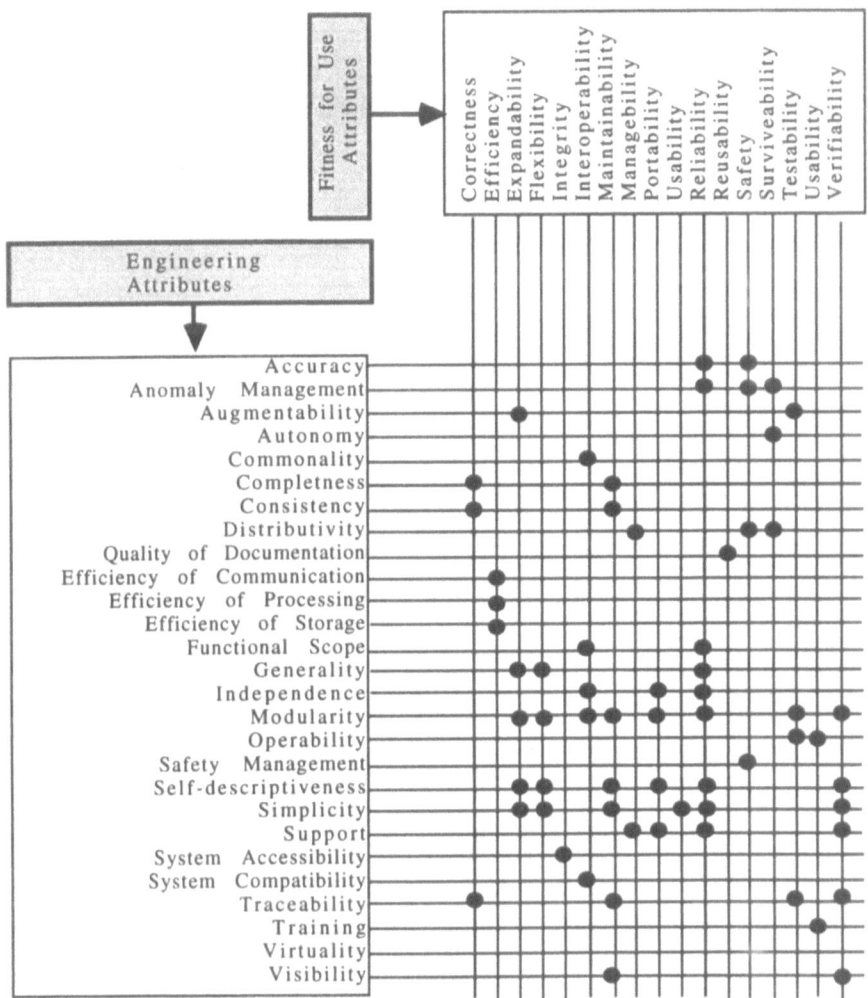

Figure 7.12: Relationship Between User Oriented Quality Factors and Engineering Attributes

There have been many attempts to make software quality – both factors related to the user and engineering attributes –, measurable. It is relatively easy to count errors per lines of code if the program is finished and in use. But, as shown above, errors are not the only quality factors and counting errors in a running program can be completely inadequate, e.g. in a flight control program.

The quality factors and engineering attributes described above are high level factors and attributes. It is not always possible to measure them directly i.e. the software product has not been started or is in the analysis or design stage. The metric is used to predict the future quality of the software system. Factors and attributes that correlate with the high level factors and attributes are measured. The relationship between these attributes and factors and the high level factors and attributes to be predicted is called a model. The following table shows examples of attributes which can be measured in order to derive the high level quality engineering attributes.

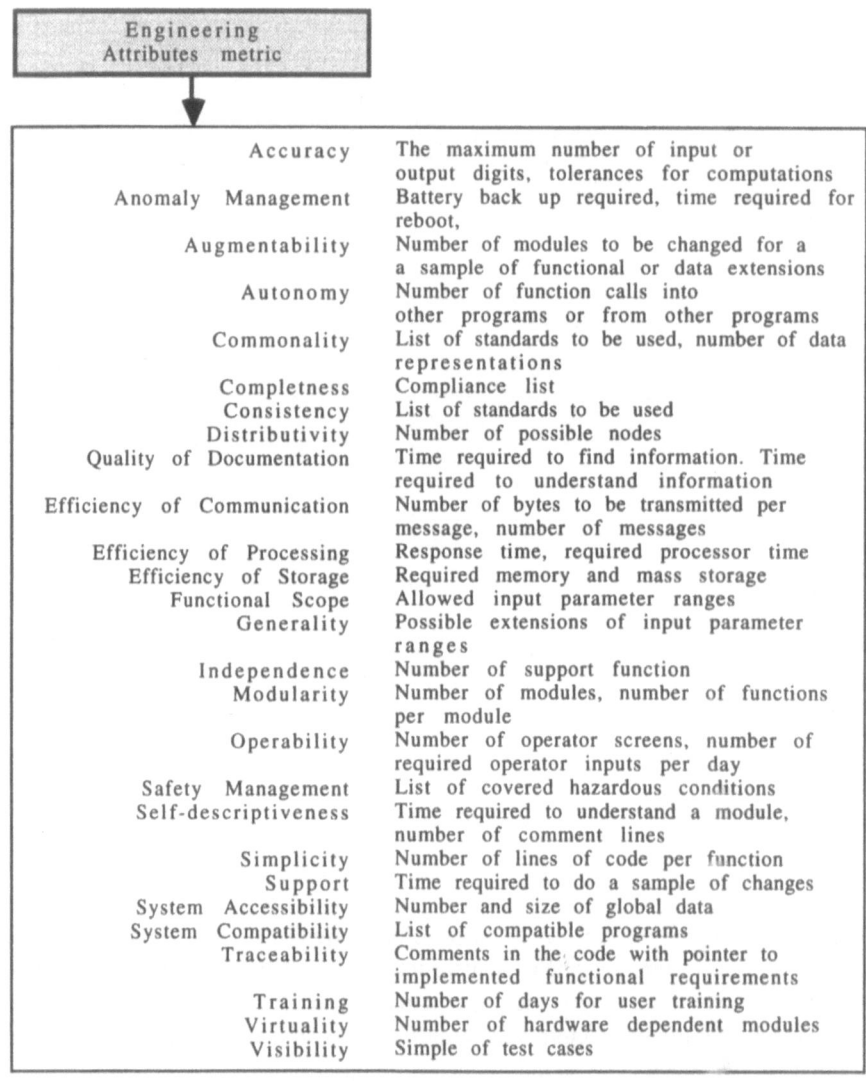

Engineering Attributes	metric
Accuracy	The maximum number of input or output digits, tolerances for computations
Anomaly Management	Battery back up required, time required for reboot,
Augmentability	Number of modules to be changed for a a sample of functional or data extensions
Autonomy	Number of function calls into other programs or from other programs
Commonality	List of standards to be used, number of data representations
Completness	Compliance list
Consistency	List of standards to be used
Distributivity	Number of possible nodes
Quality of Documentation	Time required to find information. Time required to understand information
Efficiency of Communication	Number of bytes to be transmitted per message, number of messages
Efficiency of Processing	Response time, required processor time
Efficiency of Storage	Required memory and mass storage
Functional Scope	Allowed input parameter ranges
Generality	Possible extensions of input parameter ranges
Independence	Number of support function
Modularity	Number of modules, number of functions per module
Operability	Number of operator screens, number of required operator inputs per day
Safety Management	List of covered hazardous conditions
Self-descriptiveness	Time required to understand a module, number of comment lines
Simplicity	Number of lines of code per function
Support	Time required to do a sample of changes
System Accessibility	Number and size of global data
System Compatibility	List of compatible programs
Traceability	Comments in the code with pointer to implemented functional requirements
Training	Number of days for user training
Virtuality	Number of hardware dependent modules
Visibility	Simple of test cases

Figure 7.13: Examples of Measurable Attributes

The measurable attributes used can depend on the method used for the requirements specification and design. If data flow diagrams are used the number of description levels, the number of input and output data flows per transformation, etc., can be counted. The example above shows only measurables attributes which are independent of the method used. The authors could not find publications which investigated measurement systems specific to a particular method, e.g. data flow diagrams, and the quality factors described above.

Software Quality Planning

In a quality plan the required quality factors and the methods by which they are to be measured are described. Based on such a quality metric the measure of quality for each quality attribute is defined. For instance, if the number of lines of code is used as a quality metric for simplicity then one quality requirement could be that the number of lines of code for each function does not exceed 250.

How the requirements of the quality plan can be achieved must be defined. All quality assurance methods and activities are described in the plan. These include organisational aspects, documentation standards, and coding standards. The following table shows an example of the table of contents of a quality assurance plan /BUCK79/.

1. **Purpose**
   This chapter describes the specific purpose of this particular Software Quality Assurance Plan. It lists all the names of the software covered and its intended use

2. **Reference documents**
   This chapter contains a list of all documents referenced in the plan.

3. **Quality Definitions and Metrics**
   This chapter contains the definition of the quality metric used in this project.

4. **Management**
   This chapter describes the organisation, tasks and reponsibilities for all the quality assurance activities.

5. **Documentation**
   This chapter defines all documents which have to be produced during the development process.

6. **Standards, Practices, and Conventions**
   This chapter describes all the standards to be used for documentation standards, logic structure standards, coding standards commentary testing standards.

7. **Reviews and Audits**
   In this chapter the technical reviews and audits to be conducted are defined. The time schedule for the reviews and audits have to be integrated in the time schedule

8. **Test plan**
   This chapter describes the test strategies and samples of test cases.

9. **Configuration Management**
   In this chapter all software items and the corresponding controlling, reporting and changing procedures are defined.

10. **Problem Reporting and Corrective Action**
    This chapter describes the organisational responsibilities and procedures for reporting, tracking and resolving problems

11. **Tools, Techniques and Methodologies**
    This chapter describes all the tools, techniques and methodologies which support software quality assurance

12. **Code Control**
    This chapter describes all the ways and methods to maintain and store a control version of the code

13. **Media Control**
    This chapter describes all methods to avoid unauthorised access to project development documents,. source code, etc.

14. **Supplier Control**

    This section describes how software components delivered by other vendors or subcontractors are controlled.

Figure 7.14: Example of Quality Assurance Plan

Major Quality Assurance Activities

The quality assurance activities which are most important from a technological point of view are described in sections 7 and 8 of our quality assurance plan. Because of their importance we describe these activities in a little more detail.

* *Technical reviews and audits*

The technical reviews serve a control purpose; they are used to determine whether the development process satisfies the quality requirements; whether the system will meet the user requirements; and whether the system design and implementation are technically feasible.

Technical reviews or audits are carried out by a group of between three and five persons. Each technical review is conducted as a formal meeting and is succesful only if it is properly planned, prepared, controlled and attended. The goals of technical audits and reviews is to uncover errors and inconsistencies, to verify that the software system under review meets the requirements and to confirm that the software development follows the quality standards defined in the quality assurance plan. After each review meeting, a final report must be produced. This report, or at least the final review report, is part of the documentation of the project.

In order to ensure that the requirements, design and implementation documents are reviewed independently by the actual developers, managers of a project should not participate in review and audit meetings. Managers should only be interested in the final result: whether a particular component passed its review.

The developers and reviewers are responsible for a software component meeting the functional and quality requirements. More details about audits and reviews can be found in /PRESS87/, /WALK79/, /YOU78/.

* *Testing*

The purpose of testing is to validate programs; it represents the ultimate review of specification, design and implementation. The static analysis in the technical reviews of the program code, provides global information about the program structure whereas dynamic testing investigates the runtime behaviour of a program /FAIR78/. Very often at least 40% of the development time is required for testing. The goal of testing is to find errors. Good test cases uncover as many errors as possible. However one should be aware that testing can only show the presence of errors; it cannot show the absence of errors.

As already mentioned in chapter 3, a software system can be tested by two basic strategies: white box testing and black box testing. In white box testing the creation of test cases is based on the internal behaviour of the system. Black box testing is based on the functions of a software system. White box and black box testing can be applied to modules, subsets of modules, or to the complete system. If a complete system is to be tested, the interworking of tested modules is checked. Therefore this type of test is called an integration test. Integration tests can be done step by step. First only a subset of tested modules are combined and tested. After the integration tests of this subset are finished, other modules or other tested subsets can be added for further tests. In the following figure the different test strategies are summarized.

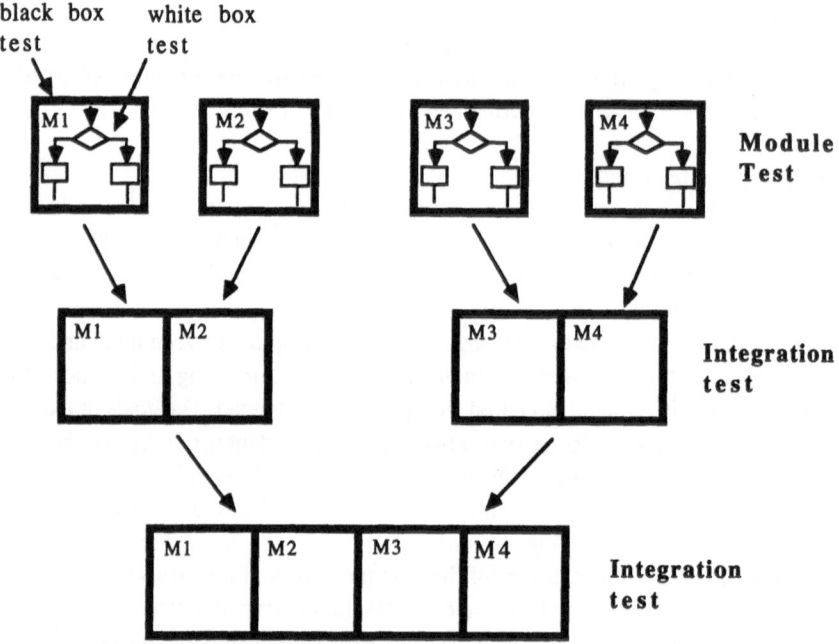

Figure 7.15: Test strategies

In all test strategies the critical success factor is the selection of test data. It is useful to describe test data, i.e. test cases, in the quality assurance plan. Test cases for black box testing should cover most of the functions of the system. The selected test cases should be both inside each permitted input data class and on the boundary of the class /ADBRCH82/.

Test cases for white box testing are intended to test the structure of a part of a program. The quality of these test cases is based on the number of statements, branches, and paths in the program which are exercised by the test data /ADBRCH82/, /DLSA78/.

7.3 Project Control

The management of a project involves controlling the development process and the products of the process. Project control is performed by the project manager Controlling a project includes three major activities:
- Gathering data about the status of the project
- Evaluation of the data gathered and decision making rearding consequent actions
- Alteration of the project plans with respect to budget, time, and quality in accordance with the results of the data evaluation.

These activities are repeated in a cycle. It is also possible that several control cycles are running in parallel in order to control different aspects of a project. In the following section these project control activities are described in more detail.

Gathering Data:
The project manager continously gathers data – facts and impressions – about the current status of the development process and the project. The following methods can provide correct information about the status of a project:
- Personal Contacts
  Talking to developers, customers, administrators,. etc. can provide much information about the morale of the development team, the technical problems occurring, etc. These informal methods can give very early signs of problems arising.
- Formal Meetings
  In meetings the current status of the project is formally discussed. The progress of the project is compared with the plans.
- Protocols of Walk-Through Meetings
  The final protocols of the walk-through meetings show the current development stage and quality of the software.
- Time Reports
  All those involved in a project report how much time they have spent on particular activities belonging to the project.
- The Project Log
  Important information about the project is recorded in the project log. This contains important statements by members of the project, managers, customers, subcontractors, etc.
- Budget Reports
  A project manager normally receives reports from administration about the actual budget. This can be compared with the planned budget and any major differences, e.g. travel expenses or telecommunication expenses, can be identified.

All the information described above is condensed to a project status report. In the next step the content of the project status report is evaluated.

Evaluate Information:
Next the project control information gathered is compared with the project plans. If there are no differences everything is clear and the project team can continue the project without changes. But in most cases, in fact nearly always, there will be differences between the project status and the plan. Major causes of deviations from the project plan can be:
- too much optimism about time required, manpower, etc.
- the customers requirements can change
- developers are assigned to other projects by top management
- cooperation problems between individual members of the project or the project teams
- unforeseen technical problems
- subcontractors are late or can not even deliver

There are many reasons why a project does nor follow its plan. A project manger has to analyse the causes and effects of deviations from the project plan. The result of this analysis will result in actions. The project plans have to be changed. If major changes of the project plan are necessary, the steering committee which is a normal feature of a project has to agree to the changes.

A project can be cancelled if the project status shows that the project will cost too much money or too much time.

Alter Project Plan
Based on the actions set out in the project evaluation phase, new project plans will be produced. This can mean that time schedules, budgets, and quality plans have to be changed. If the changes exceed the authority of the project mangers then the steering committee must be involved.

7.4 Peopleware

"Peopleware" is the title of a well known book by Tom DeMarco and Timothy Lister /DELI87/. The title expresses in an excellent way that you need more than hardware and software to make a project successful. Program development is done by people; therefore they are the most important resource. In order to implement a project people with the right technical and social skills have to be selected and assigned to positions in the project. The development team has to be led through all the ups and down of a project. A motivated team can do nearly everything. In the following sections we can only glance at this important aspect of software engineering. It could fill many books. We want to discuss at least some of the more important aspects.

7.4.1 Project Organisation and Team Structure

The organisational structure of the development team is oriented towards the work packages identified in the work breakdown structure and the time schedule. The figure below shows how the problem structure is mapped onto an organisational structure /DALY79/. The managers – line managers and chief programmers – are responsible for the interfaces with the software components developed in other groups e.g. the second level of line management is responsible for the interfaces between the subsystems.

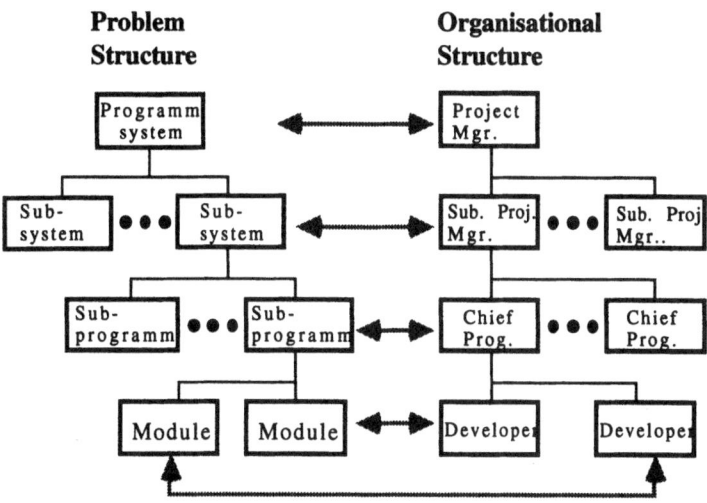

Figure 7.16: Relationship between Problem Structure and Organisational Structure

In the next step the positions created by the project organisation must be filled with the right people. This includes selecting candidates for the positions and training of them in order to enable them to perform their job in the best and most efficient way. People required for a project can belong to the more functionally oriented parts of the company, i.e. the line departements. There can be several functional units e.g. a database department, a real-time programming department, a financial application software department. In general, staffing a project means assigning people from the functional entities to positions in the project organisation. The following figure illustrates the staffing of a project.

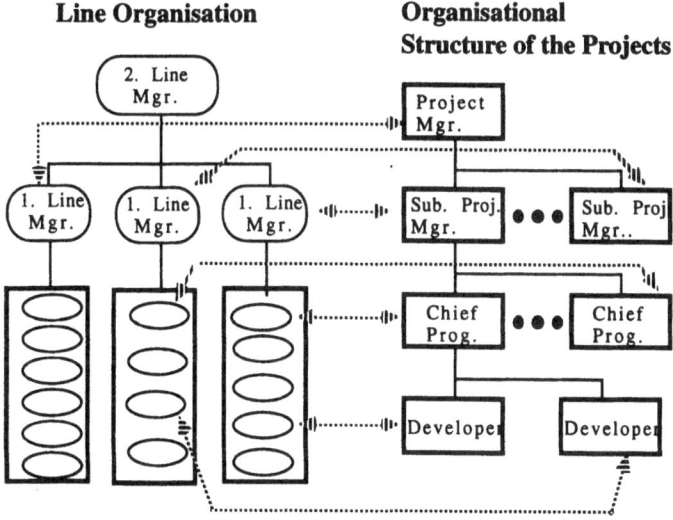

Figure 7.17:
Staffing of a Project

The figure shows the principles of embedding the project organisation into the functional organisation. The assignment of people can be done in three basic ways: functional organisation, project organisation or matrix organisation. These three basic ways of structuring project organisations or staffing projects are illustrated by a simple example. There are two projects: A and B. We show below how these two projects are structured.

– *Functional organisation*
A project is implemented either in a single functional unit or, if it is a multifunctional project, by dividing the project between the three departments X, Y and Z. The figure below shows the separate organisations for project A and project B. All decisions that cross functional bounderies are made by one person, the head of all functional organisations. This has both advantages and disadvantages. The advantage is that synergies between different projects can be optimally controlled. On the other side there are only few managers who are able to deal effectively with so much authority.

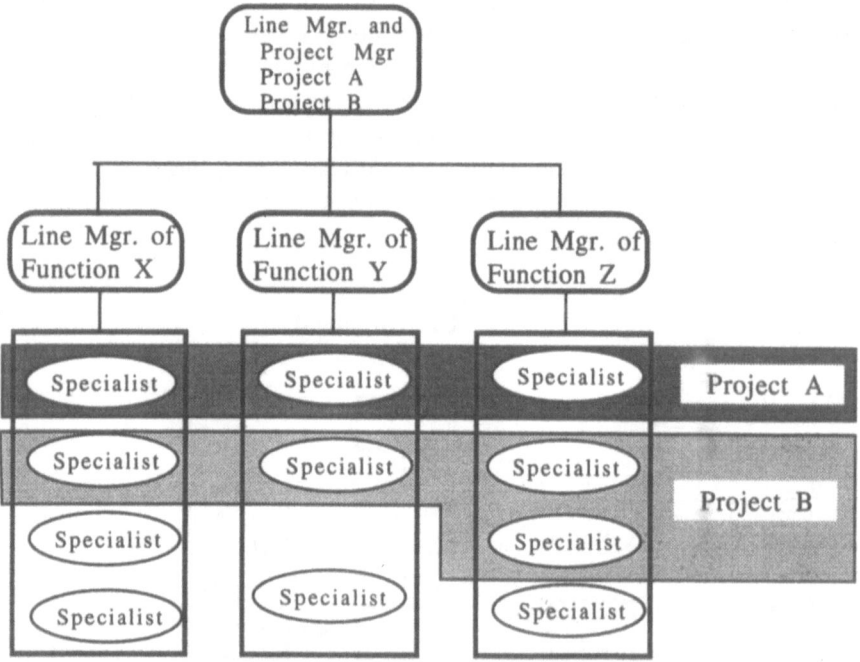

Figure 7.18: Functional Organisation

– *Project organisation*

In project organisation the functional structure and the project structure are identical. Hence the project manager is also the line manager. The project manager is given the authority, responsibility and resources to accomplish the project. The project organisation inhibits the use of common features between projects. This implies that on completion of a project or on commencement of a new project a reorganisation of the company is necessary or staff have to be retrained for a new project which requires other skills. The following figure shows the organisational structure for project A and project B.

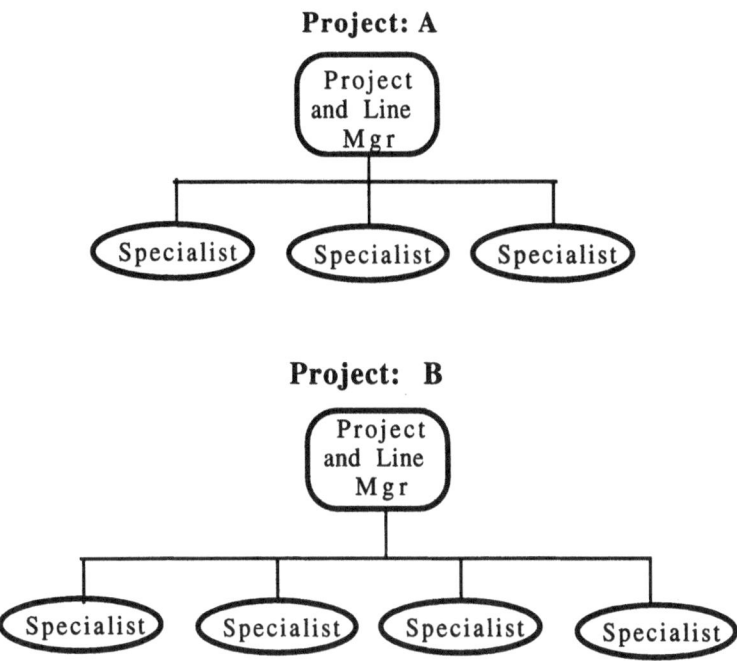

Figure 7.19: Example Project Organisation

– *Matrix organisation*

The matrix organisation tries to combine the long term orientation of functional organisation with the short term orientation of the project organisation. The project manager is given the responsibility and authority to complete the project. Line managers are responsible for providing the right resources, i.e. staff with the required skills. The figure below shows a simple two dimensional matrix organisation. Matrix organisations allow a very flexible response to new or finished projects. The major disadvantage of the matrix organisation is that there is no single person who is responsible for the success of a project.

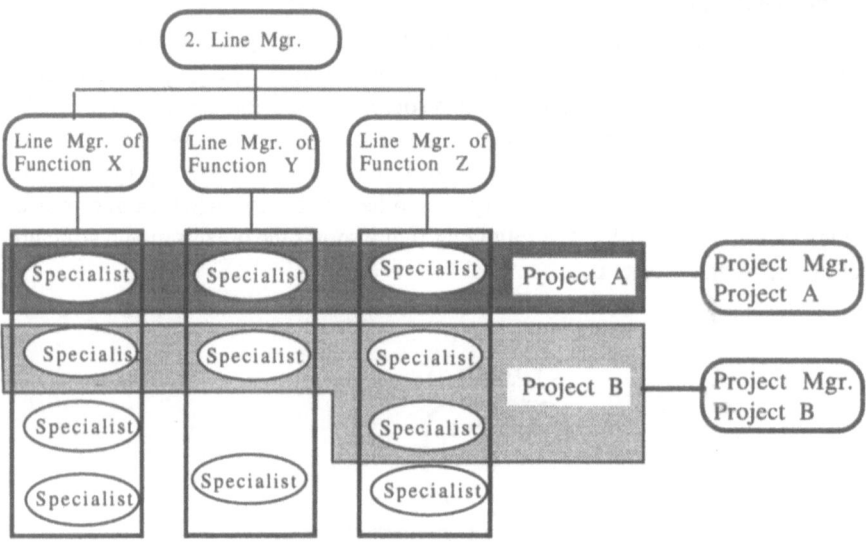

Figure 7.20: Example of a Matrix Organisation

As already explained each type of organisational structure has several advantages and disadvantages. Very often these basic organisational structures are mixed to maximise or minimize certain advantages and disadvantages. A more detailed discussion of organisational structures can be found in /THAY88/.

In addition to embedding the project organisation into the functional organisation it is necessary to organise the project team internally. Examples of such team structures are the chief programmers team, the hierarchical team, and the egoless team.

A chief programmer team consists of a chief programmer, back-up programmer, program librarian, and other auxiliary personel. The chief programmer is responsible for all technical aspects of the project or sub-project and makes all the managerial decisions /BRO75/, /THAY88/. The chief programmer is supported by the other team members.

In a hierarchical team the project leader manages senior programmers and senior programmers manage junior programmers.

In an egoless team all decisions are made by consensus. There is no central control authority and leadership responsibility rotates /THAY88/.

It is possible that several different team structures are used in one project. For example the design and implementation activities are organised using the chief programmer team and the quality assurance team is egoless. Obviously there is a relationship between the project organisation embedded into the functional organisation and the internal structure of the project team. The project manager responsible decides which team structure is used for which activities.

7.4.2 Productive Teams

Defining the project structure and embedding the project organisation into the functional organisation is only one factor in the success of a project. Perhaps the more important factor is a winning team, i.e. a team that is willing and eager to finish a project successfully. The organisation of a productive team /DELI87/ is a common management problem, not only in software development. Many books have been written about this problem e.g. /DELI87/, /BENA85/, /PETE82/, /PETE85/, /PETE87/, /ROGE86/ (this is only a more or less random selection of literature about productive teams). It is not possible here to give even an outline of the different aspects of organising a productive team. Suffice to say that good systems are not developed by only using the correct methods. A system is developed by people who are motivated, willing, and able to use the appropriate technology. Software development managers are very often technologically-oriented people and sometimes they are not aware of more personal factors.

The mythical word associated with successful teams and organisations is leadership. 'A real leader has the ability to motivate others to their highest level of achievement; then gives them the opportunity and the freedom to grow.' /ROGE86/. Behind such a simple definition there are many aspects and problems in day to day work. We do not want to write a book about this very important topic; we aim rather to write a book about technology. We recommend everybody to read books and to attend courses on leadership. A successful software project manager must also display leadership qualities.

Recommended Reading:

/THAY88/   Thayer R. H. (Ed.)
            Software Engineering Project Management
            IEEE Computer Society Press, New York 1988
            This book contains a collection of articles about various aspects of
            software project management.

/DELI87/   DeMarco T., Lister T.
            Peopleware: Productive Projects and Teams
            Dorset House Publishing, New York 1987
            This book covers mainly the human aspects, maybe the most impor-
            tant of software development.

/DEUT88/   Deutsch M. S.
            Software Quality Engineering
            Prentice Hall, Englewood Cliffs 1988
            This book is a very deep and sythematic discussion of software qual-
            ity assurance.

Control Questions:

1. What are the major planning activities?
2. What are the different phases of a project? Explain them.
3. What are the major project planning steps?
4. What is a Work BreakDown Structure (WBS)?
5. What is the realationship between WBS and Software Life Cycles?
6. Explain some basic methods for effort estimation?
7. Explain some scheduling techniques?
8. Explain some techniques for resource and budget planning?
9. Explain some software quality factors?
10. Explain the relationship between quality factors and engineering attributes?
11. What are major quality assurance activities ?
12. What are project control activities?
13. What are the basic types of team structures?

Exercises:

1. How are projects managed in your environment?
2. How do you do estimate effort?
3. What is your project organisational structure?
4. Classify your project control procedures?
5. What are your quality assurance activities?

8 Tools

The various aspects of software engineering tools and the integration of different types of tool are described with some examples.

A new term related to software engineering tools was created several years ago: CASE stands for Computer Aided Software Engineering. CASE is the automation of software development.

'The basic idea behind CASE is to provide a set of well integrated, labor saving tools linking and automating all phases of a software life cycle'./MCCLU89a/

CASE combines software tools and development methodologies, where the tools automate the software process, and the methodologies and procedures (life cycles) define the process to be automated /CHIK89/, /MCCLU89b/. According to /MCCLU89a/ a complete CASE system must have the following capabilities:

- Full life cycle coverage for different types of life cycles
- Tightly integrated toolset
- Consistency checking
- Sharing all information in a central repository
- Graphics capabilities
- Automatic code generation

The figure below shows in a simplified way the development of software using a CASE environment.

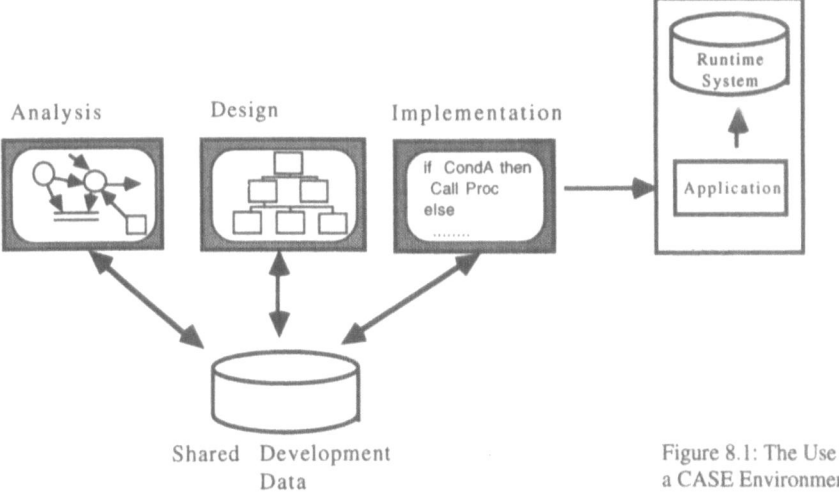

Figure 8.1: The Use of a CASE Environment

A software system can be developed in a different computer environment than the computer system on which the finished application will run.

CASE environments should facilitate transitions between the phases of the underlying development cycle. A developer must be able to return to earlier versions, to change them and to return to the point at which he was working. A CASE environment should guarantee that the different documents are updated and remain consistent.

Normally medium and large software systems are developed by a team. A CASE environment should support team work which means that team members have access to the development information or parts of it, and can read or change it. Each member of the team has access to updated and consistent development documents. All results related to a project are contained in a repository which is the heart of a CASE environment.

It is not necessary to repeat the argument that diagrams are easier to understand and allow the expression of complicated relations much clearer than text. Nearly all CASE environments support graphical representations. Diagrams are used to define program requirements, e.g. data flow diagrams and entity relationship diagrams, and to represent program designs and system structures. Diagrams are the basis for transforming a design into a program structure or even a complete program.

Tools for the different development activities can be independent of each other or closely related. This means that the output i.e. product from one tool can form the direct input for the next tool. Tools for several development activities form a coherent CASE environment.

The tools of a CASE environment are based on the underlying analysis, design and implementation methods described in chapters 3 and 4. The methods used in a project depend on the type of application program. As already mentioned other methods than those for database applications have to be used for communication methods. Therefore there are no general purpose CASE environments. A CASE environment is tailored to a particular project according to the methods used and the area of application.

In the following sections the general features of tools for the different development activities are discussed first. Then the ANSI/ECMA reference model for integrated CASE environments is described. In the last sections some examples of CASE systems are outlined.

8.1 Analysis and Design Tools

Analysis tools support a systems engineer in documenting the requirements of the user for a program to be developed. This is normally an iterative process. The analyst and the user must understand the aims of the program very thoroughly. In addition different user groups will have different views of the same problem. What this means is that an analysis document must be changed very often. Therefore many analysis tools are nothing more than editors that allow the producion and maintainence of data flow diagrams, entity relationship diagrams, etc. Such editors exist for all the analysis methods described in chapter 4. More enhanced versions of such tools allow consistency checks to be carried out. For example, in data flow diagrams it can be checked whether the structure of each information flow is defined, whether a specification exists for each transition, etc.

These tools which support the production of definitions for functional requirements can be used with other tools to design user interfaces such as menu builders and screen painters.

Fourth generation languages can be used to implement prototypes in order to investigate at least some aspects of the system in more detail. If executable specification languages are used, a prototype is produced with little additional effort.

Simulation tools are used to make more reliable statements about the response time of a program. Especially for applications with hard real-time requirements, it can be very useful to construct a simulation model of the system.

Design tools support a designer in documenting the results of his design activities. They support the documentation of module hierarchies, module interfaces, module functionalities, data structures, etc.

8.2 Implementation Tools

Implementation tools support the production of code based on the system design. Tools allow code skeletons or complete programs to be generated from design specifications.

Program skeleton codes for database access, file access, screens, program to program communication, etc. are generated automatically. For each module identified in the program design a code frame is generated. The code of each of these modules has to be added manually. Here programmers can be supported by editors which are specific to the programming language used. These support a programmer in following programming standards for variable names, procedure names, comments, etc.

Complete code can only be derived from a design which contains all the required information. This means that either the requirements or the program design is described in an executable language. It may be the possible to change the code manually. This can be especially necessary in real-time applications.

8.3 Project Management Tools

Project management tools support the different project management activities. During the planning of a project graphical tools enable the drawing of work breakdown structures. WBSs are normally changed very often during project planning. If they are available in an electronic representation they can be changed easily.

Project management tools allow a project plan to be derived from the WBS. They can be used to draw PERT diagrams, CP diagrams, and GANTT charts. Nearly all these tools can derive one type of diagram from another automatically. This means that, for instance, a GANTT chart is automatically derived from a PERT diagram. Project management tools also allow the assignment of resources to tasks to be described. Plausibility checks are executed automatically. This helps to prevent a non-sharable resource being assigned to several tasks at the same time e.g. a programmer cannot work full time on two different tasks at the same time. Project management tools use the time schedule and the list of assigned resources to automatically calculate the budget of the project.

Spreadsheet programs support a project manager by performing all the required extra calculations such as the cost of travel and communication cost. Techniques for estimating effort are very often supported by appropriate tools, especially if algorithms are used to estimate the effort.

During the implementation of the project forms facilitate the gathering of control data. These forms can be paper or computer based. Computer based forms allow reports to be produced automatically.

Word processors improve the writing of letters or program documentation. If a team working on the same project is distributed over several geographical locations an electronic mail system can be useful. It can help to improve communication within the team and to reduce travelling costs (see also section 1.5.4 about groupware).

File and database systems support the management of all project documents including the code listings, design documents, analysis documents, letters, and protocols of meetings.

8.4 Integrated CASE Environments

The previous sections outlined the possible functions of tools which correspond to the various software development activities. Tools supporting particular development activities can be based on particular specification languages, programming languages, methods, and methodologies. Tool sets are designed to assist several development activities. The output from one tool can form the input of another tool. CASE environments can be classified in various CASE classes.

The relationship between several tools supporting different activities can be more or less strong. There can be the integration of various types of tools.

In the following sections a way of classifying CASE tools is described. The subsequent sections discuss different ways in which CASE tools depend on each other.

8.4.1 Classification of CASE Environments

According to /MCCLU89a/ and /DEFH87/ five classes of CASE environments can be identified:

Language oriented:
This type of CASE environment is built around a particular programming language. The development and the production systems are the same. Code is changed, com-

piled, linked, executed and tested in the same environment. Well known examples of such CASE environments are BASIC programming systems. They include an editor, an interpreter, and debugging capabilities. Language oriented CASE environments only support one programming language.

This type of CASE environment supports only implementation activities. It does not support analysis and design activities, i.e. programming-in-the-large. Language oriented CASE systems usually do not support team work. Normally it is not possible for several programmers working on the same project to use their own programming environment and to share some information, i.e. programming-in-the-many.

Structure-oriented:

Structure oriented CASE systems are independent of a particular programming language. Instead of program code, the program structures are manipulated. The editor is the central component of such a CASE system. Such an editor supports interactive semantic analysis, program execution, and debugging. The syntax orientation of language-oriented systems has been replaced by a structure orientation.

Up to now structure-oriented CASE environments have been mainly used as teaching aids and they have found little acceptance in industry /DEFH87/. They resemble language oriented CASE systems in that they do not support programming in the large or programming in the many.

Tool kits:

Tool kits are a set of integrated tools that support one type of software development activity. This means that there are tool kits for analysis, design, implementation, testing and project management. The tool kit approach starts with the operating system which is very often the only connection between tools of the same tool kit or between tools belonging to different tool kits. Examples of tool kits for programming activities are editors, compilers, debuggers and some tools for version control and configuration management. A well known example of such a tool kit is the Unix Programmers Workbench, Unix/PWB. (Note that the word 'workbench' here has a different meaning from that used below). In Unix/PWB the Unix file system is used for tool integration.

The various tool kits support programming-in-the-large and programming-in-the-many.

Workbench:

A CASE workbench is an assembly of integrated tools for all development activities as well as tools for software project management activities. The output from the various tools can be used as input for other tools. The final product of a CASE workbench is executable code.

In general CASE workbenches support programming-in-the-large and programming-in-the-many.

Methodology companion:
A CASE methodology companion is a tool kit or workbench for a particular development method or methodology. These CASE tools help to structure the whole development process according to a particular methodology and support all the development activities. Developers are supported by help screens and menus which provide information about the status of a development project. Sometimes forcing functions do not allow the program to start the next development step before the previous step has reached a certain stage.

8.4.2 Types of Integration

The different tools of a CASE system have to be integrated in a single CASE environment which supports all development activities and several methodologies (Several tools share the same project dictionary). However this type of integration is limited to tools produced by the same vendor and sometimes even restricted to data in the same project.

The National Institute of Standards and Technology and the European Computer Manufacturers have developed a technical framework for classifying the different types of CASE tool integration /NIST91/, /CHNO92/. The following figure shows this technical framework.

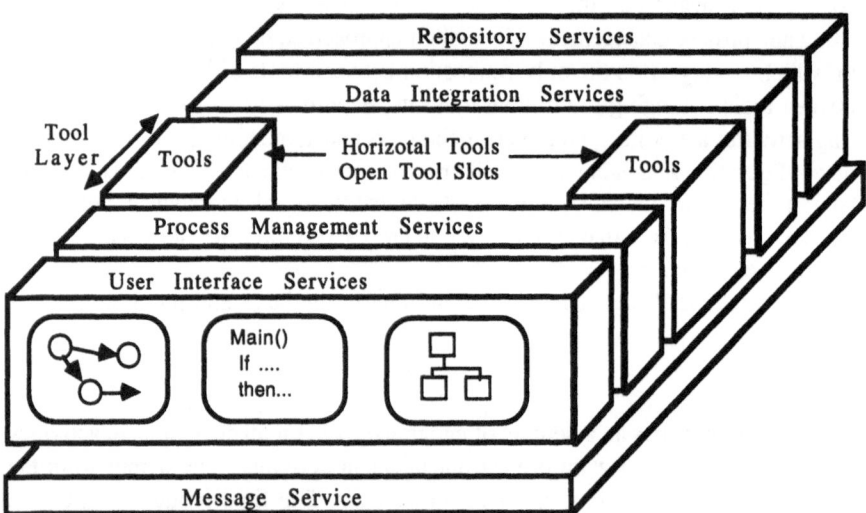

Figure 8.2: The NIST/ECMA Reference Model

Different types of tool integration can be defined /CHNO92/, based on this reference model for CASE systems.

Data integration:
The most important type of tool integration is the sharing of analysis, design, implementation and management data. There are several ways of sharing data.

Direct data transfer:
Data is exchanged directly between tools. The relevant tools are connected by filters. Filters form a very important concept in the well known Unix operating system. The results of using a tool A are transformed into input data for a tool B. This transformation is executed by filters. The following figure shows the direct data transfer between tools via a filter.

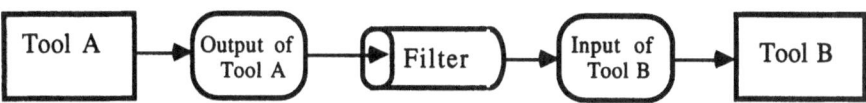

Figure 8.3: Direct Data Transfer between Tools

This type of tool integration is most efficient when real-time integration is required. However it is very difficult to implement if several tools must be combined.

Communication based transfer:
If direct data transfer is used in a distributed development environment then we have a communication based information transfer between tools. Tool A and tool B can run on separate systems. The filter function is separated into two parts. One half runs on the same system as tool A and the other half on the same system as tool B. The two parts of the filter are connected by a communication system.

File based transfer:
A very simple type of data oriented tool integration is file based information transfer between tools. The output from tool A is located on a file which is accessed by tool B. Tool B can read the file and extract the required information. In order to simplify file based tool integration, there are recommondations for structuring the content of these integration files.

Repository transfer:
All information about a software system including planning, analysis, design, implementation, and project management are stored in a CASE repository. CASE repositories are the cornerstone of several integrated software development tools as previously described. CASE repositories provide basic services for the storage and management of objects/entities and links/relations. Repositories support configuration management, naming services, security and transaction control /CHNO92/.

The data stored in a repository is data about data. Repositories provide an appropriate store for data about business entities such as data records and databases; and business processes or transformations such as customer order handling. Because a repository contains data about entities and processes and is considered a higher order of abstraction, it is often referred to as metadata.

Presentation Integration:
In order to make it easier to use several tools the same rules that govern user interfaces apply to tools. Different tools supporting different activities use the same standards for their user interactions. Today nearly all advanced user interfaces of CASE tools are based on windows. According to /WASS90/ there are four levels of presentation integration for user interfaces based on windows:
- the windows system
- the windows manager
- the user interface development tool kit
- the look and feel guidelines

System Integration:
System integration combines aspects of data integration and presentation integration based on a specific vendor system for either the development or runtime environment e.g. IBM's CASE environment AD/Cycle is closely related to IBM's Systems Application Architecture (SAA) /MMNR90/ and Digital's CASE framework Cohesion is related to Digital's Network Application Support (NAS) architecture /DIGIT90/. In the following sections IBM's and Digital's CASE environments are discussed in more detail.

System integrated CASE environments which are independent of a particular vendor are based on Unix /DUNP91/.

Control Integration:
Control integration of tools includes data integration. In addition tools which provide control integration are able to inform each other of events, activate other tools under program control, and share functions /WASS90/. A tool can transfer messages to other tools. These messages can activate particular functions. An example of such control integration is a compiler which activates the editor if a syntax error is discovered.

Methodology Integration:
Methodology integration is at the very least a combination of data and control integration. Sometimes it also includes presentation and system integration. Tools supporting several methods for each development activity are combined to give an integrated methodology companion. It is possible to transfer control from a tool supporting a particular development activity to a tool supporting another activity. Transfer of control from one tool to another tool is controlled by the steps of the applied methodology, e.g. it is only possible to activate an implementation tool when the design supported by an appropriate design tool is completed.

Management Integration:
A totally different type of tool integration is management integration. Up to now we have not considered the team orientation aspect of most software development projects. Management integration combines several of the integration concepts described above and supports
- a single user performing a particular development activity
- a development team in which each member is working on a different component of a system or is performing a particular activity
- a complete organisation where several teams are working on several projects.

Management integrated tools allow the sharing of information between members of a team and support their cooperation by control integration which transfers control from one team member to another.

8.5 Examples of Integrated CASE Environments

Based on their application architectures, e.g. SAA for IBM, NAS for Digital, all major computer system vendors offer their own CASE environments. These CASE environments allow at least the data integration of tools developed by other vendors. In the following sections we outline the CASE concepts of the two large computer system vendors, AD/Cycle of IBM and Cohesion of Digital Equipment Corporation. AD/Cycle and Cohesion cover mainly system integration features and are based on the manufacturers' repositories. The system integration features particularly support implementation activities. Screen builders, debugging tools, report processors, file systems, etc., are normally based on a particular computer system.

AD/Cycle and Cohesion allow the development of distributed programs but are focused on client/server programs. They do not support the development of cooperative programs e.g. process control systems or communication systems.

8.5.1 Cohesion of Digital Equipment Corporation

Digital's CASE environment Cohesion is closely related to Network Application Support (NAS). The goal of NAS is to implement vendor independent specifications for interfaces and services, formats to enable applications to be ported across a particular range of systems with minimal changes, to cooperate with other applications on local and remote systems, and to interact with users in a way that facilitates user portability /DIGIT91/. NAS interfaces are based on existing or vendor independent standards for application programming interfaces, data representation, communication protocols, etc. NAS products can be used and implemented on a variety of systems with the client/server model of computing.

NAS includes an application integration model which is a visual representation of an application and its interaction with its environment. An application must interact with users, data stores, other applications, and the underlying sytem. An application displays information to and accepts requests for information from the user, i.e. it supports user interaction. Information stored on various storage devices is accessed by almost any application, i.e. a data interaction. It should be possible for an application to communicate with other applications via various communication systems, i.e. application to application interaction. Finally it must interact with the system in order to obtain system resources, i.e. system interaction.

The different interactions are offered to an application via application programming interfaces, API, of the particular services. There are a set of services for each type of interaction. The following figure shows the application integration model.

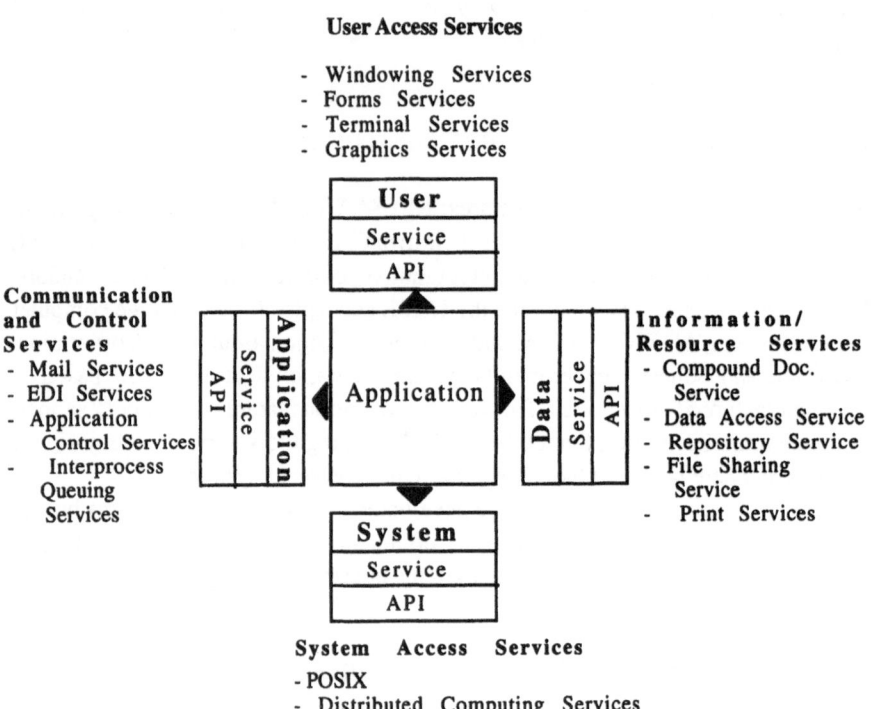

Figure 8.4: Application Integration Model

The following figure shows the NAS architecture and how the application integration model is embedded in it. The services for the different types of interactions can run on different server or client systems e.g. an application may run on a server and the related user interface server is executed on a client system such as an MS-DOS PC.

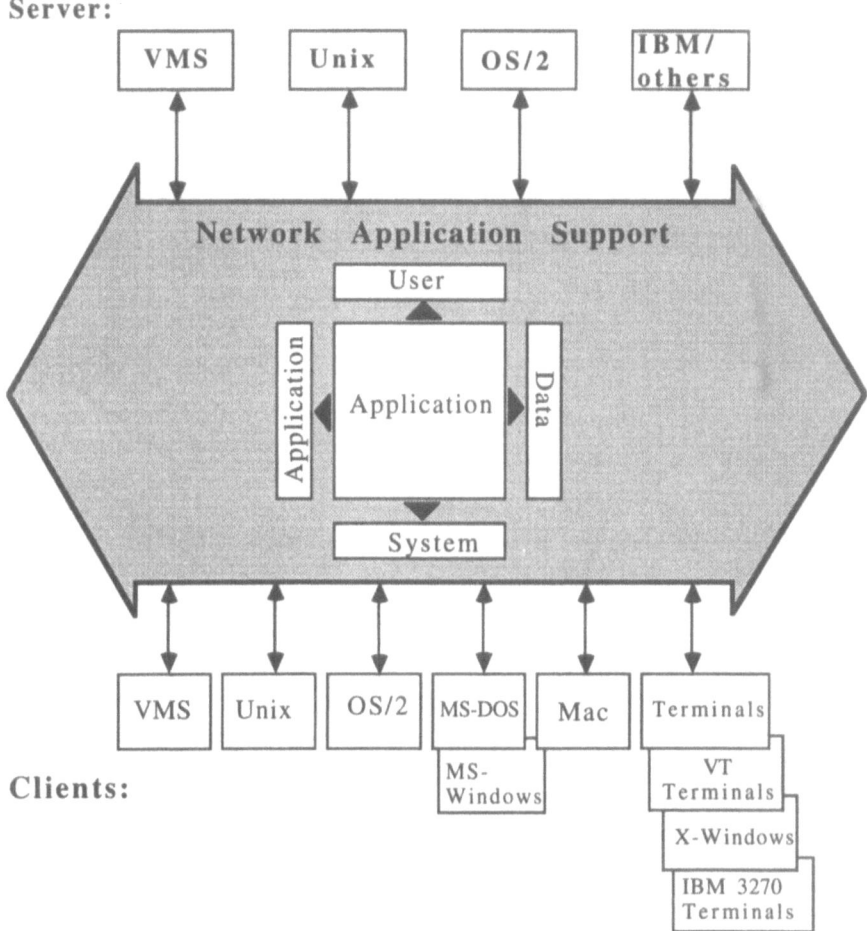

Figure 8.5: The NAS Architecture

The relationship between NAS and Cohesion is bidirectional. Cohesion tools are based on NAS and are used to construct NAS applications. Cohesion is the software development environment for NAS. Cohesion integrates Digital tools, additional vendor tools, and special customer tools. The heart of Cohesion is a repository that represents a common view of software development information. The following figure shows the structure of Cohesion and its relation to NAS.

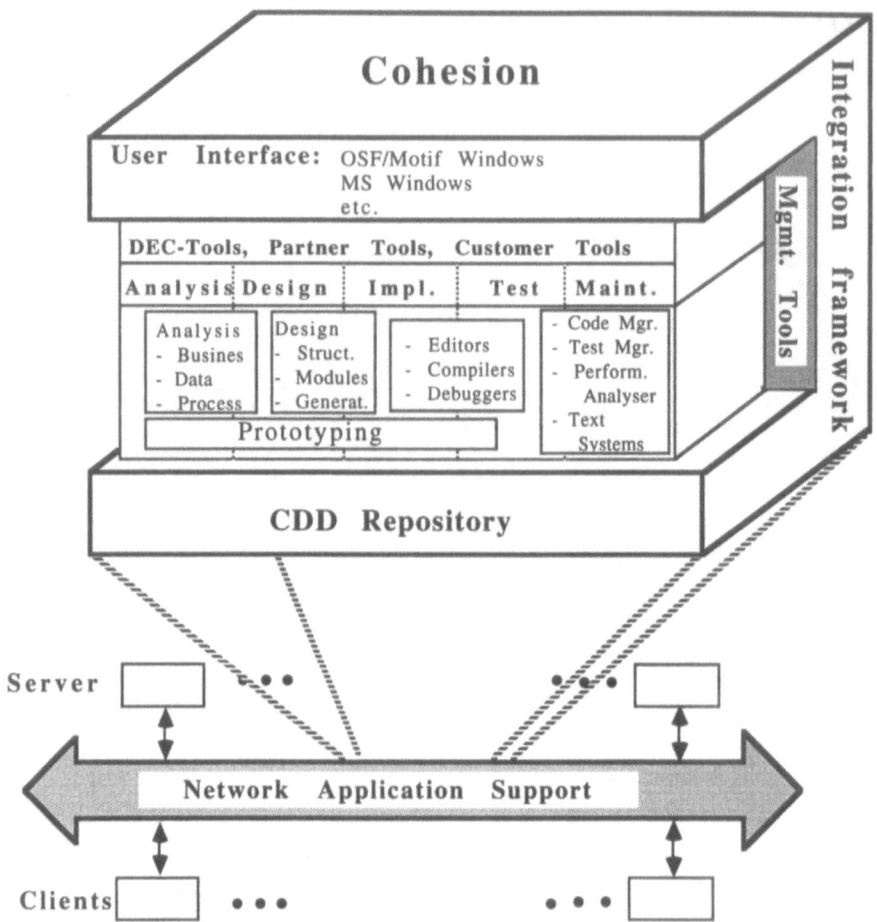

Figure 8.6: The Cohesion Life Cycle Function Model

8.5.2 AD/Cycle of IBM

IBM's System Application Architecture, SAA, is a framework for the development of portable applications which can interact with applications running on the same or different systems. SAA is a set of interface standards, coding rules and communication standards for distributed applications. An application can use three types of interfaces:

- The Common Programming Interface, CPI, which includes programming languages, generators, expert systems, query languages, dialogue, and presentation managers
- The Common User Access, CUA, which includes the various types of user interfaces such as windows, function keys, and integrated help functions

- The Common Communication Interface, CCI, supports different types of protocol, especially the facilities of IBM's proprietary communication system System Network Architecture (SNA), and communication systems which conform to the ISO/OSI standards. CCI also includes the interfaces to information systems such as data bases, texts, graphics, and compound documents, and the possibility of transferring information from one system to another.

The following figure shows the overall SAA structure. It also shows the internal structure of a system which is hidden by CPI, CUA, and CCS interfaces. The details of these features should not be visible to an application. This encapsulation allows an SAA compliant application to be run on different systems which are supported by SAA.

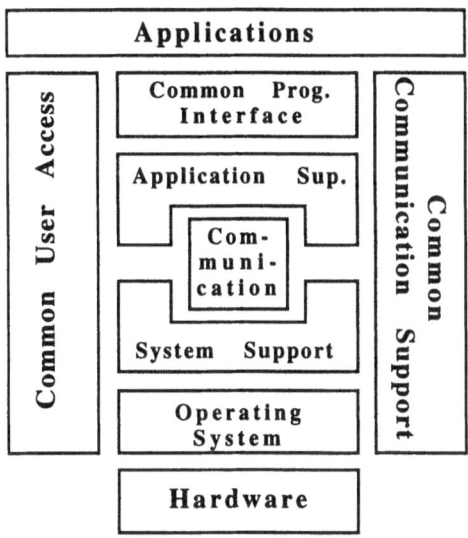

Figure 8.7: The SAA Architecture

AD/Cycle is based on SAA and involves the use of the SAA interfaces. On the other hand AD/cycle supports the development of SAA applications. Based on the AD/Cycle repository tools developed by IBM, other vendors or customers can be integrated into AD/Cycle. AD/Cycle tools can be used across all development activities or can be targeted to particular activities such as analysis and design. The following figure shows the structure of AD/Cycle and the relationship between different tool classes.

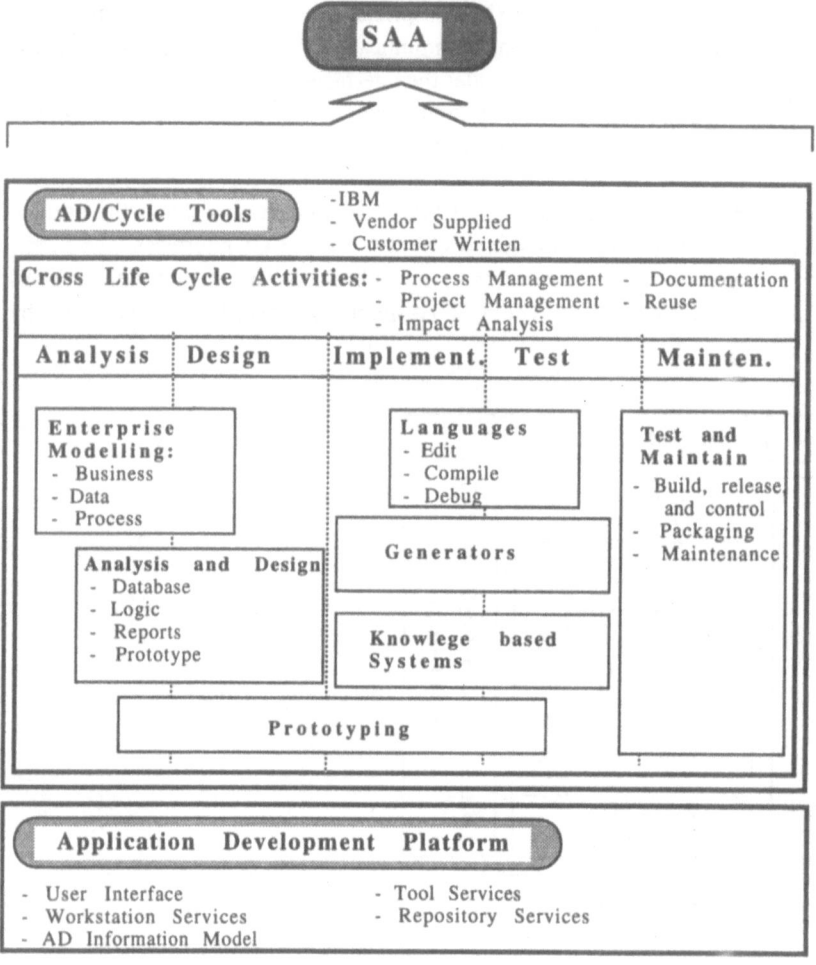

Figure 8.8: AD/Cycle Life Cycle Function Model

8.6 Method Oriented CASE Environments

Method oriented CASE environments are more or less closed systems which guide a developer through the whole development process. A developer is informed which activities have to be executed and at what time. Data produced during various development activities can easily be used in other activities supported by other tools. This is a major advantage of method oriented case environments but it can also be a disadvantage. It is difficult or impossible to reuse software developed with other methods and tools.

In the following sections some examples of method-oriented CASE environments are outlined.

8.6.1 SREM

In order to increase reliability and productivity design languages and tools have been integrated into the SYSREM/SREM system. Tools support each development phase based on the conventional life cycle. Special languages are used to represent the results of the different phases and each phase is supported by tools based on a particular language.

SYSREM/SREM and the related tools have been evaluated in several projects /SSR85/. Based on these case studies it has been recommended that Requirement Specification Language (RSL) is extended to explicitly describe concurrency and distributed processing. Changes to RSL would also imply changes to the related tools. Code generated from RSL is not efficient enough.

The following figure presents a summary of the final system /ALF85a/, an integrated set of languages, tools, databases, and methods.

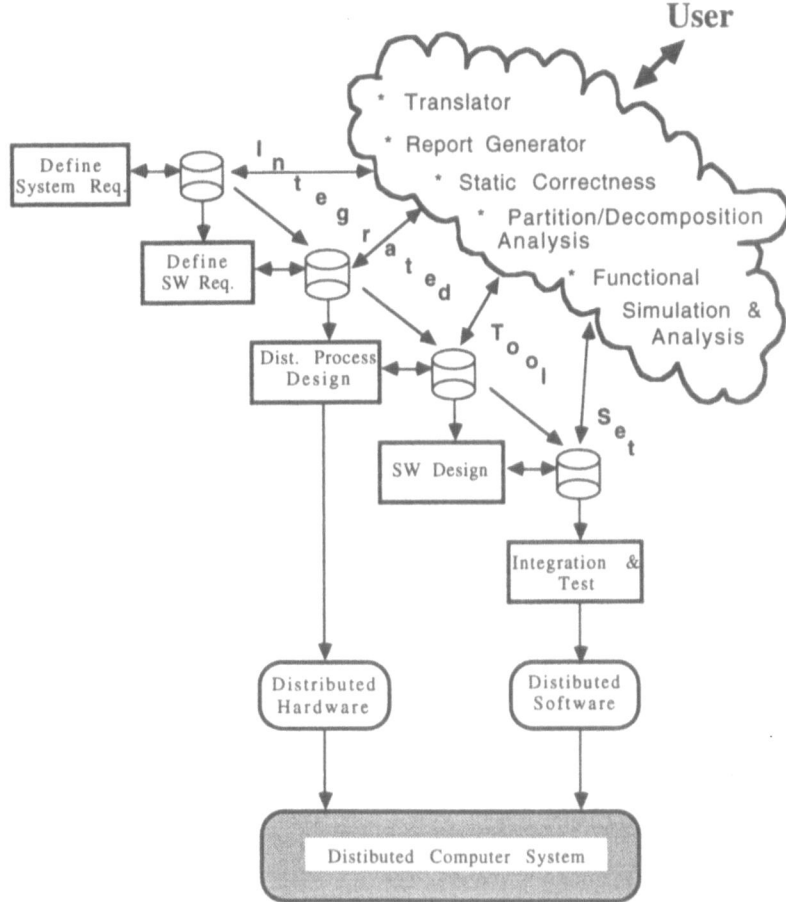

Figure 8.9: Distributed Computing Design System (DCDS) Integrated Languages and Tools

8.6.2 Estelle

Estelle was developed by the International Standard Organisation, ISO, for the specification of communication systems, i.e. communication protocols. The application of Estelle is supported by numerous tools which have been developed in several research projects, e.g. /SIBL90/, /CLLM89/, /CLM89/, /RICL89/, /SSCO89/. There are tools for the creation of specifications, the validation of specifications, implementation, the generation of test cases, and the analysis of test results. For protocol engineering – which involves the implemention of one protocol layer – the selection of tools shown in the following figure is suggested /PIAT81/, /RUDIN86/, /SIBL90/, /SIST91/.

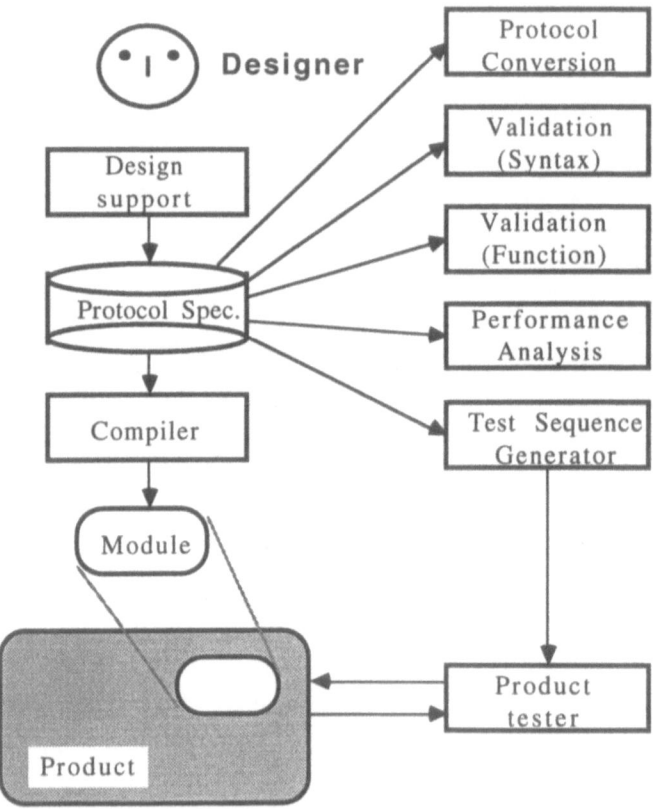

Figure 8.10: One View of Protocol Engineering

Details about Estelle and Estelle tools can be found in /TURN89/ and /QMV91/.

8.6.3 LOTOS

A set of LOTOS based tools have been developed from a research project sponsored by the European Community. Editors can be used to type in LOTOS specifications. These editors can be based on either a textual or graphical representation /BHLP91/. Simulators allow the symbolic execution of textual and graphical LOTOS specifications /CHYU91/. The LOTOS implementation workbench consists of a set of support tools and compilers. It is impossible to produce executable code from a LOTOS specification directly (only an interpretation is possible). Annotations must therefore be included in a LOTOS specification to allow a compiler to produce executable code. The following figure shows a more detailed structure of a LOTOS based development environment.

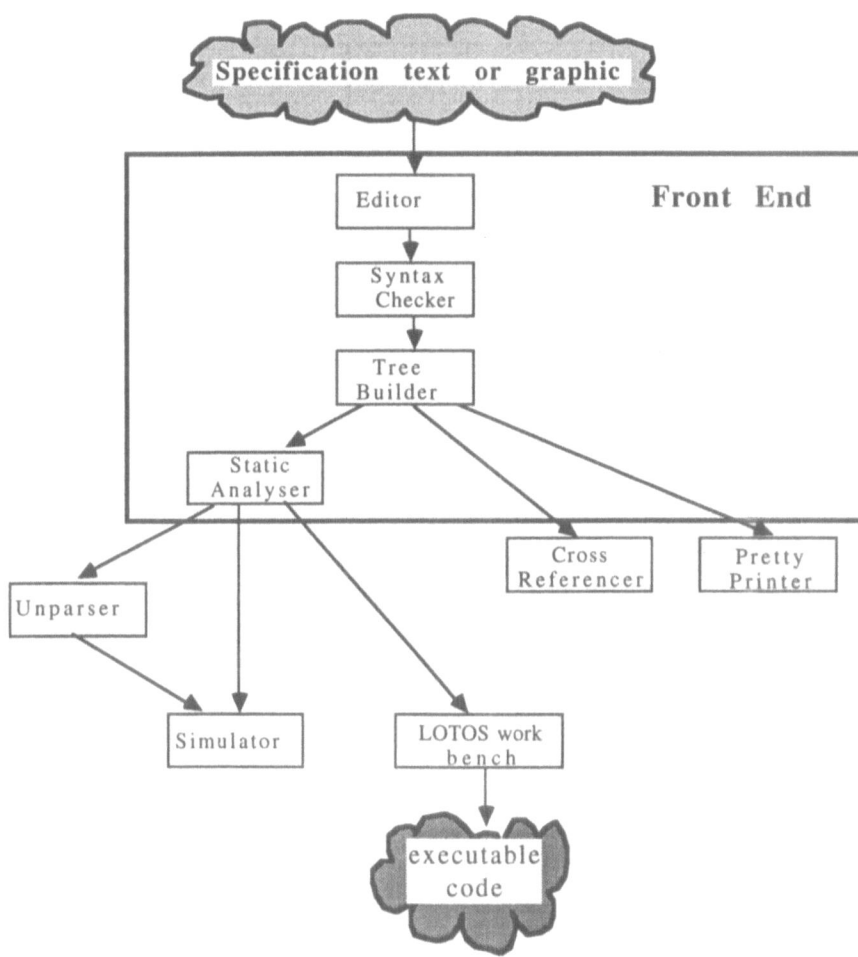

Figure 8.11: A LOTOS based Software Engineering Environment

Details about LOTOS and LOTOS tools are given in /EVD89/, /TURN89/ and /QMV91/.

8.6.4 SDL

Tools similar to those for Estelle and LOTOS are available for SDL which are very. There are tools for typing in specifications, validation, and code generation. The following figure shows the architectural context of an SDL tool set /EKEL91/.

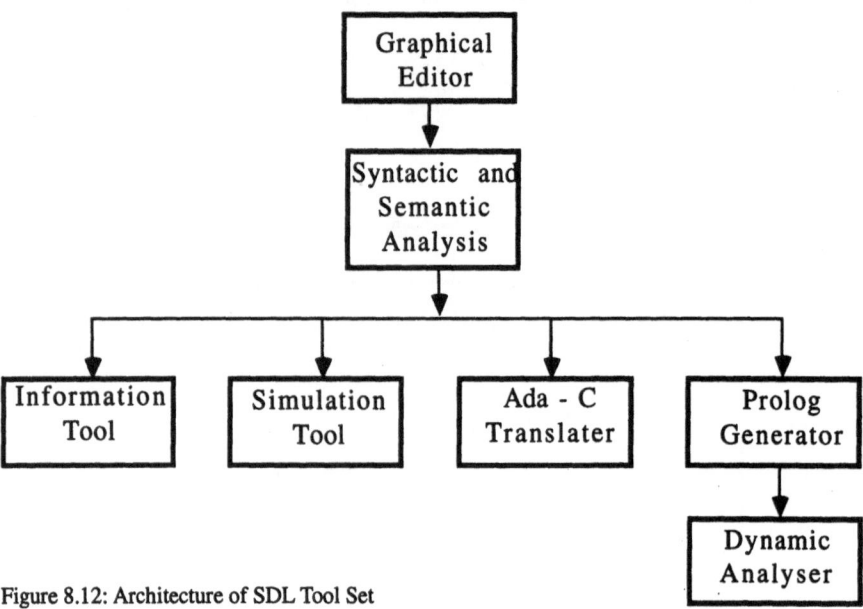

Figure 8.12: Architecture of SDL Tool Set

The system shown above is mainly an analysis tool which allows a user to look for deadlocks, output with no receivers, and unbound queue overflow.

A very extensive SDL Bibliography can be found in /SDL91/.

Recommended Reading:

/MCCLU89a/ McClure C.
        CASE is Software Automation
        Prentice Hall, Englewood Cliffs, New Jersey, 1989
        This book is an easy to read introduction to CASE. It also contain
        many examples of the various types of CASE systems.

/CHIK89/   Chikofski E. J.
        Computer Aided Software Engineering (CASE)
        IEEE Computer Society Press, New York 1989
        This book contains a collection of papers which covers all aspects of
        CASE.

Control Questions:

1. What are the capabilities of a CASE system?
2. How can tools support software development activities?
3. How are CASE environments classified?
4. What types of tool integration do you know?
5. Explain Cohesion and AD/Cycle

Exercises:

1. Which type of tools are used in your professional environment?
2. Which development activities are tool supported?
3. Which types of integration are possible?
4. Compare your CASE environment with Cohesion and/or AD/Cycle.

Part II

A detailed Example of an SEE:
Subject Oriented Programming

In this part of the book a software enginering environment is presented which incorporates many of the techniques described in the previous part. This software engineering environment is called SAPP/PASS, where SAPP stands for "Structured Analysis of Parallel Programs", and PASS stands for "Parallel Activities Specification Scheme". As the names imply it is a software environment especially designed for the development of concurrent systems.

SAPP/PASS combines the concepts of concurrent processes with decomposition concepts mainly used in sequential programs like modules, abstract data taypes and objects (see chapter 4). These passive elements are used by processes. This means processes execute functions offered by the passive elements. In SAPP/PASS the starting point for developing a software system are the identification of sets of processes and processes. Later the 'objects' used by these processes are defined. In philosophy active elements are also called subjects. Therefore we call that type of software development subject oriented development (see chapter 19).

SAPP/PASS is not a closed development environment. On the contrary it is open for the integration of existing and proved development methods. SAPP/PASS should help to demonstrate and to teach the relations between the different aspects and methods of software engineering for concurrent systems.

9 Overview

This chapter describes how the different software engineering concepts described in the previous chapters can be combined to construct a SEE for distributed systems.

SAPP/PASS is a set of methods, techniques and tools which covers many software activities such as project management, specification, design, and implementation. All development activities are supported by appropriate methods and tools. SAPP/PASS tries to integrate many well known methods and techniques in an orthogonal way. It can easily be learned step by step. It helps to show the relationships, strengths, and weaknesses of many software engineering methods as described in Part I and probably already known to the reader.

9.1 Development Goals

SAPP and PASS are languages that allow the use of several types of life cycles and incorporate many of the concepts introduced in the previous chapter. SAPP/PASS tries to implement what we can call **open software engineering**. A developer should be able to use a set of methods appropriate to the type of software system being developed. We do not want to say that some particular method or technology will solve all problems. SAPP/PASS is considered one way - certainly not the only way- of combining many proved software engineering methods. This has been the major design goal of SAPP/PASS.

In detail this means:
- SAPP/PASS allows the use of any software life cycle. A developer can choose the development method which is best for his problem.
- Existing software can be integrated into the development process of a new system. We think that this is a very important aspect because today a software system is seldom developed from scratch. Reuse of software protects investments in older developments.
- There are many software technologies which have proven their advantages. As many as possible of these techniques are integrated into SAPP/PASS. SAPP/PASS incorporates:
  - Structured analysis methods for the decomposition of a system into subsystems and concurrent processes.
  - The principal communication methods for concurrent processes such as
    - messages between processes

- shared data and shared objects
- remote procedure calls.
- Synchronisation methods related to the corresponding communication methods such as:
    - synchronous, asynchronous, and semiasynchronous message exchange
    - resource oriented synchronisation methods such as monitors.
- Different ways to describe process behaviour such as
    - explicit behaviour specification using states and transitions
    - implicit behaviour description using behaviour predicates and temporal logic
- Object oriented analysis, design, and programming methods
- Integrated project management methods
- Integrated tool concepts

The following example shows how these different methods are used in a program for the specification of an intersection traffic control system. The figure below shows an intersection controlled by traffic lights. When a car arrives at the intersection, a car detection device informs the control system that a car wants to pass the intersection. Depending on the traffic the N/S or the E/W direction will be opened or closed. The traffic is recorded in a database system in order to obtain statistics. An operator can change some control parameters such as the length of time a direction is opened.

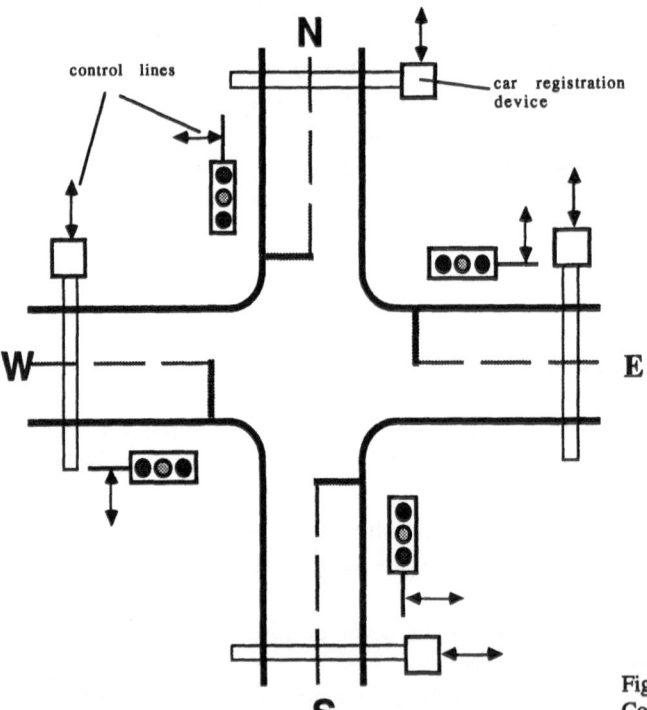

Figure 9.1: Intersection
Controlled by Traffic Lights

The following figure shows the structure of the complete control system. The environment of the control software is represented by rectangles and software system components are represented by rectangles with round corners. The example shows that several methods have to be used. The software system as a whole is represented in a way similar to structured analysis and it exchanges messages with components of the environment. It can use remote procedure calls for database access. An entity relationship method is used to describe the structure of the database.

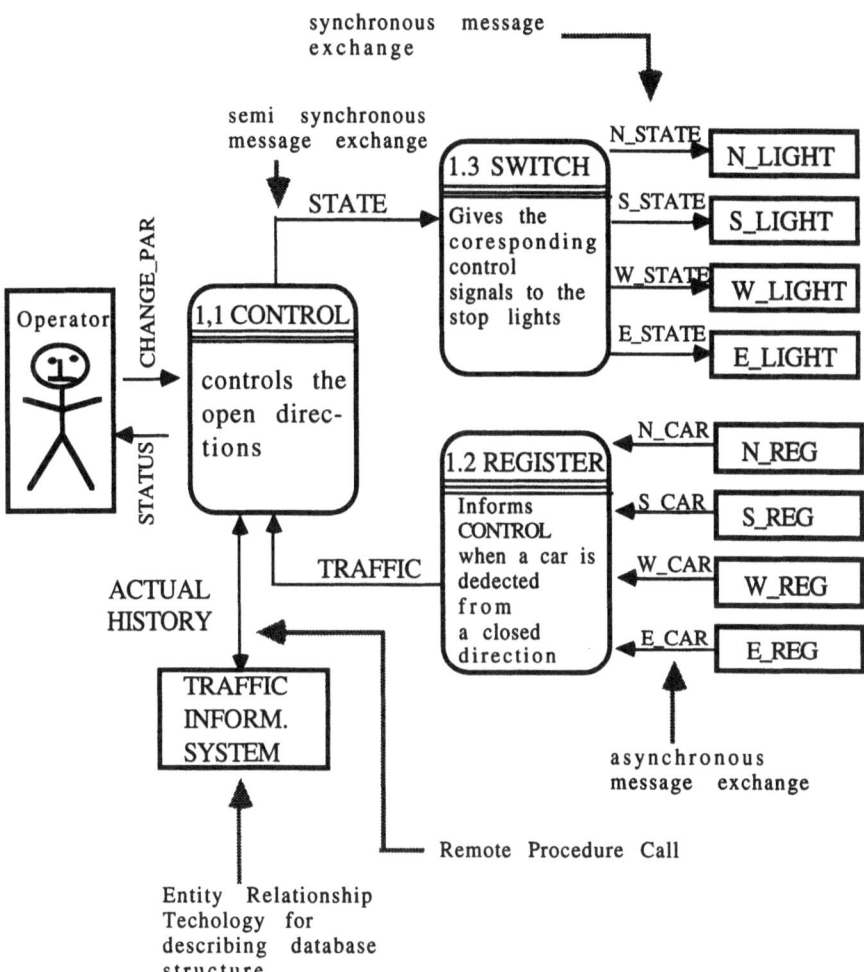

Figure 9.2 : Different Methods Used in a Traffic Control System

The following section gives a short description of how these different methods are combined.

9.2 Main Characteristics of the SAPP/PASS Methodology

As in many specification methods, system development using SAPP/PASS is done in two major steps:
- Decomposition of a system into processes and
- Description of these processes.

In order to document the results of each of these main steps special languages have been developed. The language SAPP – **Structured Analysis of Parallel Programs** – allows the description of sequences in system decomposition steps. A SAPP document shows which information is exchanged between the parts of the system under development.

PASS is a language for describing the functional requirements and, to a certain extent, the performance requirements of an embedded system. It is used to specify processes. PASS specifications can be executed. This allows one to test whether the requirements correspond to the ideas and intentions of customers and designers.

9.2.1 Decomposition of Systems into Subsystems and Processes

SAPP is based on the same ideas as dataflow diagrams (DFDs) /YOCO79/, /GASA79/, /DEMAR79/. DFDs describe the flow of data through the system by identifying sources and sinks. By using a DFD method specially tailored to the requirements of distributed systems, a system can be broken down into system subsets and processes step by step. Finally all processes and shared objects, the messages exchanged between processes and the shared objects they use, are identified.

The design of a program is a creative process. During the design process a program is structured in several components which interact with each other to meet the program requirements. The most important criterion for the quality of a design has to do with the complexity of the relations between the program components. The stronger these relations are, the worse is the design.

The quality of a design depends on the intuition /NAUR85/ and the experience of a designer. Nevertheless the use of a methodology simplifies the design process and helps to avoid errors. A basic methodology for developing software is the top-down approach, i.e. stepwise refinement. A top-down analysis starts with the main functions of a system, i.e. at the top. In the next step these main functions are further broken down to more primitive functions. These primitive functions are closer to the basic system on which the program is to run. This process of stepwise refinement is continued until the functions of the basic machine are reached.

DFDs allow a stepwise decomposition of a system into system subsets. These system subsets are called processes but in order to avoid confusion with the term process as we have been using it we will not use 'process' in conjunction with DFDs. The amount and complexity of information exchanged between these subsets determines the quality of separation. The structure of the information should be simple. Each system subset can be further decomposed into subsets and so on.

The information exchanged between subsets is also broken down in parallel with the decomposition into subsets . This method produces several layers of DFDs.

The notation for SAPP is very similar to the notation used in /GASA79/, but the symbols have a slightly different meaning.

9.2.2 Specification of Processes

A SAPP description of a system shows the processes and the types of message they send and receive but does not show the parameters of the various messages or the sequences in which the messages are sent or received. A SAPP description shows the global view of a system.

In the PASS model each system consists of a fixed number of processes and each process has a unique name. Processes send and receive messages and perform internal computations. The results of these internal computations can influence the communication behaviour of processes. The behaviour of each process is described in PASS.

In PASS the description of a process consists of:
- the input pool for synchronisation specification
- the PASS graph refinements for functional specification and
- the PASS graph for process behaviour description

The following figure shows the structure of a process specification in PASS.

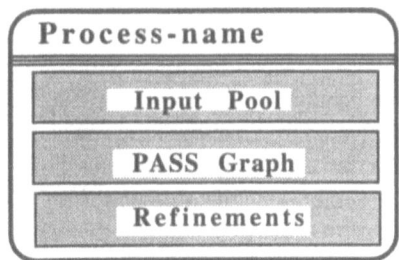

Figure 9.3: Structure of a Process Specification in PASS

PASS supports direct and indirect communication concepts as well as several synchronisation concepts related to the various communication methods.

PASS allows the use of different synchronisation concepts for direct communication. In order to define which synchronisation type is applicable for direct communication, the **input pool** concept is introduced. Each process has an input pool in which messages sent to that process can be stored. It is possible to define certain properties of an input pool such as the overall maximum number of messages or the maximum number of messages of a certain type which can be stored in it.

It is not possible for example to deposit a message in an input pool which already contains the maximum number of messages (the input pool applies the blocking strategy). The type of synchronization used is described in the input pool and depends on process and message names.

The **PASS graph refinements** contain the local variables of a process and the operations and functions defined on the local variables. The values of all local variables define the local context or the local state of a process.

Operations change the values of local variables and functions leave them unchanged. There are four different types of functions and operations.

For each message type which can be received by a process there is a *receive message specification*. The receive message specification describes the message parameters and the effect of a received message on the values of the local variables, depending on the values of the message parameters and the current values of the local variables.

For each message type which is sent by a process, there is a *send message specification*. This describes the message parameters and how the values of the message parameters are obtained from the values of the local variables.

The *internal operation* specification describes how an internal operation changes the values of the local variables. In addition to changing the values of the local variables, an internal operation can yield several results. For example a 'push' operation on a stack of limited depth can have the result 'done' or 'stack full'. The behaviour of a process can be influenced by these results. They are therefore called 'communication relevant' results. The internal operation specification also describes when an internal operation delivers a particular communication relevant result.

Internal functions check the state of the internal variables of a process. They allow the state of the local variables to influence the communication behaviour of a process. An internal function delivers different results according to the state of the local variables which in turn can influence the behaviour of the process. Each of these communication relevant results can be delivered by a subset of the states. For example, a check function of a counter can have the results 'below limit' or 'limit'. In all states where the value of the counter variable is below a certain limit the execution of the check function delivers the result 'below limit'. In all other states the result is 'limit'.

Local variables and related operations and functions can be combined to objects which can be incarnations of object classes. These object classes can be derived from other classes. In other words, all the object oriented concepts can be applied to the specification and implementation of PASS graph refinements.

Internal operations and functions can use functions and operations defined on shared objects. This is the only way in which processes have access to shared objects. If processes have access to the same shared objects, PASS does not allow any exchange of messages. This restriction avoids the interleaving of synchronisation mechanisms for direct and indirect communication. For more details see section 4.3.

The **PASS graph** describes the sequences in which a process sends messages, receives messages and executes functions and operations. The PASS graph gives a summary of the communication behaviour of a process. It does not show the parameter values of messages or the specifications of operations and functions. These belong to the PASS graph refinements.

Instead of using state transitions, other techniques such as transition expressions and temporal logic can be used to describe process behaviour. PASS will be introduced by using a state transition oriented technique. Later we will show how this state transition technique can be transformed into other description methods.

The different features of PASS used for describing the PASS graph, the PASS graph refinements, and the input pool are introduced in the following sections. An example gives a first impression of a PASS specification.

Example of a PASS Specification
To give a first impression of PASS, a short example is explained. The following figure shows the SAPP specification of a very simple example

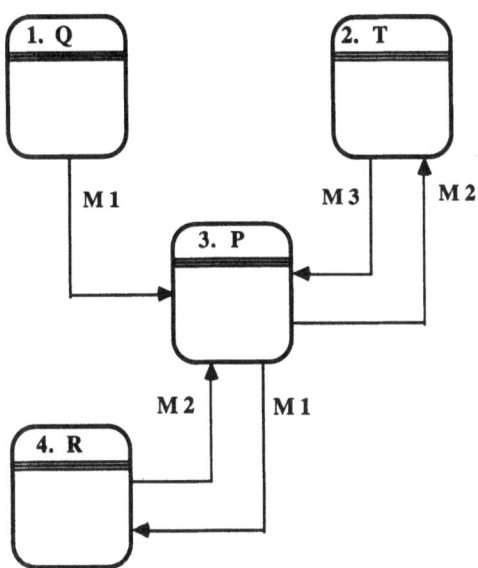

Figure 9.4: SAPP Specification of an simple Example

The process P in the system above is shown in more detail in the figure below.

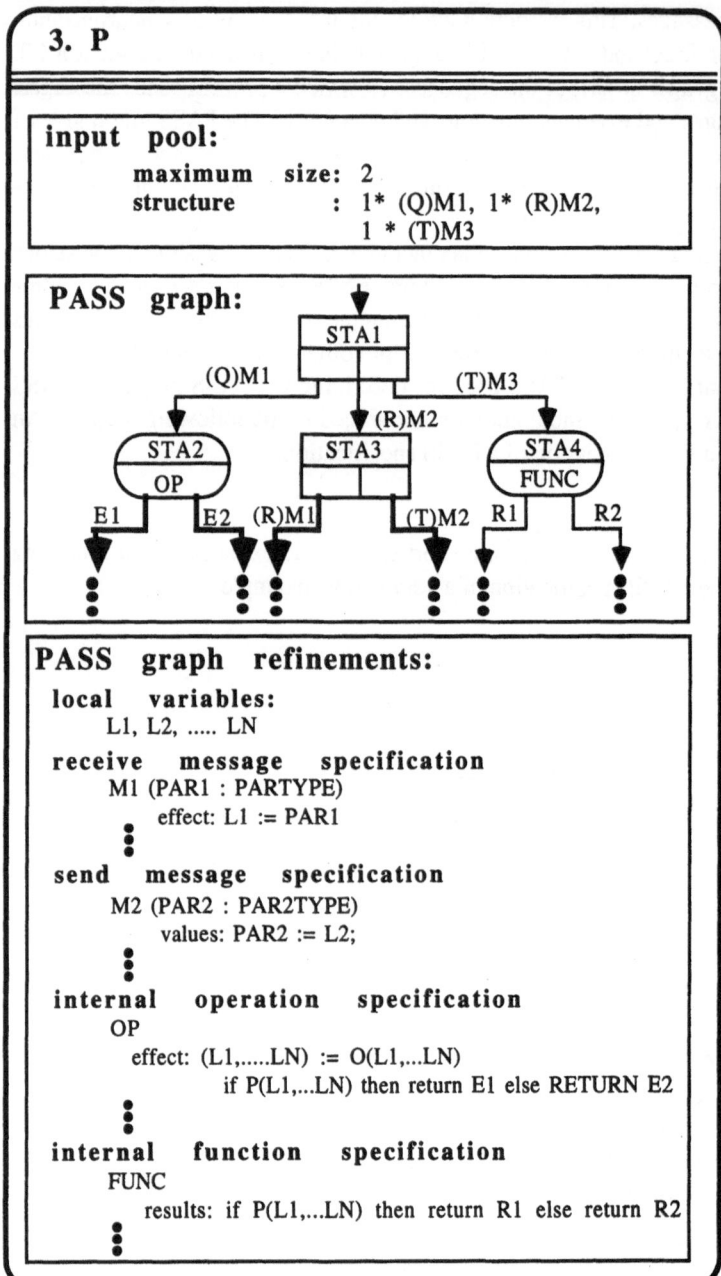

Figure 9.5: An Example of a Process Specification

The input pool clause shows that process P has a maximum input pool size of two slots. The input pool is structured. Only one message from each of the other processes can be in the input pool at a time.

The PASS graph shows that state STA1 is the initial state; it is marked with a small arrow. In this state the message type M1 from process Q, the message type M2 from process R and the message type M3 from process T are expected, i.e. state STA1 is a receive main state. If the message (R)M2 is in the input pool, the transition to state STA3 is executed. In State STA3, the message type M1 is offered to process R and the message type M2 is offered to process T. State STA3 is a send main state.

In state STA2, which is reached if the message (Q)M1 is accepted, the internal operation OP is executed. This means that the values of local variables are changed. The operation OP can have the results E1 or E2. Depending on the result, the transition to a new main state is performed. State STA2 is an internal operation main state.

State STA4 is an internal function main state. In this state the function FUNC is executed. A function checks the values of the local variables. Depending on the result, a transition to a new main state is executed without changing the values of the local variables. In the example, the function FUNC can have the result R1 or R2.

In the PASS graph, only the communication behaviour can be seen. It does not contain the message parameters, the definition of the internal operations, etc. These are specified in the PASS graph refinements.

The PASS graph refinements are separated into five clauses. The local variables clause contains the names and types of the local variables in a process.

In the receive message specifications clause, all message types which can be received are described in more detail. In our example, the message type M1 has the parameter PAR1 of type PAR1TYPE. If messages of this type are received, the value of the parameter is copied into the local variable L1 (effect clause). The meaning of the messages being sent is described in the send message specifications clause. Messages of type M2 have a parameter of type PAR2TYPE.

The send message specification of a message type describes how the values of the message parameters are derived from the values of the local variables. In our example the value of the parameter is equal to the value of the local variable LI.

The internal function specification clause specifies how the results of a function depend on the values of the local variables. In our example, the function FUNC delivers the result R1 if the predicate P is true; otherwise the result is R2.

The internal operation specification clause describes the internal operations. It defines how the values of the local variables are changed by the different operations and what results the different changes produce. In our example, the local variables are changed as defined by the operation O. If the predicate Q is true after the changes the result is E1, otherwise E2.

9.3 SAPP/PASS Based Development Activities

The SAPP/PASS development activities have a close relationship to the structured analysis of systems. A SAPP/PASS methodology does not prescribe the sequence of a certain set of activities. The sequence in which the SAPP/PASS development activities are executed depends on the life cycle used. In this sense the SAPP/PASS activities most be arranged according to the development life cycle used. The activities described below need not be executed exactly in the order given. Normally they are interleaved. Before the function of a component can be described, the system must be broken down into components. Some parts of the system can be broken down after the components identified in a previous decomposition step have been described completely. A software life cycle and the development activities described below define the steps of a SAPP/PASS methodology.

1. System decomposition

During this activity the components of the system under development are defined, including the relations to the environment. This includes the integration of existing software systems. Each reused software system is considered as a PASS subsystem or process. The interfaces of existing software are described in PASS terms. Existing software sends and receives messages in the same way as pure PASS subsystems or processes. This means that it may be necessary to cover existing software with an adaption layer which adapts existing software to the PASS philosophy.

2. Informal description of sytem components

The functional and non-functional requirements of the components identified in system decomposition are described informally. Here a mixture of natural language, tables, structured language, diagrams, etc., can be used.

3. Description of the relations between system components

System components exchange information either via shared data and objects or via messages. During this activity the type of message exchange and the structure and meaning of the information to be exchanged are defined. For the description of the information structures formal languages or subsets of programming languages can be used. The meaning of the information to be exchanged can be described in natural language.

4. Specification of the input pool

In this activity, the type of message exchanged is specified. The receiver of a message defines the related type of synchronisation. This is done defining the size, structure and attributes of an input pool.

5. Specification of the process behaviour

The specification of the behaviour of a process defines another detail of a process. For this specification a state transition system such as the PASS graph or another behaviour specification language can be used.

6. Specification of the PASS graph refinements

For the specification of the PASS graph refinements any specification method for sequential programs can be used. Today we would recommend object oriented techniques. This could mean that in the refinements of different processes, objects of the same class could be used. In principle a complete set of classes is identified for a software system and objects of those classes are used in the refinements of several processes. This also allows the use of object classes developed during other projects.

Existing software developed in a non-object oriented way can also be integrated into the refinements. Some functions and operations can be implemented on the basis of existing software, e.g. data base systems.

7. Design of the communication system
The exchange of information is normally implemented using an existing programming environment. If processes exchange messages but are located on the same computer system then the information exchange can be implemented on the basis of shared memory. Processes exchanging information and running on different computer systems have to use a network. Many operating systems offer facilities for exchanging information between processes. Based on these facilities a communication system must be defined which meets the requirements of PASS.

8. Implementation of the communication system and the input pools.
The SAPP/PASS oriented communication system defined in activity 7 above has to be implemented on the basis of available communication functionality.

9. Implementation of the PASS graphs.
The PASS graphs have to transformed into executable code. Normally PASS graphs are automatically transformed into standard languages like C or C++. The code for the PASS graph also uses the code of the SAPP/PASS oriented communication system (activity 8).

10. Implementation of the PASS graph refinements.
The PASS graph refinements are developed like normal sequential programs.

If the SAPP/PASS development activities are ordered according to the conventional live cycle then the activities are executed exactly in the order described above. If an incremental life cycle is used acitivity 1 is executed first and after that activities 2 to 10 are repeated several times.

9.4 SAPP/PASS Based Project Management

A software development project can be planned and controlled using a SAPP/PASS methodology. The activities described above are the basis of a work break down structure. The required resources and time can be estimated for each activity and system component . Ordinary scheduling techniques can be used to describe a project schedule. The hierarchical manner of a time schedule can be similar to the system hierarchy.

The structure of SAPP/PASS program specifications allow the definition of quality parameters. These include the number of hierarchy levels, the number of components per subsystem, the number of messages received or sent to a component, and the number of parameters per message. Quality features can be defined for a project based on these values.

9.5 SAPP/PASS Based Tools

Tools exist for the methods used in each step of the SAPP/PASS technique. There are tools for the documentation of specifications, consistency checks, validation, code generation, code optimisation and project management. The various tools are based on different theoretical concepts. The particular part of the PASS semantics can be defined in several ways.

The semantics of message exchange can be expressed in PROLOG rules or in graph replacement grammer. Tools for the validation of the communication behaviour based on these semantic definitions can be developed.

Different methods for transforming essential parts of PASS specifications into different types of programming languages allow the implementation of automatic code generators.

9.6 Experience

SAPP/PASS has been developed for more than ten years. First the basic methods had to be applied to practical problems, especially for the implementation of communication software and process control systems. The limitations of these first versions of SAPP/PASS have lead to permanent changes and enhancements. Various techniques and methods have been added and removed.

Practical experience was gained by implementing the following ISO/OSI communication protocols:
- LLC Type 2 protocol /TSMLA90/
- Transport protocol (OSI layer 4) class 0 /FASCH91/
- Session protocol (OSI layer 5) which was implemented in Pascal /FLCHEF87/
- Presentation protocol (OSI layer 6) which was implemented in Pascal
- Remote Operation Service Element (ROSE, OSI layer 7)
- Association Control Service Element (ACSE, OSI layer 7)
- Remote Database Access (RDA, OSI layer 7)
- Manufacturing Message Service (MMS, MAP protocol)

PASS was used for specifying several programs for controlling technical processes. Control programs for physical experiments were specified in PASS and implemented in PEARL (a programming language for the implementation of technical control software, see chapter 14) and in hardware /BESO85/.

The control program for a glass tube production line was also specified in PASS and implemented in PEARL. In this case the behaviour of the technical process was also specified and implemented. The implementation of the technical process was used as a test bed for the process control software /BABA85/.

PASS was used by various people who were not familiar with this technique. PASS and the use of the tools can be learned very easily. The tools generate the complete code for the PASS graph and a code frame for PASS graph refinements. The structure of the PASS tools reflects the different activities involved in process description. Thus the PASS methodology forces the implementer to produce a well structured design.

In order to give an impression of the productivity increase we only want to mention that it took 3 weeks to get an prototype of the LLC type II protocol starting with reading the concerning IEEE standard the first time. In general, we assume that SAPP/PASS can improve development efficiency up to 50 %.

Control Questions:

1. What are the development goals of PASS?
2. What programming concepts are used for the intersection control system?
3. What are the main characteristics of SAPP?
4. What are the main characteristics of PASS?
5. What are the SAPP/PASS development activities?
6. What are the characteristics of SAPP/PASS based project management?

Exercises:

1. What are the main techniques supported in the software development methodology which you currently use?
2. Identify in your environment some software applications and analyse the software technologies used.
3. Identify an existing or planned software system and try to describe its structure with SAPP.
4. Describe the interaction of a program with the user in PASS.

10 Decomposing a System

This chapter describes the application of system decomposition methods in SAPP/PASS. The way how a system is broken down into components is shown by an example.

A software system mostly interacts with its environment. The environment can be a technical process, another software system which does not belong to the system to be developed, or users who type in commands and get back results. Another name for the system environment is the system context. The requirements of a software system under development depend highly on the system context. Therefore the decomposition of a system is executed in three steps:
- Analysis and decomposition of the system context,
- Analysis of the system to be developed and break down of the system into process sets
- Break down of process sets into processes.

The language SAPP is used to describe the results of the decomposition steps.

10.1 Decomposition of the System Context

The specification of a system is started by creating a context diagram which shows the external entities and the system to be defined. The system and the external entities exchange sets of messages. Message sets consist of several lower level message sets or messages. Message sets and messages are given names which identify their type. Message sets of the same type consist of either message sets or messages of the same type. Messages of the same type have the same name, the same number and type of parameters.

Message sets contained in a context diagram are the starting point of the message dictionary (MD).

The initial context diagram and MD is refined step by step by breaking down only the external entities. The decomposition of the external entities stops when only external entities and the system exchange messages. The decomposition of the context is shown in the following example.

Example:
The following figure shows the initial context diagram of the intersection control system example from the last chapter.

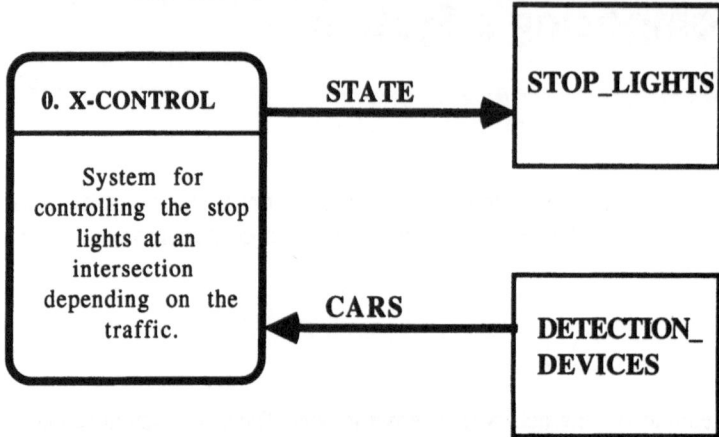

Figure 10.1: Intersection Control Context Diagram Level 0

The system to be designed is called 'X-CONTROL'. It receives the message set 'CARS' from the external entity 'DETECTION_DEVICES' and it sends the message set 'STATE' to the external entity 'STOP_LIGHTS'. If message sets are exchanged bold or douple lined arrows are used.

The message directory (MD) is shown in the figure below.

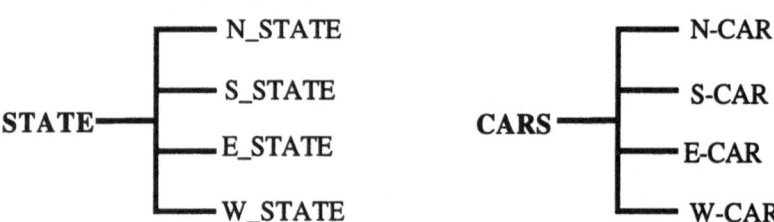

Figure 10.2: Initial Message Directory of the Intersection Control System

The message set 'STATE' consists of 4 messages. The names of the messages are N_STATE, S_STATE, E_STATE and W_STATE. The message directory also contains the specification of the message parameters of each message. Message parameters have a name and a type similar to procedure parameters. The message parameters will be added to the message dictionary in later development activities. This is described in subsequent chapters.

The context diagram has to be refined again because the external entities and the system to be to be defined exchange message sets. The next diagram shows the result of this refinement step.

At this level of refinement messages are only exchanged between external entities and the system to be defined. The refinemnt of the context is completed.

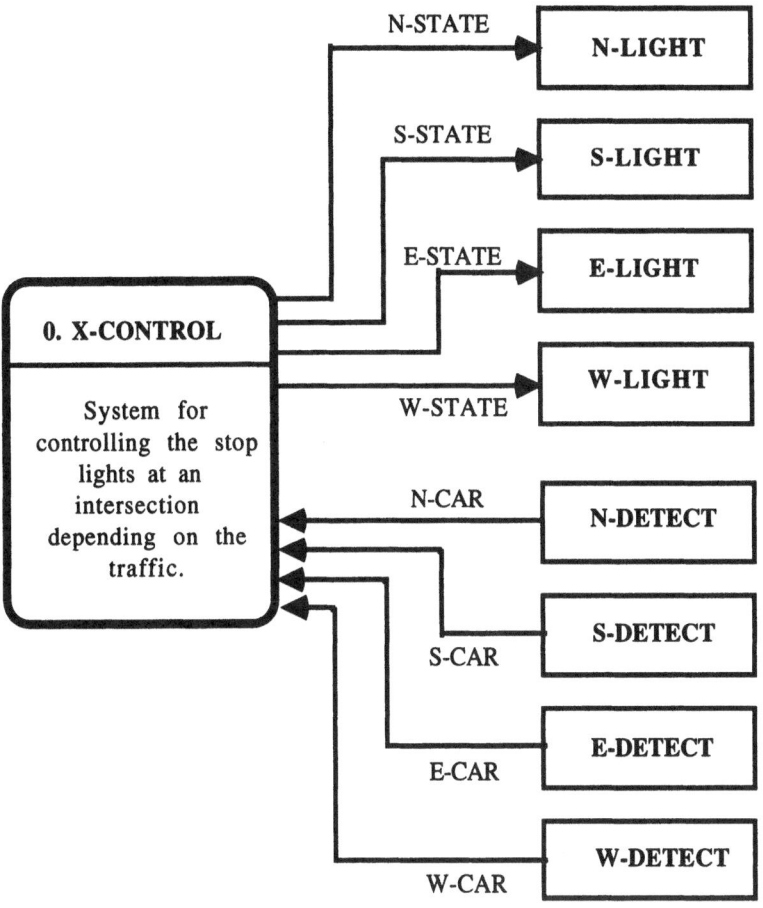

Figure: 10.3 Intersection Control Context Diagram Level 1

10.2 Decomposition of Systems into Process Sets

In the next step the system to be defined is broken down. This is done in a similar way to the context analysis. A system is refined into components which exchange messages or message sets and messages with external entities, as described in the previous section. The components of the system are refined step by step until they only exchange messages. Subsystems which only exchange messages with their environment, external entities or other subsystems are called process sets.

In order to describe the results of the decomposition steps a notation similar to /GASA79/ is used. This notation is introduced using a different example from the intersection control system, which is not complex enough to show all the possibilities of the SAPP language.

The following figure shows the final context diagram of our new example.

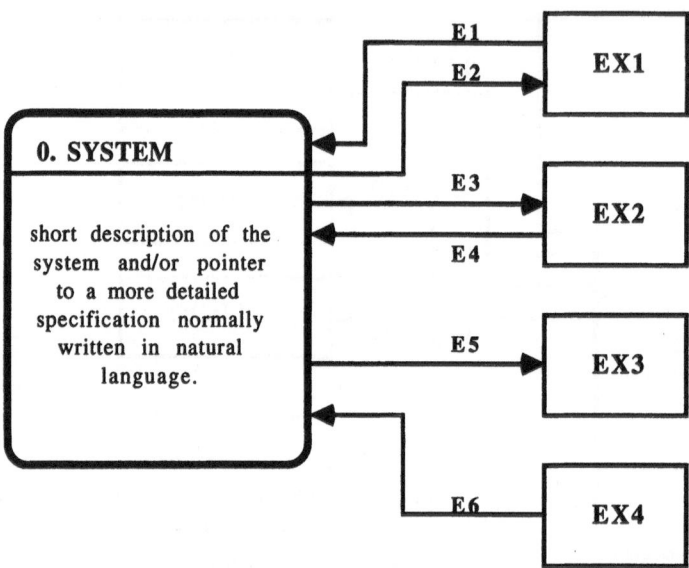

Figure 10.4: Context Diagram of a Complex Example

In the first decomposition step our example is broken down into two subsystems. The result is shown in the following figure.

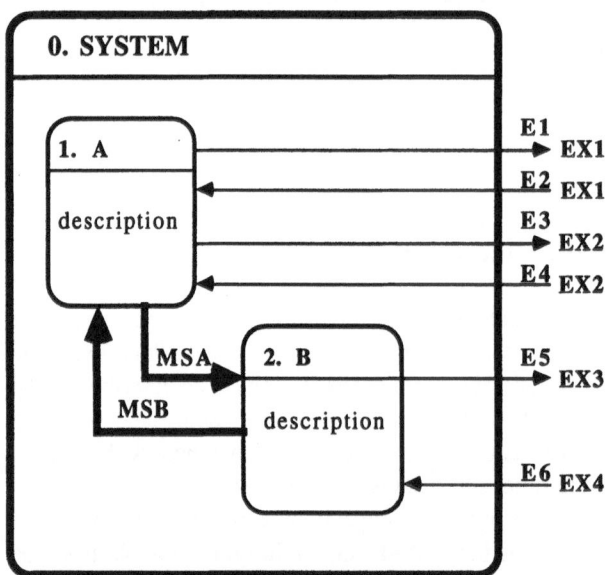

Figure 10.5: System Decomposition-Level 1

The system has been decomposed into two components, A and B (For convenience we use very short names).

Component A sends the message set MSA to component B and component B sends the message set MSB to A. The structure of these message sets and their meanings are described in the message dictionary. Natural language can be used to describe the meaning of a message set.

The messages exchanged with external entities are also assigned to one of these components. The messages E1, E2, E3, and E4 are processed by component A and the messages E5 and E6 are processed by component B.

In the next step component A and component B are further broken down. The result of this refinement step is shown in the next figure.

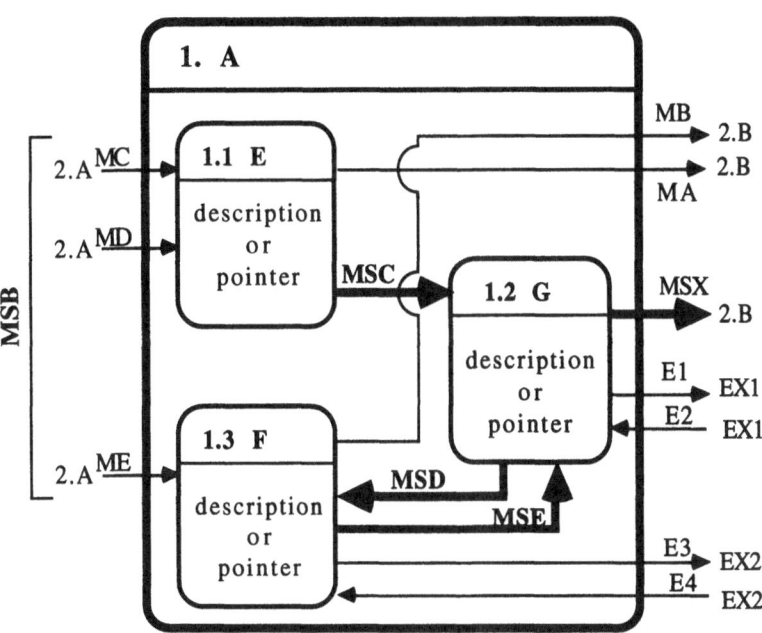

Figure 10.6: Decomposition of Component A: Level 2

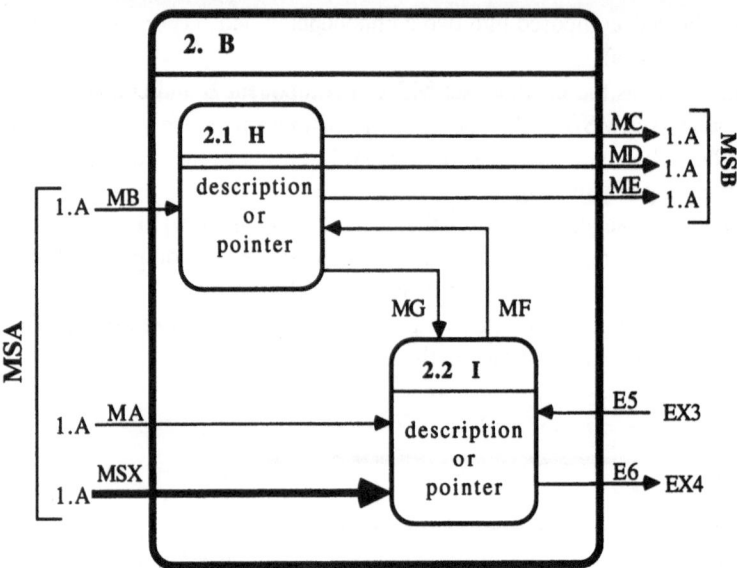

Figure 10.7: Decomposition of Component B: Level 2

In the decomposition of the component B, component H only exchanges messages with other components; therefore it is a process set. The following figures show the decompositions of components E, F, G, and I.

Components K and L of E are process sets because they only exchange messages with their environment.

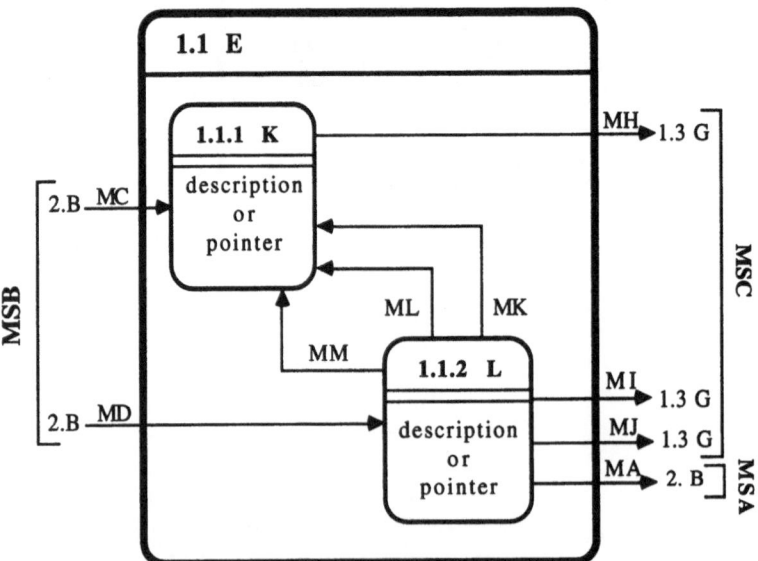

Figure 10.8: Decomposition of Component E: Level 3

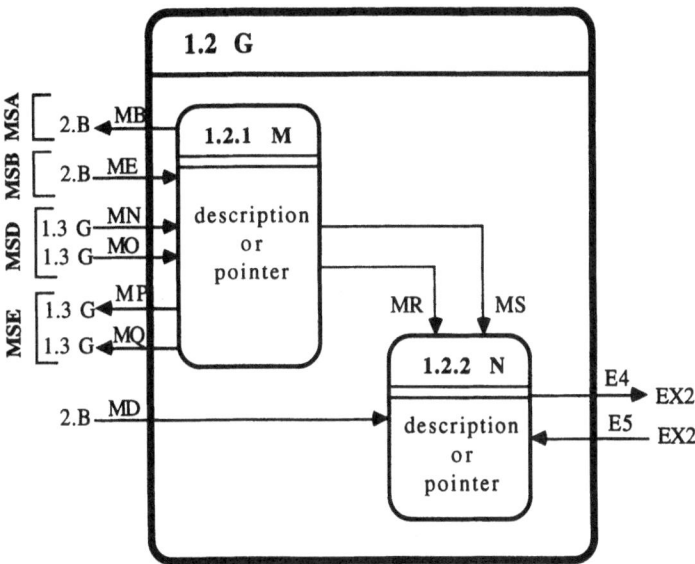

Figure 10.9: Decomposition of Component G: Level 3

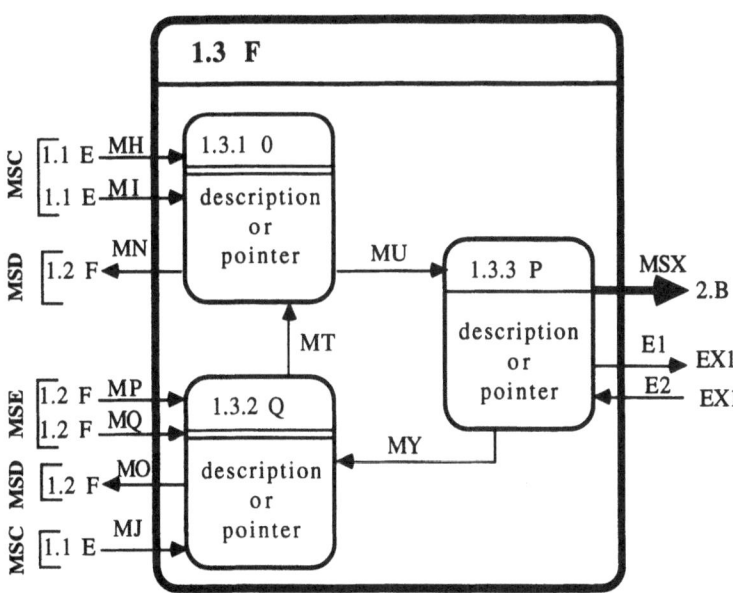

Figure 10.10: Decomposition of Component F: Level 3

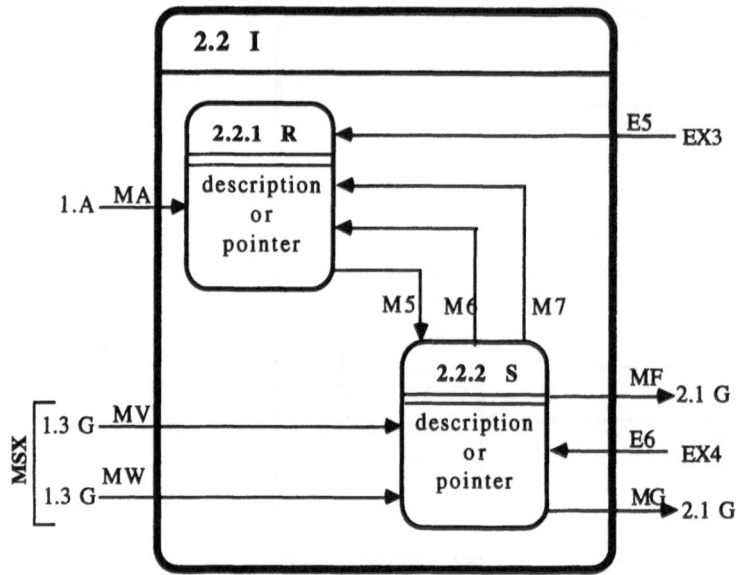

Figure 10.11: Decomposition of Component I: Level 3

Component P of G is not a process set and is further broken down. The result of this decomposition step is shown in the figure below.

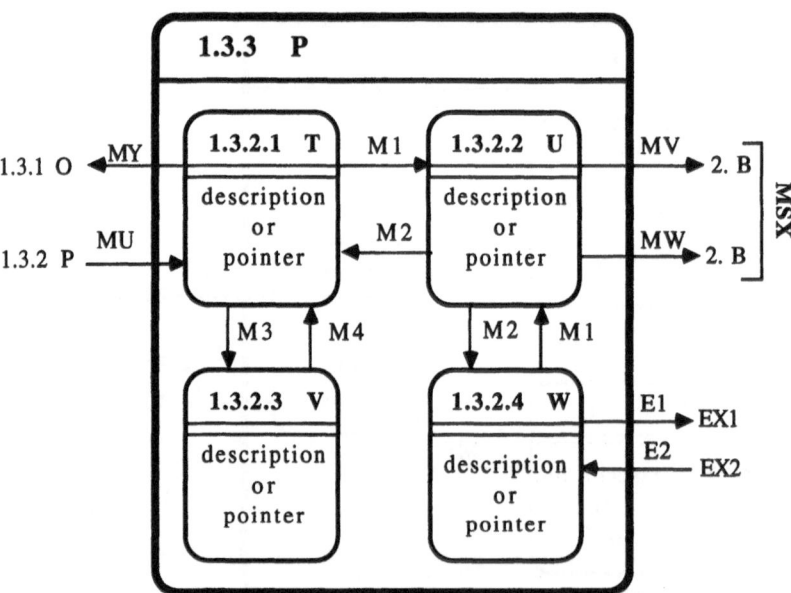

Figure 10.12: Decomposition of Component P: Level 4

The result of decomposing a system into components is a system consisting of process sets which exchange messages. The structure showing all the process sets and all the messages which they exchange is shown below.

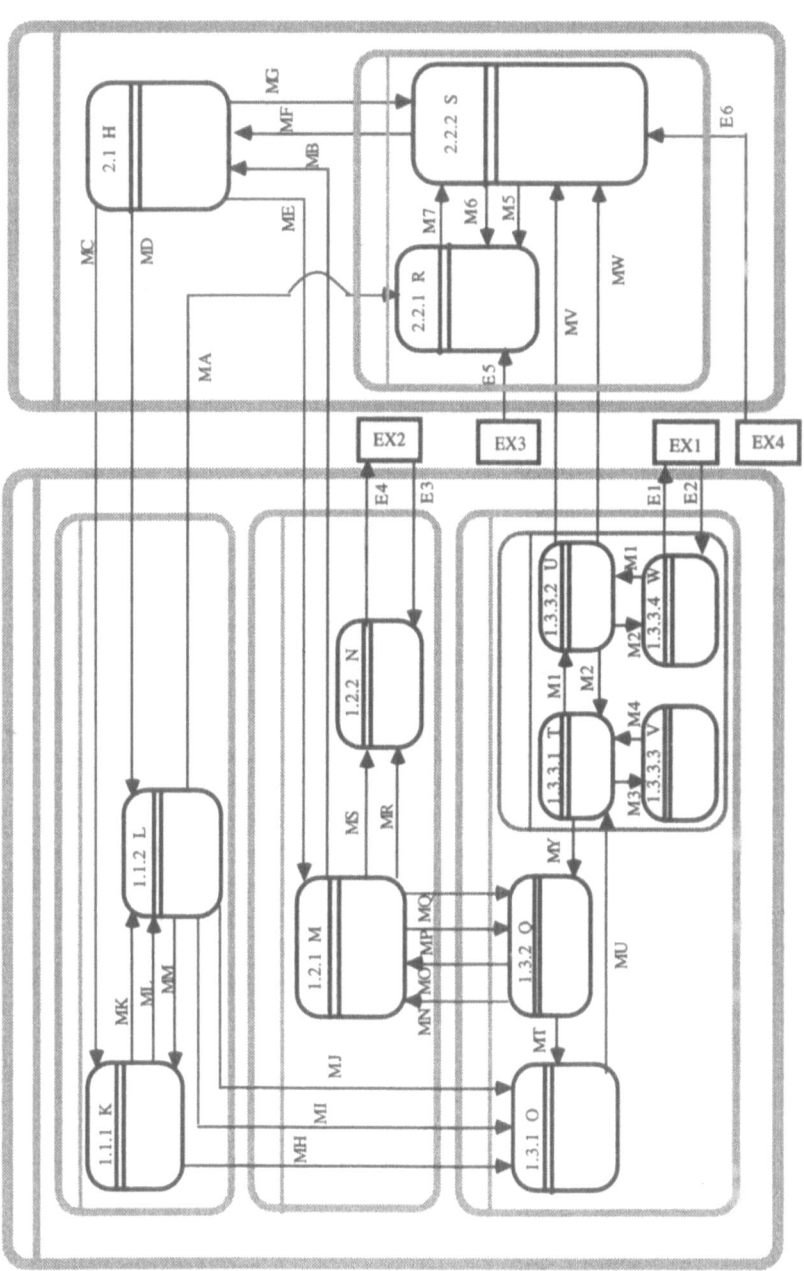

Figure 10.13: Resulting Process Set Structure from the Previous Example

After decomposing a system into process sets the message dictionary contains all message types exchanged between the process sets. The message dictionary does not have to contain a complete definition of all message types, i.e. the number and type of all message parameters. Message type specifications can be completed over the whole development process. It is only neccessary to have an intuitive understanding of the meaning of each message. This intuitive understanding can be described in the message dictionary in natural language.

For simple systems a decomposition into system components is not necessary. The system itself is the only process set which exchanges messages with the environment. The intersection control system example is a single process set.

10.3 Decomposing Process Sets into Processes

In the next development step each process set is broken down into processes. This decomposition can be done by intermediate process sets. Processes or intermediate process sets in the same process set can communicate via messages or shared objects; processes in different process sets can only communicate with each other via messages.

The decomposition of process sets into processes is performed in several steps.

1. Introduction of interface processes
An interface process is assigned to each process set. This interface process is represented by its process set to all other process sets. Therefore interface processes have the name of the process set they represent.

Interface processes receive and send all messages from or to other process sets through their interface processes.

Messages received by an interface process from another are forwarded to processes inside the appropriate process set. The internal process to which a message is forwarded by an interface process can depend on the message type, message parameter values and the current state of the interface process. Processes inside a process set that want to send a message to another process set, send this message to the interface process of their process set. The interface process forwards the message to the interface process of the target process set.

Based on the previous example the figure below shows the process set K which exchanges messages with the process sets H, L, and O.

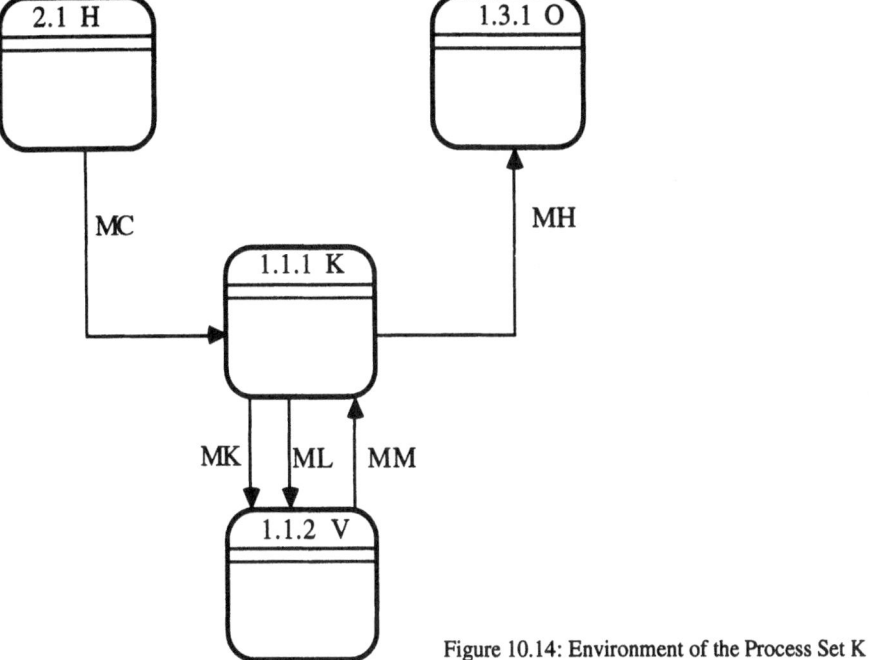

Figure 10.14: Environment of the Process Set K

The interface process K receives and sends all external messages from and to other process sets. The following figure shows the process set K and its interface process which has the same name.

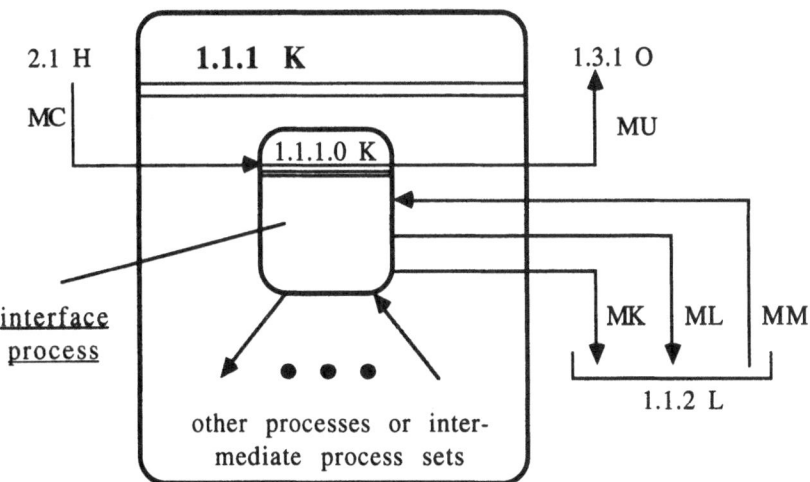

Figure 10.15: Process Set K and its Interface Process

2. Decomposing process sets and intermediate process sets

In a second sequence of decomposition steps, process sets are broken down into intermediate process sets and processes. Processes and intermediate process sets within the same process set, including interface processes, can exchange information via messages or shared objects. As described previously an object consists of a data structure and a set of operations which is the only way of accessing the data structure (This is described in the following sections). The figure below shows the decomposition of the process set K into the processes K1 and K2 and the intermediate process set K3.

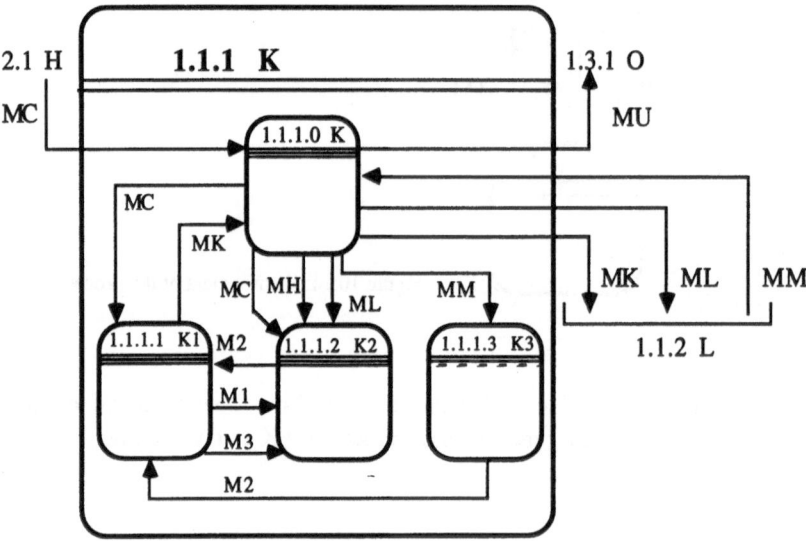

Figure 10.16: Decomposition of the Process Set K

The process set K is decomposed into the processes K1 and K2 and an intermediate process set K3.

Intermediate process sets are decomposed in the same way as process sets. Intermediate process sets are also represented by an interface process to other processes and process sets. The following figure shows the decomposition of the intermediate process set K3 into the processes K4 and K5.

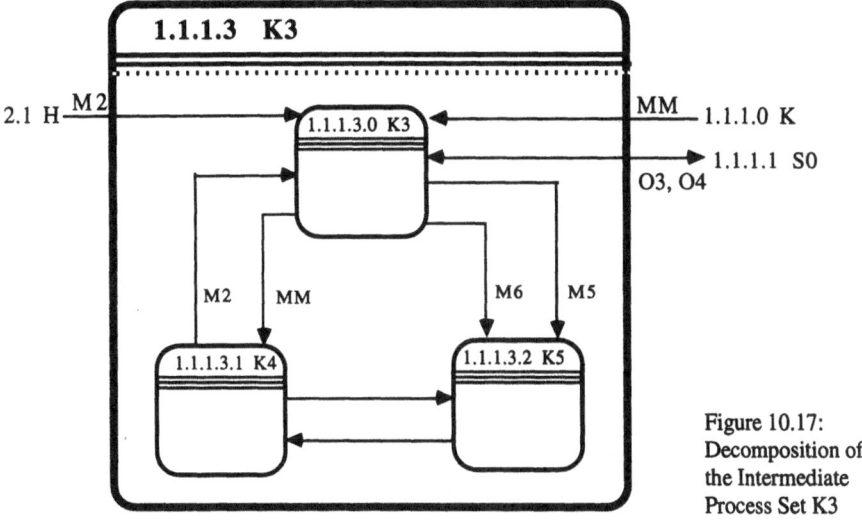

Figure 10.17:
Decomposition of
the Intermediate
Process Set K3

Intersection Control System

The intersection traffic control system is a very simple system. The whole system is
one process set and there are no intermediate process sets. The figure below shows
the decomposition of the intersection control system into processes.

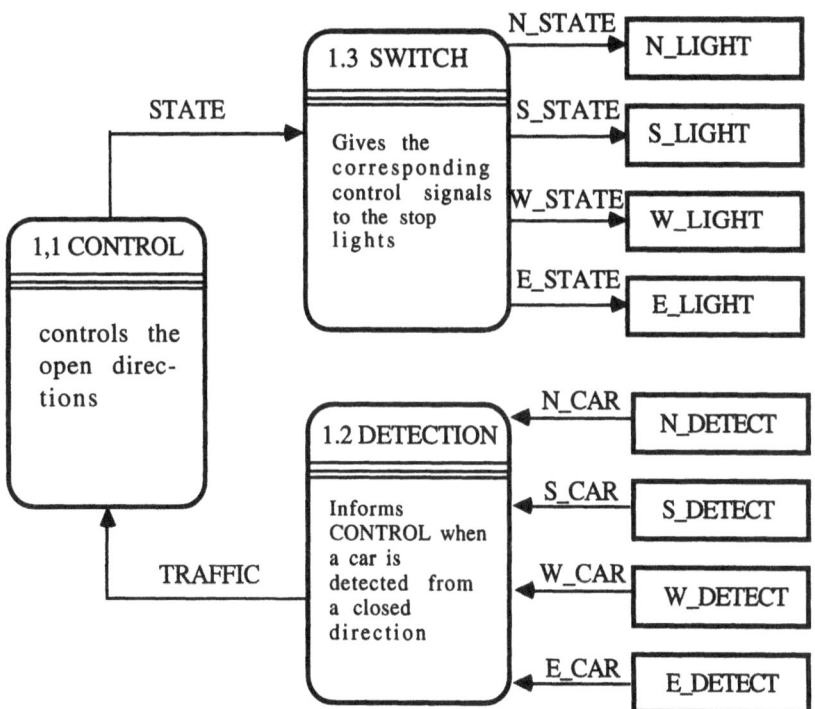

Figure 10.18: Decomposition of the Intersection Control System.

The process 'DETECTION' is informed by the detection devices whether cars have arrived at the intersection and it informs the process 'CONTROL' whether a car has arrived from one of the closed directions. The process 'CONTROL' decides whether the open direction has to be switched and informs process 'SWITCH' if this is required. The process 'SWITCH' changes the open direction by switching the particular traffic lights on or off.

10.4 Shared Objects, Process Clusters, Process Groups

Up to now only process communication and synchronisation based on messages has been considered. Processes can also exchange information via shared objects. The operations and functions of a shared object can be performed by several processes or process sets. Several processes can initiate the execution of the same or different operations and functions of the same object concurrently. Therefore the execution of the operations and functions of a shared object must be synchronised in order to keep the state of the object consistent. The figure below shows an example of a shared object.

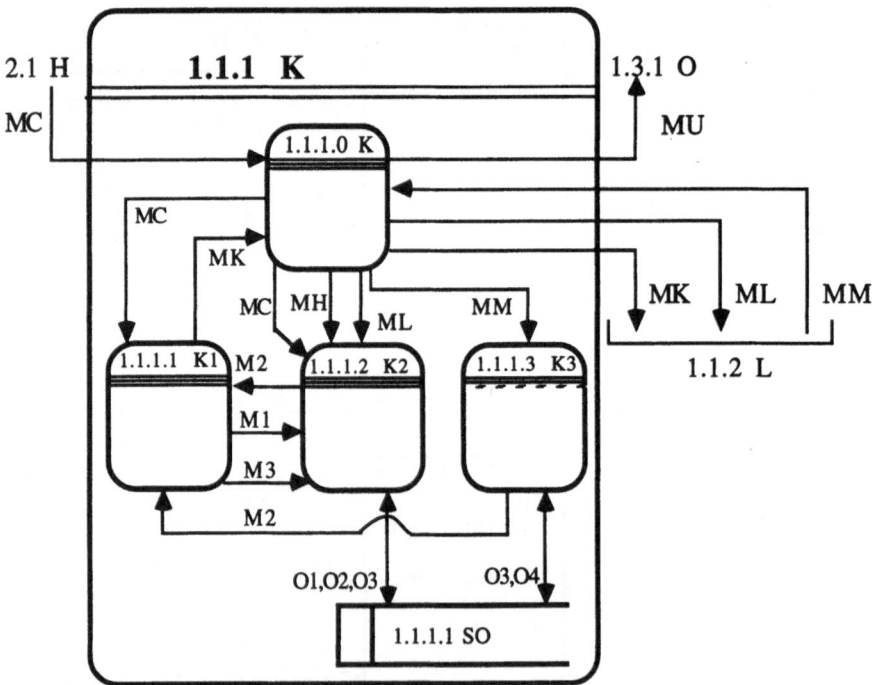

Figure 10.19: Shared Objects

The process K2 and the intermediate process set K3 share an object called SO. The operations O1, O2, O3, and O4 are defined on the object SO. The process K2 executes the operations O1, O2, and O3. The intermediate process set K3 executes the operations O3 and O4. Access to the object SO is synchronised using resource oriented synchronisation methods such as monitors or path expressions. The specification of the synchronisation requirements are part of the specification of SO. If processes or intermediate process sets exchange information via shared objects they are not allowed to communicate via messages. This restriction helps to avoid interleaving of message-based and shared object-based synchronisation methods.

The object OS is shared by the process K2 and the intermediate process set K3. If a shared object is used by an intermediate process set then all operations which are executed by this intermediate process set must be executed by the corresponding interface process. If a process inside the process set needs information from this shared object the interface process can give this information to the process either via messages or another shared object.

Cooperating processes which share objects, for example a database, form a **process group** or **process cluster**.

10.5 Process Clusters

Processes identified in a SAPP specification which share the same objects form a process cluster.

The PASS specifications of processes belonging to a process cluster look like those of normal processes. However in the PASS graph refinements, functions and operations on shared objects can be used.

Because several processes can use shared objects simultaneously it is necessary to synchronize the access. Procedure oriented concepts such as monitors are appropriate for this kind of synchronisation.

The functions and operations on shared objects cannot be used in receive and send message specifications. This prohibits message exchange and access to common objects which would cause synchronization interference. For the same reason processes in a process cluster are not allowed to exchange messages with each other. They must communicate via common objects.

The structure of a process cluster is shown in the following figure.

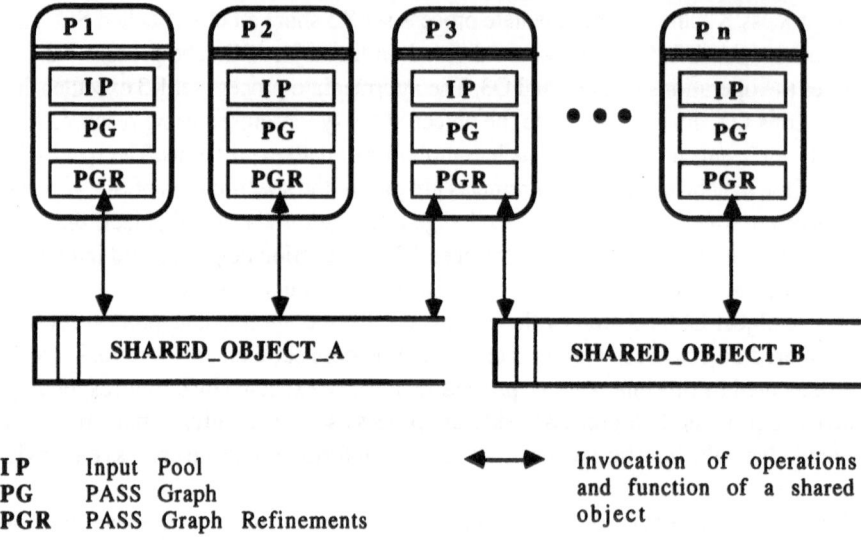

I P	Input Pool		Invocation of operations
PG	PASS Graph		and function of a shared
PGR	PASS Graph Refinements		object

Figure 10.20: Structure of Process Clusters

10.6 Process Groups

In a SAPP specification processes and process groups cannot be distinguished.

A process group as a whole has a name and it is not possible to identify processes inside a process group, i.e. group processes, from the outside. If a process sends a message to a process group the sender does not know which of the processes in the process group will accept the message. Similarly a process receiving a message does not know whether the message has been sent by an ordinary process or a process inside a group. A process group appears from outside to be a normal process.

A process group as a whole has an input pool. The individual processes inside the group do not have input pools. The following figure shows the structure of a process group.

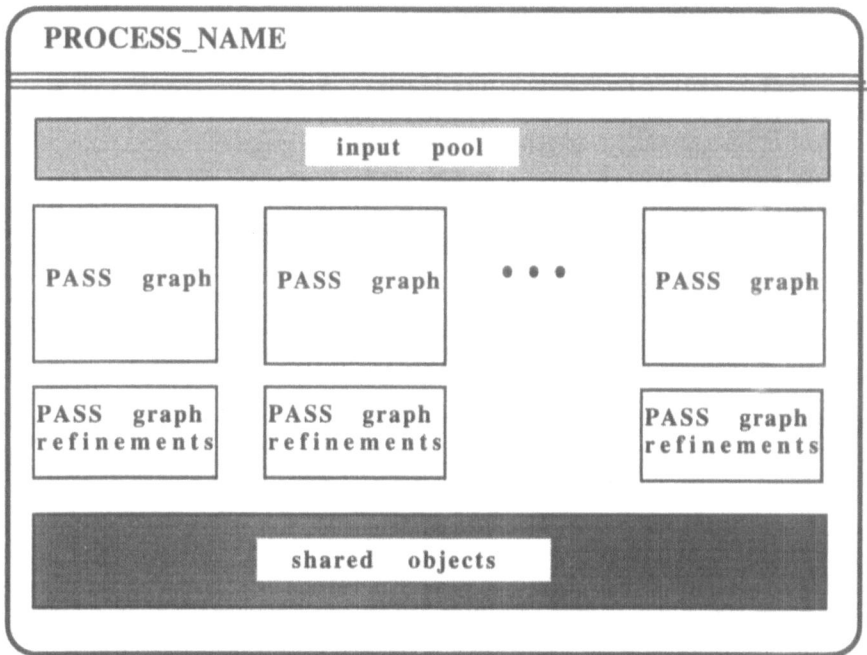

Figure 10.21: Structure of Process Groups

It is possible to solve client/server problems more efficiently using a process group. For example a data base can be considered a shared object. Some processes however cannot access the database directly. They are located on different nodes of a computer network and a remote procedure call mechanism is not available. The access from remote processes (client processes) to a database is implemented by a server process. Client processes send their requests via messages to the server process which executes the requests and sends the results back via messages. Instead of one server process, a process group can be used. A message arriving at the server group can be dealt with by one of the server processes which is not busy. It is not necessary for the client process to know which server process is used. The client sends its request to the process group and receives the answer from the process group. The figure above shows the general structure of a process group. The server processes in a process group are usually identical. Different processes in a process group are also allowed. PASS does not impose any restrictions here.

Control Questions:

1. What is the starting point of a SAPP specification?
2. What are the three basic elements of a SAPP specification?
3. What is the difference between message sets and messages?
4. What is the difference between subsystems and process sets?
5. What are the structuring elements of SAPP?
6. What are interface processes?
7. What are intermediate process sets?
8. What are the characteristics of shared objects?
9. What are the characteristics of process clusters?
10. What are the characteristics of process groups?

Exercises:

1. Identify a process control system in your environment and describe its structure in SAPP.
2. Describe your organisation in terms of SAPP. For example a department corresponds to a process set and a person corresponds to a process, etc..

11 Process Communication and Synchronisation

This chapter describes how different communication methods are introduced into PASS.

In SAPP/PASS both direct and indirect communication are supported. Both communication methods have their advantages. Indirect communication can be implemented more efficiently on systems with shared memory, whereas direct communication is more efficient for the implementation of cooperative distributed systems.

11.1 Direct Process Communication and Synchronisation

For direct communication processes exchange messages. In PASS messages have a name and parameters. The message name identifies the type of the message. The message parameters contain the data transferred from one process to the other. Messages of the same type have the same message parameters. Message parameters have a name and a type. The message parameter type specifies which type of data is allowed to be transferred via a particular parameter.

Processes receive messages from other processes via input pools. Messages from other processes are deposited in the input pool of the receiver. A message deposited in an input pool consists of the name of the sender, the message name, and the parameter values. Input pools provide the interface for the message exchange. The input pool is also used as an interface to the system context. Input pools allow the specification of the message exchange with users and technical processes. The receiving process removes the messages from the its input pool in sequences defined in its behaviour specification.

Input pools also determine the synchronisation method when transferring a message. Each process has an input pool with certain properties. The following sections describe these properties in detail.

11.1.1 Maximum Size

An input pool has a maximum size defined by the user. This specifies how many messages can be stored in the input pool.

An input pool of size zero means that only synchronous messages can be sent to the owner of this input pool.

If the maximum size of an input pool is greater than zero, messages which are sent to the process are buffered in its input pool. This means that a sender will not be blocked if space is available in the input pool of the receiver.

An input pool of size 'dynamic' means that the number of messages which can be stored in such an input pool depends on the properties of the hardware system on which the particular process runs. The memory necessary for this input pool will be allocated at runtime. A sending process will be blocked if no further memory is available for slots in the input pool. This is the way pure asynchronous message exchange is implemented.

An input pool can contain several messages of the same type from the same sender. A process expecting such a message receives the oldest one, i.e. a first in, first out strategy is used. A message accepted by the receiving process is removed from the input pool. The following figure shows the principle of the input pool.

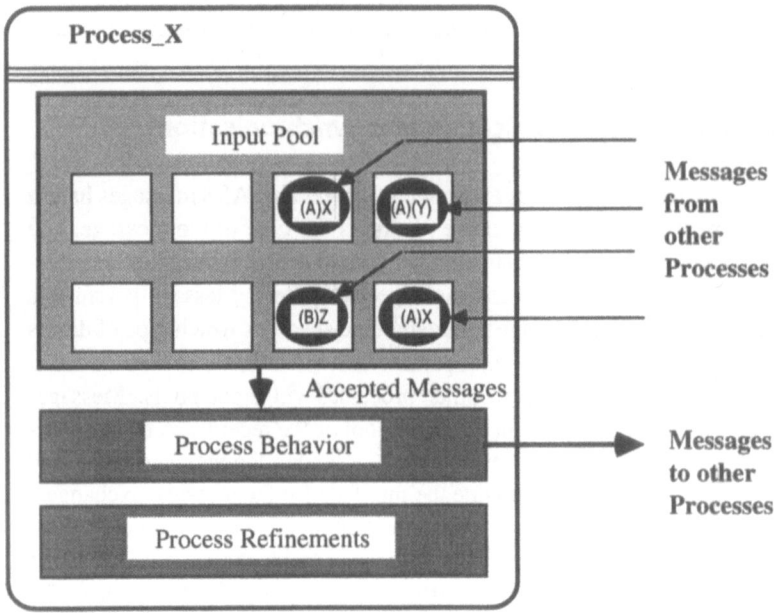

Figure 11.1: The Input Pool Concept

The example above shows an input pool with eight slots. Four slots are occupied by messages. The input pool contains three messages from process A. Two are of type X and one is of type Y. The other message in the input pool is from process B and is of type Z. The specification of the process behaviour defines in which order messages are removed from the input pool and in which order messages are sent to other processes. This is discussed further in the next chapters.

11.1.2 Attributes

If a process repeatedly sends messages of the same type to a process with an input pool then the input pool can already contain a message of this type. In such a case different strategies can be specified.

If space is still available in the input pool the message is marked with a time stamp. Messages of the same type and from the same sender can be identified by their time stamps. The time stamps show the sequence in which these messages have arrived. A process wanting to accept such a message will receive the oldest one and the others will remain in the input pool. This is the default strategy in PASS for handling identical messages in an input pool. This strategy is called **blocking strategy**.

The time stamp described above allows the specification of different strategies to cover the case of a message arriving which is the same as one already in the input pool. If the input pool is full and it contains a message of the same type as the message being offered then the oldest identical message is replaced by the offered message. This strategy is refered to as **replace the oldest**.

Instead of replacing the oldest one the newest message can be replaced. This strategy is called **replace the newest**.

PASS also allows the user to specify that only one copy of a message can be held in the input pool. If a message is already in the input pool the new message can be discarded; this is called a **discard strategy.** Alternatively the message in the input pool will be replaced by the new message; this is called a **replace strategy**. The next figure shows an example of the input pool attributes of a process.

discard   : (P1)A
replace oldest : (P1)B

Figure 11.2: Specification of Input Pool Attributes

In this example messages of type A from process P1 are discarded if the message (P1)A is already in the input pool. The oldest message of type B from process P1 is replaced if the input pool is full and a message of type B from process P1 is already in the input pool.

The sender of a message cannot distinguish whether a message is deposited in the input pool, discarded, or replaced. In all cases the message is transmitted by the sender.

The standard strategy, the blocking strategy, is used for messages not mentioned in an input pool attribute specification.

If the general process name and general message name are used, the strategy described above can be defined for message types, for messages from a particular process, or for all messages. The next figure shows an example of an input pool attribute description using the general process and general message name.

discard   : (P1)A
replace oldest : (P1)*, (P2)B
replace newest: (P2)C

Figure 11.3: Specification of Input Pool Attributes Using General Names

In the example above, all messages of type A from process P1 are discarded if a message of this type is still in the input pool. The oldest message from the process P1 will be replaced by any message arriving from process P1 if no slot is available for the arriving message. The same policy for messages of type B from process P2 applies. For messages of type C from process C the replace newest strategy is applied.

11.1.3 Structure

If the blocking strategy is used as an input pool attribute, the designer of a system can define a structure for the input pool. In addition to the total size of an input set, it can be specified that only a certain number of identical messages, only a certain number of messages from one process or only a certain number of messages of the same type can be in the input pool. The figure below shows an example of an input pool structure.

input pool
    size   :   1 0
    structure   :   3* (P3)D
    attributes :   discard (P3)D

Figure 11.4: Specification of an Input Pool Structure

In this example the input pool can contain 10 messages, and the structure definition is always valid. Only three messages (P3)D can be in the input pool at any time. If process P3 tries to send a message of type D and three messages (P3)D are already in the input pool the strategy defined in the input pool attributes is used. In this example the discard strategy is executed. If an input pool structure specifies that a message can be in the input pool zero times then the message exchange for this message is synchronous. This allows the type of message exchange to be specified individually for each message.

11.1.4 Time Restrictions

A reaction time for the different messages in an input pool can be defined independently of their attributes and structure. The reaction time specifies the length of time in which a process can accept a message. An example of an input pool specification with a reaction time clause is shown below:

reaction time: $1s < (P3)D < 5s$

In this example the reaction time clause defines that a message (P3)D will stay in the input pool at least one second and at most five seconds.

Instead of only absolute numbers it is also possible to specify a length of time together with a probability. A message will be removed from the input pool in the specified time period with the given probability. An example of this kind of reaction time definition is shown below:

reaction time: $1s < (P3)D < 5s$ **probability:** 90%

This reaction time definition means that a message (P3)D is removed from the input pool in 90 percent of all cases within the specified time period.

In a reaction time clause the general process name '(*)' and general message names can also be used. This allows reaction times for messages of a certain type or from a certain process to be defined.

A reaction time definition of $0.5s < (*)A < 1.0s$ means that all messages of type A stay at least 0.5 seconds and at most 1 second in the input pool. The reaction time clause allows guaranteed reaction times to be specified. It is a way of defining the required performance of a program. This is very important in process automation.

11.1.5 Application of Input Pools

Input pools are also used to define the communication of software processes with technical processes and human users.

Interaction of Software Processes with Technical Processes
When a software process transfers data to a technical process this is normally done via registers. The data is written to a register in the particular subprocess of the technical process.

If a software process requires that the technical process opens or closes a switch it sends the message OPEN or CLOSE to the appropriate component of the technical process. The following figure shows the logical structure.

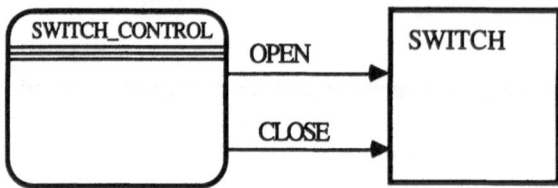

Figure 11.5: Communication Software Process – Technical Process

The process SWITCH_CONTROL writes a particular bit pattern into a register of the component SWITCH in order to send the messages OPEN or CLOSE. This bit pattern causes SWITCH to execute the appropriate operation, i.e. to open or close the switch. This command register of the component SWITCH can be considered as an input pool of the process SWITCH. The input pool of process SWITCH has one slot and the attribute 'replace oldest' because the content of a register is overwritten and the sending process is never blocked.

If a component of the system context should send a message to a software process this can be considered in the same way. If a software process obtains values from a register in a hardware component then this register is considered as an input pool slot of the software process. This slot is reserved for messages from the particular hardware process.

Interrupts from components of the technical process can be considered as messages without parameters.

Communication of Software Processes with Human Users
The communication between software processes and human users via standard I/O devices can also be modelled using input pools. Standard outputs of software processes are messages to the human users. The screen of a terminal can be considered as the input pool of the process 'human user'. Input from a keyboard can be deposited in the input pool of the particular software process in the same way as normal messages.

11.2 Indirect Communication

In PASS, processes can also exchange data via shared objects. These shared objects consist of a set of data and some access operations. The operations allow the set of data to be read or processed. Several processes can use the operations of a shared object concurrently. They can only be invoked in the refinements of a process. The invocation of the operations of a shared object must be synchronised. In the example shown in the figure below the monitor concept is used to define the synchronisation of a shared object.

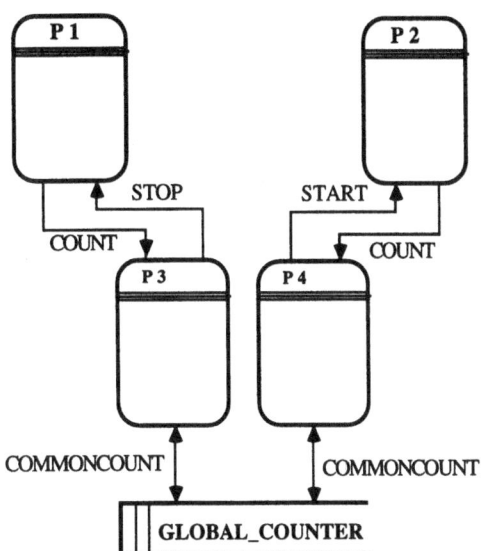

Figure 11.6: Communication Structure of a Process System with a Process Cluster

The process P1 sends messages of type COUNT to the process P3 and the process P2 sends messages of the same type to the process P4. The processes P3 and P4 belong to the same process cluster. The process P3/P4 sends messages of the types STOP and START to the process P1/P2. If the process P3/P4 receives a message of type COUNT a local variable located in the PASS graph refinements which belong to the process and a global variable located in the common part of the PASS graph refinements are incremented. The global counter is incremented by process P3 and process P4. The incrementation of the local counter is part of the receive message specification and the incrementation of the global counter COUNT is executed in an internal operation. In this internal operation the operation COMMONCOUNT which is defined in a shared object is invoked. The current value of the common counter COUNTER is transferred from the shared object to the PASS graph refinements specific to the process via an operation parameter. The following figure shows the specification of the shared object GLOBAL_COUNTER.

shared oject: GLOBAL_COUNTER

global variables:
    COUNT : integer;

begin monitor:
    COMMONCOUNT (PARAM : integer)
        effect: COUNT := COUNT + 1;
                PARAM := COUNT;
end monitor;

Figure 11.7: Example of a shared Object

Because the operation COMMONCOUNT can be called simultaneously by the processes P3 and P4, its use must be synchronized. In the example the operation COMMONCOUNT is placed in a monitor. Only one process can be in a monitor at any time. Another process which tries to execute a function within a monitor will be blocked until the first process has left the monitor.

Instead of sharing such simple objects, several processes can have access to a large and complex database. The database can be considered a shared object.

Control Questions:

1. What are the characteristics of direct communication?
2. What is a PASS input pool?
3. How is the maximum size of an input pool defined?
4. What are the attributes of an input pool?
5. How is the structure of an input pool defined?
6. What restrictions can be applied to an input pool?
7. How can the input pool concept be used to describe information exchange with the environment?
8. What are the characteristics of indirect communication?
9. What are the characteristics of shared objects?

Exercises:

1. Identify in your personal environment where direct and indirect communication is used between programs and people ?
2. Identify cases where indirect communication is more or less effective than direct communication.
3. Which type of program communication is mainly used in your professional environment?

12 Process Behaviour

This chapter explains how various methods for describing behaviour can be used in PASS. The use of behaviour expressions as an alternative to PASS graphs is described.

The behaviour of a process defines the sequence in which it sends messages, receives messages, and executes internal functions and operations. As already discussed there are several ways to specify the behaviour of a process. We introduce below a state transition model for the specification of behaviour. This has some extensions which allow the specification of time requirements, priorities, etc. These extensions are introduced to make it more convenient to specify practical applications. This type of state transition system is called a PASS graph.

In principle a developer can use a method of his own choice. In this section we show how a state-oriented specification can be transformed into a transition-oriented specification.

12.1 The PASS Graph

The communication behaviour is specified as a state transition diagram. The communication behaviour of a process depends on the messages received or sent by the process and the data state. All these dependencies are specified in the PASS graph. As the name implies the PASS graph is described graphically by nodes and lines with arrows between nodes. The nodes correspond to the main states of a process and the arrows describe the permissible transitions between the main states.

The transitions from one main state to another can have four different causes. A transition can be triggered by sending messages, receiving messages, the results of internal functions and the results of internal operations. Four corresponding types of nodes are possible in a PASS graph. In a node which represents a 'send' state, a process offers messages and executes the transition associated with the message sent. In a 'receive' state, a process waits for messages and executes the transition associated with the message received. The influence of the context on the communication behaviour is described by internal function nodes and internal operation nodes. Arrows leaving internal nodes are marked with the possible results of the internal functions and operations performed. The transitions determined by these results are executed.

12.1.1 Send Messages

The graphical representation of a send node is a box from which thick (douple width) arrows begin (see figure below).

Each box is divided into three fields. The first field contains an optional state name. The state name is only for documentation and has no influence on the semantics. The second field can contain a priority list and the last field can contain a timer value for a timeout. The meaning of these two fields, priority and timeout, is discussed later in this section.

It is possible to offer different messages, possibly to different processes, in the same send state; this is represented by the number of arrows which leave the node.

The type of the message offered and the name of the process to which a message is to be sent are marked on each arrow. For example (P)M means that the message of type M is offered to the process P.

The following figure shows an example of a send node. In this example the messages (P1)M1 and (P2)M2 are offered in state STA.

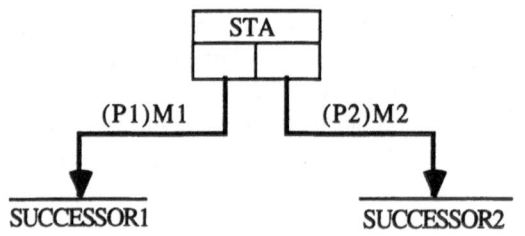

Figure 12.1: An example of a Send Sode

If a process can send one of its offered messages then the appropriate transition is executed. A message which is offered can be sent if space is available in the input pool of a suitable process or if a suitable process without an input pool, i.e. with input pool size = 0, accepts the offered message directly, i.e. at a rendezvous. A process is blocked in a send state until one of the messages offered can be sent.

In the above example the process executes the transition to the state SUCCESSOR1 if the message (P1)M1 is sent. If the message (P2)M2 is sent the transition to the state SUCCESSOR2 is executed.

A process sends several messages simultaneously if the arrows are marked with a message term. This connects several messages by an and operation. Arrows marked with a message term can only be executed if all messages in the message term can be sent. The messages in a message term cannot be sent singly. Either all are sent or none.

The next figure shows a send node with a transition marked with a message term.

If the process can send the messages (P1)A and (P2)B, it can perform the corresponding transition. If it is only possible to send message (P1)A, nothing happens because (P1)A can only be sent if it is also possible to send (P2)B and vice versa. Alternatively the message (P3)C is offered. If message (P3)C can be sent the transition to state SUCCESSOR2 is executed.

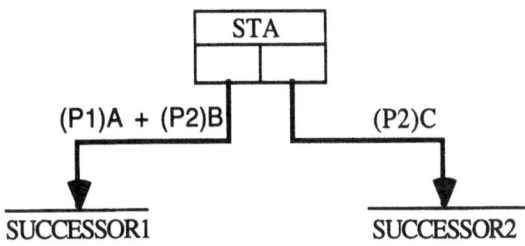

Figure 12.2: An Example of a
Send Node with a Message Term

Time-out

If no messages can be sent a process is blocked. This blocking can be limited by a timer. The maximum blocking time can be specified in the time-out field of the send node. If none of the offered messages can be sent in the specified time period, the process performs the transition marked with TIMEOUT (see figure below).

The timer can have a fixed value or can be evaluated at random. In the former case a time interval is specified and the process is blocked for the specified length of time. The value of the timer is assigned when the process reaches the particular node. The next figure shows a send state with a time guard. If none of the messages offered can be sent after a length of time (between 2 and 4 seconds) then the process executes the transition marked with TIMEOUT.

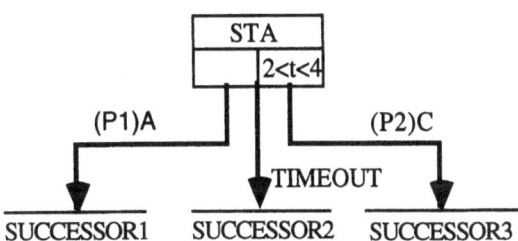

Figure 12.3 : An Example of a
Send Node with a Time Guard

If an exact length of time is specified in the timeout, for example, t = 3, a process offers the messages only for the specified length of time. If none of the messages can be sent during this time the transition TIMEOUT is executed.

Priorities

It is possible that a process can perform more than one transition if more than one of the messages offered can be sent. In such a situation a process has to decide which transition to execute. One possibility is that a process chooses a transition at random; this occurs if the priority field is empty. Alternatively, the different transitions can have priorities. A process executes the highest priority transition. The priorities are specified in the priority field of the send node.

It is possible to write either the value of the priority or its name in the priority field. The name of the priority is a reference to a priority definition. The figure below shows a send node with reference to a priority definition in the priority field.

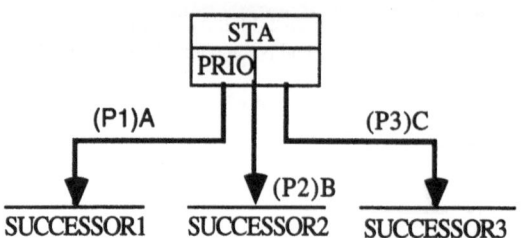

Figure 12.4: An Example of a Send Node with Priorities

PRIO: (P1)A = 1
      (P2)B = 2

In the example shown above the message (P1)A has the highest priority and message (P2)B the second highest priority. No priority is explicitly assigned to message (P3) which therefore has the lowest priority by default. The transition with the lowest number has the highest priority. Transitions to which no numbers have been assigned have the lowest priority. If two messages have the same priority i.e. both can be sent, and no other message with a higher priority can be sent, one of the two is chosen at random. In the example above only static priorities are used but it is possible to define dynamic priorities. The definition of a dynamic priority consists of n static priority definitions. Each definition is numbered starting at one. After starting the system the first definition of the priority is used the first time that a process arrives at a state with dynamic priority. The next time the process reaches this state the second definition of the priority is used, and so on. If the state has n priority definitions, then the message to be sent is selected randomly after it has been reached for the n+1'th time.

Continous dynamic priorities can be defined using a successor priority. The static priority definition is followed by a 'continue' clause. This continue clause specifies the index of the priority definition which is valid the next time the state is reached. The figure below shows an example of a definition of dynamic priority.

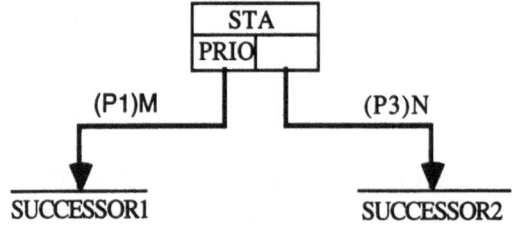

PRIO: 1. (P1)M = 1
         (P2)N = 2

      2. (P2)N = 1
         (P1)M = 2
         continue 1;

Figure 12.5: An Example of a Send Node with Dynamic Priorities

When the process reaches the state for the first time the message (P1)M has a higher priority than the message (P2)N. The second time the process reaches this state (P2)N has the higher priority. Priority definition 2 also states that priority definition 1 is valid the third time. Priority definition 2 is valid the fourth time, and so on.

So far, the dynamic priority has been shown only to depend on how many times a process has already reached a certain state, but it can also depend on the values of local variables. The following figure shows an example of dynamic priorities which depend on a local variable LOCALVAR.

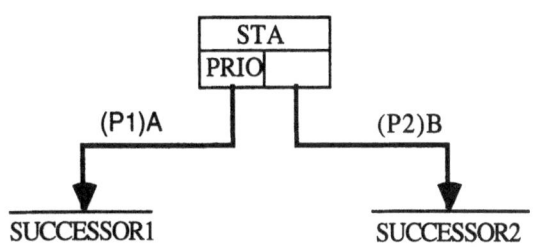

Figure 12.6: A Send Node with Dynamic Priorities depending on Local Variables

PRIO: if LOCALVAR <= 5 then (P1)A = 1, (P2)B = 2
              else (P1)A = 2, (P2)B = 1;

If the local variable LOCALVAR has a value less than or equal to 5 the transition marked with (P1)A has the higher priority, otherwise the transition marked with (P2)B has the higher priority.

12.1.2 Receive Messages

The graphical representation of a receive node is very similar to that of a send node. It is a box with thin arrows as outgoing lines.

Each box is divided into three fields like with send nodes. All three fields have the same meaning as for send nodes.

The receipt of different messages, possibly from different processes, is allowed in a single receive state. Each arrow leaving the node represents a possible message. The type of the expected message and the name of the process which sends the message are marked on each arrow. For example (P)M means that a message of type M is expected from process P. The next figure shows an example of a receive node. In this example the messages (P1)A, (P2)B, and (P3)C are possible.

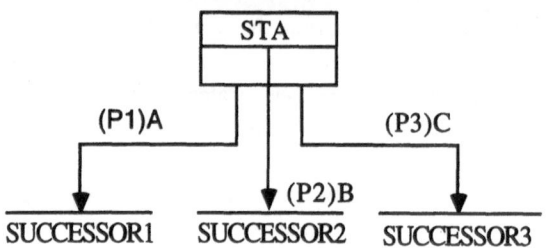

Figure 12.7: An Example of a Receive Node

If a process receives one of the expected messages then the appropriate transition is executed. In the above example the process executes the transition to the state SUCCESSOR1 if the message (P1)A is accepted. If message (P2)B or (P3)C is accepted, transition to state SUCCESSOR2 or SUCCESSOR3 occurs.

A process with an input pool whose size is greater than zero and which contains an expected message removes the message from the input pool and executes the transition to the appropriate successor state. In the case of message terms, all messages of the term must be in the input pool. They are all removed when the appropriate transition is executed.

A process is blocked until an expected message is put into the input pool.

If a process has an input pool of size equal to zero a sender has to give a message directly to the receiver. This means that the receiver has to wait until the right message is offered or the sender has to wait until the receiver accepts the message. This kind of message exchange is called a synchronous or rendezvous message exchange.

A process can expect a particular message type independent of the sending process. An arrow marked with (*)M means that a process expects a message of type M independent of the sending process. Similarly (P)* means that any message type from process P is accepted. This implies that receive message specifications exist for all message types which can be sent by the corresponding process. If an arrow is marked with (*)* any message will be accepted. The symbol * is called a general message or general process name.

Time-out

If none of the expected messages can be received the process is blocked. As in send states, this blocking can be limited by a timer. The maximum blocking time can be specified in the time-out field of the receive state symbol. The definition of the timer value is the same as for send nodes. If none of the desired messages arrives within the specified time period the process performs the transition marked with TIMEOUT.

Priorities

It is possible that a process can execute more than one transition if more than one of the messages expected is offered. In this case the process has to decide which transitions are to be executed. This is a similar situation to send nodes. One way to resolve such a conflict is to choose a transition at random. A process does this if the priority field is empty. In PASS, transitions can have priorities. In this case a process performs the permissible transition with the highest priority. The priorities for receive nodes can be defined in the same way as for send nodes.

12.1.3 Internal Functions

The influence of the context of a process on its communication behaviour is described using internal nodes in which an internal function is evaluated. The transition to be executed in the PASS graph and thus the communication behaviour, depend on the value of the function. Since the result of the internal evaluation is deterministic, exactly one transition is executed. There are no priorities and there is no time-out. An internal function does not change the data state and a process cannot be blocked if it performs an internal function. The way the results of internal functions are evaluated from the context of a process is described in the PASS graph refinements.

The graphical representation of an internal function is an oval with single-line arrows for the transition. The lower half of the oval contains the name of the internal function. The upper half contains the optional state name. Each outgoing line is marked with the result of the evaluation leading to the transition.

The following figure shows an example of an internal function.

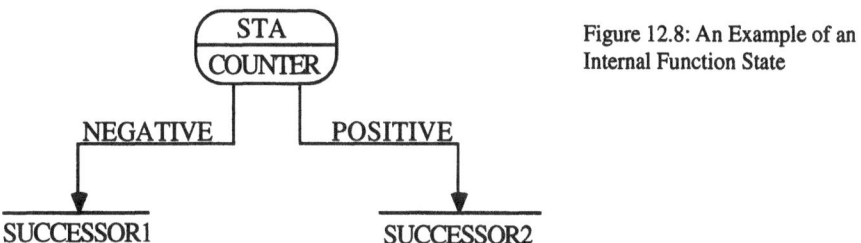

Figure 12.8: An Example of an Internal Function State

In the internal function state STA the process evaluates the internal function COUNTER. The possible results are NEGATIVE or POSITIVE. If the result is NEGATIVE the transition to the state SUCCESSOR1 is performed and if POSITIVE to the state SUCCESSOR2.

12.1.4 Internal Operations

A process can change its context without receiving a message. This occurs at an internal operation node in the PASS graph. The effect of an internal operation on the context is described in the PASS graph refinements. The result can influence the communication behaviour. Arrows leaving an internal node are marked with the possible results where these results influence the communication behaviour. Internal operations are deterministic, similar to internal functions. This implies that there are no priorities and no time-outs.

The graphical representation of an internal operation is an oval with thick lines for the transitions. The lower half of the oval contains the name of the internal operation. The upper half contains the optional state name. Each outgoing line is marked with the outcome of the internal operation leading to this transition. A common use of an internal operation is to provide an error exit.

The next figure shows an example of an internal operation state.

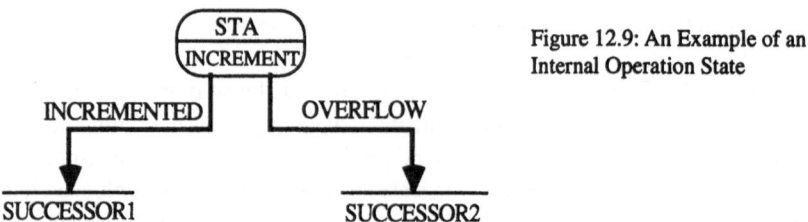

Figure 12.9: An Example of an
Internal Operation State

In the internal operation state STA, the internal function INCREMENT is evaluated. The possible results are INCREMENTED or OVERFLOW. If the result is INCREMENTED a transition to state SUCCESSOR1 occurs and if the result is OVERFLOW a transition to state SUCCESSOR2 occurs.

12.1.5 Process Pointer Variables

As explained above it is only possible to describe the sender or receiver of a message statically, in the PASS graph.

In PASS, a process can declare variables of the type 'process pointer'. The values of these variables can only be process names. They can only be set or changed if a process receives a message. The name of the sender can be stored in a process pointer variable. If the name of the sending process is stored in a process pointer variable during a receive transition, the name of the process pointer variable is written beside the corresponding arrow. The name of a sender is often stored with the general process name, i.e. the symbol * as process name.

The next figure shows an example of storing the name of a sending process in a process pointer variable.

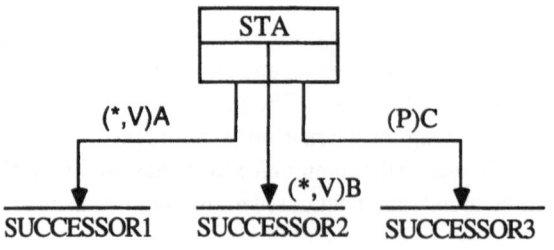

Figure 12.10: Process Pointer
Variables in Receive Nodes

The process in state STA expects messages of type A or B from any sender, or the message C from process P.

When a message of type A or B arrives, the name of the sender is stored in the process pointer variable V. If the process receives the message (P)C, the process pointer variable is unchanged.

Process pointer variables can specify indirectly the destination to which a process should send messages. The name of the destination is contained in a process pointer variable. The following figure shows an example using process pointer variables in send nodes.

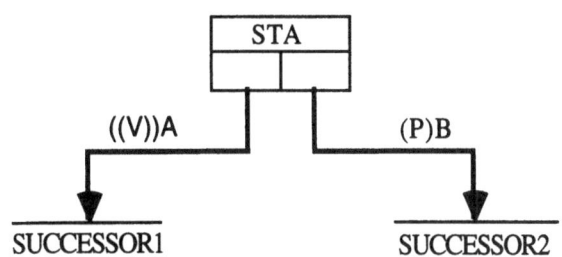

Figure 12.11: The Use of Process Pointer Variables in Send Nodes

In state STA the process should send a message A to a process whose name is contained in the process pointer variable V.

A process expecting a message can define the sender process indirectly. Instead of using a process name, a process pointer variable can be used. The message is expected to arrive from the process whose name is contained in the process pointer variable.

The following figure shows an example of using process pointer variables in receive nodes.

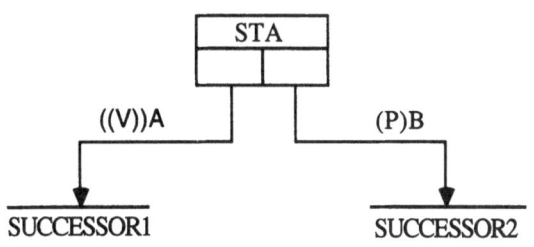

Figure 12.12: The Use of Process Pointer Variables in Receive Nodes

In state STA the corresponding process expects a message of type A from a process whose name is contained in the process pointer variable V.

The values of process pointer variables can only be changed by receiving messages but can be read by any internal functions or internal operations and when sending messages.

The use of process pointer variables is demonstrated in the following, more complex, example. The figure below shows the relevant part of the PASS graph.

process: SERVER

Figure 12.13 An Example
of the Use of Process
Pointer Variables

PASS graph:

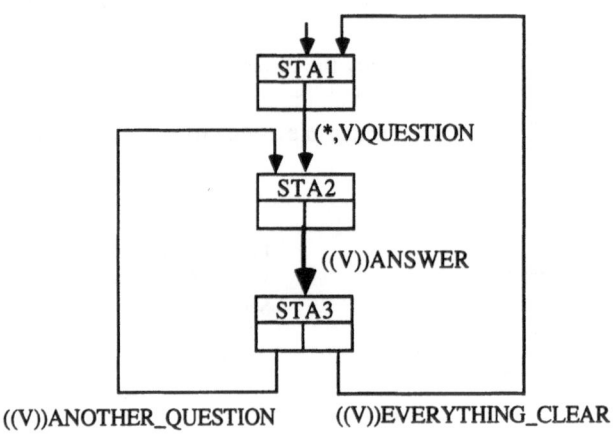

((V))ANOTHER_QUESTION   ((V))EVERYTHING_CLEAR

In state STA1 the process SERVER is waiting for the message type QUESTION from any process. If a message of type QUESTION arrives the name of the sender is stored in the process pointer variable V. In state STA2 the process SERVER sends as an answer a message of type ANSWER to the sender. This is possible because the name of the sender is contained in V. In state STA3 the process SERVER expects a response to its answer. The answering process must send a message of type ANOTHER_QUESTION or of type EVERYTHING_CLEAR.

12.1.6 Time Requirements in PASS Graphs

Software time requirements are very important (as outlined in chapter 2) especially in process control . A specification technique for process control software must contain features to specify time requirements. These define the maximum time allowed for executing a certain sequence of actions.

All permissible action sequences of a process are described in the PASS graph. Therefore time requirements are part of PASS graphs. They define the maximum time allowed to take a process from one state to another following a certain time-critical path. It is not necessary to define time requirements for all possible sequences of states. Time requirements are only specified for time-critical paths. These are defined by a sequence of states. The figure below shows an example of a PASS graph with two time-critical paths.

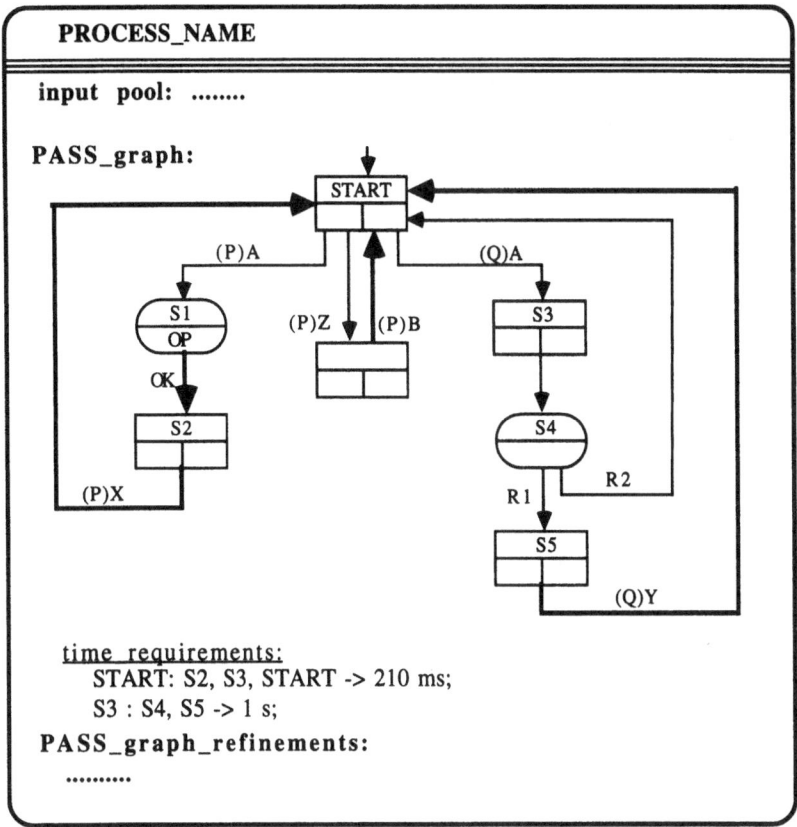

PROCESS_NAME

input pool: ....

PASS_graph:

time requirements:
    START: S2, S3, START -> 210 ms;
    S3 : S4, S5 -> 1 s;
PASS_graph_refinements:
    ....

Figure 12.14: PASS Graph with Time Critical Paths

The first time-critical path defines a loop. After 210 ms the process must execute the loop from state START via the states S2 and S3 back to state START. The second time-critical path definition shows that the process must reach state S5 within 1 second after message (Q)C is available. Because critical paths are specified by state names each state in a critical path must have a name.

The time requirements defined for a critical path must be fulfilled by the implementation or else it is not correct.

The time for a critical path starts as soon as the transition from the start state of a critical path to its successor state can be executed. In our example the time starts when the message (P)A or (Q)C is in the input pool if the message exchange is asynchronous, or is offered by the processes P or Q if the message exchange is synchronous. If a message is already in the input pool or is offered by the sender the time starts when the process reaches the start state of a critical path. If the start state of a time-critical path is an internal node, i.e. an internal operation or function, the time starts as soon as the process reaches that state.

Each state can belong to several critical paths.

12.1.7 A Textual Notation for PASS Graphs

The graphical oriented technique for describing PASS graphs can be impractical for automatic processing of PASS graphs; therefore a line oriented textual notation is introduced. This textual notation is especially useful in tools for editing PASS graphs and automatic code generation from PASS graphs, as described in chapter 14. In textual notation each transition is basically described by three items: current state, cause of transition, and successor state. The basic concept varies depending on the type of the current state.

For send nodes each transition is described in the following way:

CURRENT_STATE, t, (DESTINATION)MESSAGETYPE,
priority: N,SUCCESSOR_STATE

The letter t stands for transmit and it prefixes all lines which describe the transitions starting from a send node. A send state time out is described in the following way:

CURRENT_STATE, **t, time:** TIMER_VALUE, SUCCESSOR_STATE

The key word time prefixes the timer value. The next figure shows an example of a send node described in textual notation.

graphic:

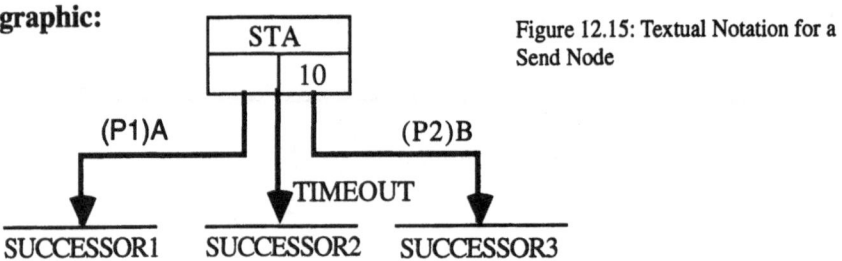

Figure 12.15: Textual Notation for a Send Node

textual:

STA, t, (P1)A,   SUCCESSOR1
STA, t, (P2)B,   SUCCESSOR2
STA, t, time: 10, SUCCESSOR3

The textual description for receive nodes is similar to the notation for send nodes. Instead of the prefix t the prefix r is used.

Internal function node transitions are described in the following way:

CURRENT_STATE, f ,FUNCTION_NAME.RESULT, SUCCESSOR_STATE

The letter f is the prefix of transitions starting from internal function nodes. The figure below shows an example of an internal function node described in textual notation.

graphic:

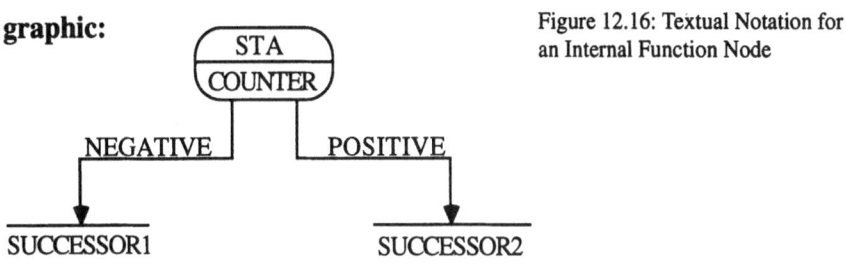

Figure 12.16: Textual Notation for
an Internal Function Node

textual:

STA , f, COUNTER.NEGATIVE, SUCCESSOR1

STA , f, COUNTER.POSITIVE , SUCCESSOR2

The textual description of internal operation nodes is similar to the notation for internal function nodes. The prefix .o is used instead of the prefix f.

12.1.8 The Combined Use of Priorities and Structured Input Pools

Lifelocks and deadlocks caused by unfair strategies can cause problems in parallel programs e.g. a certain state of a process that has no defined priorities. In this state a process always accepts the same message when this message is continuously offered. This behaviour can cause deadlocks for other processes. They offer their messages but they are never accepted.

In the following example, the combined use of input pool structures and dynamic priorities is shown. This avoids deadlocks and lifelocks caused by unfair strategies.

A process SERVER receives messages of type QUESTION from the processes CLIENT1 and CLIENT2. The following figure shows the communication structure of this example. The process SERVER sends the message type ANSWER to both client processes.

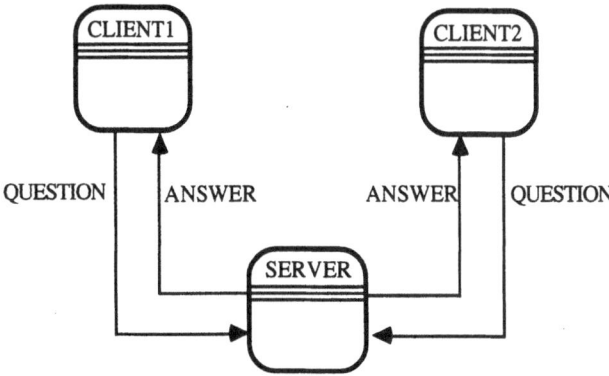

Figure 12.17: Communication Structure of a Server/Client Example

The process SERVER has an input pool for 5 messages. The following figure shows the communication behaviour of all three processes.

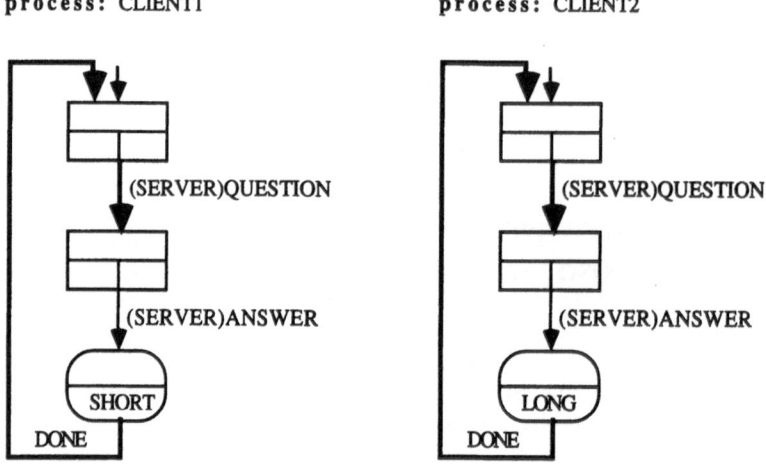

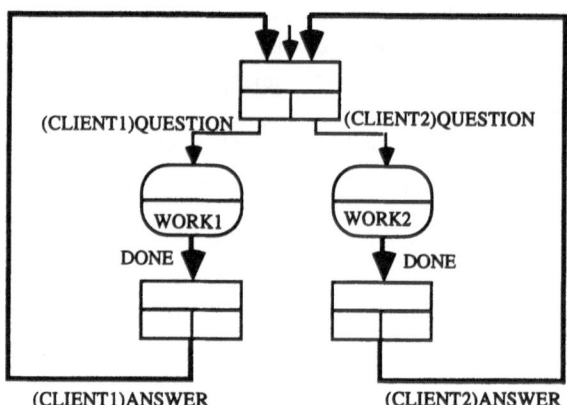

Figure 12.18: PASS Graphs of the Processes

If CLIENT1 is a very fast process, CLIENT2 can be blocked for ever. CLIENT1 fills up the input pool with its messages. CLIENT2 cannot deposit its messages and is blocked. Before SERVER can accept the first message, CLIENT1 is already offering its next message. When SERVER removes a message from its input pool one of the offered messages can be deposited in the input pool. In PASS no strategy is defined for these kind of conflicts. We assume that CLIENT1 obtains the free slot and can send its message. CLIENT2 remains blocked.

Before SERVER can remove its next message, CLIENT1 is already offering another message. This can happen repeatedly. If the scheduling strategy for the input pool is unfair, CLIENT2 is always blocked.

This problem can be solved by defining a suitable structure for the input pool of the server. Three input pool slots are reserved for messages from CLIENT1 and two slots for messages from CLIENT2. CLIENT2 can now deposit its messages but this causes a new problem. CLIENT2 can deposit two messages in the input pool. If SERVER prefers the messages from CLIENT1, CLIENT2 will be blocked when it offers the third one.

If CLIENT1 is fast enough and SERVER prefers messages from CLIENT1 then CLIENT2 will be blocked for ever.

This problem can be solved by using dynamic priorities. The next figure shows the corresponding priority definition.

process: SERVER

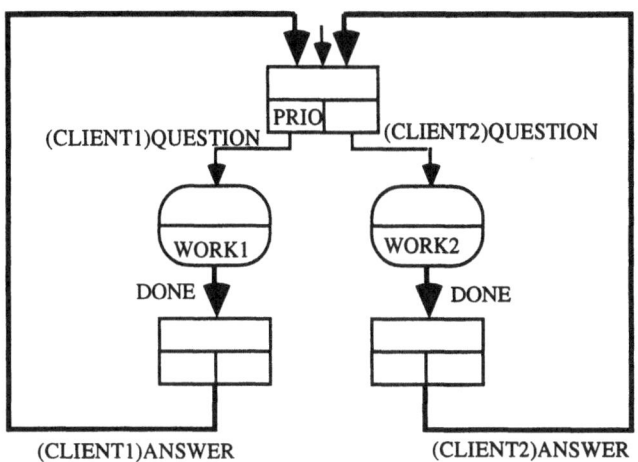

PRIO: 1. (CLIENT1)QUESTION = 1
             (CLIENT2)QUESTION = 2

          2. (CLIENT1)QUESTION = 2
             (CLIENT2)QUESTION = 1
                continue at 1

Figure 12.19: Dynamic Priorities for a Fair Server Strategy

SERVER prefers messages from CLIENT1 the first time and from CLIENT2 the next time.

The input pool structure together with dynamic priorities allows fair strategies to be defined.

12.2 PASS Graph Macros and PASS Graph Types

In a process PASS graph the same communication sequence can be executed in different parts of the PASS graph. In such a case it would be necessary to describe the same sequence several times. To avoid this, PASS allows the definition of macros so that parts of the communication behaviour of a process can be described separately. A PASS graph uses macro nodes where the communication behaviour is described in a macro. A process reaching a macro node executes the corresponding macro.

The symbol for a macro node is a rectangle divided into several fields. The field in the middle contains the optional name of a macro node and the name of the corresponding macro. The other fields, the state fields, contain state symbols with state names which represent communication nodes or internal nodes. These are states inside the macro. Each of these states must appear in the corresponding macro expansion. They are the states where a process can enter a macro.

A macro node defines how the corresponding macro is embedded into the PASS graph.

The next figure shows an example of a PASS graph in which macros are used. The nodes MACRO1 and MACRO2 are macro nodes. The macro MACROEX is executed in these macro nodes. A process reaching the macro node at the state field MAC1, executes the macro MACROEX starting at the state MAC1. The same is true for MAC2.

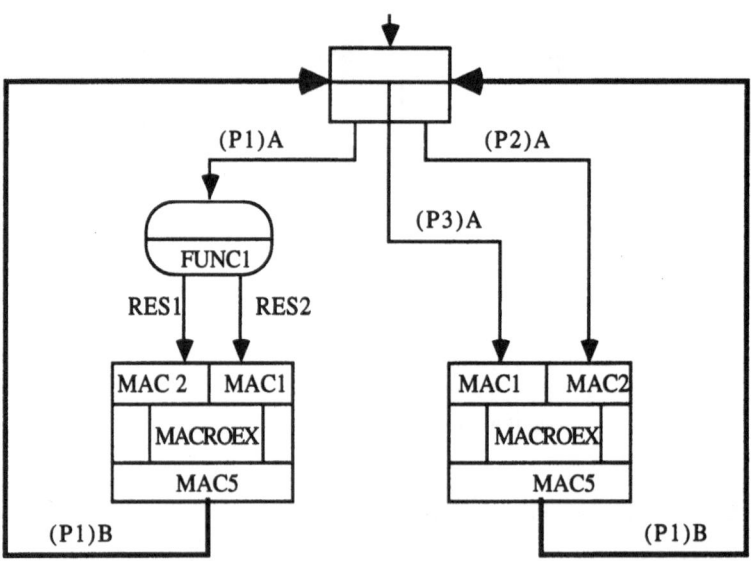

Figure 12.20: PASS Graph with Macro Nodes

The following figure shows the macro definition of MACROEX.

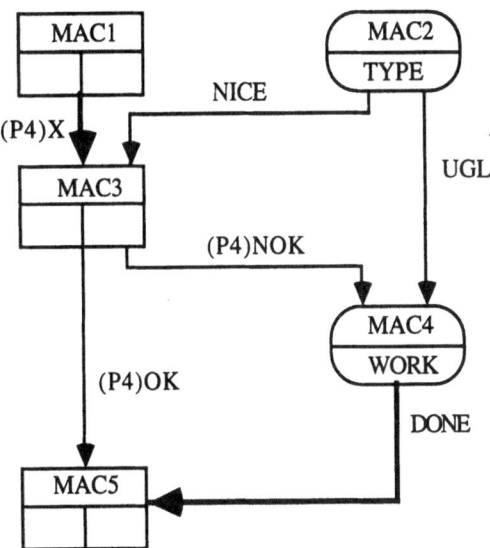

Figure 12.21: Macro Definition MACROEX

Macro types

A macro can only be used in the PASS graph of one process. A macro which is used in different processes must be defined in each of these processes. It is possible to define macro types to avoid this. Instead of using actual process names, formal sender and receiver names are used.

A process which needs a macro of a certain type introduces it with a declaration. In the declaration the formal process names are replaced by actual process names. The next figure shows an example of a macro type definition. In this macro type the formal names F1 and F2 are used instead of the actual process names.

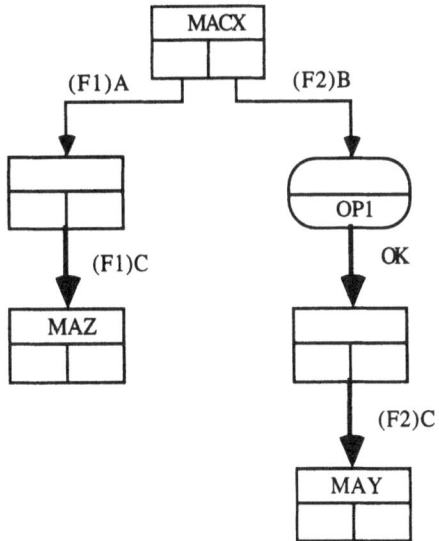

Figure 12.22: Definition of a Macro Type

In the macro declaration the formal names F1 and F2 are replaced by the process names P1 and P2.

declare MACRONAME **of type** EXAMPLE **where** (F1=P1, F2=P2);

For processes in which macros of a certain type are declared and used, receive and send message specifications must exist for the message types received and sent in the macro and the macro type. The internal operations and functions used in the macro type must also be defined. These operations and functions can be different in the different processes. Macros are only means by which PASS graphs can be structured and do not include a PASS graph refinement.

In order to leave a macro empty, transitions are sometimes necessary. Empty transitions are executed without any effect on the environment or the variables. The symbol for an empty transition resembles the symbol for internal functions but there is no function name in the appropriate field and the transition is not marked.

The following figure shows a PASS graph with a macro. The macro is left via an empty transition.

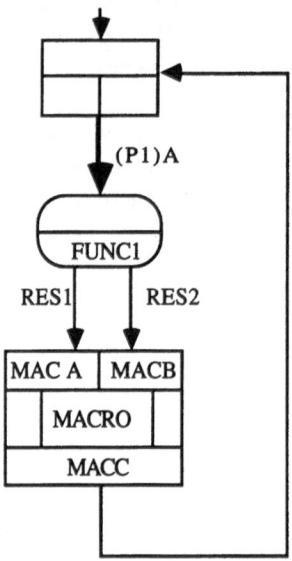

Figure 12.23: The Use of Empty Transitions

The extension of the above macro MACRO is shown in the figure below. The state MACC is a state which is left by an empty transition.

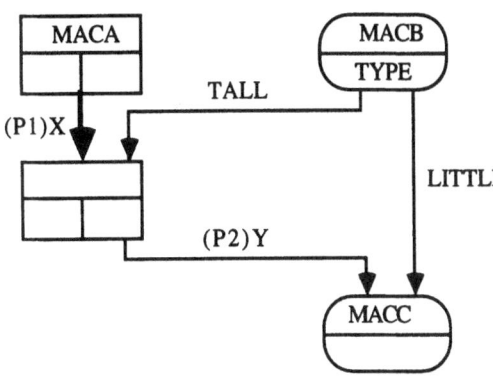

Figure 12.24: Macro Definition
with an Empty Transition

PASS Graph Types

It is also possible to define PASS graph types in a similar way as macro types. PASS graph types are described in the same way as normal PASS graphs. Instead of actual process names, formal names are used in the messages sent and received. The formal names are replaced by actual names in the declaration of a PASS graph for a certain process.

Macros can be used in PASS graph types. The macro definition in the specification of a PASS graph type uses formal names instead of actual names.

When macro types are used in a PASS graph type definition, the formal names in the macro declaration are replaced by the actual names used in the PASS graph type definition. Processes whose communication behaviour are defined by declaring the PASS graph, must contain the send message, receive message, internal function and internal operation specifications in the PASS graph refinements.

12.3 Behaviour Expressions instead of PASS Graphs

The current version of PASS describes the behaviour of processes using the permissible sequences of states. As already discussed, the initial state and the permissible sequences of transitions can be used to specify the behaviour of processes instead of describing the permissible sequences of states. The permissible sequences of transitions can be specified explicitly by expressions defining the possible sequences or by requirements which must be fulfilled by a history of transitions /SCME82/. A well known technique for explicitly describing the behaviour of processes is the calculus of communicating systems (CCS) /MILN80/.

Based on CCS, PASS can specify the behaviour of processes using behaviour expressions instead of PASS graphs. The current version of CCS does not allow all aspects of the behaviour of PASS processes to be specified, e.g. priorities and time-outs are not contained in the current version of CCS. CCS is only considered below as far as it allows the specification of PASS processes.

It is easy to derive the equivalent CCS behaviour expressions from a PASS graph which does not contain priorities or time-outs.

PASS graph   **CCS: Behaviour Expression**

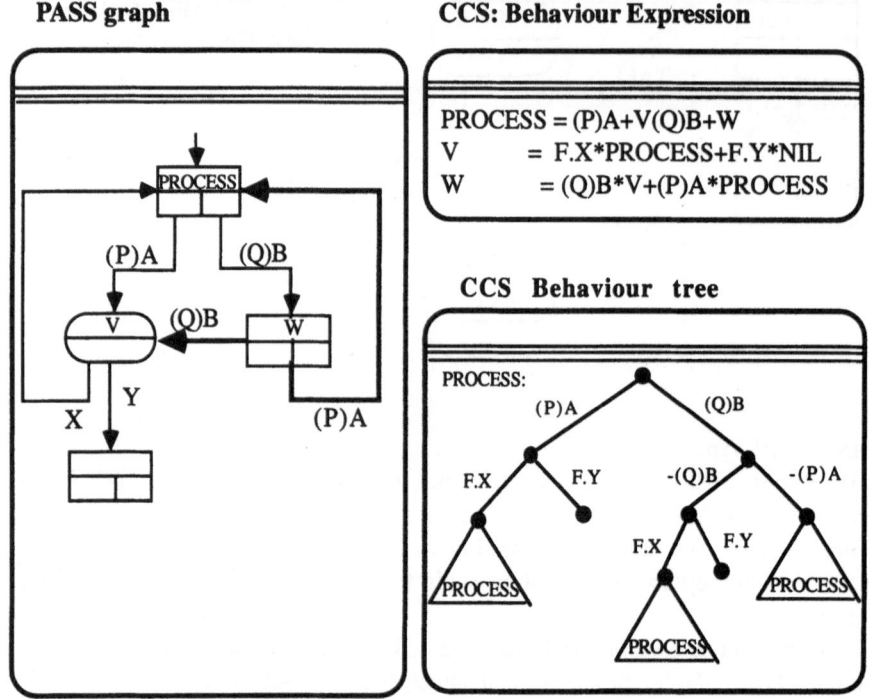

Figure 12.25 : Transforming PASS Graphs into Behaviour Expressions

The method for transforming a PASS graph into a CCS behaviour expression is very
simple:

- Each node in a PASS graph is given a name i.e. state name.
- For each node in a PASS graph, a behaviour expression is defined which has the
  same name as the corresponding state or node in the PASS graph.
- Each transition is a sequential behaviour expression of the type:

ACTION * SUCCESSSOR

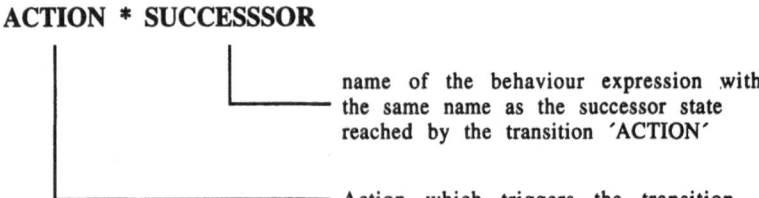

- The behaviour expression for a state is constructed by applying the alternative
  operator to all behaviour expressions corresponding to the possible transitions
  from a state.
- Results of internal functions and operations are considered interactions with the
  PASS graph refinements.

The method described above results in a CCS process system without parallelism. CCS parallel processes only interleave with each other and therefore no real parallelism is possible. Instead of a PASS graph, one or several CCS processes which can also be connected by the parallel operator can be used. Parallelism in CCS implies the interleaving of the CCS process behaviour expressions. This kind of parallelism is therefore not visible from outside the particular PASS process. CCS processes which describe the behaviour of a PASS process can exchange messages, i.e. signals. However no refinements exist for these messages. They are only used for synchronization between CCS processes and cannot be seen from outside the PASS process. CCS can only be used to describe the behaviour of one PASS process. When a PASS process sends or receives messages, the behaviour expressions interact with the input pool.

The semantics of sending and receiving messages is the same as for PASS graphs except that the permissible sequences are described differently. This also means that in different PASS processes belonging to the same system, different specification techniques can be used for the process behaviour. It is up to the designer to choose the best specification technique for defining the behaviour of a process.

The reasons why we prefer PASS graphs are:
- We think that a graphical method is more convenient to use than expressions
- CCS expressions are not powerful enough to express all PASS features namely timeouts, time requirements, and 1/n, n/1 transactions.

Control Questions:

1. What is the symbol for sending messages?
2. What is the symbol for receiving messages?
3. What is the symbol for invoking internal functions?
4. What is the symbol for invoking internal operations?
5. What different types of time-outs are allowed in PASS?
6. What types of priorities are allowed in PASS?
7. What are process variables?
8. Describe some examples of the combined use of structured input pools and priorities?
9. What are PASS graph macros and PASS graph types?
10. How are PASS graph types embedded in a PASS graph?
11. How can PASS graphs be transformed into behaviour expressions?

Exercises:

1. Express some parts of your own personal behaviour in the form of a PASS graph.
2. Express the behaviour of your travel department as a PASS graph.

3. Express the interaction between the user and an application program in your environment as a PASS graph.

4. Transform some of the PASS graphs above into behaviour expressions.

13 Refinements of a Process

This chapter describes how specification and programming techniques for sequential programs are incorporated into PASS.

The semantics of sent messages, received messages, operations, and functions are defined in the refinements of a process. These contain a detailed specification of each activity used in the behaviour description. In the following sections, the relationship between behaviour specifications and refinements is described in more detail. Then specification techniques for refinements are discussed, especially the application of object-oriented specification, design and implementation.

13.1 PASS Graph Refinements

The PASS graph describes only the communication behaviour, because it depends on the communication history and the values of the local variables. A message can have parameters. The parameters and their types are not shown in the PASS graph. The arrival of a message can change the values of the local variables, depending on their current state and the values of the message parameters. This effect of messages on the state of the local variables and the specification of the message parameters is contained in a receive message specification. The message parameters and how their values are obtained from the state of the local variables must be specified for the sending process. This is defined in a send message specification. In the PASS graph only the name and the possible results of an internal function are shown. A PASS graph does not show how the results are obtained from the values of the local variables; this is contained in an internal function specification contained in the PASS graph refinements.

For each internal operation, there is an internal operation specification which describes how the execution of the operation changes the values of the local variables. It also describes how the different results are obtained from the state of the local variables. In the following sections the PASS graph refinement is discussed in more detail.

13.1.1 Receive Message Specifications

There is a receive message specification for each message type which can be received by a process. This describes the parameters of the particular message type and the effect on the local variables if the message is accepted. The receive message specification of a message type is only valid for a particular process and can be different in different processes. The number and type of parameters must be the same but the effects on the internal state can be different. This is in many ways similar to different people hearing or reading the same text but each understanding it in a different way.

The following points hold true when a process accepts a message:

1. If the message is in an input pool then it is removed. If the receiving process does not have an input pool the sender can execute the appropriate transition
2. The state of the local variables is changed according to the receive message specification.
3. The process executes the transition to the appropriate successor state.

These three steps are indivisible. Either all three steps are executed or none.

When a process accepts a message term the corresponding receive message specifications are executed in any sequence. A variable which is changed in several receive message specifications has an undefined effect on the local state. A process expecting message terms is not allowed to change a local variable in more than one relevant receive message specification. This condition can be checked statically. The next figure shows an example of a receive message specification.

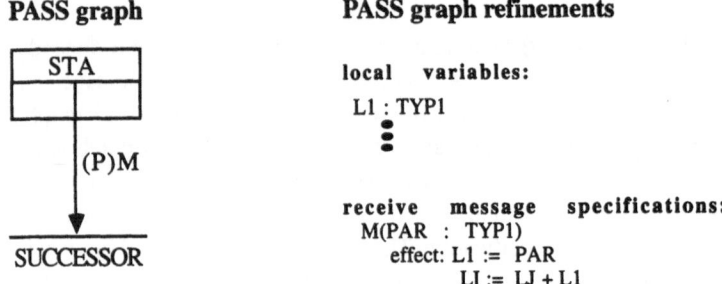

Figure 13.1: Example of a Receive Message Specification

The PASS graph refinements in the above figure show that the message type M has the parameter PAR of type TYP1. If a message of type M is received the value of the parameter is copied in the local variable L1 and the new value of the local variable LI is the sum of the values of the variables LJ and L1.

13.1.2 Send Message Specification

Each message sent by a process has a send message specification in the PASS graph refinements. The send message specification describes the message parameters and how the parameter values are obtained from the state of the local variables.

A process which should send a message, first evaluates all the message parameter values and then offers the messages to the corresponding processes.

The send specification for the same message type can be different in different processes. The number and type of the parameters must be the same but in each process the parameter values can be evaluated in a different way.

The next figure shows an example of a send message specification.

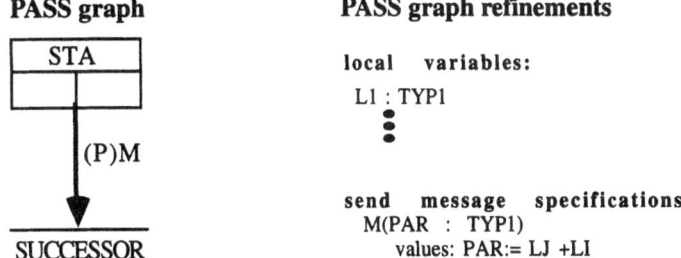

PASS graph

STA

(P)M

SUCCESSOR

PASS graph refinements

local   variables:

L1 : TYP1

send   message   specifications:
M(PAR : TYP1)
values: PAR:= LJ +LI

Figure 13.2: Example of a Send Message Specification

The send message specification in the above example shows that the message type M has one parameter called PAR. The value of this parameter is the sum of the local variables LI and LJ.

13.1.3 Internal Operation Specification

The internal operations change the local state and can give differing results. These results can influence the communication behaviour of a process.

When a process performs an internal operation:

1. The internal state is changed according to the internal operation specification.
2. The corresponding transition is performed in the PASS graph depending on the end condition.

The following example shows an internal operation node and its internal operation specification.

PASS graph:

STA
INCREMENT

INCREMENTED   OVERFLOW

SUCCESSOR1   SUCCESSOR2

PASS graph refinement:

local   variables:

L1 : TYP1

internal   operations
specifications:
INCREMENT
effect: L1 := L1 + 1
if L1 < 10 then
return INCREMENTED
else
return OVERFLOW

Figure 13.3: Example of an Internal Operation Specification

The internal operation INCREMENT increments the internal variable by one. If the value of the variable is less than ten after the execution of the operation, the result INCREMENTED is returned to the PASS graph where the transition to state SUCCESSOR1 is executed. If the local variable L1 is greater than or equal to ten, the result OVERFLOW is given to the PASS graph and the transition to state SUCCESSOR2 is executed.

13.1.4 Internal Function Specification

The internal functions check the local state of processes. An internal function returns a result which depends on the local state of a process. The result of an internal function initiates a particular transition in the PASS graph. Internal functions do not change the local state of another process.

Internal functions with identical names are allowed in different processes but the internal function specifications in the corresponding PASS graph refinements are completely independent. Internal functions with the same name but in different processes can even produce different results.

The following figure shows an example of an internal function node and the internal function specification of the internal function executed.

PASS graph: **PASS graph refinement:**

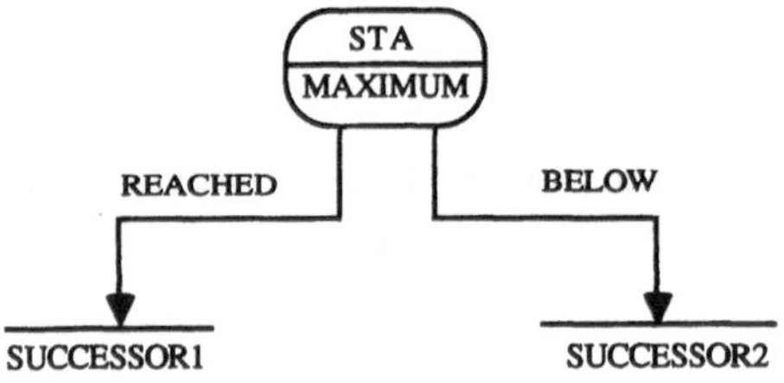

```
local    variables:

L1 : TYP1
  .
  .
  .

internal    functions
specifications:

MAXIMUM
    results:  if (LI+LJ) < 10 then
                         return BELOW
              else
                         return REACHED
```

Figure 13.4: Example of an Internal Function Specification

If the sum of LI and LJ is less than 10 then the process executes the transition marked with BELOW. Otherwise the transition marked with REACHED is executed.

13.2 Specification Techniques for Refinements

13.2.1 Hierarchy of Modules

In the examples above, pseudo-code was used to describe the functions and operations of the PASS graph refinements. In addition it had been assumed that the refinements consisted of a single data structure, the local variables of a process, and as well as a corresponding set of operations related to sent messages, received messages, internal functions, and internal operations. Refinements can be very complex and therefore it is useful to separate refinements in modules according to some module definition. Each module can be considered as an abstract data type which encapsulates a data structure and its operations. These operations are either a receive message specification, send messages specification an internal function specification or internal operation specification.

Other low level modules can be used in order to implement these final set of modules which contain all receive message specifications, send message specifications, internal functions and internal operations; this is usual in normally complex programs. In PASS the behaviour specification can be regarded as a main program which calls the operations of underlying modules. The following figure shows refinements structured in several layers of modules.

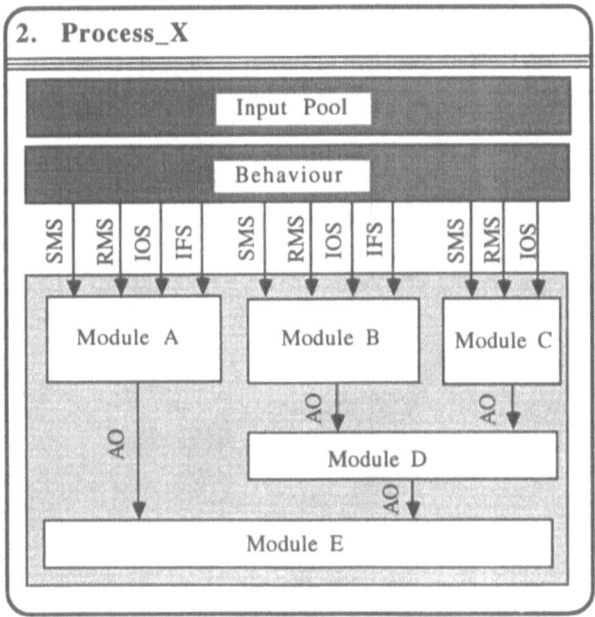

SMS	Send Message Specifications
RMS	Receive Message Specifications
IFS	Internal Function Specification
IOS	Internal Operation Specification
AO	Auxilary Operation Specifications

Figure 13.5: Refinements Structured in Modules

In the example above, the send specifications, receive specifications, internal operations, and internal functions are defined in the modules A, B, and C. For the specification of these modules, operations are used which are defined in module D and E.

For modules, it is possible to use any specification technique used for sequential programs, i.e. natural language, a formal specification technique such as algebraic specification or a programming language.

The choice of the technique depends on the experience and personal taste of the specifier and on how close the specification should be to the implementation.

An overview of specification techniques for sequential programs is given in Part I (chapter 4) of this book or in /PRESS87/, /YATS86/, /CONN85/, /PETE80/, /BALZ82/ and /GRIES81/.

13.2.2 Object Oriented Technologies

The refinements of a process can be regarded as a set of objects belonging to object classes. In order to define these object classes all aspects of object oriented development technologies can be used that is abstraction, encapsulation, inheritance, and polymorphism. Different objects of the same object class can be used in the refinements of several processes. In principle one or several hierarchies of object classes can be defined for each software system specified in SAPP/PASS. The objects that are only used in the refinements of a particular process are the private objects of that process.

The following figure shows a simple system specified in SAPP/PASS and a hierarchy of classes which is the basis for the refinements specification. The objects contained in the refinements of PROCESS_A and PROCESS_B may be incarnations of process classes which have been developed for the complete SAPP/PASS system.

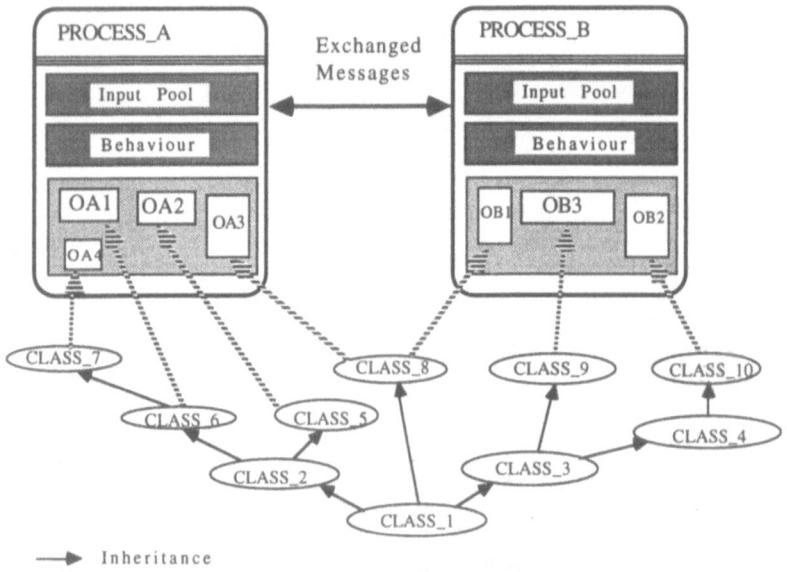

Figure 13.6: Application of Object-Oriented Techniques in SAPP/PASS Specifications

A hierarchy of classes can be developed for a system of concurrent processes specified in SAPP/PASS. These classes can be used to specify the refinements of each process. In addition to this class hierarchy for the whole system special classes for subsystems or even single processes can be defined.

Processes are active elements. Active elements are also called subjects. These subjects call methods of objects, which means they use objects. Therefore SAPP/PASS can be called a Subject Oriented Programming Technique. This more philosophical aspect of SAPP/PASS is discussed in detail in chapter 19.

13.3 Shared Objects

The operations of a single object can be executed by several different processes. Operations and functions of a shared object can be called in the internal operations and functions of a process. Processes which share objects comprise either a process group or a process cluster (see chapter 11.5). The following figure shows processes which share an object.

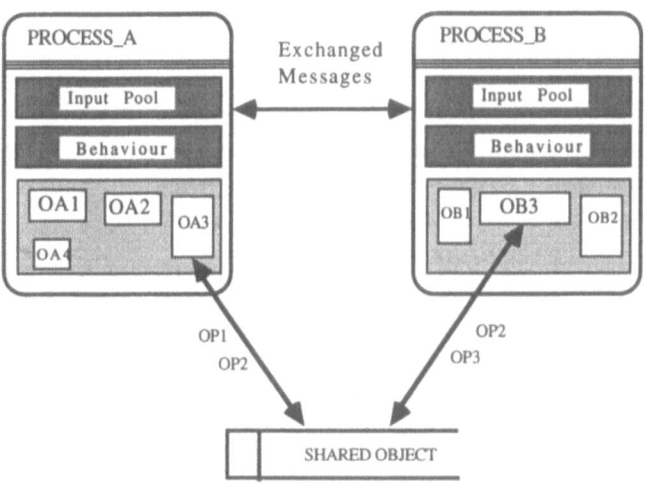

Figure 13.7:
Processes which
share an Object

In the example above, operations OP1 and OP2 of SHARED OBJECT are called in object OA3. In OB3 the operations OP2 and OP3 of SHARED OBJECT are called in the refinements of PROCESS_B. In order to keep shared objects in a consistent state, the operation execution of shared objects must be synchronised. This means that the specification of a shared object will consist of three major parts:
– The specification of the data structure
– The specification of the operations.
– The specification of the synchronisation.

The next figure shows an example of a process system with a process cluster.

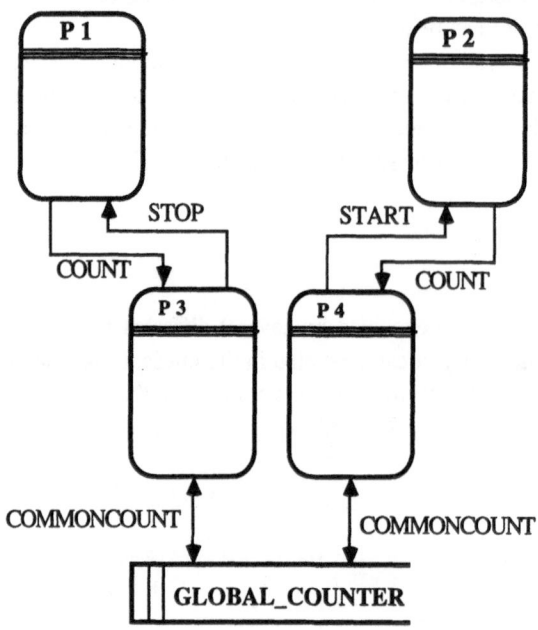

Figure 13.8: Communication Structure of a Process System with a Process Cluster

Process P1 sends messages of type COUNT to process P3, and process P2 sends messages of type COUNT to process P4. Process P3 and process P4 belong to the same process cluster. Process P3/P4 sends messages of the types STOP and START to process P1/P2. If process P3/P4 receives a message of type COUNT a local variable located in the PASS graph refinements specific to the process and a global variable located in the common part of the PASS graph refinements are incremented. The global counter is incremented by process P3 and process P4. The incrementing of the local counter COUNTER is part of the receive message specification whereas the increment of the global counter COUNT is executed in an internal operation called SUM.

The following figure shows the PASS description of process P3. Process P4 is similar to process P3 except that it receives messages from process P2 instead of process P1.

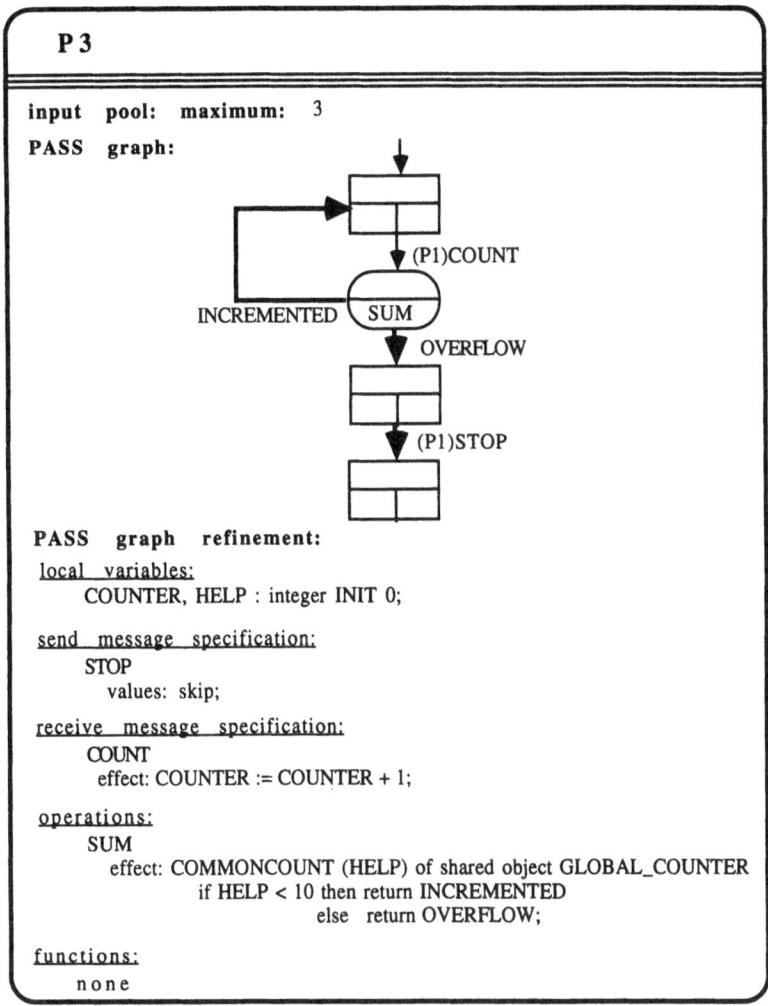

P 3

input pool: maximum: 3

PASS graph:

(P1)COUNT

INCREMENTED SUM

OVERFLOW

(P1)STOP

PASS graph refinement:

local variables:
COUNTER, HELP : integer INIT 0;

send message specification:
STOP
values: skip;

receive message specification:
COUNT
effect: COUNTER := COUNTER + 1;

operations:
SUM
effect: COMMONCOUNT (HELP) of shared object GLOBAL_COUNTER
if HELP < 10 then return INCREMENTED
else return OVERFLOW;

functions:
none

Figure 13.9: Specification of a Cluster Process

In the internal operation SUM, the operation COMMONCOUNT defined in the
common PASS graph refinements is invoked. The current value of the common
counter COUNTER is transferred from the common PASS graph refinements to the
process specific PASS graph refinements via the parameter HELP. Depending on the
value of the parameter, the results INCREMENTED or OVERFLOW are given to
the PASS graph.

The following figure shows the specification of the shared object
GLOBAL_COUNTER.

---

shared oject: GLOBAL_COUNTER

<u>global variables:</u>
   COUNT : integer;

begin monitor:
   COMMONCOUNT (PARAM : integer)
    effect: COUNT := COUNT + 1;
          PARAM := COUNT;
end monitor;

Figure 13.10: Example of a Shared Object

Because the operation COMMONCOUNT can be called simultaneously by the processes P3 and P4 its use must be synchronized. In the example the operation COMMONCOUNT is placed in a monitor. Only one process can be in a monitor at any time. Another process which tries to execute a function within a monitor will be blocked until the first process has left the monitor.

Data Bases:
An important case of a shared object is a database. Normally databases are shared by several programs which can be regarded as processes or process sets. For these programs the database is the only way to exchange data. The following figure shows two programs which share a database.

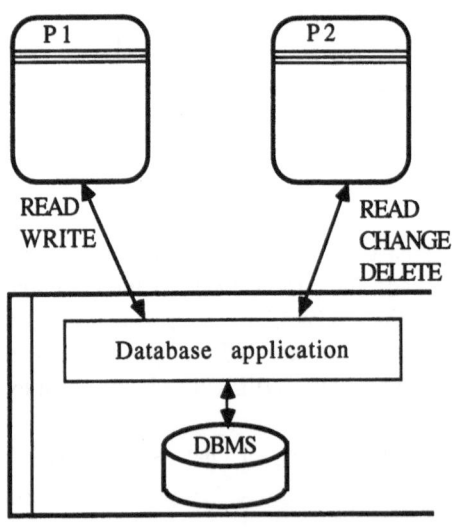

Figure 13.11: Processes sharing a Database System

DBMS: Database Management System

13.4 Process Types

A software system can consist of several more or less identical processes. Each of these processes has the same input pool structure, the same behaviour and the same refinements. The only difference is that these processes do not communicate with the same processes. Process types can be used to structure a complete process system. A process type includes an input pool PASS graph and PASS graph refinements. Like PASS graph types, formal process names are used in the PASS graph instead of actual process names. The PASS graph refinements include the specifications of all internal functions, internal operations, and messages sent or received.

A process of a certain type is incarnated by a declaration. In a declaration the formal names used in the PASS graph are replaced by actual process names as in PASS graph declarations.

It is possible to use macros and macro types in the PASS graph description of a process type. This is analogous to the use of macros and macro types in PASS graph types.

The next figure shows the specification of a process type.

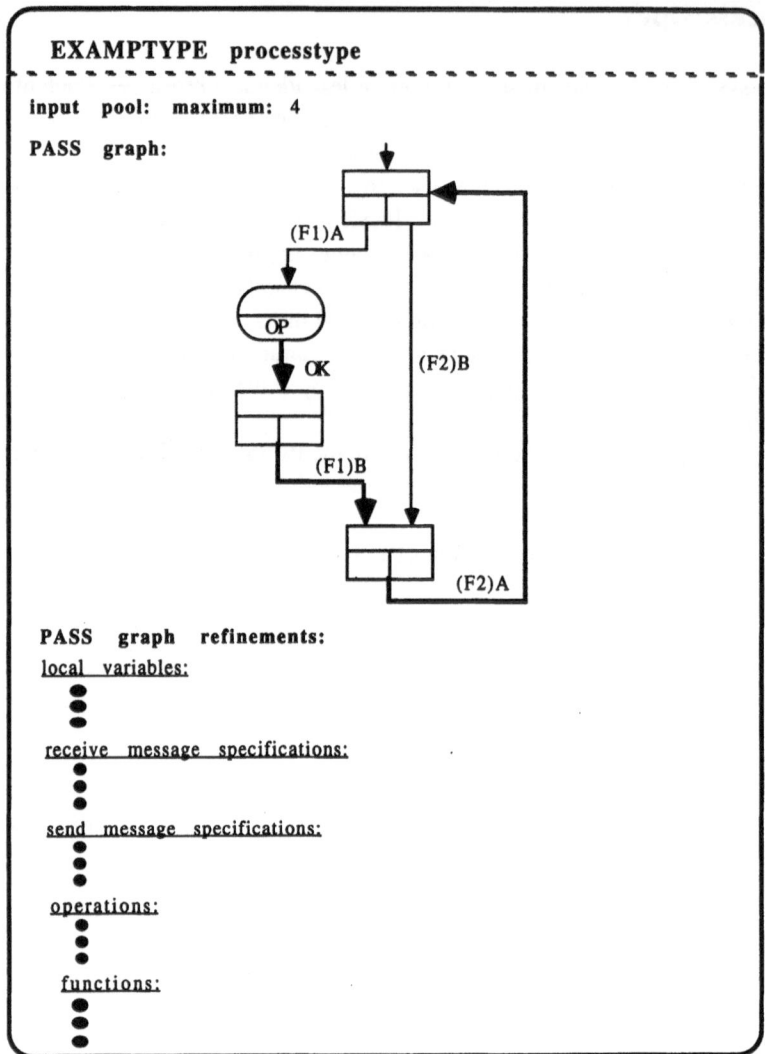

EXAMPTYPE processtype

input pool: maximum: 4

PASS graph:

PASS graph refinements:
local variables:

receive message specifications:

send message specifications:

operations:

functions:

Figure 13.12: Specification of a Process Type

In the following process declaration the name of the declared process is EXPROCESS and the formal names F1 and F2 in process types PASS graphs are replaced by the names P1 and P2.

declare EXPROCESS of type EXAMPTYPE where (.F1=P1,F2=P2);

It is possible to use incarnations of a process type as processes in process groups and process clusters. Functions and operations defined in the common part of the PASS graph refinements can be used in these processes.

If a process type is defined, functions and operations can be used in the PASS graph refinements. These functions and operations must be defined in the common part of the PASS graph refinements. This means that such a process type can only be used in process groups and clusters.

Process group types and process cluster types
Process group types and process cluster types can be defined in a similar way to process types.

The specification of a process group or process cluster type is very similar to that of a process type. Formal process names are used in the PASS graphs of cluster or group processes. A process group or cluster of a certain type is created by a declaration. In the declaration the formal names are replaced by actual names.

Process types can be used in the definition of a process group type or process cluster type. If process types are used the formal names in the process type definitions are replaced by formal names used in the process group or process cluster type specification.

Control Questions:

1. What are PASS graph refinements?
2. What are receive message specifications?
3. What are send message specifications?
4. What are internal function specifications?
5. What are internal operation specifications?
6. How can the module concept be used for refinement specifications?
7. How can object-oriented techniques be used for refinement specifications?
8. What are shared objects in PASS?
9. How are shared objects used?
10. How can the access to shared objects be specified?
11. What are process types?
12. How are incarnations of process types introduced into a specification?

Exercises:

1. How can your standard programming methodologies be used for the specification and development of refinements?
2. What is the SAPP oriented structure of a database application?
3. What are database transactions in an SAPP/PASS context?

14 Implementation of SAPP/PASS Specifications

This chapter describes how SAPP/PASS specifications are transformed into different types of programming languages.

One major goal of SAPP/PASS is to allow the easy transformation of a specification into executable code. The structure of the code, i.e. the design, is very close to the structure of a SAPP/PASS specification.

The PASS process code consists of a part which is dependent on the environment and an a other part which is independent of the it. The former implements
- message sending
- the input pool and message reception
- the timer mechanism
- the process interface to a scheduler if several processes are executed on the same processor. A scheduler assigns the processor to a process for a certain period of time.

The code which is independent of the environment consists of
- the PASS graph code
- the implementation of the PASS graph refinements.

The code structure of a process specified in PASS is shown in the following figure.

PASS Process

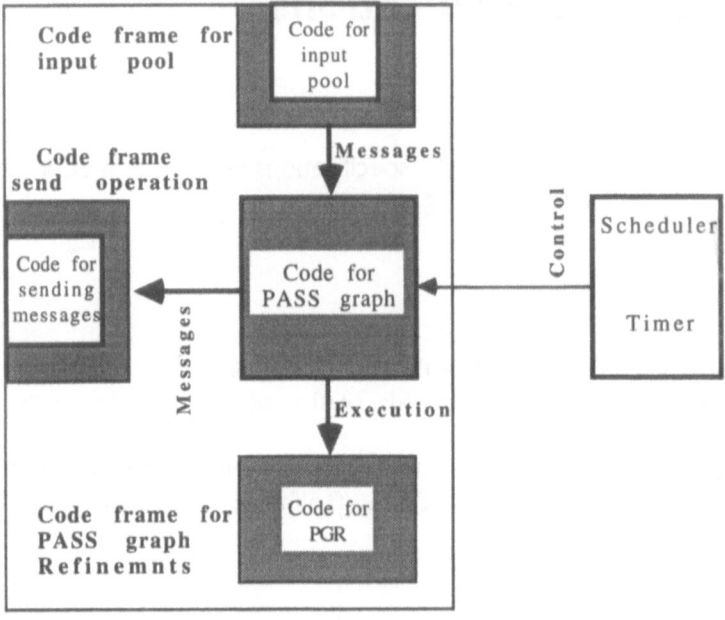

| | System dependent code |
| | System independent Code |

Figure 14.1: Code Structure of a PASS Process

The following figure shows the code structure of a system of concurrent processes specified in PASS.

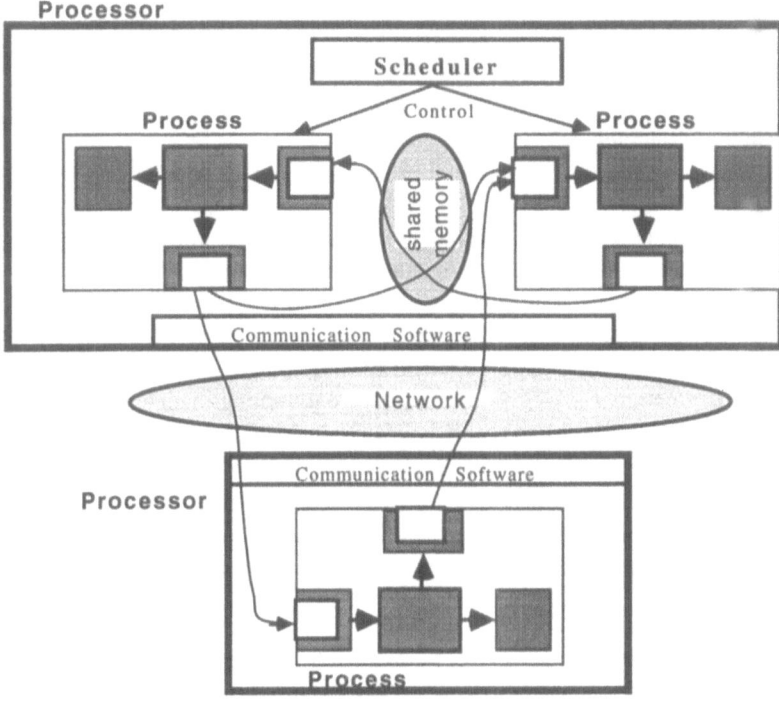

Figure 14.2: Code Structure of a System of Processes Specified in PASS

The above figure shows three processes: two processes are running on the same hardware system, the third process has its own processor. The processes running on the same hardware exchange messages using shared memory. In order to communicate with the other process a communication system has to be used. A scheduler on the system distributes the processor times to the two processes.

The implementation of exchanging messages and assigning processor time to processes can be based on available operating system facilities. Operating systems such as Unix already contain a process concept and functions for exchanging information between processes. A SAPP/PASS-oriented runtime environment which covers the required functionality should be based on an available operating system. A prototype of a runtime environment has been developed for MS-Windows /TISCH89/, /LIEB89/ and for a Transputer system /GREI89/.

The implementation of PASS graph refinements is dependent on the specification language used. It is therefore assumed that implementations of PASS graph refinements are derived using this specification language and the target programming language.

Only implementations of processes, PASS graphs and input pools are considered below. The implementation of these parts of a PASS specification depends on the properties of the target system being used for implementation. The facilities of the target system can be used in order to implement message exchange, scheduling and timing functions. The functions of the target system can be provided as operating system calls or they can be embedded in a programming language. In order to illustrate the transformation of a PASS specification into executable code we use three types of programming languages:

- Programming languages with parallel processes and send and receive operations.
- Programming languages with parallel processes, common objects and appropriate synchronisation methods – semaphores and monitors
- Sequential programming languages.

In the following sections an example of each of these language types is given to show the transformation of PASS processes into programming languages. In these examples not all aspects of PASS are considered. In certain cases it can be neccessary to introduce additional processes in order to communicate with the software system environment. To exchange messages with the environment using standard I/O devices additional processes must be implemented (see /BABA85/), i.e. device drivers. These aspects are not considered in the examples below in order to keep them simple.

14.1 Parallel Programming Languages with Message Operations

14.1.1 Language Overview

A variation of distributed PEARL /FLHO83/ is used to demonstrate the implementation of PASS graphs and input pools with this type of programming language. Distributed PEARL is based on PEARL /PEARL81/ and was designed for the implemention of distributed automation control programs. The language contains parallel processes and operations for exchanging messages. Distributed PEARL allows messages to be sent or received and it is also possible to offer or to expect different messages, i.e. guarded regions, at the same time. The semantics of the send and receive operations are very close to that of PASS. Messages can be exchanged both synchronously and asynchronously. Each PEARL process can have an input buffer. The size of the buffer is defined in the same way as in PASS but it is not possible to define structures or attributes. These restrictions are neglected here.

14.1.2 Implementation of PASS Graphs, Input Pools and Message Exchange

As described in the above section distributed PEARL contains nearly all the PASS concepts. It is only necessary to map the different PASS concepts onto the corresponding features of distributed PEARL.

The PASS input pool concept and message exchange actions are mapped to the input pool and send and receive operations of distributed PEARL.

A PASS process corresponds to a process in distributed PEARL. It is called a task.

Each send state of a PASS graph is represented in distributed PEARL by a label followed by sequential statements and a guarded region. The name of the label is representative of the state name. The values of the parameters of the offered messages are computed in the sequential statements. This corresponds to the execution of the send message specifications.

In a guarded region a process offers alternative messages. A process which can send a message performs the corresponding REACTION clause. The REACTION clause of a send state contains only a 'jump' statement to the label which marks the code sequence of the successor state.

The following figure shows an example of the transformation of a PASS send state into a code sequence of distributed PEARL.

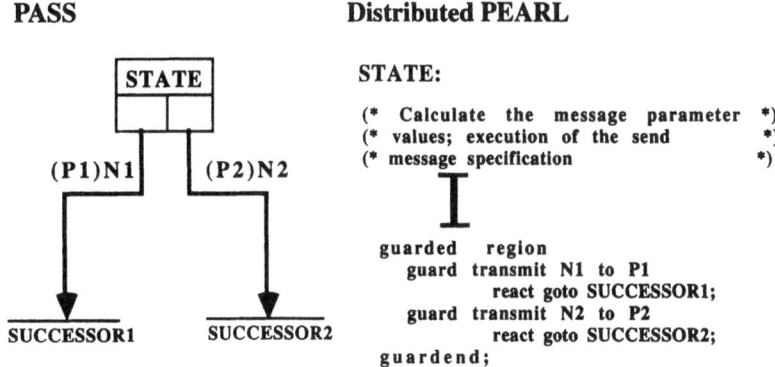

Figure 14.3: Transformation of a Send State into Distributed PEARL

The transformation of PASS receive states into distributed PEARL code sequences is similar to the transformation of send states. Each receive state in a PASS graph is represented by a label whose name is identical to the state name and by a guarded region where the different alternative messages are expected. When one of the expected messages is received, the process continues working and performs the REACTION clause of the message received. The reaction clause contains the code belonging to the specification of the receive message. Afterwards the process branches to the code sequence of the successor state.

The next figure shows an example of the transformation of a receive state with a time-out transition into a PEARL code sequence.

PASS   **Distributed PEARL**

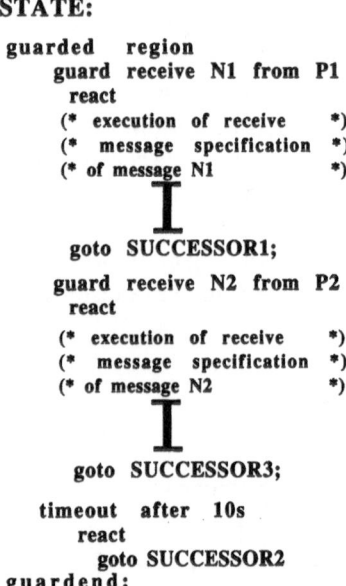

STATE:

```
guarded    region
     guard  receive  N1 from  P1
     react
     (* execution  of  receive      *)
     (*  message   specification    *)
     (* of message  N1              *)

            goto  SUCCESSOR1;

     guard  receive  N2 from  P2
     react

     (* execution  of  receive      *)
     (*  message   specification    *)
     (* of message  N2              *)

            goto  SUCCESSOR3;

     timeout   after   10s
          react
                goto SUCCESSOR2
guardend;
```

Figure 14.4: Transformation of a Receive State into Distributed PEARL

The transformation of the internal PASS states easily can be achieved by normal sequential program statements.

14.2 Parallel Programming Languages with Common Objects

14.2.1 Language Overview

Programming languages with common objects, use shared variables for communicating. Different processes can access common objects simultaneously and therefore the use of these objects must be synchronized. There are many mechanisms to solve synchronization problems. A well known synchronization mechanism is the use of semaphore variables. Semaphore variables are positive integers. Two operations are defined on semaphore variables: the V-operation where the value of a semaphore variable is incremented by one and the P-operation where the value of a semaphore variable is decremented by one if the value is greater than zero. A process wanting to execute a P-operation on a semaphore variable having the value zero will be blocked until another process increments the semaphore variable.

14.2.2 Implementation of Input Pools and Message Exchange

To implement a process system which is specified in PASS in a parallel language which supports shared variables and semaphores for synchronization, it is necessary to simulate the message exchange in accordance with PASS semantics. This simulation will be demonstrated using global variables and semaphores. A complete simulation of the PASS message transfer with common objects and semaphores is very difficult. We therefore make the following restrictions:
- Each process has an input pool greater than zero
- The PASS graphs of the processes involve send states with only one possible transition, i.e. only one message is offered.

With these restrictions input pools can be implemented using a buffer module with the following functions:
- A 'write' procedure which is called by sending processes that should send messages to the owner of the input pool. In this procedure the sending process has to decrement a semaphore before a message can be put into the buffer. This semaphore is initialized by the number of messages that can be deposited in the buffer and shows how many places in the buffer are vacant. If the semaphore cannot be decremented, the buffer is full and the calling process is blocked. If the semaphore can be decremented, the message is put into the buffer and another semaphore, the deposit semaphore, is incremented. This signals to the owner of the pool that a new message has been put into its buffer. The deposit semaphore is initialized with 0.
- A 'read' procedure which is called by the process that owns the buffer and should receive the message. A parameter of this procedure contains the name and sender of the expected message. If this message if found in the buffer, it is removed and the semaphore which tracks the number of available buffer places is incremented. If the message is not in the buffer, a return code 'not found' is given to the owner process, otherwise the return code is 'found'.

The buffer module described here is a very simple one. Buffer pools with structures and other attributes which are used in the PASS specification need more complex buffer modules.

14.2.3 Implementation of PASS Graphs

In section 14.1 a parallel programming language with input pool concepts and message exchange operations very similar to PASS was used to implement PASS. The PASS graph would be mapped into code and the implementation considered code-driven.

There is an other additional possible implementation solution for parallel languages with shared objects and sequential languages. Instead of converting the information about process behaviour contained in PASS graphs into code sequences, it can be converted into data. Here the implementation is data-driven.

Languages such as distributed PEARL cannot have data driven implementations because it is not possible to check which messages are in an input pool without removing messages.

Code Driven

In code driven implementations of PASS graphs, each send node corresponds to a code sequence whose structure is shown in following figure.

PASS   **Code**

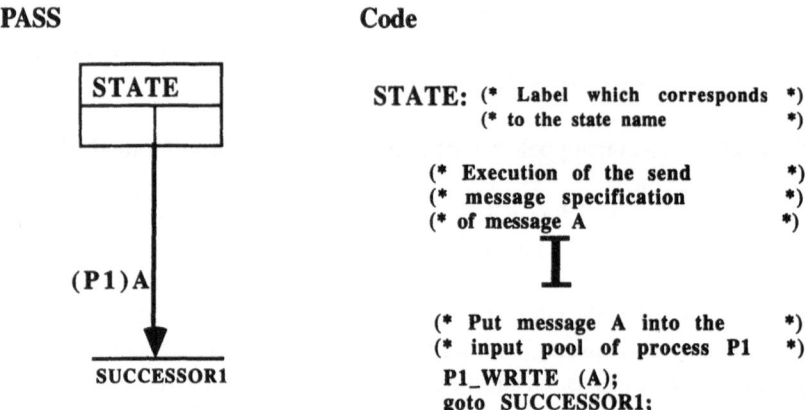

Figure 14.5: Send Nodes with simulated Message Sending

The structure of this code is very similar to the code structure used in distributed PEARL. First the values of the message parameters are computed and then an attempt is made to send the message by calling the send procedure of the receiver. A sending process remains blocked in the send procedure until the message can be placed in the input pool of the receiving process (see description of send procedure). When a message is sent, the process branches to the code sequence belonging to the successor state.

The code sequence for receiving messages is more complicated because several messages can be expected simultanously. Its structure is shown in the figure below.

PASS   **Code**

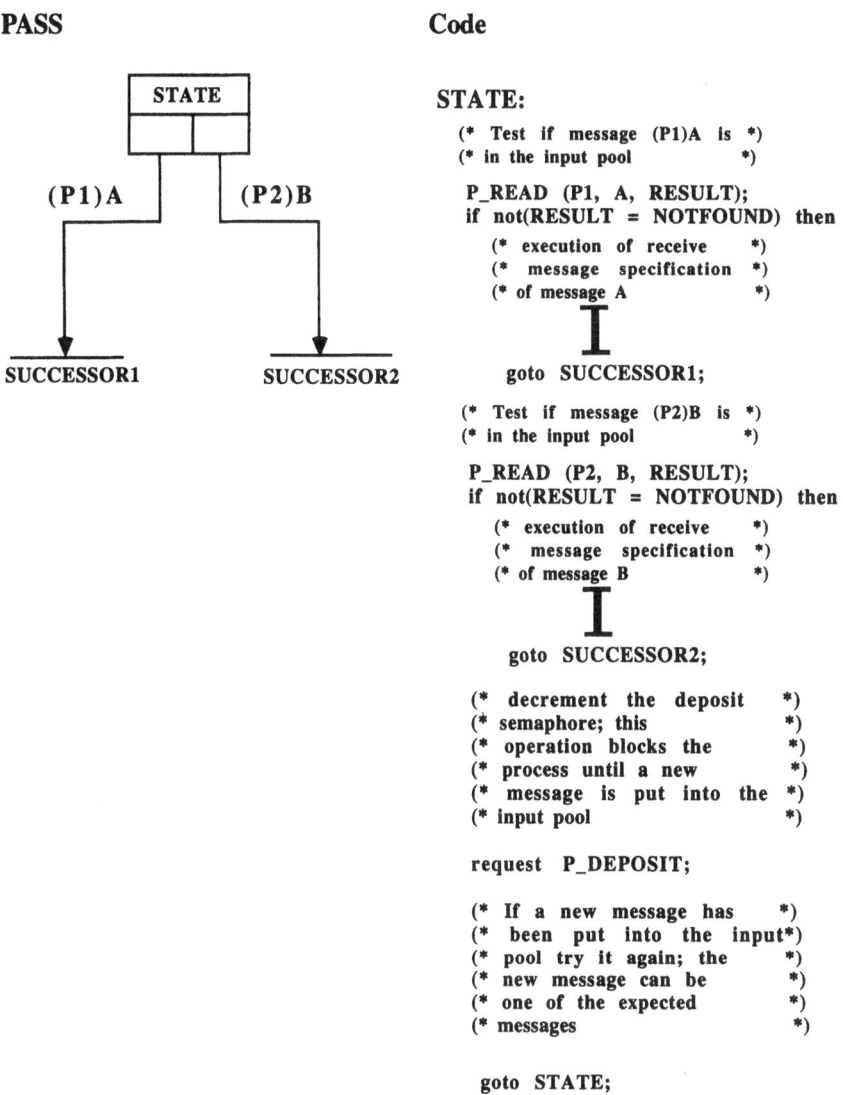

STATE:
```
(* Test if message (P1)A is *)
(* in the input pool        *)

P_READ (P1, A, RESULT);
if not(RESULT = NOTFOUND) then
    (* execution of receive     *)
    (* message specification    *)
    (* of message A             *)

              I

    goto SUCCESSOR1;

(* Test if message (P2)B is *)
(* in the input pool        *)

P_READ (P2, B, RESULT);
if not(RESULT = NOTFOUND) then
    (* execution of receive     *)
    (* message specification    *)
    (* of message B             *)

              I

    goto SUCCESSOR2;

(* decrement the deposit     *)
(* semaphore; this           *)
(* operation blocks the      *)
(* process until a new       *)
(* message is put into the   *)
(* input pool                *)

request P_DEPOSIT;

(* If a new message has      *)
(* been put into the input   *)
(* pool try it again; the    *)
(* new message can be        *)
(* one of the expected       *)
(* messages                  *)

    goto STATE;
```

Figure 14.6: Receiving Messages simulated by using Common Objects and Semaphores

A process checks whether a required message is in its input pool by calling the read operation. If the required message is in the buffer, it is removed and the parameter values are returned to the calling process. The value of the returned parameter 'found' shows that the required message is in the buffer. Now the code for the appropriate receive message specification is executed and the process branches to the code sequence of the successor state. If the required message is not in the input pool this is signalled by the return code value 'not found'. Then a process checks whether another expected message is in the input pool.

If none of the expected messages is in the input pool a process tries to decrement the deposit semaphore (see the receive procedure described above and shown in the above figure). The process is blocked until another process puts a message into the buffer and increments the deposit semaphore. Now the appropriate process checks again whether one of the expected messages, possibly the new message, is in the buffer.

Data Driven

All states and transitions of a PASS graph are stored in two arrays: the state array which contains all states and the transition array which contains all transitions /URB87/.

The following information is stored in an element of a state array:
- the state type: send, receive, function, operation
- indices identifying the possible transitions in the transition array
- the time for time guards if it is a receive or send node and the name of the internal operation or function if it is an internal operation or function state.

All states are identified by their indices in the state array.

Each element in the transition array represents a transition and contains the following information:
- the name of the triggering event,
- an index pointing to a transition array element which contains an alternative transition
- an index pointing to a state array element containing the description of the successor state.

The following figure shows an example of a PASS receive node and the corresponding description in a data structure:

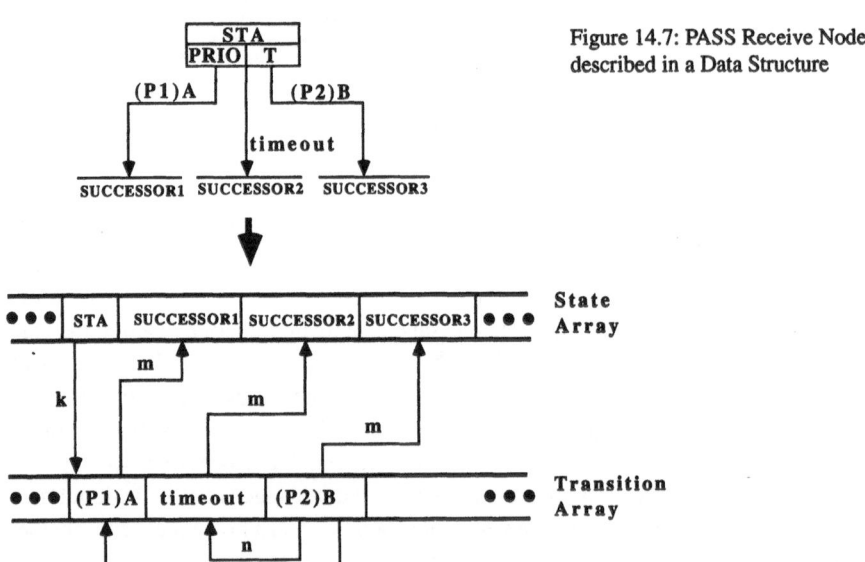

Figure 14.7: PASS Receive Node described in a Data Structure

The element in the state array describing a state X contains the index k of the transition array element which inturn contains the enabling condition of the permissible transition: receiving the message (P1)A. This transition array element contains the index l of a transition array element containing the description of an alternative transition (receiving the message (P2)B), and the index m of a state array element containing the description of the corresponding successor state SUCCESSOR_1.

Processes in the programming language representing PASS processes interpret data belonging to the structure described above. The code which interprets the data consists of four parts: code for handling receive states, send states, internal function states and internal operation states. In these, code segments procedures called mapping procedures, are called to identify the procedures which implement the receive message specification, send message specification, internal function specification and internal operation specification. The following figure shows the structure of a data driven implementation of a PASS process.

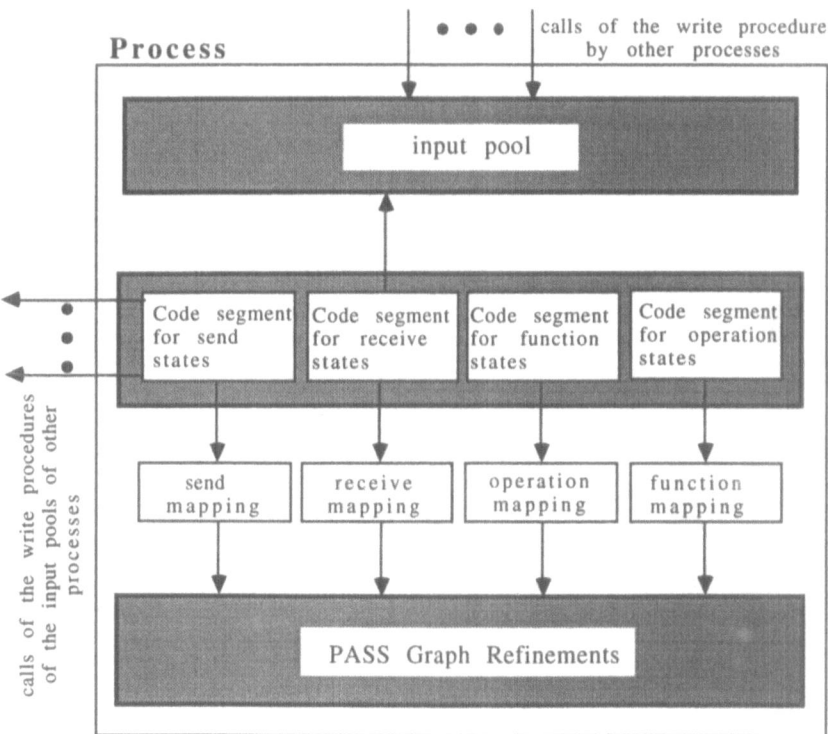

Figure 14.8: Data driven Implementation Structure of a PASS Process

The implementation of sending and receiving messages is identical to the implementation used in the code-driven version. The procedures implementing the message exchange are called in the mapping procedures.

14.3 Sequential Programming Languages

In the previous section (14.2) it was only necessary to simulate the message transfer. Sequential programming languages also have to simulate processes and message transfer. This simulation can be based on the facilities of an operating system.

14.3.1 Simulation of Processes

Each PASS process in a sequential language is represented by a procedure (henceforth called process procedure). The invocation of a process procedure implies that the process obtains control. The main program which gives control to the different process procedures contains the scheduling strategy. The main program calls the different process procedures, i.e. polls, using some suitable strategy. The program structure for data driven implementations is shown in the following figure.

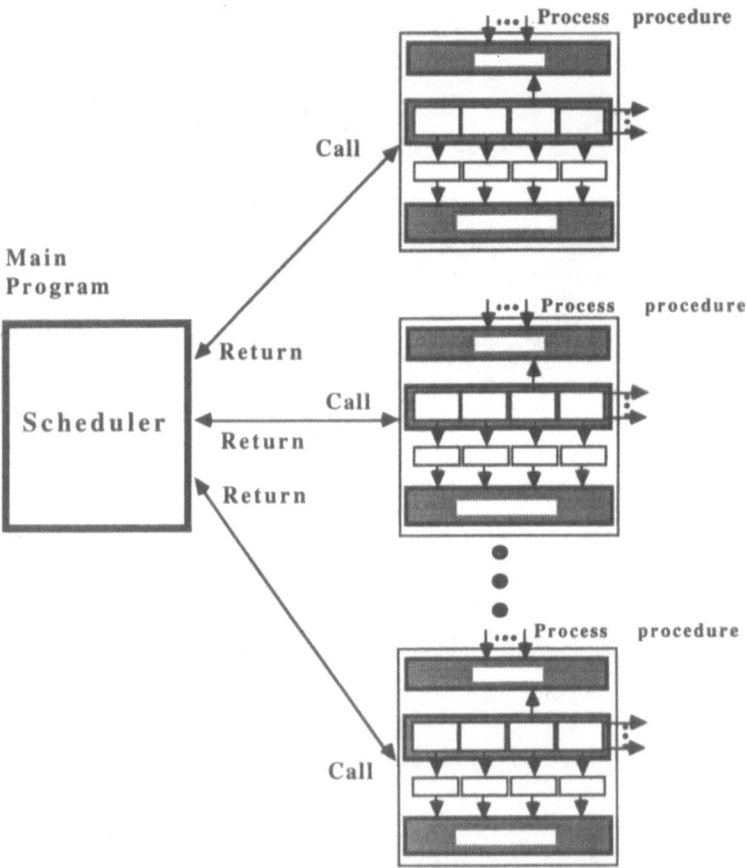

Figure 14.9: Structure of a Process System in a Sequential Language

If a process is blocked because it cannot send a message or an expected message cannot be received, the corresponding process procedure stores the current state and executes a 'return from procedure' statement. The next time the process procedure is called it will continue in that state. The current state of the process is stored in a process procedure variable since it must be remembered after completion of the process procedure call. This also applies to the local variables of a process. Therefore they are defined in the main program and are passed to the process procedure as parameters. If a process is code driven, the first statement in the process procedure is a 'jump' to the code sequence representing the current state. The following figure shows the structure of a process procedure if the process behaviour is code-driven. The parameter CURRENT_STATE_PX contains the current state of process PX.

```
procedure PX (LIST_OF_VARIABLES, CURRENT_STATE_OF_PX)
    begin
       goto CURRENT_STATE_OF_PX); (* indirect branch *)
       STATE_1:
```

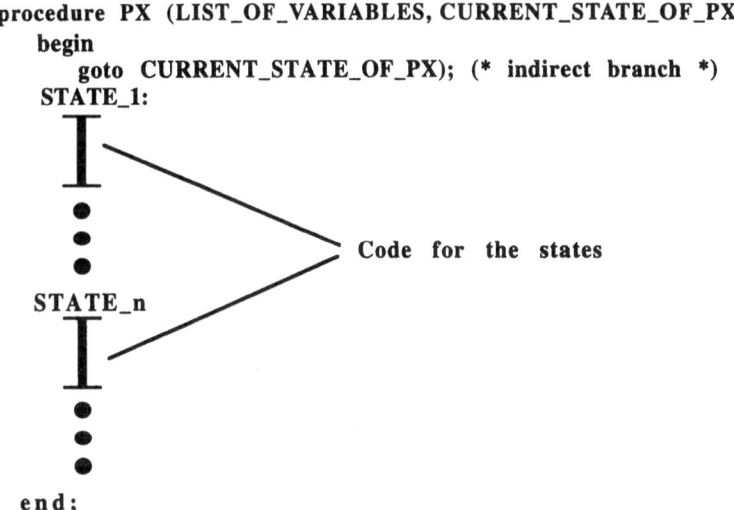

Figure 14.10: Structure of Code Driven Process Procedures

In the data-driven version nothing need be done because the current state variable contains the index of the state array element containing the current state. The structure of process procedures is the same as the structure of the data driven processes in section 14.2.3.

14.3.2 Implementation of Input Pools and Message Exchange

The restrictions stated in section 14.2 apply to the translation of a PASS specification into sequential language code, i.e. alternative sending is not allowed and all processes have input pools.

The input pool can be implemented as a buffer module with similar procedures as described in section 14.2.2:

- A 'write' procedure which places a message in a pool. A return parameter shows whether it was possible to put the message in the pool.
- A 'read' procedure which removes a message from the input set. A parameter contains the name of the sender and the message type. If the message is in the input pool, the message is removed from the buffer and the message parameter values are given to the caller together with a positive return code. If the message is not contained in the buffer, a negative return code is returned.

14.3.3 Implementation of PASS Graphs

The PASS graphs of a process can be implemented in a similar way to that discussed in section 14.2.2. The process behaviour can also be code or data driven.

Code-driven
If a process cannot place an offered message in the input pool of the receiver, it will receive a negative return code. In the previous version, a process is blocked in the 'write' procedure. Conceptually a process should be also blocked here except that this is not possible in sequential languages. Because each process in PASS is mapped onto a procedure, a process returns control by executing a return statement.

The following figure shows the code for send states.

PASS   **Code**

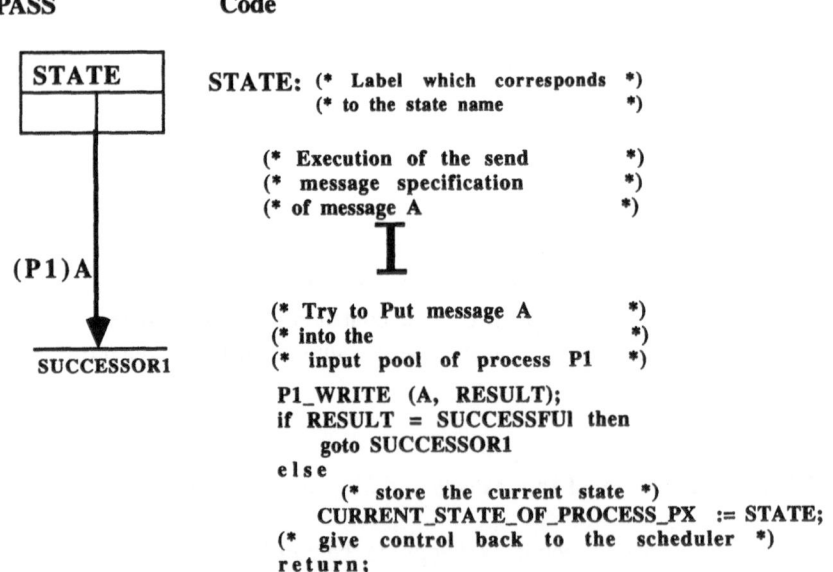

Figure 14.11: Message Sending simulated in an Sequential Language

The code sequence for receive states is shown in the next figure.

PASS

Code

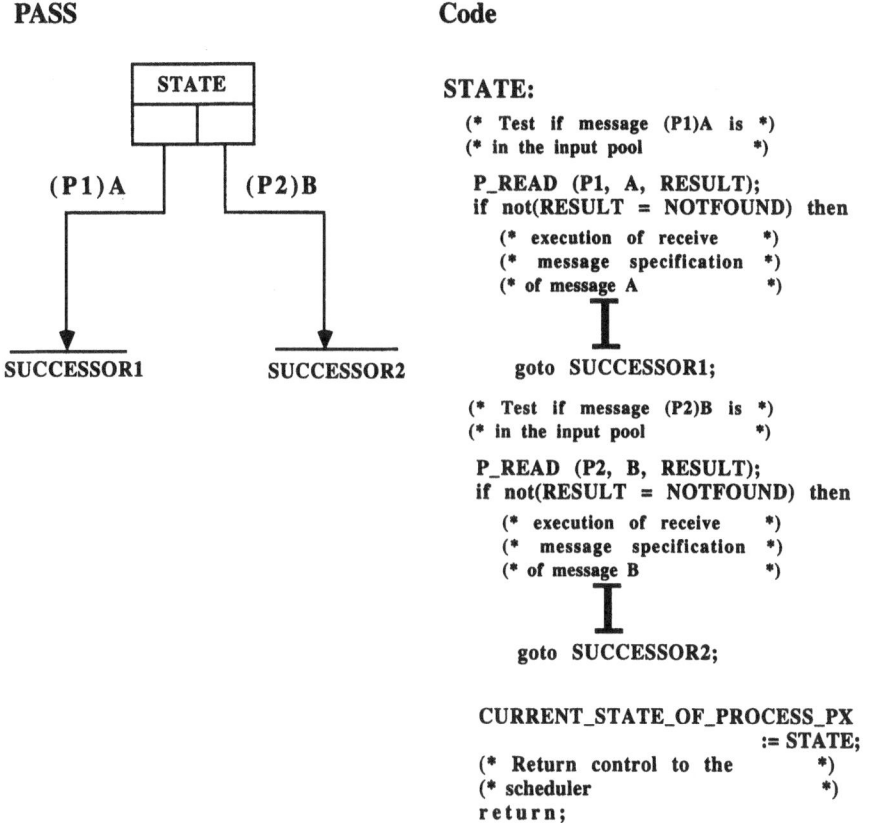

STATE:

```
(* Test if message (P1)A is *)
(* in the input pool          *)

P_READ (P1, A, RESULT);
if not(RESULT = NOTFOUND) then

    (* execution of receive      *)
    (*   message specification  *)
    (* of message A              *)

    goto SUCCESSOR1;

(* Test if message (P2)B is *)
(* in the input pool          *)

P_READ (P2, B, RESULT);
if not(RESULT = NOTFOUND) then

    (* execution of receive      *)
    (*   message specification  *)
    (* of message B              *)

    goto SUCCESSOR2;

CURRENT_STATE_OF_PROCESS_PX
                    := STATE;
(* Return control to the      *)
(* scheduler                  *)
return;
```

Figure 14.12: Messages Receiving simulated in a Sequential Language

Data-driven
The structure of the data driven process procedures is the same as that of parallel languages with shared variables. The procedures for sending and receiving messages are the same as for the code-driven version (see section 14.3.2). Instead of executing a P-operation on the deposit semaphore a return statement is executed. This means that control is returned from the process procedure to the main program, i.e. the scheduler. Returning control means that a process, i.e. a process procedure, is blocked.

Control Questions:

1. What is the code structure of a PASS process?
2. What is the code structure of a complete software system developed using SAPP/PASS?
3. What are the major characteristics of distributed PEARL?
4. How are input pools implemented in distributed PEARL?
5. How are PASS graphs mapped into distributed PEARL?
6. How are refinements mapped into distributed PEARL?
7. How can semaphores and shared data be used to simulate message exchange?
8. Which concepts are used to map a PASS graph into a programming language?

Exercises:

1. What are the properties of a concurrent programming language in your environment?
2. How can PASS programs be mapped into this programming language?
3. How can PASS programs be mapped into Fortran?
4. How can the interaction of PASS programs with their environment be implemented?

15 SAPP/PASS
Based Project Management

This chapter describes how general project management methods are applied in a project which is implemented using SAPP/PASS methods.

15.1 SAPP/PASS Based Program Development Activities

The order in which the SAPP/PASS development activities are carried out depends on the life cycle to be used and the development activities based on SAPP/PASS which were described in section 9.3.

If the conventional life cycle is used the development activities are carried out in the order in which they are described. If the evolutionary or incremental life cycle is used the different development activities are interleaved.

15.1.1 Context Identification

The first activity is the identification of the context in which a software system is to be used. The software system requirements are defined in terms of the relation to the context. This includes different user classes, other programs on the same or remote computer systems and technical processes. The description of the context includes the interactions of each context entity with the system to be developed. These interactions can be regarded as SAPP/PASS messages or shared data, i.e. the messages have a type and parameters.

In addition to this abstract specification of the interaction between external entities and the program to be developed, the implementation of the interaction must also be specified. If an external entity is represented by a user or user class the interaction between the user and the program is implemented by standard I/O. This means that the context specification will include the different screens that are used for communication between the user and the program. The name of the screen is the message type and the different fields in the screen are the message parameters. The functions related to a screen and its data are informally described. The operations invoked by each screen are defined. This means that a complete user manual is the final result.

The same considerations apply to the interaction between the program to be developed and the entities of a technical process. Instead of standard I/O devices, process I/O devices such as analogue I/O, digital I/O, and signal I/O are used. Entities of technical processes are valves, switches, stepping motors, etc. Their behaviour in relation to the control program can be also described in PASS. An implementation of the behaviour of external entities can be used as a test bed.

Interrupts can be seen as messages from an external entity to the program.

The interaction with already existing programs can be considered, simular to the communication between users and technical processes. Functions of existing programs are invoked by messages. The results are also received from existing programs via messages. In order to implement these, it may be necessary to implement some adaption procedures.

A different type of interaction between programs takes place if they share data. A system to be developed can share data with an existing program. This means that the new system has access to already existing data bases.

The context specification can be regarded as the requirements specification of a new system.

Depending on the life cycle which is used it may be that the context specification must not be completed before other SAPP/PASS activities can be performed. It is possible that only parts of a context are considered in a first version of the program. Other parts can be deferred for further investigation.

15.1.2 Decomposition

After some context specification activities, the system to be defined is broken down into smaller pieces. Each component or process set is refined in a stepwise manner. The task of each component, process set or process is informally described.

In parallel to this, the messages which are exchanged between the various components, process sets and processes are identified. This means that the names of these messages are specified, some or all of the parameters are defined and the meanings of the various message types are informally described.

During the decomposition activities, the design of the system is specified. Components of the system and how they work together are identified.

It is not necessary to decompose a system in one step. Some components can be identified as far as the process level. Others can only be specified very vaguely. They are defined in more detail in a later step.

15.1.3 Process Specification

The specification of a process follows straightforwardly the structure of a process.

Input pool specification:
The features of the input pool should be specified first. The maximum size of an input pool is an indication of how closely this process cooperates with other processes. An input pool size of zero, i.e. synchronous message exchange, couples a process very closely to its partners.

Behaviour:
After a first draft of an input pool specification the behaviour of a process is defined. The specification of the process behaviour is started with the main paths. In succeeding steps exception handling is added.

If the same behaviour pattern occurs in different branches of the process behaviour macros should be defined. This allows the hierarchical description of process behaviour.

Refinements
The refinements are the last detail of a process. The parameters of the messages and the local data of the process are finally defined. The refinements are specified as sequential programs and already existing programs are integrated. If object oriented development techniques are used object classes which can also be used in refinements of other processes should be identified.

Shared refinements, i.e. objects, are specified if the refinements of the processes which have access to them are already defined.

It is not necessary to specify the processes sequentially. It may become necessary to switch from one process to another, for example, if a new parameter is required for a message, at least two processes are involved. The refinements of the sending and receiving processes must be adapted.

15.1.4 Process Implementation and Test

The implementation follows exactly the concepts described in the previous chapter. The standard parts of the code can be generated by suitable tools.

Communication between processes and between processes and external entities requires special attention. Five cases can be distinguished:
- The communicating processes are located on the same processor
- The communicating processes are located on different processors
- The process communicates with an external entity which is a human user
- The process communicates with an external entity which is a technical process
- The process communicates with an external entity which is another program

All these types of message exchanges should be implemented using existing operating systems. The underlying operating systems e.g. UNIX and Windows NT, provide functions which make it much easier to implement process communication. All multiuser or multitask operating systems contain process concepts and the related communication and synchronisation mechanisms. The SAPP/PASS concepts can be mapped onto these mechanisms. In the most simple case this means that each PASS process is mapped onto one process of the operating system. Communication systems based on various protocols such as ISO/OSI or TCP/IP can be used to implement communication between processes on different processors. Standard I/O packages can be used to implement the communication with the users.

A program can be tested step by step in accordance with the structure of a program based on SAPP/PASS development concepts.

Refinement tests:
The process refinements are implemented using methods which are common in standard sequential programming and are tested using available debuggers.

Behaviour test:
The behaviour of a process as specified and implemented is compared with the communication behaviour of the environment.

Input pool test:
The specification of the input pool is tested to see whether it meets the intended synchronisation requirements.

Process test:
The interworking of all the components of a process as described above, are tested to see whether they work in the right way. Test tools simulate the environment of a process.

Communication:
The implementation of the various communication mechanisms can also be tested separately.

Subsystem test:
When the above tests have been completed the subsystems can be tested. The environment of a subsystem can be simulated using test tools.

System test:
After subsystem tests the complete system can be tested. In a first step the context is simulated, then the system can be incorporated step by step into the complete context.

15.2 Project Management Activities

15.2.1 Planning a Software Project

In planning a project, the first decision is which type of life cycle is to be used. The planning steps are carried out, based on this life cycle.

Planning a software project means decomposing a system into work packages and assigning people to particular work packages for a certain period of time. The different decomposition steps of SAPP can be considered as part of a WBS. The highest level of a WBS corresponds to the SAPP decomposition steps:

1. Decomposition of the environment
2. Decomposition of the system.
   The following figure shows the corresponding WBS diagram.

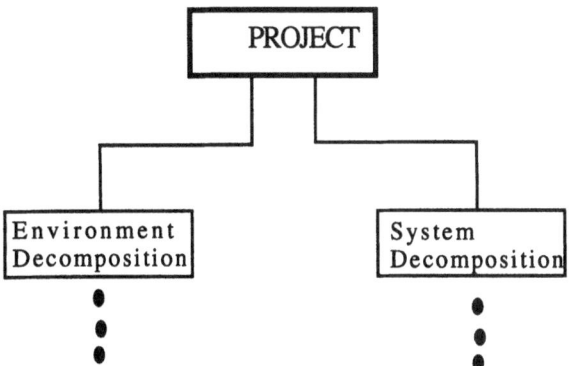

Figure 15.1: WBS Level one if SAPP/PASS is Used

The components, process sets and processes which are defined in step 2 correspond to the work packages. Following the decomposition steps in SAPP, each work package is refined step by step. The SAPP decomposition hierarchy is part of the corresponding WBS. How the different parts of a SAPP hierarchy are inserted in a WBS depends on the life cycle used. The following figure shows a WBS based on SAPP/ PASS and a conventional life cycle.

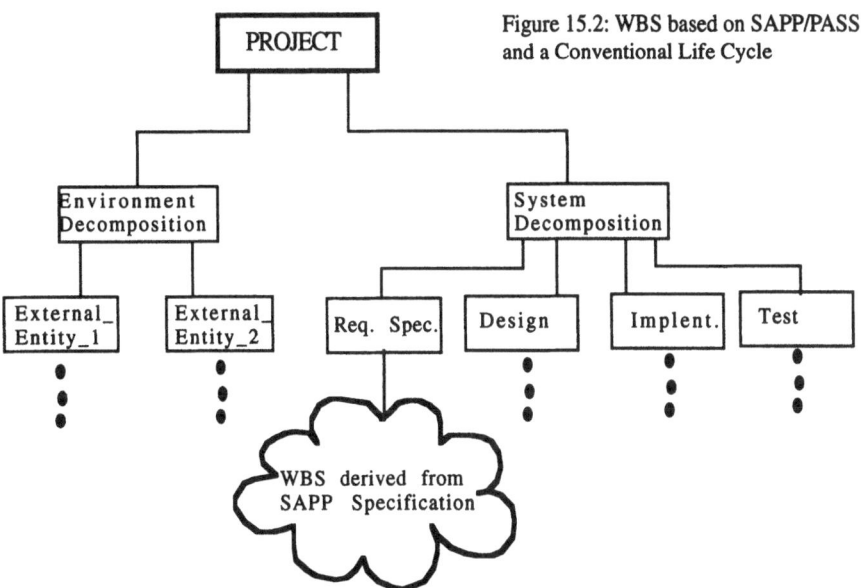

Figure 15.2: WBS based on SAPP/PASS and a Conventional Life Cycle

If an incremental life cycle is used instead the conventional life cycle the WBS is as shown in the figure below.

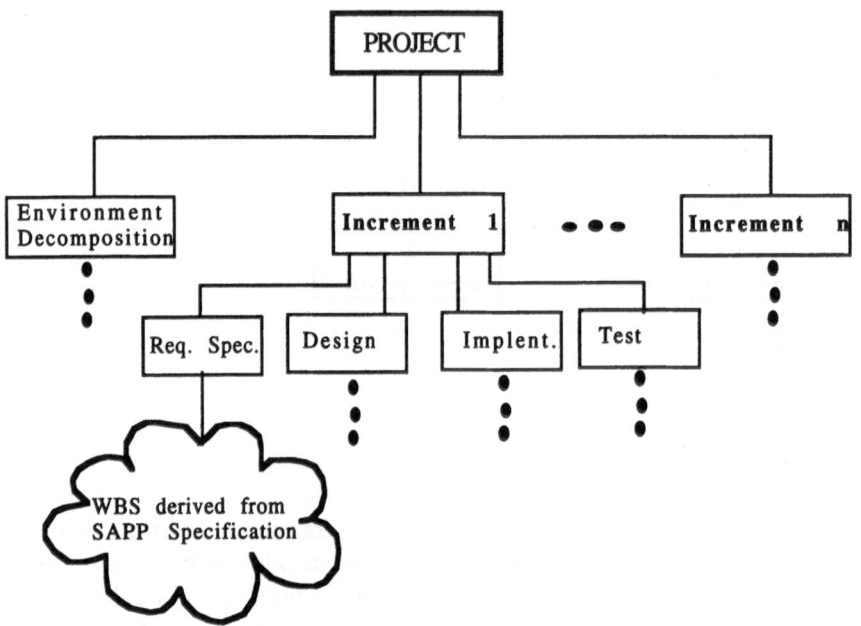

Figure 15.3: WBS based on SAPP/PASS and an Incremental Life Cycle

Each work package on the different WBS levels is described using planning information. The figure below shows a suggestion for a planning form for each work package. The planning forms are based on the corresponding SAPP symbols for components, process sets and processes. Each of the coresponding planning form is identical. The following figure shows a planning form for a process set.

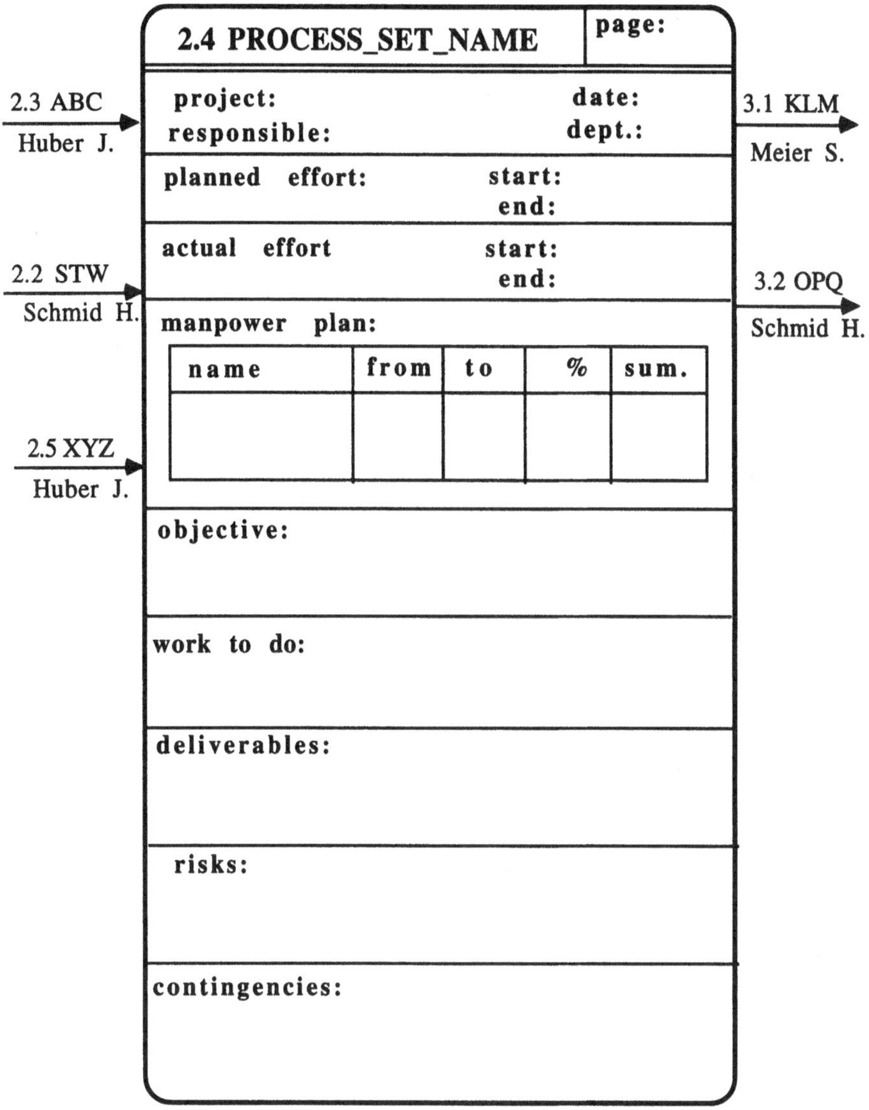

2.4 PROCESS_SET_NAME	page:

2.3 ABC
Huber J.

2.2 STW
Schmid H.

2.5 XYZ
Huber J.

3.1 KLM
Meier S.

3.2 OPQ
Schmid H.

project: date:
responsible: dept.:

planned   effort: start:
                           end:

actual   effort   start:
                           end:

manpower   plan:

name	from	to	%	sum.

objective:

work to do:

deliverables:

risks:

contingencies:

Figure 15.4: Planning Form for a Process Set.

Components, process sets and processes, exchange message sets and messages with each other. The planning form contains the names of the work packages, the same as the names of the components, process sets and processes, to which message sets and messages are sent and from which message sets and messages are received (the related work packages). The name of the person responsible is shown in addition to the name of the work package. The communication structure of the specification also defines the communication structure of the development team. Each developer knows the names of the developers responsible for the work packages.

The different SAPP decomposition levels imply a hierarchy of work packages and also a hierarchy of responsibilities. A developer responsible for a certain work package also has to communicate with the developer responsible for the work package at the above level.

15.2.2 Project Organizing, Directing and, Controlling

The organisation of a project involves assigning people to different work packages for a certain period of time. In addition, it must be defined who is responsible for each work package. The hierarchy of responsibilities is related to the different SAPP decomposition levels. There is a project manager for the entire system under development. Depending on the size of the project, there is a project leader for each component and process set. Several components and process sets can be assigned to the same project leader as work packages. The communication paths between project leaders and developers are defined by the communication structure specified in SAPP. Project leaders who are responsible for components and process sets which exchange message sets or messages must also communicate with each other.

Directing a software project mainly involves maintaining the communication paths between the project leaders and the developers responsible for the various work packages. Developers responsible for related work packages must also communicate in order to define the details of the messages exchanged between their work packages. Each developer responsible for a work package can arrange meetings with developers responsible for related work packages. The results of these meeting are documented in the minutes of the meeting. The developer responsible for the work package of the level above receives the minutes of these meetings in order to keep him informed.

Depending on the size of the project several levels of project leaders or project managers can be required. This hierarchy is also along the hierarchical structure of the program to be developed. The developers responsible for work packages that belong to the same work package of the level above report to the developer responsible for that higher work package. A developer receives status reports from all developers responsible for work packages which belong to his work package. Status reports appear very similar to work package specification forms. They contain information about effort consumed, development delays, risks, next actions, etc.

In summary, the project organisation is a mxture between network and hierarchical structures and follows closely the structure of the program to be developed.

15.3 Quality Assurance

Quality control can be performed easier if quality can be measured and does not only depend on a subjective view. Measured results define quality to a certain extent. This does not mean that subjective factors are not important; many important quality factors cannot be measured e.g. it is difficult to measure why different people prefer different types of user interfaces.

In this section we want to concentrate on measurable aspects of programs based on the SAPP/PASS software engineering environment. We want to give an impression of how these measurable control values affect the engineering attributes described in chapter 7. For each of these control values a maximum value, minimum value and average value can be measured and each of these values gives an indication of the quality of a system. Tools allow these control values to be can be evaluated more or less automatically. Currently there is not enough data available to allow precise values to be assigned to quality estimators. We can only describe some ideas how SAPP/PASS control values relate to the quality criteria described in /DEU88/.

The following examples of control values can be defined in SAPP/PASS:

SAPP oriented control numbers:
- number of external entities
- number of different messages sent to or received from external entities
- decomposition levels in each component
- number of subcomponents in each component
- number of messages received per component
- number of messages sent per component
- number of shared objects such as data bases
- number of reused shared objects such as existing databases
- number of reused subsystems, i.e. parts of former projects

PASS oriented control values:
- size of input pools
- number of states in PASS graphs
- number of internal operations and functions
- number of results per internal function or operation
- number of parameters per message received from or sent to other processes
- number of parameters of messages sent to or received from external entities
- number of different object classes used in refinements
- number of class levels
- number of different refinements where objects of the same object classes are used
- number of reused classes, functions etc.

Implementation control values:
- number of processes per processor
- number of messages sent to or received from processes on other processors
- transmission time for messages exchanged between processes executed on the same processor.
- transmission time for messages exchanged between processes executed on different processors depending on the transmission system.
- number of failures per year per transmission line

- number of remote procedure calls in refinements
- number of user I/O's, i.e. the number of screens
- number of I/O fields per screen
- number of user screens which cannot be used if one processor fails
- number of reused software modules in refinements
- number of operating system processes or threads which are required to implement one PASS process.

Depending on particular features of a system implementation, other control values can be added, e.g. the number of interrupts per second which can be handled.

It was explained in chapter 7 how quality attributes are mapped to engineering attributes /DEUT88/. SAPP/PASS allows some of the control values to be converted directly to quality attributes. Other control values are only used as control indicators via engineering attributes. Some possible relationships between quality attributes, engineering attributes, and SAPP/PASS control values are discussed below.

Correctness:
Completeness, consistency, and traceability are directly supported by SAPP/PASS, e.g. tools can check automatically whether a specification is complete. It can be checked whether there is a receiver for each message which is sent or whether there is receive message specification for each message to be received, etc.

Efficiency:
Efficiency of communication:
- number of parameters per message received from or sent to other processes
- number of messages sent to or received from processes on other processors
- running on the same processor.
- number of failures per year per transmission line
- number of remote procedure calls in refinements
- number of parameters per message received from or sent to other processes

Efficiency of processing:
- decomposition levels of each component
- number of class levels
- number of results per internal function or operation
- number of internal operations and functions
- number of different object classes used in refinements
- number of class levels
- number of processes per processor
- number of remote procedure calls in refinements
- number of operating system processes or threads which are required to implement one PASS process.

Efficiency of data storage:
- number of shared objects such as data bases
- number of reused shared objects such as existing databases
- number of different object classes used in refinements
- number of different refinements where objects belonging to the same object classes are used
- number of reused classes, functions etc.

Further control values must be added, especially for database oriented applications /DEMAR82/.

Expandability:

This quality attribute is supported by the following engineering attributes: extendability, generality, modularity, self-descriptiveness and simplicity. These engineering attributes are directly supported by SAPP/PASS, especially modularity, self-descriptiveness, and simplicity.

Integrity:

This quality attribute is covered by SAPP/PASS itself.

Interoperabilty:

The SAPP/PASS approach supports a standard philosophy for interfaces between different programs and the integration of existing programs into a SAPP/PASS based program.

Maintainability:

The related engineering attributes – completeness, consistency, modularity, self-descriptiveness, simplicity, traceability and visability – are mainly covered by the following SAPP/PASS control values:
- the number of different messages sent to or received from external entities
- the number of decomposition levels in each component
- the number of subcomponents in each component
- the number of received messages per component
- the number of sent messages per component
- the number of shared objects such as data bases
- the number of reused shared objects such as existing databases
- the number of reused subsystems, i.e. parts of former projects
- the number of of states in PASS graphs
- the number of internal operations and functions
- the number of different object classes used in refinements
- the number of class levels
- the number of different refinements where objects of the same object classes are used
- the number of reused classes, functions, etc.
- the number of operating system processes or threads which are required to implement one PASS process.

Manageability:
This is an inherant property of SAPP/PASS. The decomposition concepts in SAPP/PASS allows a problem to be broken down into manageable pieces. After changes have been made tools can check the consistency of a changed specification.

Portability:
Programs based on SAPP/PASS can be ported easily to their operating system or hardware platforms. Those parts which are dependent on the target system are clearly defined and separated from the operating system and those parts which are independent of the hardware.

Usability:
– the number of user I/Os, i.e. the number of screens
– the number of I/O fields per screen
In addition to these control values, other control values depending on the application, can be defined, e.g. the number of inputs required to obtain a particular information.

Reliability:
It is necessary to define control values for the following engineering attributes: accuracy, anomaly management, functional scope, generality, and independence. These control values depend on the application. The engineering attributes modularity, self-descriptivenes, simplicity, and support are covered by the SAPP/PASS development methodology.

Safety:
It is necessary to define control values for the engineering attributes accuracy and anomaly management. Distributivity is inherent in programs developed according to SAPP/PASS.

Survivability:
Apart from anomaly management the engineering attributes autonomy and distributivity are directly covered by SAPP/PASS.

Testability:
This aspect is mainly covered by the SAPP/PASS methodology itself. The different components of a SAPP/PASS based program can be tested independently and separately.

Verfiability:
Verifiability is characterised by the engineering attributes modularity, self-descriptiveness, simplicity, support, traceability, and visibility. These are also mostly covered by the SAPP/PASS methodology.

The direct relationship of quality attributes and engineering attributes to SAPP/
PASS, or to control values which SAPP/PASS supports, provide a high degree of
quality assurance.

Recommended reading:

/DEMAR82/ DeMarco T.
                Controlling Software Projects - Management, Measurement and Esti-
                mation
                Yourdan/Prentice Hall, Englewood Cliffs, 1982
                This book provides a detailed example how control   values can
                be found for structured analysis and design.

/DEUT88/ Deutsch M. S.
                Software Quality Engineering
                Prentice Hall, Englewood Cliffs 1988
                This book is a very deep and sythematic discussion of software qual-
                ity assurance.

Control Questions:

1. What are the major development activities of the SAPP/PASS methodology?
2. What is context identification?
3. What is system decomposition?
4. What are the steps in process specification?
5. What are the SAPP/PASS implementation and test steps?
6. What are the SAPP/PASS-oriented project management activities?
7. How is a SAPP/PASS-oriented project planned?
8. How is a SAPP/PASS oriented project organised directed, and controlled?
9. What is quality control for a SAPP/PASS oriented development project?

Exercises:

1. What is the difference between the project management methods which you currently use and the SAPP/PASS oriented methods?
2. What are your quality assurance strategies?

16 PASS Based Computer Aided Software Engineering

The different methods which can be used to develop tools are described It is shown how theoretical approaches can be applied to software engineering tools.

The basic concepts of SAPP/PASS are:
- structured decomposition
- graphical representation of system structure
- structured specification of processes i.e. synchronisation, behaviour, data types
- graphical specification of process behaviour

In this chapter tools and the associated concepts are described. These tools allow
- consistency checks
- prototyping
- automatic code generation

With these concepts all the properties described in chapter 8 can be supported in principal. Not all conceivable tools have yet been implemented. The development of tools has been concentrated on areas where we expected conceptual problems. In the following sections either the concepts for the tools or the tools themselves are described.

16.1 Tool Concepts for Structured Decomposition

There are no problems in principle in developing tools which can draw message flow diagrams to describe the message dictionary, and to perform consistency checks. The symbols for message flow diagrams (MFDs) are very similar to the symbols used for data flow diagrams (DFDs) /DEMAR79/, /YOCO79/, /GASA79/. There are only a few restrictions in using the different symbols, e.g. message arrows are not allowed between system subsets which have access arrows to the same object. This means that tools for drawing and analysing MFDs can be used which are very similar to tools used for data flow diagrams. An overview of different tools based on data flow diagrams is given in /MCCLU89a/. These tools also contain facilities for describing and managing data dictionaries (DDs). The close relationship between DDs and MDs implies that the functions of DDs can also be applied to MDs.

16.2 Tools for Describing Processes

A PASS specification of a process has the following main parts:
- input pool
- PASS graph
- PASS graph refinements.

Tools can be developed for each of these parts to support the description of PASS processes.

Tools for describing input pools are very simple and no problems in principle are expected. A specification tool for input pools is a simple menu which asks for the different properties of the input pool.

Tools for describing PASS graph refinements depend on the method used. The PASS graph refinements (PGR) are mainly independent of the other parts of a process description and are more or less a data type with a certain number of operations and functions i.e. receive message specifications, send message specifications, internal operations and internal functions. Therefore any method for specifying data types and related tools can be chosen. We have not yet developed special tools for PGRs.

To describe PASS graphs an editor called PATE – PASS Transition Editor – was developed. PATE is a menu driven program which operates on the textual representation of a PASS graph called a PASS table. A textual notation was chosen for the editor in order to avoid the problems common to all graphical editors. We wanted to concentrate on problems specific to PASS.

As described in section 12.1.7 each line in the textual notation corresponds to a transition in the PASS graph and consists of four items:
- current state
- event type
- event
- successor state

In addition each PASS entry which represents a transition can have an info-line. This can contain comments or be used to document the history of changes in a PASS graph.

The procedures supplied by PATE for manipulating and managing PASS graphs are accessible via menus and can be divided into four groups:

INPUT/OUTPUT:
The input/output procedures are used to store, load and print a PASS table according the requirements of the user. It is also possible to store a PASS graph as text. This allows the use of ordinary text editors to manipulate PASS graph descriptions.

EDITING:
Special functions are provided for editing PASS graphs and their state and event names. PASS entries and info-lines can be added, deleted and manipulated in several other ways.

CONSISTENCY CHECKING:
Sinks, sources, islands and unreachable states in a PASS graph can be detected by special checking procedures.

OPTIMISATION:
States and transitions in a PASS graph can be removed in such a way that both the original and the optimised PASS graphs are equivalent with respect to the sequence of events.

SUBSETTING:
This function is only important when developing communication software. The subsetting operations discard unnecessary transitions and paths.

The special PATE features – error checking, optimisation and subsetting – are described in more detail below.

16.2.1 Consistency Checking

The PASS transition editor, PATE, provides two kinds of error checking mechanisms: implicit or local error checking, and explicit or global error checking.

Implicit error checking:
Implicit error checking relates to a subset of transitions which are affected by the specification of new transitions. In order to avoid invalid transitions in a PASS graph new PASS entries which do not satisfy certain consistency conditions are rejected. The consistency conditions reflect the fact that a PASS graph must be deterministic. For example, it is not possible to specify a transition twice or to include transitions which are identical except for their successors. This kind of local error checking is always done automatically when a new transition is added to a PASS graph.

Explicit error checking:
Explicit error checking can also be regarded as global error checking since the whole PASS graph is searched for specification errors. A special menu supplies a set of procedures which can detect errors of the following kinds:

Sinks and sources:
A PASS graph can be checked for states which have no direct successors (sinks) or predecessors (sources).

Unreachable states:
Every PASS graph has an entry point which is also called the starting state. All other states in a PASS graph must be reachable from this entry point, i.e. there must be a path between the starting state and every other state. States which are not reachable from the starting state, i.e. islands, are marked by a special procedure.

Islands:

An island denotes a set of states which is not reachable from the other states in a PASS graph.

These errors are not always obvious in large PASS graphs and are usually hard to detect during the specification process.

16.2.2 Optimisation

The optimization operations are based on minimisation algorithms from the theory of finite state machines /AHUL77/.

The possibility of optimizing a PASS table is based on the fact that only the sequence of events and the relations between them is relevant for the PASS graph specification. As every event in a PASS graph corresponds to special program code produced by the generator, the deletion of an event results in a smaller PASS table and also reduces the amount of program code produced for the specific application. There is a special optimization procedure which compresses a PASS table in such a way that the original and the optimized PASS graph are equivalent in the sense that both graphs have the same sequences of events. In many cases a PASS graph contains transition sequences with identical parallel transition events. This means that starting from different PASS graph states identical sequences of events can be found which lead to the same successor state. If such a constellation is detected in a PASS graph the following optimization can be performed. Instead of keeping identical event sequences with different state names in the PASS graph, one representative transition sequence is chosen. All other transition sequences whose events match the events of the representative transition sequence can be replaced by the representative transition sequence. The figure below shows a very simple part of a PASS graph which can be used to demonstrate the optimization described:

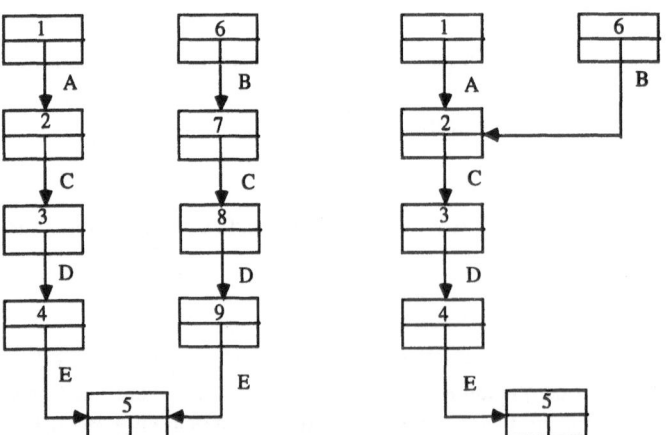

Figure 16.1: Optimization of identical Transition Sequences in a PASS graph

The original graph on the left of the figure has identical sequences of events C-D-E starting from state 2 and state 7 and leading to the common successor state 5. Changing the arc of event B from successor 7 to successor 2 does not change the possible event sequences, as shown in the graph on the right. This optimization saves 3 transitions and 3 states.

In a protocol specification state names or parts of state names mostly represent certain semantics, e.g. a connection is established in the states CONNECTEDxx. Since there is a merging of state names or a complete discarding of classes of state names in the optimisation described, the clearness and readability are reduced. Therefore an optimization should only be performed before the transformation of the PASS graph into program code. The complete specification should only be used for maintenance.

In extensive protocol specifications as in the PASS specification of the full ISO-Session-layer /ISO8326/, /ISO8327/, /FLCHEF87/, the above optimization step leads to an 8% reduction in the number of transitions from 5540 to 5081 and a 19% reduction in the number of states from 1462 to 1183.

16.2.3 Subsetting

The user or application requirements of certain communication systems may not make full use of all the facilities provided. According to the ISO/OSI model, services are represented by service primitives. In a PASS specification of communication software service primitives are implemented by messages.

PATE provides a function for removing service primitives represented by messages when a complete communication service is not requested. This allows a flexible adaptation of the communication service to the user requirements. If a PATE user wants to remove a certain facility from a communication service specification, he must to declare to PATE the service primitives, i.e. messages, which provide these facilities. These events will no longer occur. PATE discards all these transition entries and reduces the PASS table. Paths to the next state with more than one predecessor are also removed.

The figure below shows an example of a graph in which the receive events R3 and R4 should be removed. After deleting transition R3, the successor state 4, and the transition O1, the deletion must stop because state 7 is also reachable from state 8. Discarding event R4 implies deletion of the succeeding event O2 and the succeeding paths with states 7, 10, 13. The path consisting of states 8, 11, 14 is erased up to state 14 because state 14 can be reached from state 15.

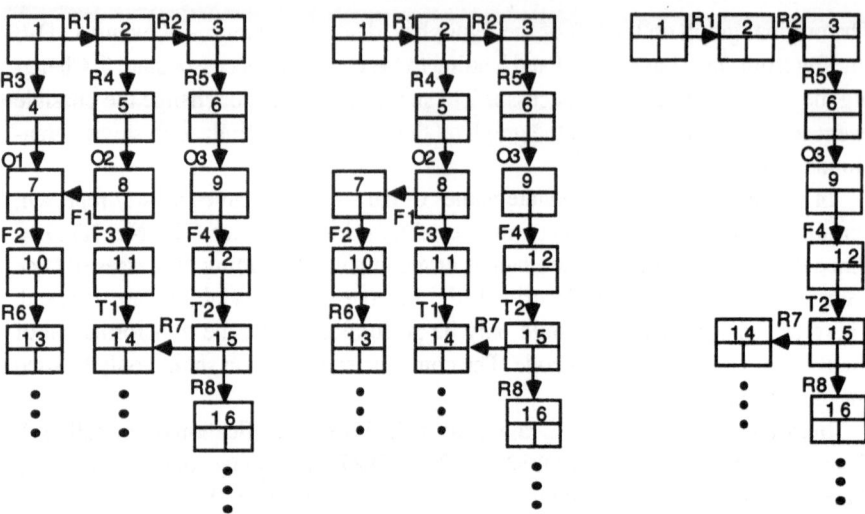

Figure 16.2: Example of subsetting

An example of subsets of communication services is the session layer protocol of the ISO/OSI mode /ISO8326/, /ISO8327/. This protocol specification allows only the required parts of a communication service to be implemented when the user requirements are limited. Functional units provide certain facilities. They are formed from a set of service primitives. Functional units themselves are combined into subsets which are negotiated by the peer entities during the establishment of the connection. The subsetting facilities in PATE were successfully used to produce different subsets of the session layer service.

16.3 Validation Tools

Validating a specification means checking whether a process is correct. Two aspects of correctness can be distinguished:
- A system must have certain properties, e.g. livelock free, deadlock free which are independent of the application. This is implicit correctness.
- A specified system must do what a designer has intended. This is explicit correctness.

Both aspects of correctness can be supported by tools. For PASS these tools are based on the formal description of the PASS semantics in PROLOG and in a graph replacement system (see following sections).

16.3.1 Prolog Based Validation Tools

Foundations:

In /NMMF87/, the semantics of PASS is described in PROLOG. PROLOG is a programming language for writing programs in a declarative style. A declarative program consists of a set of facts and rules. Facts describe a true relationship between individuals or objects. Facts of the same type are called relations. Rules describe the dependencies of facts on a group of other facts /CLME81/.

A PASS specification can be translated into PROLOG facts and rules. The facts describe an actual PASS specification. The rules define when a process can execute which transitions. These rules are defined independent of any special processes and therefore they define the semantics of PASS.

Translating PASS specifications into PROLOG:

The communication structure, the input pool definitions and the PASS graphs of a PASS specification are transformed into PROLOG facts. The PASS graph refinements are translated into PROLOG facts and rules. The facts contain the definition of the local variables and their initial values. The rules describe the functions and operations of PASS graph refinements. The figure below summarises the different transformations.

PASS Specification

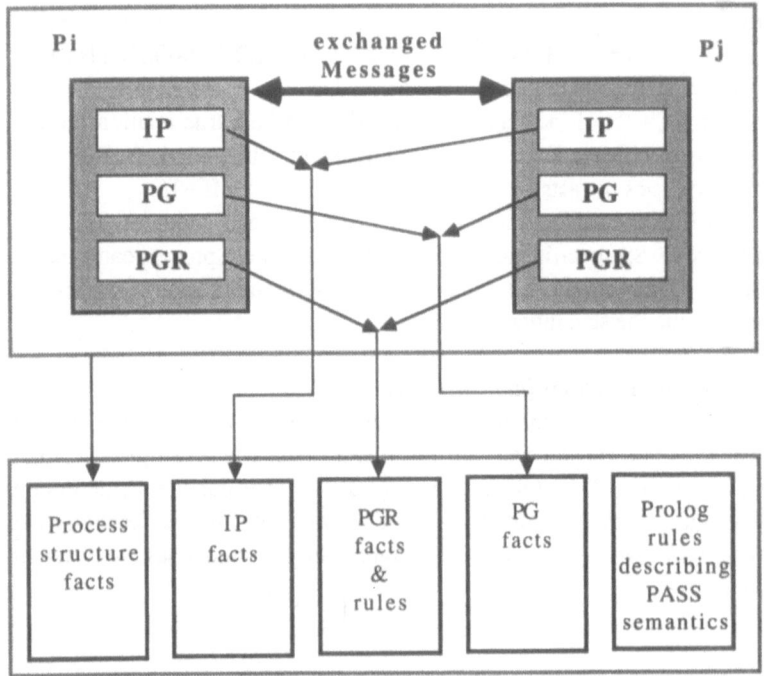

Description in PROLOG

IP   : Input Pool
PG   : PASS Graph
PGR : PASS Graph Refinement

Figure 16.3: Transformation of PASS Specifications into PROLOG

In the following clauses, the transformations are discussed in more detail.

Communication Structure:
The PROLOG relation proclist contains the identifiers of all processes of a system. For the PROLOG system it is assumed that all processes are incarnations of a process type. The relation proctype describes which processes are of which type. The parameter binding, i.e. the mapping of the formal process names onto real process names, is contained in the relation procpar. The following list summarizes these relations /NMMF87/:

proclist (<plist>:PID*)   <plist> is a list of all existing processes

proctype (<pid>,<ptype>)   process <pid> is of type <ptype>

procpar (<pid>,<ppar>,<pida>)   formal process parameter <ppar> is bound to
                                       process <pida> for process <pid>

The notation <TYPE>* is used to denote a list containing objects of type <TYPE>.

Input Pool:
The relation pool contains information about the input pool.

pool   (<ptype>,<size>,<struclist>:STRELE*)
              'size' contains the input pool size

STRELE   (<pid>,<mid>,<number>) number of messages of type mid from
              process

The other attributes of input pools can also be added to the relation pool but are not
considered here.

PASS graph refinements
The relation lvarlist contains a list of the local variables of a process.

lvarlist   (<pid>,<lvlist>:LVID*) <lvlist> is a list of local variables belonging
              to process <pid>

The list of the local variables, lvarlist, contains all local variables specified in the
PASS graph refinements and variables which correspond to the message parameters.
If a message is accepted by a process the parameter values are copied to the appropriate variables.
    The rules for the receive message specifications operate on these variables as
representatives of the message parameters. The 'send' message specifications ini-
tialize the values of the corresponding variables. The values of these variables are
copied to the message parameters if the corresponding message can be sent. These
message parameter representatives are introduced to simplify the PROLOG program.
    The initialization of the local variables is described in the relation initlv.

initlv   (<ptype>,<lvid>,<value>) for processes of type <ptype> local vari-
              able <lvid> is initially set to <value>.

PASS graph

The PROLOG facts corresponding to the PASS graph of a process also contain information about the message parameters and their representatives.

The relation unit defines the initial main state of a process.

init   (<ptype>, <sid>) processes of type <ptype> start at main state <sid> (state identifier)

PASS graphs and message parameter mappings are described in three kinds of relations: send-node, rev-node and op-node.

The relation send-node contains information about a certain send node. This includes a list of possible transitions, triggering messages, and parameters of the different message types. The definition of the send node relation is shown below:

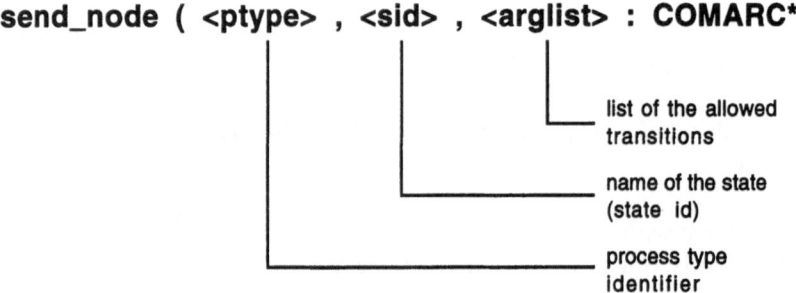

The elements of the list <arglist> describe the possible transitions and the triggering messages. The structure of these list elements is defined as follows:

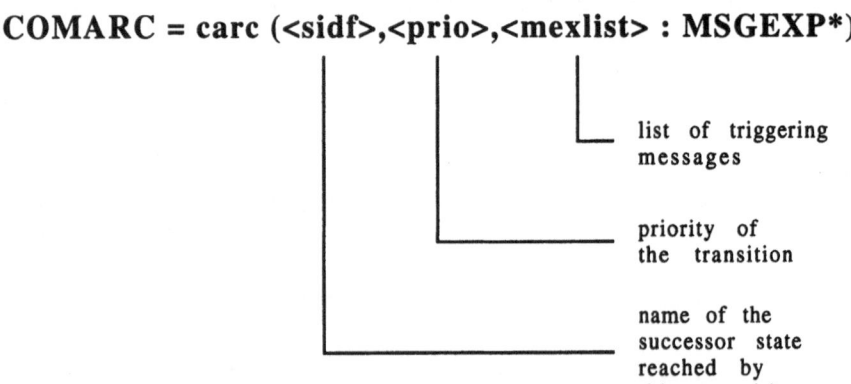

When several messages must be sent to trigger a transition, i.e. a message term, the message descriptions are defined in the list <mexlist>. The elements of this list have the following structure:

MSGEXP = (\<mid\>,\<ppar\>,\<mpslist\>, : MPSSPEC*)

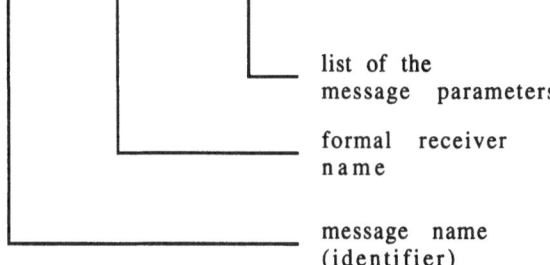

list of the
message   parameters

formal   receiver
name

message   name
(identifier)

The parameter list contains the mapping of the parameters to the corresponding elements in the local variable list. The structure of the list elements \<mpslist\> is shown below.

MPSSPEC = mpsp (\<mpid\>,\<lvid\>)

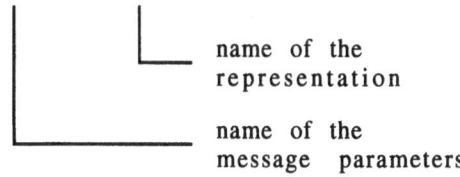

name of the
representation

name of the
message   parameters

Similarly a fact of type rev-node comprises information about a certain receive node and the receive arcs initiating from it:

ref-node (\<ptype\>,\<sid\>,\<arclist\>; COMAR(*))

Here formal process names in expressions refer to names of senders.

For simplicity the internal function nodes and the internal operation nodes are described in PROLOG as one type of fact. The relation which describes an internal operation or internal function node is defined as follows:

op_mode (\<ptype\>,\<sis\>,\<op\>,\<arglist\> : OPARC*)

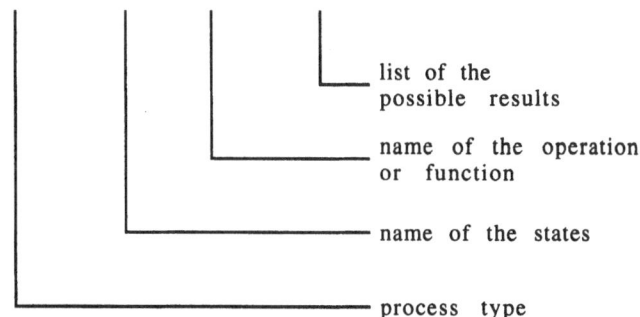

list of the
possible   results

name of the operation
or function

name of the states

process   type

The list <arglist> comprises the possible results of the function or operations performed.

OPARC = oarc (<sidf>,<value>)

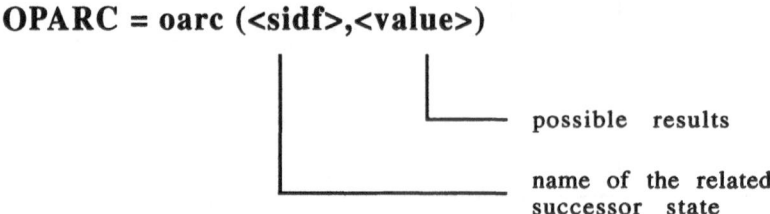

       possible   results

       name of the related
       successor   state

In the field of parallel processes the problem of the five philosophers is often used to demonstrate synchronization problems. Five philosophers are sitting at a round table. On the table there are five plates of spaghetti and five forks, arranged as shown in the figure below.

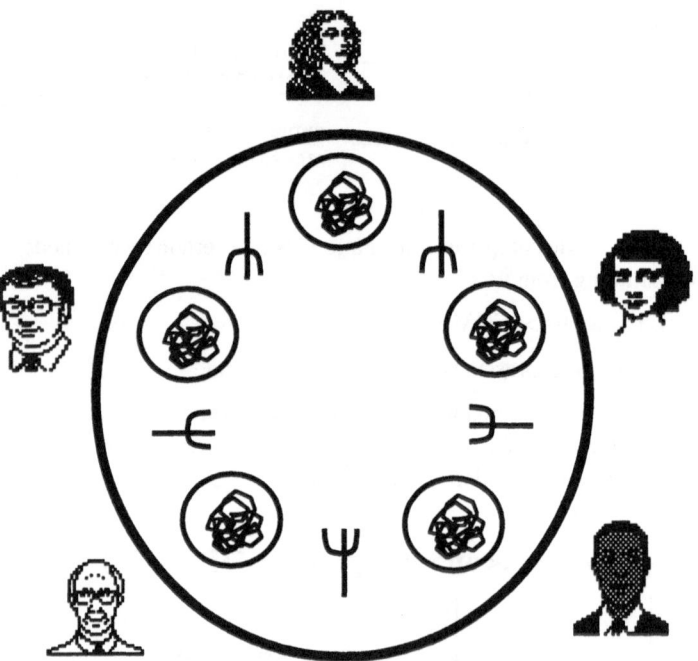

Figure 16.4: The Table of the five Philosophers

The table is surrounded by five chairs each labelled with the name of a philosopher. Their names are PHIL0, PHIL1, PHIL2, PHIL3 and PHIL4.

A philosopher is expected to think for most of the time, but when he feels hungry he goes to his chair and tries to pick up the forks on either side of his plate. If a philosopher can pick up both forks then he can start eating. When he is finished he puts the forks down. If either one or both of the forks is in use, the hungry philosopher waits until both the forks have been put down.

The PROLOG representation of the five philosopher problem is shown below /NMMF87/:

proclist ((ph0,ph1,ph2,ph3,ph4,f0,f1,f2,f3,f4)).

proctype(ph0,ph).	procpar(ph0,f1,f0).	procpar(ph0,fr,f4).
proctype(ph1,ph).	procpar(ph1,f1,f1).	procpar(ph1,fr,f0).
proctype(ph2,ph).	procpar(ph2,f1,f2).	procpar(ph2,fr,f1).
proctype(ph3,ph).	procpar(ph3,f1,f3).	procpar(ph3,fr,f2).
proctype(ph4,ph).	procpar(ph4,f1,f4).	procpar(ph4,fr,f3).
proctype(f0,f).	procpar(f0,ph1,ph1).	procpar(f0,phr,ph0).
proctype(f1,f).	procpar(f1,ph1,ph2).	procpar(f1,phr,ph1).
proctype(f2,f).	procpar(f2,ph1,ph3).	procpar(f2,phr,ph2).
proctype(f3,f).	procpar(f3,ph1,ph4).	procpar(f3,phr,ph3).
proctype(f4,f).	procpar(f4,ph1,ph0).	procpar(f4,phr,ph4).

lvarlist(ph,(hungry)).lvarlist(f,()).
init(ph,s1).   init(f,s1).
pool(ph,0,()).   pool(f,0,()).

rcv_node	(ph,s1,(carc(s2,0, (mexp(get,fl,()), mexp(get,fr,()))))).
op_node	(ph,s2,eat, (oarc(s3,success))).
send_node	(ph,s3, (carc(s4,0, (mexp(give,fl,()), mexp(give,fr,()))))).
op_node	(ph,s4, think, (oarc(s1, success))).
send_node	(f,s1, (carc(s2.0, (mexp(get, phl, ())), carc(s3,0, (mexp(get,phr, ())))))).
rcv_node	(f,s2, (carc(s1.0, (mexp(give, phl, ()))))).
rcv_node	(f,s3, (carc(s1.0, (mexp(give,phr, ()))))).

query (ph, eat, ()).
eat(ph, (), Result):-
Result=full   /* this line is generated manually*/

query (ph, think, ()).
think (ph,(), Result):-
Result=exhausted   /* this line is generated manually*/

PROLOG rules defining the PASS semantics

Coding the PASS semantics in PROLOG is more difficult than transforming a given specification into PROLOG; Fortunately however, this has only to be done once. PASS is based on an extended finite state model. The PROLOG rules which implement the semantics of PASS have to define the conditions for transitions. First the state structure of a single process is defined /NMMF87/

STATE   = s(<pid>,<sid>, <lvlist>:VAR*, <pool>:MESSAGE*)
VAR   = var(<vid>,<value>)
MESSAGE = msg(<pids>, <mid>,<pidr>,<mplist>:VAR*)

At any point in time, the state of a process <pid> is defined by its main state <sid>, the list of its local variables <lvlist>, and the list of messages in its pool <pool>. Each local variable is represented by its identifier <vid> and its value <value>; a message is defined by its sender <pids>, its identifier <mid>, its receiver <pidr>, and the list <mplist> of message parameters.

The global state of a system is defined as the cross product of all process states. The initial global state of the five philosopher problem, e. g., is given by

s(ph0,s1,( ),(),)
s(ph1,s1,( ),(),)
s(ph2,s1,( ),(),)
s(ph3,s1,( ),(),)
s(ph4,s1,( ),(),)
s(f0 ,s1,(),(),)
s(f1 ,s1,(),(),)
s(f2 ,s1,(),(),)
s(f3 ,s1,(),(),)
s(f4 ,s1,(),(),)

The states are simple because in the PASS specification of the philosopher problem none of the processes has local variables.

If processes uses synchronous message passing a message causes main state changes in the sending and receiving process. That means that in the STATE structure of the relevant processes, the components <sid> are changed. In the receiving processes the local variable component <lvlist> is also changed according to the receive message specifications.

If processes communicate asynchronously, a main state change is performed in the sending process and the message is added to the input pool of the receiving process. This means that the component <pool> is changed in the state structure of the receiving process. Parts of the semantic rules also describe whether these state changes are allowed.

If a process which owns an input pool of size greater than zero accepts a message the message is removed from the input pool and the corresponding main change and receive message specification is executed. This means that the components <sid>,

<lvlist>, and <pool> of the STATE structure are changed. The changes in the components <sid> and <pool> are defined using semantic rules. The changes in the component <lvlist> are described by rules corresponding to the receive message specifications.

Internal functions or operations which are executed cause the corresponding PROLOG rules to be evaluated. As already described, these rules must be derived manually from the PASS specification. These rules can change the components <sid> and <lvlist>, i.e. only operations.

PROLOG based validation tools

In the previous section the transformation of a PASS specification into PROLOG was described. For communication structures, input pools, PASS graphs and some parts of PASS graph refinements and variables, the transformation from PASS into PROLOG can be done automatically. A program is available for this automatic transformation. The PROLOG program automatically derived from a PASS specification contains all the necessary information about the system behaviour. This information about a system and the rules for PASS semantics, construct an expert system for a particular system originally described in PASS. Basically this expert system knows all about those execution paths which start at a state x, end at a state y, and produce or accept the sequence S of messages. The expert system can answer questions about /NMMF87/:

- paths of length I (PROLOG goal step (X,Y,S),
- paths of a maximum length N, PROLOG goal steps (X,Y,S,N)
- paths of arbitrary length, PROLOG goal reach (X,Y,S)

The different PROLOG goals indicate the types of questions which can be put to such an expert system. Parameters in these questions are the initial and the final state and the corresponding sequence of events. When asking the system whether one of the goals - step (X,Y,S), steps (X,Y,S,N), or reach (X,Y,S) - can be satisfied, each of the parameters X,Y,S can be either instantiated, in which case its value is given, or uninstantiated, requiring the expert system to find suitable values using all the information about the specified system. Thus a system can be asked a number of different questions: e.g. when asking step (X,Y,S) with all parameters instantiated the system will return true if a given state Y can be reached from a given state X producing the required sequence S of events, sending and receiving messages, in one step. The states X and Y can be in the PASS graphs of different processes. When asking the same question with only Y instantiated, the expert system will return all states Y reachable from a given state X in a single event, together with the corresponding observable event sequences, etc.

These expert systems allow the behaviour of a process system to be analysed and can determine whether a system does what it was intended to do.

16.3.2 Validation Tools Based on a Graph Replacement System

Foundations:

The behaviour of a program can be described using a linear notation, as is usually done, or using a graph. A graph consists of a set of nodes and arcs between these nodes. The nodes and arcs can be marked, leading to a marked graph.

Marked graphs can be changed by replacing parts with other subgraphs. The allowed changes of a graph can be described by replacement rules, also called a graph grammar. Replacement rules define that a subgraph of a graph, the left hand side of a rule, can be replaced by a particular subgraph, the right hand side of a rule. A set of rules comprises a graph replacement system. There is a well founded theory for these graph replacement systems /NAGL79/. PASS semantics, or parts of them, which can be described as a graph replacement system can also be formally defined.

In /FEDER86/ a graph replacement system for PASS was developed. This graph replacement system does not describe all aspects of PASS. It describes the semantics of sending and receiving messages without timeouts and priorities. The basic principles of this approach are described in the following sections.

The Program Graph:

A system specified in PASS is transformed into a program graph. A program graph describes a complete system of processes in a way which allows the use of the PASS replacement rules. The program graph of a system is based on the PASS graphs. These are translated into a slightly different representation and some additional nodes and lines are added. These contain information about the current states of the different processes, the state of the input pools, i.e. the messages in the pool, etc.

When transforming a system described in PASS, each node in a PASS graph is represented by a node in the program graph also known as an action node. Corresponding to the node types in PASS graphs, action nodes in program graphs are marked with 'send' for a send node, 'rec' for a receive node, 'oper' for an operation node and 'func' for a function node.

The transitions in PASS graphs are represented in program graphs by nodes marked with 'trans'. Arcs lead from an action node to a transition node and from the transition node to the succeeding action node. The sequence – action node, transition node, action node – corresponds to a transition in a PASS graph.

Additional arcs lead from transition nodes to enabling nodes marked with the enabling condition, messages or results of a transition.

An enabling node which is connected to an action node marked with 'rec' or 'send' is marked with a message type name. An enabling node which belongs to an action node, marked with 'oper' for operation or 'func' for function, is marked with the name of an operation or function and the corresponding results. If a transition node has more than one enabling node, then the enabling conditions represented by each node must be true for the corresponding transition, i.e. the message terms to be executed.

Process input pools are represented by input pool nodes. Input pool nodes are marked with their size, structure etc. Arcs lead from an enabling node containing expected messages, i.e. a receiving node, to the node representing the input pool of the process. An arc leads from a send enabling node to the input pool node of the receiver.

An arc also leads from a node marked with 'cs' for current state node to the action node of a process representing the initial state.

The different node types in program graphs are connected by different line types. The list below summarizes the different node- and line types.

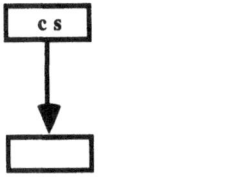

current state node, from this node

the successor arc points to the current action node

action node marked with: send, rec, oper, func

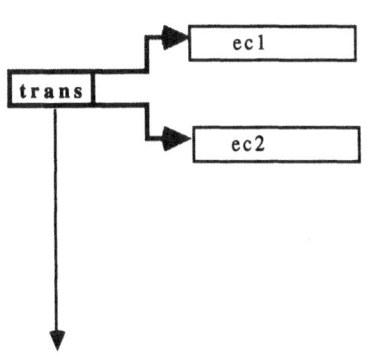

transition nodes with enabling nodes; conected by transition arcs which point from the transition node to the enabling node. Enabling nodes are marked with the enabling conditions i.e. messages, results

successor arc which points from trans nodes to the action node which is reached by the transition represented by the transition node

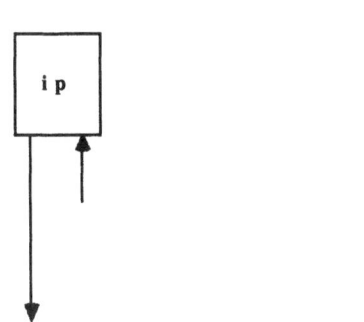

node which represents the input pool of a process

input pool arcs which point from enabling nodes marked with message names to the input pool of the receiver or the input pool arcs which points from the input pool node to an enabling node marked with the name of an expected message

Figure 16.5 : Line and Node Types in Program Graphs

The figure below shows an example of a program graph. Part of the dining philosopher problem specification, one philosopher process and one fork process, is transformed into a program graph.

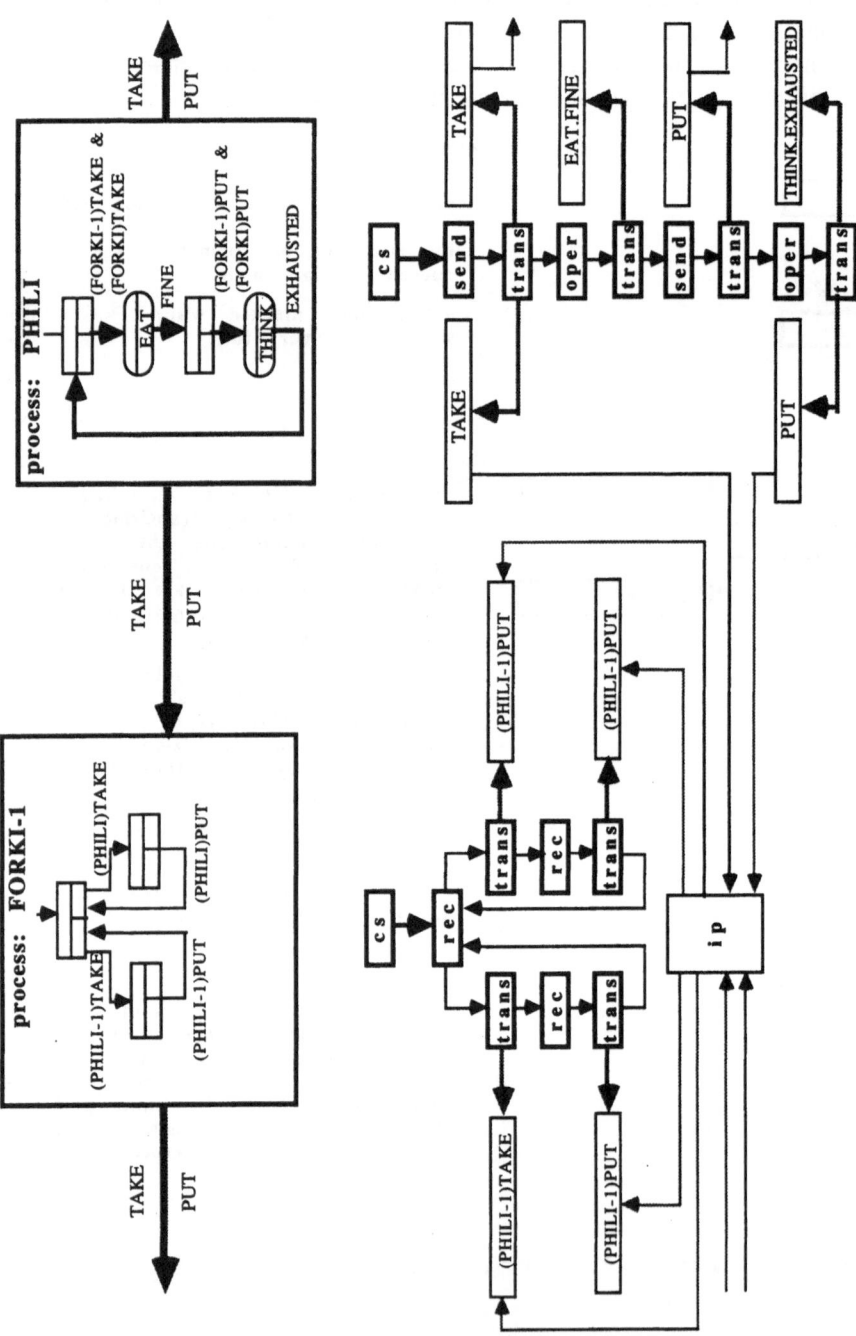

Figure 16.6: Program Graph of Parts of the 5 Philosopher System

Graph replacement system defining the PASS semantics:
The dynamic behaviour of processes is modelled by changes in program graphs. These changes are defined for housekeeping nodes, arcs, and markings of nodes. It is possible to define processes that run in parallel or interleaved. Processes which can run in parallel can run on different processors and those which can only run interleaved should run on the same processor. Processes on different processors run in parallel until they have to communicate with processes running on other processors.

The possibility of modelling real parallelism is a great advantage of the PASS approach.

The changes allowed to program graphs are defined by rules similar to grammatical production rules. These rules define an abstract interpreter for PASS. A process which can execute a transition removes the arc pointing from the 'cs' node to the current state and introduces a new arc which points from the 'cs' node to the successor node, i.e. the new current state.

The input nodes are marked with the state of the corresponding input pool, i.e. the messages in the input pool, and the attributes of the input pool.

If a message is added to or removed from an input pool, the graph production rule also defines the changes to the corresponding markings.

The complete set of rules is described in 28 pages in /FEDER86/. A good knowledge of the principles of graph replacement systems is necessary to understand an example of a full replacement. Therefore no example is given here. This chapter is designed only to give an insight into the different ways to describe PASS semantics.

PASS validation tools based on the graph replacement system:
The graph derived from a PASS specification contains similar information about a specified system as the corresponding PROLOG statements. Instead of PROLOG rules the PASS semantics are contained in graph replacement rules which interpret a PASS specification. The graph necessary for the graph replacement rules, called GRR, is derived automatically from a PASS specification. The GRRs are implemented in PASCAL (3200 lines). The behaviour of a PASS system can be observed in this simulation /FEDER86/. Special tools based on this interpreter have been produced. The use of these tools is demonstrated in the following example /AND89/.

Example:
Two processes, P1 and P2, have to exchange data packets but before either process can send the data it needs permission from the receiver. When the process has received this permission it sends the data. After sending the data it returns to its initial state. Each process can either obtain permission to transmit data and then transmit it, or give the other process permission to transmit and accept the packet of data transmitted. It is forbidden for both processes to send data at the same time. The figure below shows these two processes and the messages they exchange.

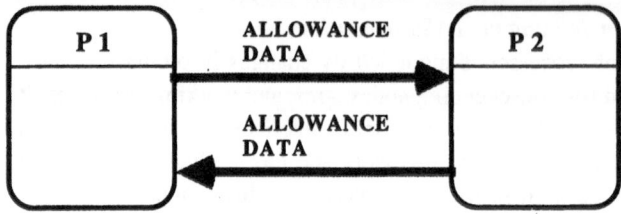

Figure 16.7: Communication Structure of two Processes

The PASS graphs of the two processes are shown in the following figure.

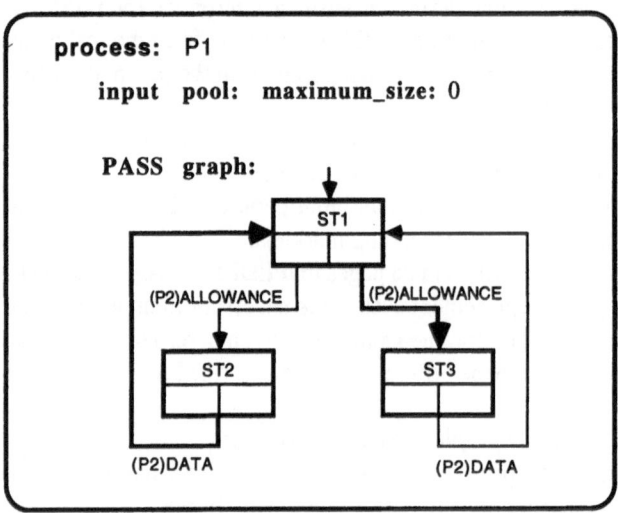

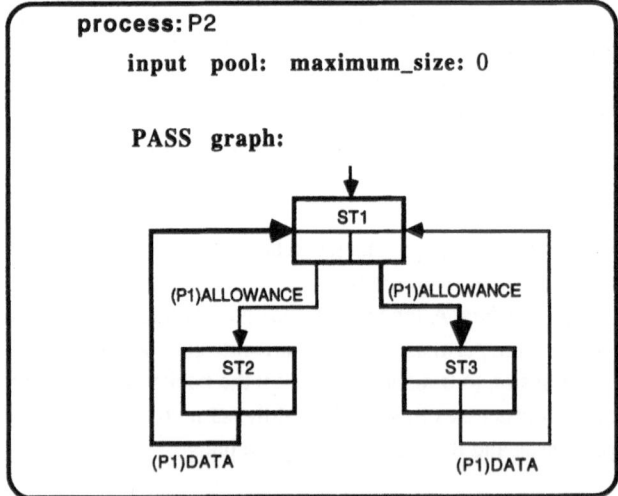

Figure 16.8: PASS Graphs of the two Processes

Preparation of the validation

The validation program assumes that the specification of the PASS graphs are contained in files. After starting, the validation program asks for the names of these files. When all PASS graphs have been loaded the validation program needs some information about the configuration namely:

- The number of processes belonging to the process system under investigation.
- The number of processors and the assignment of processes to the different processors.
- The priorities of processes running on the same processor.
- The scheduling strategy used.

The following figure shows the menu which asks for this information.

processor name:	PROCESSOR1	
scheduling:	NIL	
Process :	P 1	X
	P 2	

Figure 16.9: Configuration Menu of the Validation Program

The first section of the menu shows the name of the processor. In our example this is the processor 'PROCESSOR1'. The next section asks for the scheduling strategy. This information is only necessary if more than one process is running on the same processor. 'NIL' means that each process is running on its own processor. The last section shows the names of all processes in the system. The process assigned to the processor currently being considered is marked by 'X'. In our example process P1 is assigned to processor 'PROCESSOR1'.

In the next menu the validation program asks for the properties of the input pools. In our example both processes have an input pool of size zero, i.e. the message exchange is synchronous.

Validation:

The validation program based on the graph replacement system allows the automatic or manual simulation of a system of processes. In our example we have chosen a manually driven simulation.

After starting the program a window is opened on the terminal screen for each process. In our case only two windows are necessary, one for process P1 and another for process P2. The current state and the possible transitions from that state are shown in these windows. A field below the windows displays the name of the processors on which the processes are running. Below that field there is a menu in which the user is asked for the next transition that has to be executed for each process. The following figure shows the content of the screen after starting the validation run.

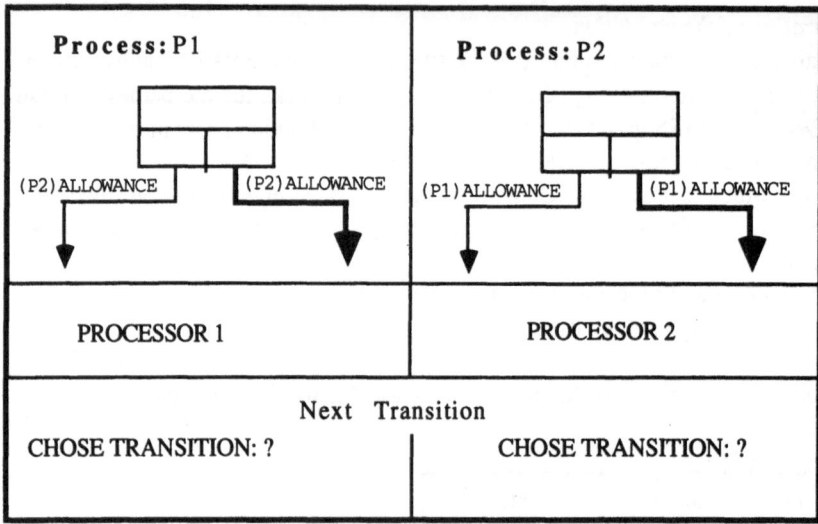

Figure 16.10: Screen Content after Starting the Validation Run

In our example two transitions can be executed:
- P1 sends 'ALLOWANCE' to P2
- P1 receives 'ALLOWANCE' from P2

If the user wants process P2 to receive the message (P1)ALLOWANCE, then process P1 must execute the appropriate send transition since synchronous message exchange enforces transitions in at least two processes, the sender and receiver. When both processes have executed their transitions the menu shown in the figure below appears on the screen.

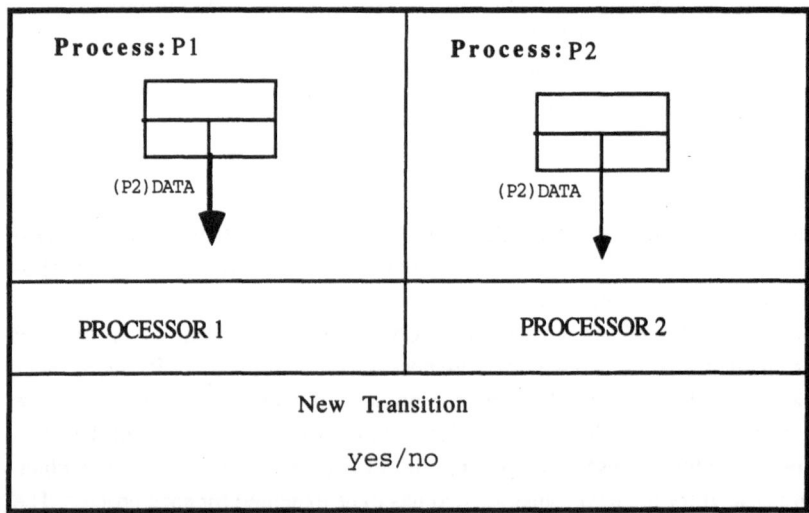

Figure 16.11: Screen after the first Transitions

In this way a system of processes can be tested step by step. The simulator described above allows one to check whether a system has the intended behaviour and also allows one to test whether a system has deadlocks.

16.4 Concepts for Implementation Tools

According to the structure of a PASS specification, code can be generated for input pools, PASS graphs and PASS graph refinements. Code generation for PASS graph refinements depends on the specification language used and therefore is not considered further here.

Currently a generator exists which produces PASCAL or C code for PASS graphs and input pools using the implementation concepts discussed in section 15.

In addition, this generator produces procedure headers for all required operations and functions. To obtain a complete program, the procedure bodies have to be added according to the functions and operation in the PASS graph refinements.

We have implemented two generators, one which produces executable code and one which produces data driven code for PASS graphs /URB87/.

Both generators were applied to the PASS graph of the ISO session protocol /ISO8327/. The code produced has the following memory requirements when compiled with the IBM PASCAL_VS compiler for VM/CMS systems:

Code driven: 413 322 KB
Data driven: 51 688 KB

For the time measurement a representative sequence of messages was used: establishing a section connection, data transfer, ending a connection:

Code driven: 11 280 microseconds
Data driven: 7 994 microseconds

16.5 Concepts for Project Management Tools

The central component of project management tools is a database containing all information about the project /MCCLU89a/, /BALZ89/. If SAPP/PASS is used as a development technology all information about work packages such as work package specifications, status reports, minutes of meetings and letters, is stored in the data base. The type of database required for SAPP/PASS is probably very similar to the databases used for other project management tools. The tools which produce different types of project management reports are much the same as project management tools. The general requirements for project management tools are described in ./MCCLU89a/.

Special PASS oriented tools support the counting of quality values such as the number of levels, the number of processes per process set and the number of different message types. For each project these values can be stored in a database. For later projects the values from older projects can be used to develop a quality metric.

Control Questions:

1. Which different tools are required for an integrated software development tool set?
2. What tools are neccessary to support the development of SAPP specifications?
3. What tools are neccessary to support the development of PASS specifications?
4. How can tools support the optimisation of PASS graphs?
5. How can tools be used for the creation of behaviour subsets?
6. What concepts can be used for the development of validation tools?
7. How can PROLOG be used for the implementation of PASS validation tools?
8. How can graph replacement systems used for the implementation of PASS validation tools?

Exercises:

1. What are your basic requirements for a SAPP tool?
2. Where can behaviour subsetting be used in your environment?
3. What are your requirements for a validation tool set?
4. Would you prefer code or data-driven code generation of PASS graphs?
5. How can your project management tools be used for the management of projects using SAPP/PASS?

17 A SAPP/PASS Based
Software Engineering Environment

This chapter provides an example of a SAPP/PASS based SEE. Several tools support the development of a program from the design to the final program. These tools are based on the general concepts described in the previous chapter.

The first stage of an integrated tool set has been implemented, based on concepts described in the previous chapter. This tool set allows the decomposition of a system into concurrent processes, the specification of the processes, and the automatic generation of C-code. It has been successfully used in several projects. One of these projects is described in more detail below to illustrate the use of the tool set.

17.1 Basic Concepts of the 3C Tools

This chapter explains the basic concept of the 3C product set and gives a detailed description of each tool. What is presented covers only a subset of the SAPP/PASS methodology. 3C is currently working on the implementation of tools for the full set of the SAPP/PASS methodology.

Tools have to support the creative process in the SAPP/PASS environment by means of structuring, visualisation and automation. The following four main aspects which have been implemented in the 3C tools provide this support.

- SAPP/PASS is based on graphical methods and representations, so graphical editors which implement SAPP/PASS techniques are the adequate approach.
- SAPP/PASS is an operational approach; to gain the benefits of this approach one has to develop code generators that can transform the graphical specificition into code.
- The information of the SAPP and PASS descriptions of a system allow rapid prototyping; therefore tools are needed to test the behaviour of specified systems before the start of the implementation phase.
- An automatic management facility which is completely integrated into the set of tools is neccessary for the use of complex tools as described above. By this means the user can do the work effectively.

As a result the tools were implemented to run under a graphical environment. 3C selected Windows by Microsoft to allow the use of the tools on PCs. 3C developed the following tools which implement the SAPP/PASS methodology.

List of 3C Tools

SYSMAN   tool to organize work at the system level

PROCMAN   tool to organize the work at the specification level and manage the output of the code generator

SAGE   graphical editor for the definition and analysis of systems described in SAPP

PAGE   graphical editor to implement the process specification in PASS

IPET   graphical editor to specify the input pool for every process

WINE   simple text editor used for refinement specification

SYCO   programm to generate code from SAPP graph

PACO   code generator which transforms a PASS specification of a process type into code

PRATE   programm which generates a runtime system to test and simulate the behaviour of the process and the system.

17.1.1 SYSMAN – The System Manager

The SYSMAN is the most important tool for the management of systems. The system manager provides the user with the essential information about a system: the graphical layout, the names of the processes, the process types and messages. From SYSMAN the user can call the systems analysis tool called SAGE, the input pool editor, the process type manager or can edit messages. SYSMAN also maintains the source code created by the code generators, and calls other tools belonging to the system which provide important informatioin.

The following figure shows the maon screen of SYSMAN.

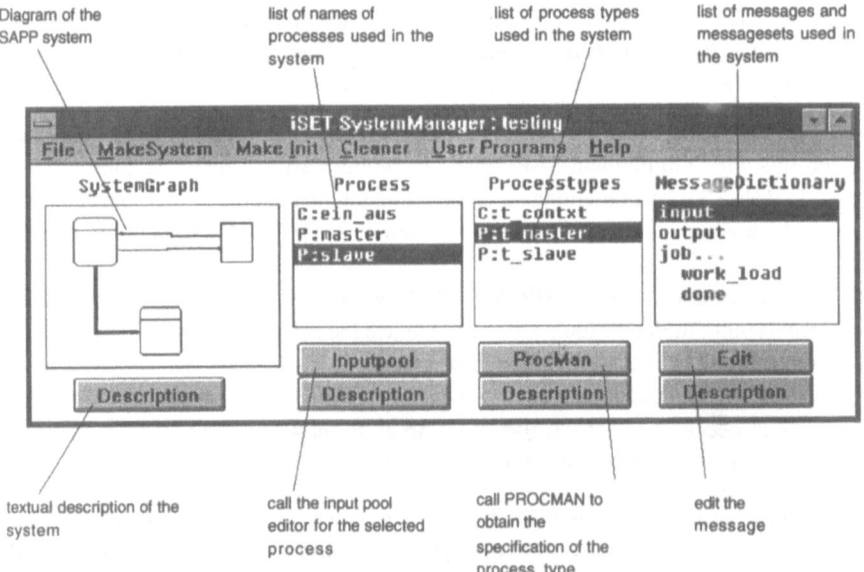

Figure 17.1: Main Screen of SYSMAN

The menu of the SYSMAN reveals the following features:

File	creates a new system or opens an existing system
MakeSystem	start the system generator and all other related tools such as compilers, linkers etc.
MakeInit	maintain the initialization code of processes
Cleaner	maintain the source code generated
UserPrograms	link other application under development to the system
Help	call help engine to obtain support

17.1.2 PROCMAN – The Processtype Manager

ProcMan is the tool which manages the specification of process types. From PROCMAN the user can call the graphical specification editor PAGE, start the codegenerator or edit the source code of the refinements which has been generated. The PROCMAN allows the user to work at the high specification level using symbols and names declared within the specification. He can select and edit refinements or messages without knowing anything about their representation or location on the computer system.

The following figure shows the main menu of PROCMAN.

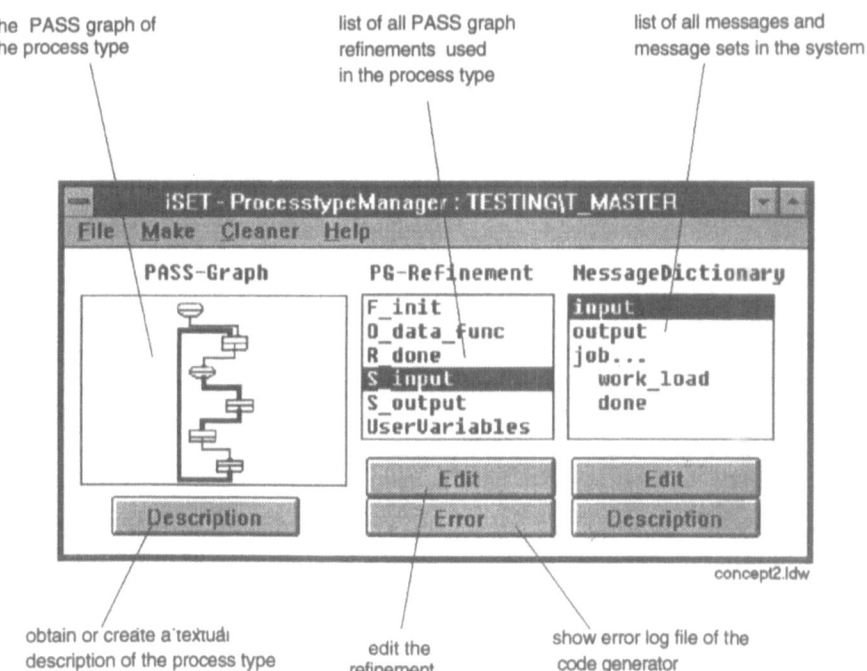

Figure 17.2: Main Menue of PROCMAN

The menu of the PROCMAN contains the following features:

FILE   opens a process type specification / calls SYSMAN / prints process type

MAKE   calls the code generator to transform the PASS graph into code

CLEANER   deletes old refinements that are no longer needed or reuses them

HELP   calls the help engine to get support

17.1.3 SAGE – The Systems Analysis Graphical Editor

The following figure shows the SAGE editor. This editor is used to define a system using the SAPP method. A system is defined by processes and process sets which communicate with each other.

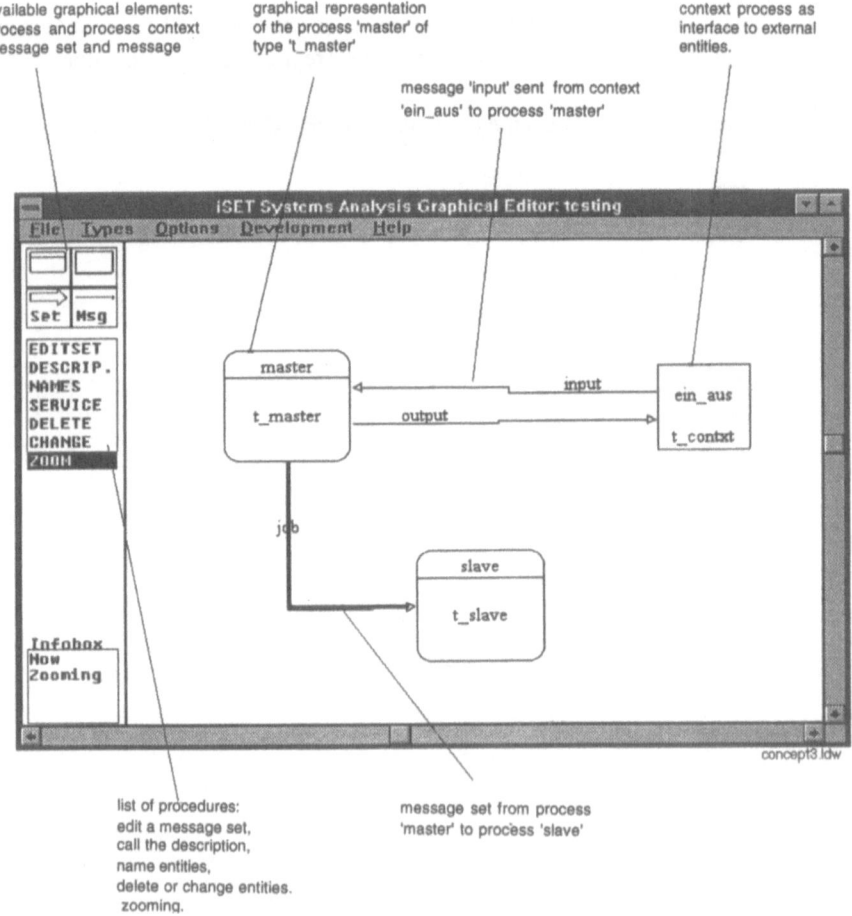

Figure 17.3: Example of the Use of SAGE

The menu of SAGE contains the following items:

FILE   Save the graph / leave the editor
TYPES   maintain all the symbols in the graph
OPTIONS   tool settings
HELP   call the help engine

17.1.4 PAGE – The PASS Graph Editor

PAGE allows easy and fast creation or maintenance of PASS specifications. To create a graph the user simply clicks on the graphical symbol for a node of the state
machine and places it somewhere on the drawing area. To create a transition between two nodes the user chooses TRANS in the function menu, clicks on the first
node and clicks on the second node. PAGE automatically creates the required transition including routing the transition from the start node to the end node. This feature
allows the complex graphical aspects of a graphical specification language to be
dealt with satisfactorily.

available graphical elements: starting node of the   PASS specification of the progress type
Send node/Receive node   state machine   'T_MASTER' which is part of the System
Operation node/Function node   'TESTING'

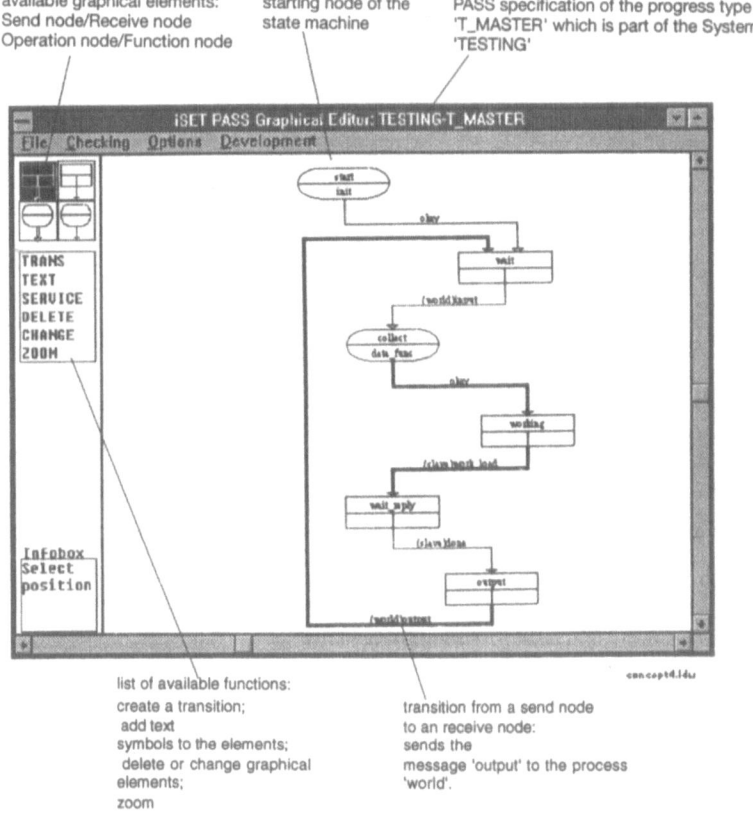

list of available functions:

create a transition;   transition from a send node
 add text   to an receive node:
symbols to the elements;   sends the
 delete or change graphical   message 'output' to the process
elements;   'world'.
 zoom

Figure 17.4: Example of PAGE Menue

The PAGE menue contains the following commands:

FILE   opens a process type, leaves editor

CHECKING analyzes the graph for errors

OPTION   tool settings

17.1.5 IPET – The Input Pool Editor

The input pool editor allows the treatment of received messages. The user can specify strategies such as blocking, replacing, or deleting to obtain the desired behaviour of the input pool. A test mode allows the input pool specification to be tested by sending messages to the pool and observing how the input pool deals with the messages.

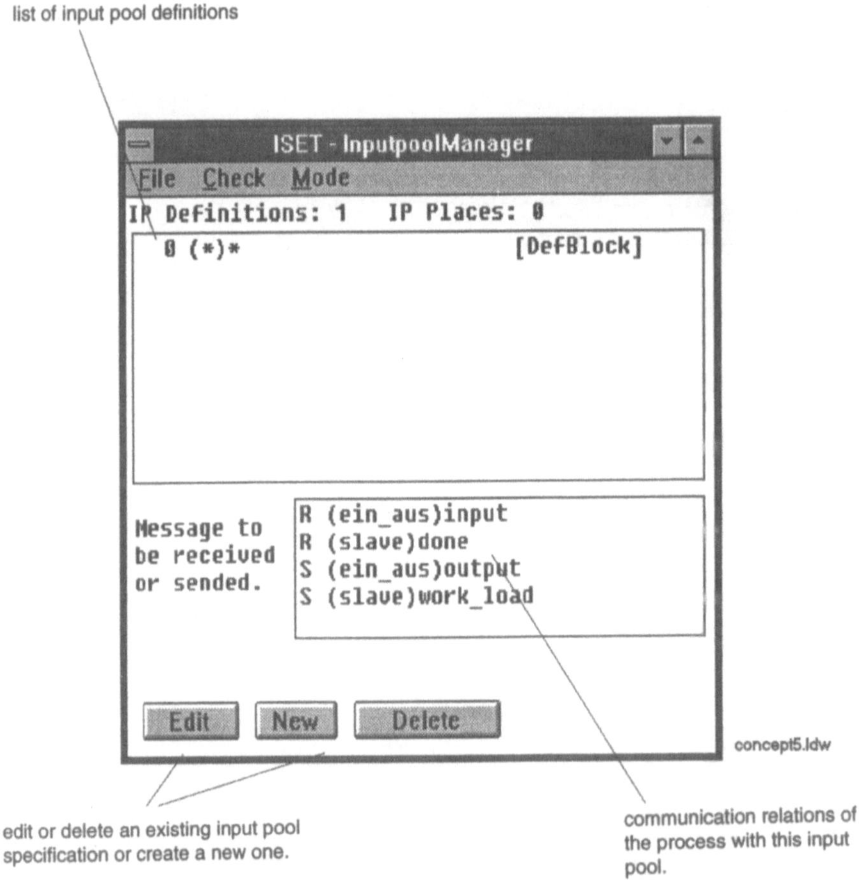

list of input pool definitions

ISET - InputpoolManager

File   Check   Mode

IP Definitions: 1   IP Places: 0

0 (*)*   [DefBlock]

Message to
be received
or sended.

R (ein_aus)input
R (slave)done
S (ein_aus)output
S (slave)work_load

Edit   New   Delete

concept5.ldw

edit or delete an existing input pool
specification or create a new one.

communication relations of
the process with this input
pool.

Figure 17.5: Example of the Use of IPET

The menu of the IPET contains the following items:

CHECK checks the input pool specification for errors.

MODE switches from edit to test mode, tests the specification by creating messages and simulating the behaviour of sending processes.

17.2 CASE Study – Software Project Using the 3C Tools

This section describes the use of the SAPP/PASS methodology in a software project. First detailed information about the procject is provided and then the use of SAPP and PASS are described. We cannot provide all the details because this would fill another book; but we have described the most important aspects of the development process and every major step in the project.

  The project is the implementation of a logistics system that can be used in the brewing industry.

17.2.1 Description of the Brewery Project

To understand this logistic system we have to provide some background about the problems at the brewery. Once the beer has been brewed and filled into bottles, the cases of beer are brought into a big warehouse. From there the cases are picked up by fork lift trucks and taken into the yard where trucks are waiting to be loaded. Many trucks arrive every day and expect to leave the brewery as fast as possible to deliver the beer to the customers. Sometimes truck owners had complained about waiting too long to get loaded. The loading of the trucks was organised by a fore-man. He received a bundle of order forms and distributed the work to the drivers of the fork lift trucks. The brewery wanted to have more control over the process of loading the trucks. They developed a concept to overcome the lack of information. This specified that the following basic requirements must be met:

* The trucks must register when they enter the brewery and also when they leave.
* The trucks can only be loaded at specified loading zones.
* The trucks must wait in queues until they are called by number into the loading yard.
* The loading of the trucks must be confirmed by the operator via a data input panel.
* All data must be collected in a database where it can be used for statistical purposes.

This would enable the brewery to keep track of each individual transaction in the process of loading trucks. The data collected could be used to identify time consuming processes and bottlenecks and so improve the logistics of the brewery. 3C was asked to carry out the project. The figure below shows the solution as it was implemented by 3C.

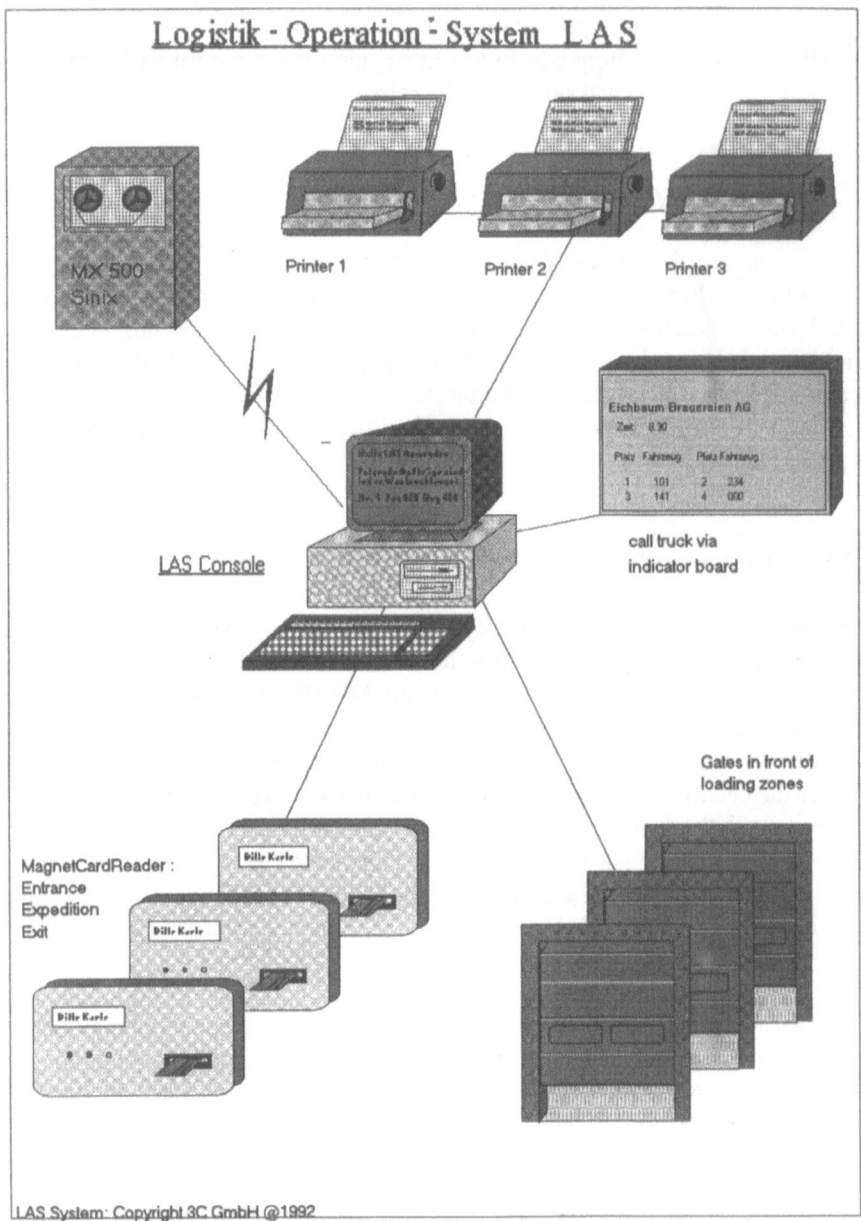

Figure 17.6: Structure of the Brewery Logistic System

The operation of the system:
Each truck has an individual number which is stored on a magnetic card. The driver must register the truck in a magnetic card reader in order to enter the brewery. The

computer receives the message and also the corresponding order form an attached UNIX system. and opens the gate so that the truck can enter. The computer checks whether there is an order for the truck that has just entered. If so, the order is marked 'can be processed'. The operator picks this order and starts to carry it out. The computer determines the best loading zone at which to process the order and starts printing instructions at the various locations in the warehouse. Workers take these instructions and start putting the order together at the designated area. Meanwhile the truck which has been waiting in the queue is now called via an indicator board to the designated position in the yard. When the order is completed the foreman opens the gate which is designated by the computer. The fork lifts start loading the truck. Once this is completed the gate is closed and the computer knows that the truck is loaded. Now the position is available for the next order. The truck can leave the yard . At the exit the driver must put the magnetic card into the reader to open the gate and thereby leave the brewery.

Thus every major process state and transition has been registered. It is even possible for the system to run in automatic mode without an operator. The system has only to wait until the truck reaches the brewery.

17.2.2 The Use of SAPP/PASS to Implement this Concept

We have described the concept in detail above; we now describe its implementation with SAPP/PASS using the 3C tools. The following pages describe the use of the tools in a 'How to do' manner to give an impression of how the system leads the user throught the different phases of the implementation.

We start at the very beginning by calling SYSMAN to create a new system. SYSMAN opens and shows the following screen:

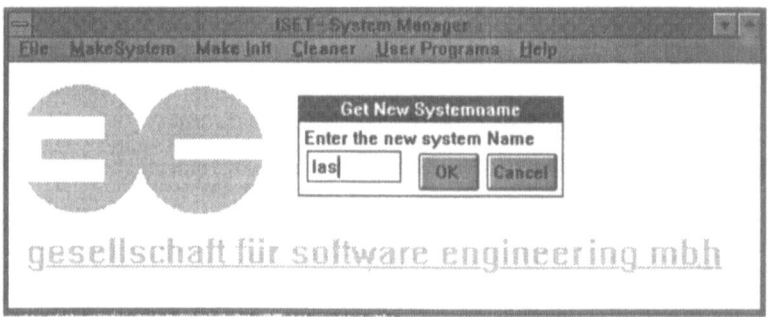

Figure 17.7 : Opening Screen of SYSMAN

The user selects FILE/NEW and enters the name of the new system. In our example we enter 'LAS', the name of the project. A text editor is called and requests that a description of the new project is entered:

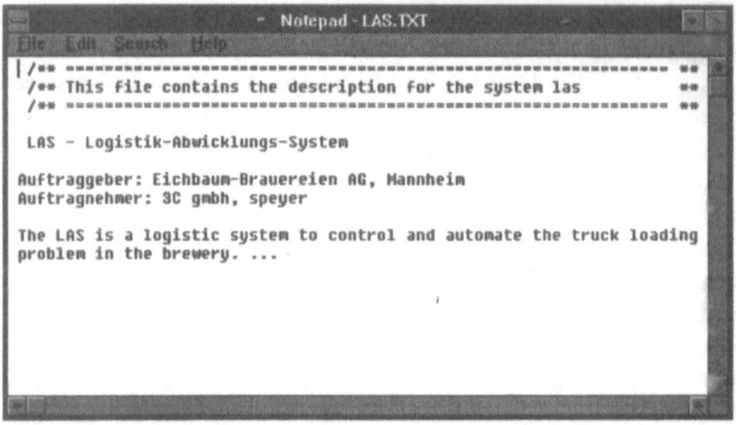

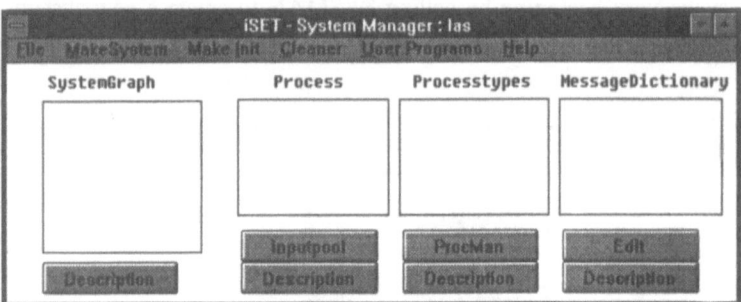

Figure 17.8: Input Screen for the Input of an Informal System Description

This file is the system description file and can be opened from the SYSMAN tool level. Of course any other tool to maintain this description can be used. The editor is registered in a database and can be replaced by any other tool. After the initial information such as a requirements catalog or a textual description of the main aspects has been entered the next screen appears. This shows SYSMAN with no further information available:

Figure 17.9: Screen for Starting SAPP/PASS Specifications

SYSMAN has created all the directories and files needed to manage the new system. The next step is to call the systems analysis tool SAGE and to enter the system description. The user clicks on SystemGraph; this calls SAGE which displays the mask shown below. The user can now start to define the system using the SAPP method.

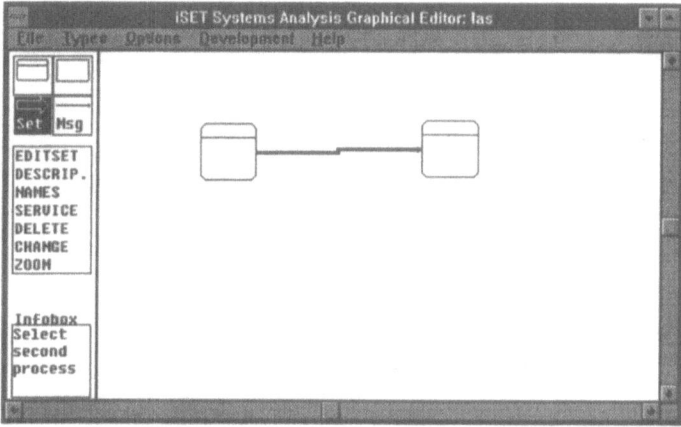

Figure 17.10: Screen for the SAPP Specification

The figure shows the SAGE screen after the creation of two processes and a message set.The analysis of the logistics of the brewery leads to the following set of processes:

- A process to manage the data transfer with the UNIX system
- A process to mangage an SQL database interface
- A process to interact with the user via an graphical user interface
  A process to control the communication with all peripheral devices of the system via subprocesses.
- A process that serves as print server
- A process that communiates with magnetic card reader terminals and implements the neccessary protocol.
- A process that performs the communication with the indicator-board and implements the device specific protocol.
- A process that controls the state of the gate and sends messages when the state changes.
- A kernel process set that manages the data and control flow.
- Context processes for the printers, the magnetic card reader terminals, the gates, the indicator-board and the UNIX connection.

The graphical layout shown below is the result of this analysis of the system:

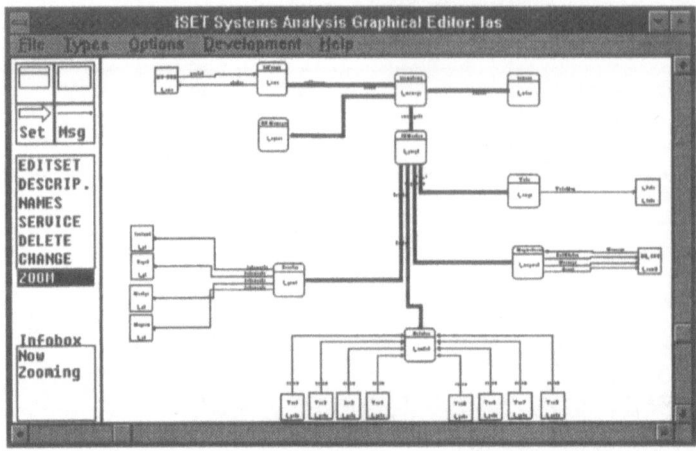

Figure 17.11: SAPP Specification of the Brewery Logistics System

In addition to creating processes and context processes the user must define the communication between these entities by defining messages and messages sets. The figure below shows how to enter a message set:

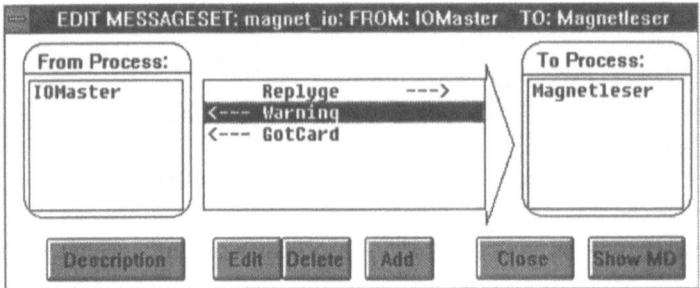

Figure 17.12: Screen for Describing Messages

It is easy to add messages to a message set or delete them. A message set defines the various messages exchanged between processes. That means that it can be used as a protocol between other processes. Thus it is possible that the list 'From Process' or the list of potential receivers 'To Process' contains more than one name. The user can now print the system graph; this is shown below:

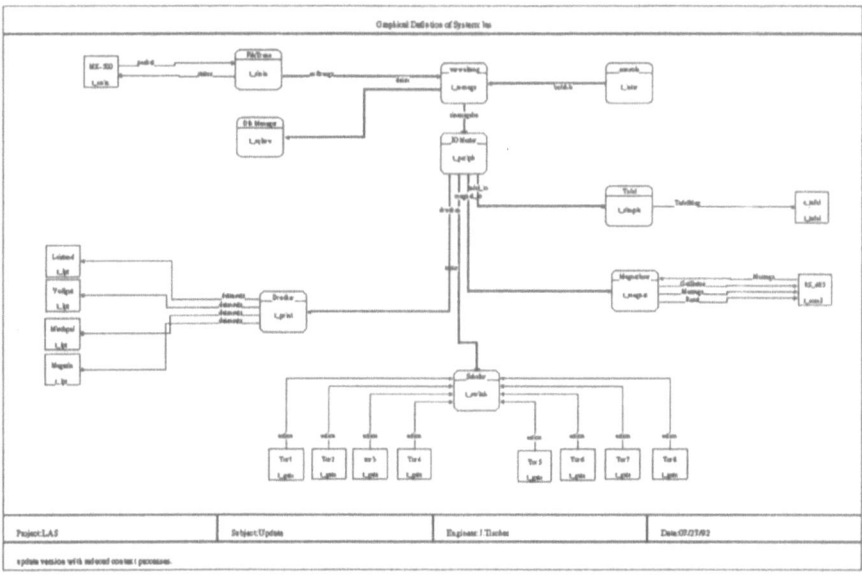

Figure 17.13: Print Out of the SAPP Specification of the Brewery Logistics System

After defining the system the user leaves the editor and returns to SYSMAN. SYSMAN takes all the new information and creates all files and code frames neccessary to prepare the work for the next step, the specification of the individual process types. After this has been done SYSMAN displays all essential information about the system: all process names and process types and a message dictionary containing all messages and message sets used in the system:

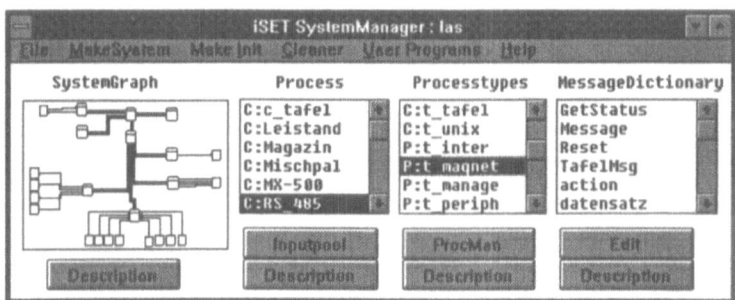

Figure 17.14: Overview of the SAPP Specification of the Brewery Logistics System

At this point the user should select a process type and call PROCMAN to proceed with the specification of individual process types. PROCMAN displays the following screen:

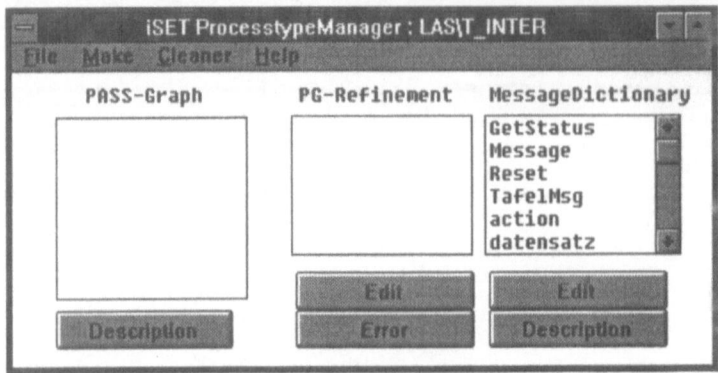

Figure 17.15: Screen for the Input of PASS Specifications

The only information available is the message dictionary. Now the graphical editor is called to create a new process type using PASS. The user clicks on the empty rectangle and PAGE, the graphical specification editor, is activated so that the user can start specifying the solution using a full graphical approach. To show more details we select the process type 'T_MAGNET' and show PAGE with a zoomed area of the graph:

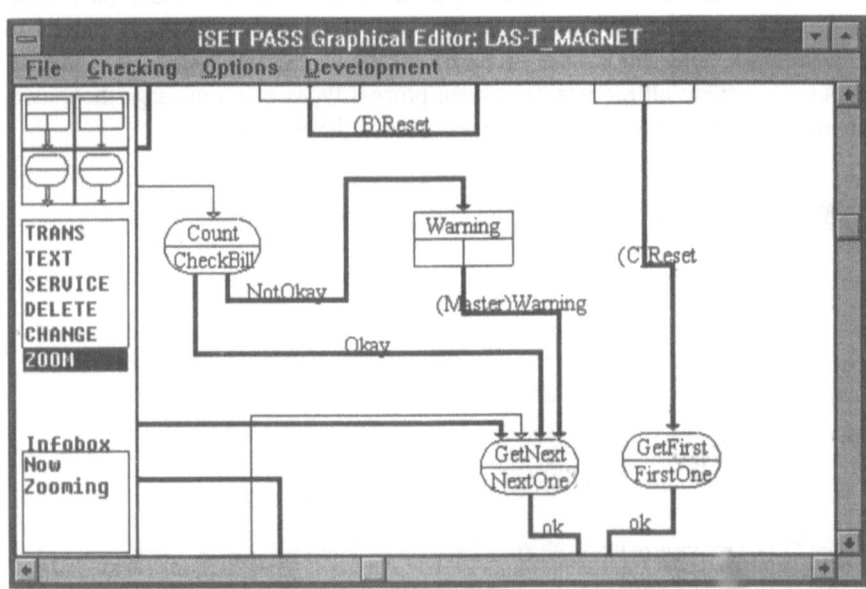

Figure 17.16: Input Screen for PASS Graphs

The different node and transition types of the PASS method can be seen. For instance consider the operation node *Count* on the left side of the screen. In this state the process calls the function *CheckBill* which performs a check of the status information of each magnetic card reader station. The results of this check are *Okay* or *NotOkay*. If the result is *Okay* then the process performs a transition to the *GetNext* state otherwise the process performs a transition to the send node *Warning* in which the message *Warning* is sent to the process *Master* in order to inform the operator that there is a malfunction of a magnetic card reader station. After this message has been transmitted we reach the *GetNext* state. *Master* is a formal parameter which means that it is just a place holder for a parameter that will replace it. The translation of formal parameters into actual parameters is done later by the system code generator.

After the process type has been specified we obtain the graph shown below:

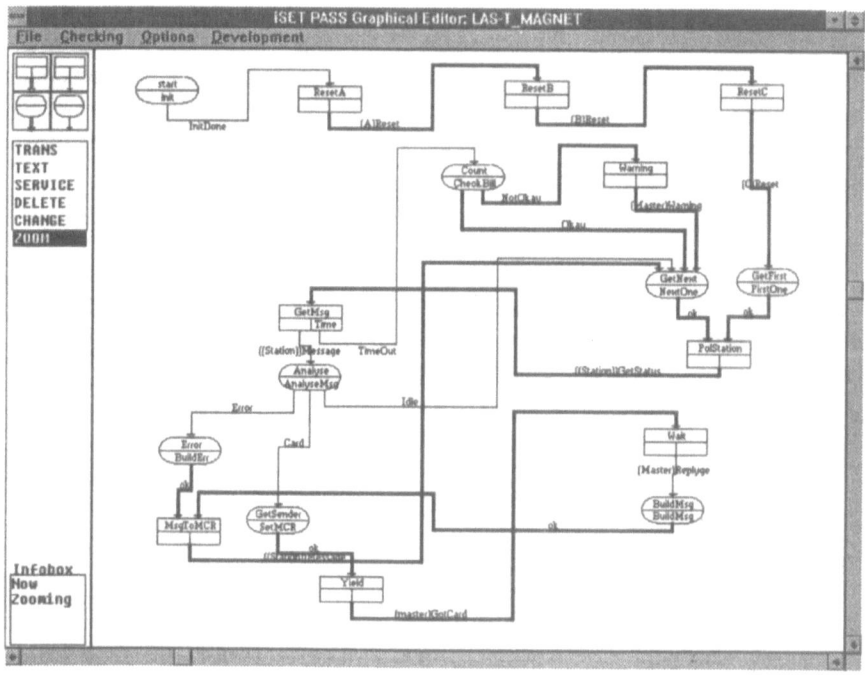

Figure 17.17: PASS Graph of a Process Type of the Brewery Logistics System

After exit from PAGE a code generator is started that transforms the specification into code. All information is extracted and PROCMAN can present new information about the particular process type. A list of all refinements and a drawing of the graphical layout of the specification are generated:

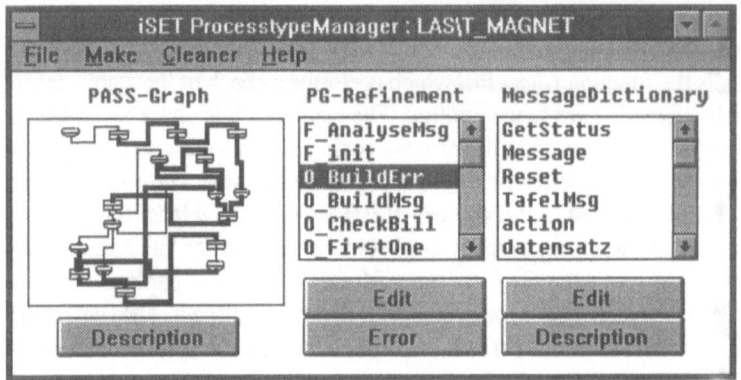

Figure 17.18: Screen for Generating the Template for the PASS graph refinements

The code generator transforms the graph into an C-code and generates code frames that can contain the refinement code. Also all the code is generated to prepare the message routing for this process type. Here is an example of a refinement generated for the PASS function 'AnalyseMsg' that produces the results 'Card','Error' and 'Idle'. These symbols can be used directly in the C-code. The generator has generated the preprocessor definitions.

```
#include "c:\3c_iset\systems\LAS\T_MAGNET\PGR_CODE.H"
#include "c:\3c_iset\systems\LAS\T_MAGNET\PGR_USER.C"
int   T_MAGNET_F_AnalyseMsg(ptr_lcb)
_3C_USER_T_MAGNET *ptr_lcb;
{/*3C begin*/
  /*3C* +--------------------------------------------+ */
  /*3C* | FUNCTION SPECIFICATION :   |   AnalyseMsg  | */
  /*3C* +----------------------------+---------------+ */
  /*3C* |      possible results   :  |      Card     | */
  /*3C* |                         :  |      Error    | */
  /*3C* |                         :  |      Idle     | */
  /*3C* +----------------------------+---------------+ */
  /*3C_code_3C*/


} /*3C end
```

Figure 17.19: Automaticaly generated C Code Frame for the PASS Graph Refinements

These steps are repeated until all process types in the system have been specified. After this you go back to SYSMAN and calls IPET to specify the input pool structure of every process. The IPET menue appears on the screen and the user enters the input pool strategy for the selected process:

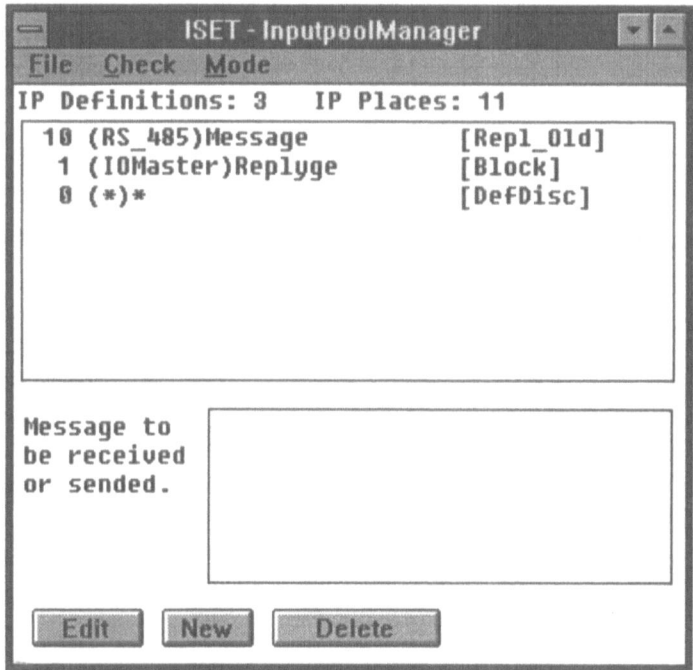

Figure 17.20: Screen for the Specification of Input Pools

Here it is even possible to test the input pool strategy. The user can enter test mode and send messages to the input pool. He can then watch how the input pool reacts and what happens to the messages. Further the input pool definition can be checked to detect semantic errors such as rules which never apply because other rules block the input pool.

Returning to SYSMAN all information needed to start the system code generator is available. This generator uses all the available information to generate code for the message transport, message routing, process scheduling, process interpretation etc. When all information is available SYSMAN can be made to call the compilers and linkers and try to generate a complete system or the runtime generator PRATE can be called. This generates a runtime environment to test and simulate the process system allthough only a few process have been implemented completely. Early prototyping of a complex process system is a very valuable feature because it allows the user to correct design errors in early stages of the project.

Controll Questions

1. What are the basic concepts of the SAPP/PASS based SEE?
2. What are the related tools?
3. Which software engineering activities are supported by which tools?
4. What is the relationship between these tools and the SAPP/PASS methodology described in chapters 9 and 15.

Exercises

1. What type of SEE and related tools do you use?
2. What strengths and weaknesses does it have in comparison to our SEE?
3. How can you combine your current SEE with SAPP/PASS tools?

18 SAPP/PASS Applications and Experiences

This chapter explains how SAPP/PASS can be used for the development of distributed programs and what experience has been gained with it so far.

18.1 Development of Communication Software

The use of SAPP/PASS to describe the behaviour of communication software is demonstrated using a very simple example.

Two applications A and B which run on different computers should communicate with each other. For simplicity we assume that A should send only one byte at a time and B never sends data to A. The host systems are connected by a very simple network consisting of only a direct line. The error rate of the line is high; therefore simple communication software on each host system should help to reduce the incidence of error. It is assumed that a parity bit and a simple acknowledgement mechanism is sufficient. This means that application A gives a data byte to a communication software entity A (also called a protocol entity below) which adds a parity bit and initiates the transmission via the network, in this case a direct line. At the other end the data is received by a communication software entity B, which checks the parity. If this is correct a positive acknowledgement is sent to entity A and the data byte is given to application B. If the parity is wrong, B sends a negative acknowledgement to entity A which sends the data again until it receives a positive acknowledgement.

The figure below shows the processes which represent different parts of the communication system.

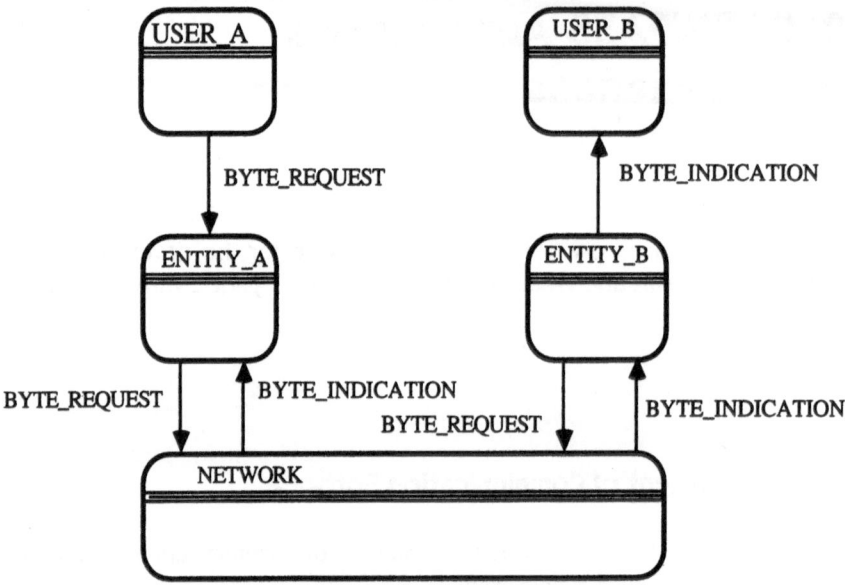

Figure 18.1: Simple Communication System

The applications, i.e. the protocol entities and the transmission line, are modelled by processes. The data sent by application A is given to ENTITY_A as a parameter of the message BYTE_REQUEST. Application B receives data from ENTITY_B as the value of the parameter of the message BYTE_INDICATION. The processes ENTITY_A and ENTITY_B communicate with the process NETWORK which models the behaviour of the transmission line.

The next figure shows the complete PASS specification of the process ENTITY_A.

ENTITY_A

input   pool: maximum   size: 5
structure: 4 * (USER_A)BYTE_REQUEST
                  1 * (NETWORK) BYTE_INDICATION

PASS   graph:

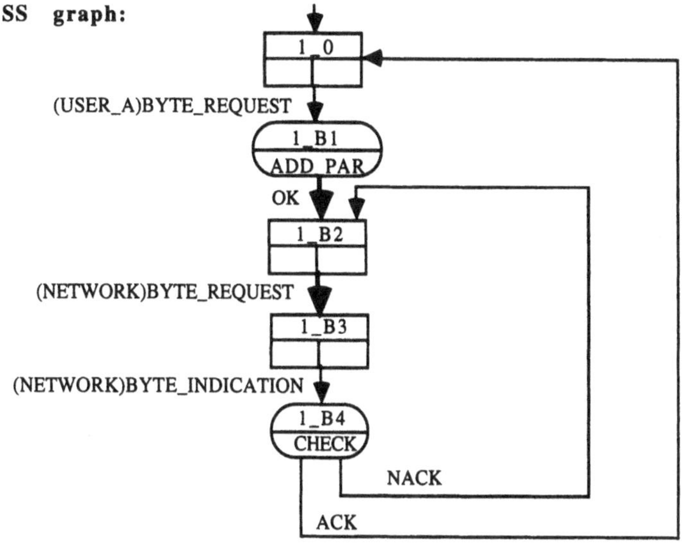

```
                              │
                         ┌────▼────┐
                         │  1_0    │◄──────────────────────┐
                         └────┬────┘                       │
    (USER_A)BYTE_REQUEST      │                            │
                         ┌────▼────┐                       │
                         │  1_B1   │                       │
                         ╲ ADD_PAR ╱                       │
                         └────┬────┘                       │
                     OK       │       ┌──────────┐         │
                         ┌────▼────┐◄──┘          │         │
                         │  1_B2   │              │         │
                         └────┬────┘              │         │
   (NETWORK)BYTE_REQUEST      │                   │         │
                         ┌────▼────┐              │         │
                         │  1_B3   │              │         │
                         └────┬────┘              │         │
 (NETWORK)BYTE_INDICATION     │                   │         │
                         ┌────▼────┐              │         │
                         │  1_B4   │              │         │
                         ╲  CHECK  ╱              │         │
                         └────┬────┘              │         │
                              │        NACK       │         │
                              ├───────────────────┘         │
                              │  ACK                        │
                              └─────────────────────────────┘
```

PASS   graph   refinements:

<u>local variables:</u> SEND_BYTE, RECEIVE_BYTE : BYTE

<u>receive message specification</u>
    BYTE_INDICATION (PAR : BYTE)
        effect: RECEIVE_BYTE := PAR;

    BYTE_REQUEST (PAR : BYTE)
        effect: SEND_BYTE := PAR;

<u>send message specification:</u>
    BYTE_REQUEST (PAR : BYTE)
        value: PAR := SENDBYTE;

<u>internal functions:</u>
    CHECK
        results: if RECEIVE_BYTE = '11111111' then return ACK else return NACK

<u>internal operations:</u>
    ADD_PAR
        effect: (* add the correct parity to the value in SEND_BYTE *)
                (* and return OK to the PASS graph   *)

Figure 18.2: PASS Specification of Communication Software

In the **input pool clause** of the example, a maximum size of 5 messages is specified. The input pool is structured. At most 4 messages from the application (BYTE_REQUEST) can be stored in the input pool. If the application tries to deposit a fifth message, it will be blocked until at least one message has been removed from the input pool by the process ENTITY_A. One slot of the input pool is reserved for messages from NETWORK. This is necessary so that ENTITY_A can obtain acknowledgements for data which it has transmitted.

In the **PASS graph** the initial state 1_0 is marked by a small arrow. In state 1_0 the process ENTITY_A awaits a message of type BYTE_REQUEST from application A. The parity bit is added to the user data in state 1_B1 by performing the internal operation ADD_PAR. In state 1_B1 the data byte is given to the provider by sending the message BYTE_REQUEST to the process NETWORK. Now in state 1_B3 process ENTITY_A waits for the acknowledgement. The acknowledgement is given to process ENTITY_A by the message BYTE_INDICATION from process NETWORK. In state 1_B4 the contents of this message is checked whether it is a positive acknowlegement (ACK) or a negative acknowledgement (NACK). If the acknowledgement is positive, the process continues to state 1_0, otherwise to state 1_B2 in which case the user data is sent again.

In this example pseudo-code is used to specify the **PASS graph refinements.** These are divided into five clauses:

- The local variable clause containing the declaration of all local variables of the process. The process ENTITY_A has the two local variables SEND_BYTE and RECEIVE_BYTE which are both of type BYTE.
- The receive message specification clause in which all messages received by the process are described. In our example the message BYTE_REQUEST has one parameter called PAR of type BYTE. The effect of receiving this message on the local variables is described in the effect clause of the receive message specification. If the message BYTE_REQUEST is received the value of the parameter PAR is copied into the local variable SEND BYTE.
- The send message specification clause in which all messages sent by the process are described. In our example the message BYTE_REQUEST has the parameter PAR of type BYTE. The send message specifications describe how the values of the message parameters are derived from the values of the local variables. In our example the value of the parameter is equal to the value of the local variable SEND_BYTE.
- The internal operation specification clause in which the internal operations of the process are specified. In our example the only internal operation, ADD_PAR, is specified in natural language for simplicity. The specification of an internal operation must also define which results are given to the PASS graph. In our example the only possible result is OK.
- The internal function clause in which the internal functions are specified. The dependence of the various results of an internal function on the values of the local variables is specified in the internal function specifications. The only internal function in our example has the result ACK if the local variable RECEIVE_BYTE has the value 11111111, otherwise the result is NACK. This

means that if the value of the message parameter **BYTE INDICATION** received form the process **NETWORK** is 11111111, then this is a positive acknowledgement and all other values are negative acknowledgements.

Specification of ISO/OSI protocols:
The communication between different computer systems has become very important. Different systems cooperate to provide certain services to their users. Because of the complexity of the services and the variety of systems involved, communication protocols can also be very complex. Layers are used as a general method for structuring complex problems. In the ISO Reference Model for Open Systems /ISO7498/ (ISO Reference model for OSI), complex communication protocols are structured in layers where each layer is further structured in protocol entities. An entity uses the services of entities in the layer below (the service provider) for communicating with another entity in the same layer (a peer entity).

The service provided by a layer is described in terms of service primitives. These can be considered as interactions between service users and service providers.

The service provider and the service user exchange the service primitives via Service Access Points, SAPs. Each entity uses and provides certain service access points. For a layer N the relationship between the SAP provided i.e. the entity, and the SAP used is called an N-mapping. The SAP concept is a way of addressing the entities. The reference model says nothing about how SAPs can be implemented. The following figure shows the structure of a protocol layer according to the ISO/ OSI model. The protocol, i.e. the communication between entities in the same layer, is executed indirectly. The protocol data units or PDUs, which contain information exchanged between peer entities, are given to the service provider as parameters of service primitives. Then service provider delivers the PDUs as the parameters of a corresponding service primitive to the peer entity.

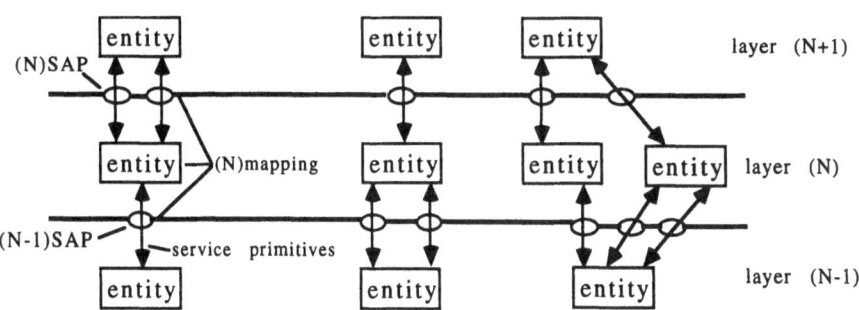

Figure 18.3: Mapping in Protocol Layers

It is possible to have several entities in the same system. Normally a connection crosses the boundaries of a system. The entities of a layer N in one system from a subsystem /ISO7498/.

If a subsystem is described in terms of the specification technique PASS each service primitive is associated with a message and each entity with a process which executes the protocol. It is possible to have several processes in an entity but for simplicity we disregard this possibility. The N-mapping is to be done by a layer management facility which is also a process in terms of PASS. Only this process has information about the N-mapping. All the service primitives, i.e. messages, sent to a layer are received by this housekeeping process. One message parameter contains the identifier of the SAP via which this message has arrived. The housekeeping process forwards the message to the target entity.

If an entity should send a message, this is sent to the housekeeping process which forwards the message to the layer administrator below or above. With this architecture the entities are not concerned with the N-mapping. This corresponds to the protocol standards which also describe the communication protocols independently of the mapping. The following figure shows the communication structure of an N-subsystem.

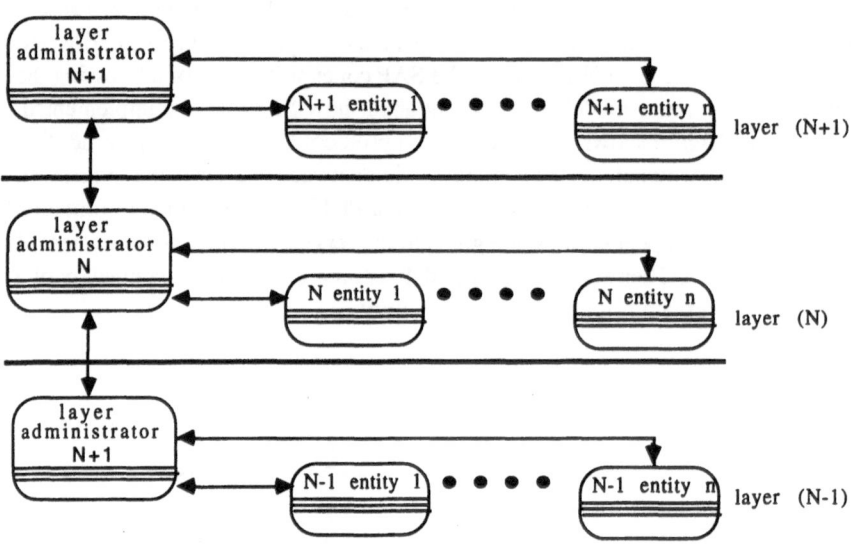

Figure 18.4: PASS Communication Structure of an N-subsystem

The communication structure can be simplified if only the communication protocol is specified. As already mentioned above, the N-mapping does not concern the protocol itself.

Only the service of layer N-1 is important when specifying the protocol of layer N; not the protocol of layer N-1.

In the structure discussed above an entity is specified dependent on a housekeeping process but it must also be possible to specify an entity, i.e. protocol, independent of this special environment. From the point of view of the protocol it is only important whether a service primitive, i.e. a message, is invoked from the layer below or above. The N-mapping can be disregarded.

Those aspects of the layer below which are important for the entity under consideration, i.e. the service provided, can be expressed in terms of possible sequences of service primitives and the parameter value dependence. This can be described by one or several PASS processes.

The same considerations lead to similar results for the layer above.

With these simplifications we come to the general structure used for protocol specifications, shown in the next figure. This structure contains only aspects which are important for a protocol, i.e. entity, specification.

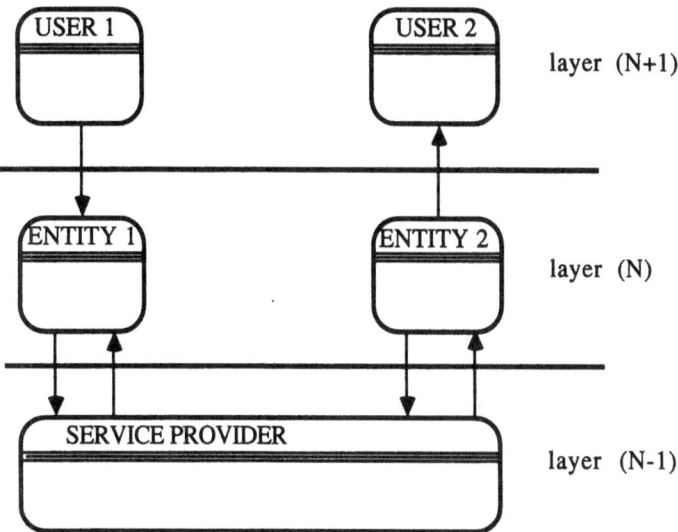

Figure 18.5: PASS Communication Structure of a Protocol Specification

However we want to use the same protocol specification in both contexts. PASS allows this. An entity can be specified as a process type. This process type can be used in systems where one is only interested in the protocol or where one is interested in the subsystem. It is only necessary to declare a specific entity with the corresponding communication partners. Below the declaration for the N-subsystem and the protocol specification are shown. 'USER' and 'PROVIDER' are the formal names used in the process type specification.

a) declare   N_ENTITY_1 of type PROTOCOL where
              (USER = LAYER_ADMINISTRATOR_N,
              PROVIDER = LAYER_ADMINISTRATOR_N)

b) declare   ENTITY_1 of type PROTOCOL where
              (USER=USER1, PROVIDER = SERVICE_PROVIDER);

18.2 Development of Process Control Software

In order to demonstrate the use of PASS in developing process control software the intersection traffic control system is used. The figure below shows the SAPP specification of the control system.

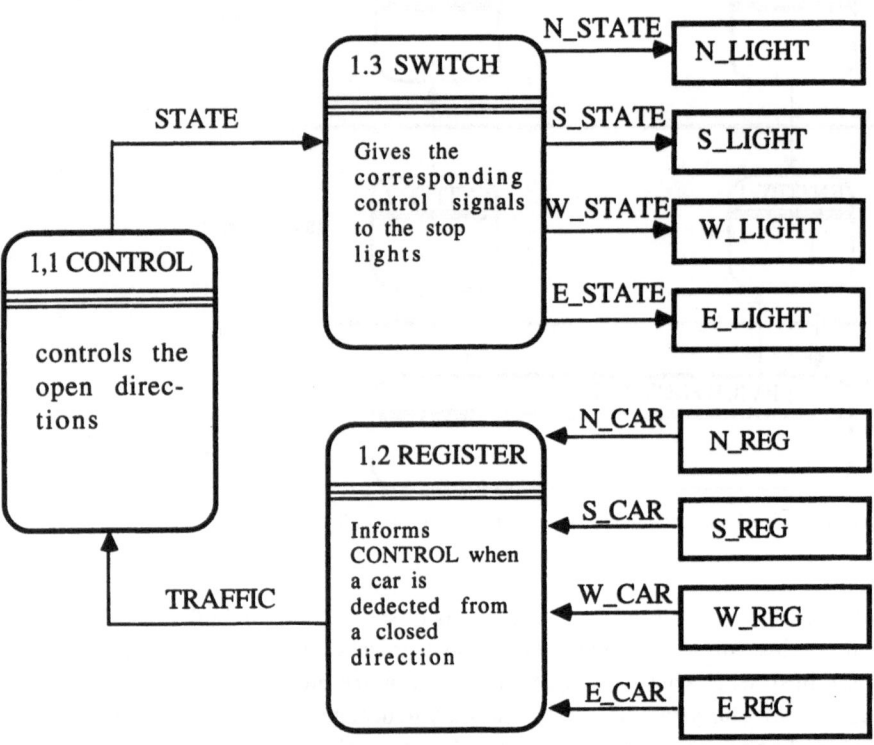

Figure 18.6: Structure of the Intersection Control System

After decomposing a system into processes it is necessary to investigate the behaviour of the external entities. These can be considered as predefined processes. In order to understand the behaviour of external entities, their behaviour in the interaction with processes can also be described in PASS. In our example the behavior of the external entities N_REG, S_REG, E_REG, and W_REG is identical. Therefore we can define a process type which describes the behaviour of all these external entities. The following diagram shows the PASS specification of this process type.

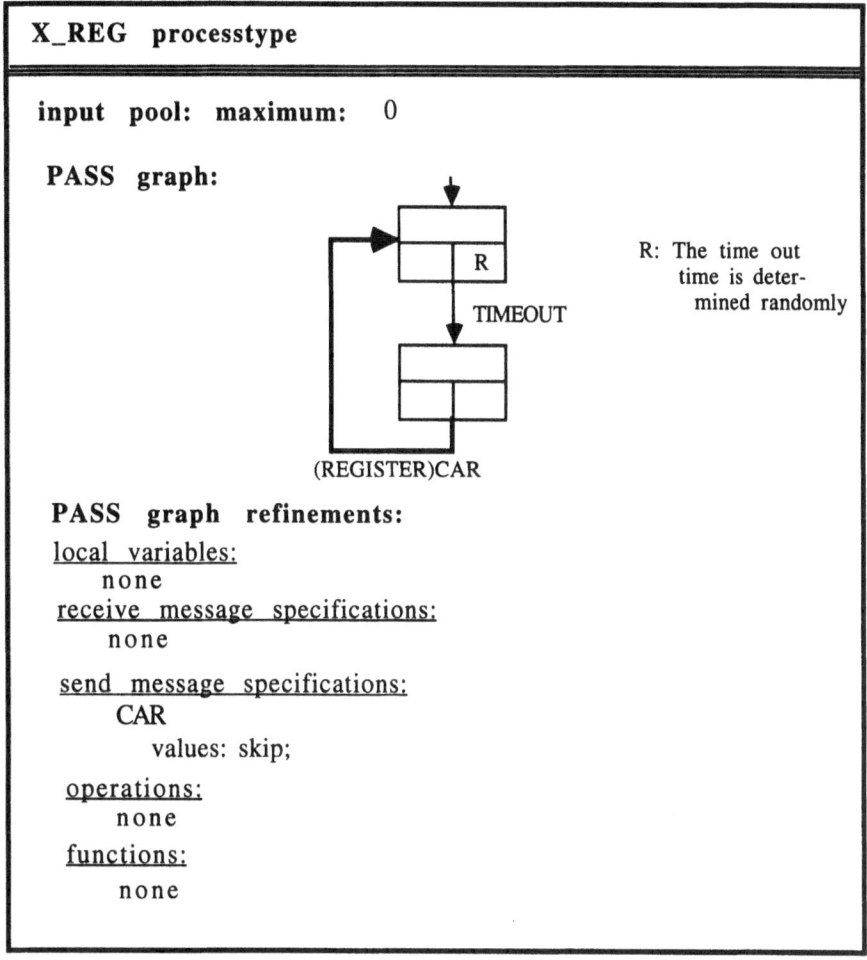

Figure 18.7: PASS Specification of a Process Type which describes external Entities

The process type described above sends the message of type CAR to the process REGISTER with random delays between successive messages. This corresponds to the arrival of cars at random times. The following declarations create four processes of type X-REG. These processes correspond to the external entities representing the car detection devices:

declare N_REG of type X-REG
declare S_REG of type X-REG
declare W_REG of type X-REG
declare E_REG of type X-REG

The figure below shows the specification of the process REGISTER.

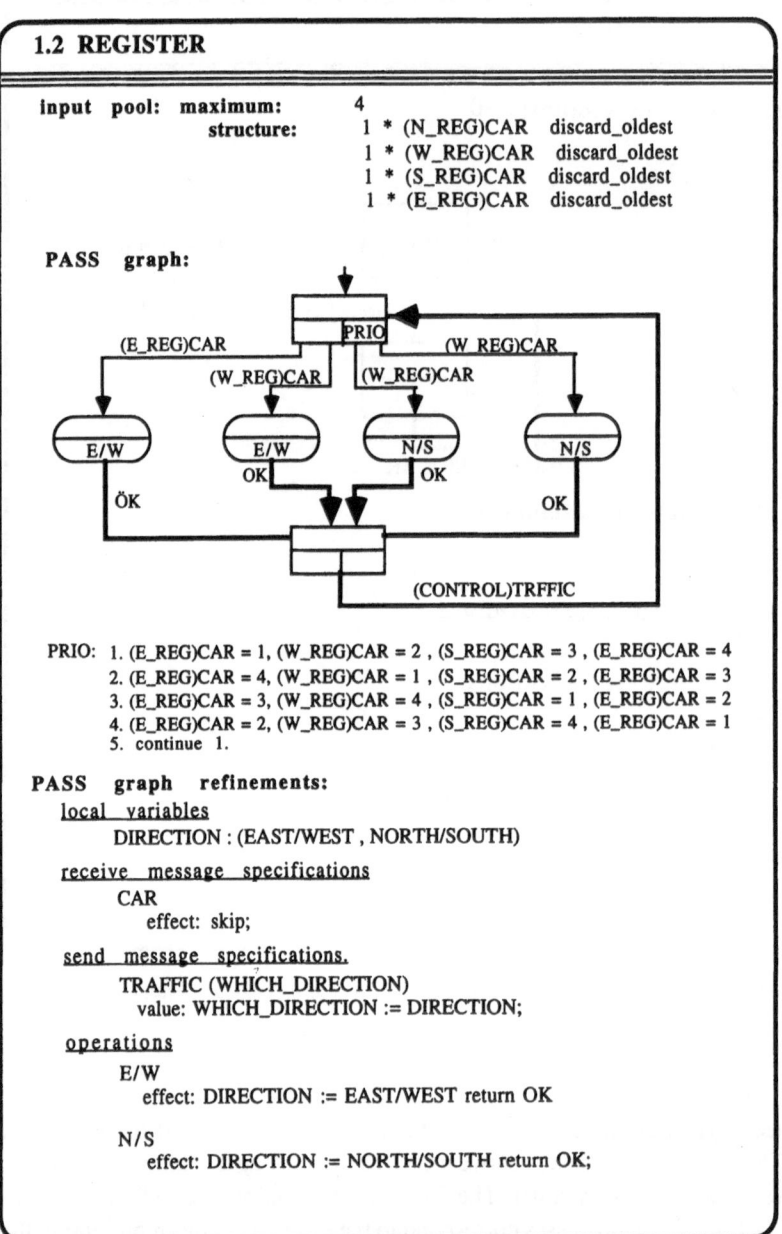

Figure 18.8: PASS Specification of Process REGISTER

This process receives messages of type CAR from the car detectors declared above. The process REGISTER informs the process CONTROL from which directions cars have been detected. The PASS specification of the process CONTROL is shown in the figure below.

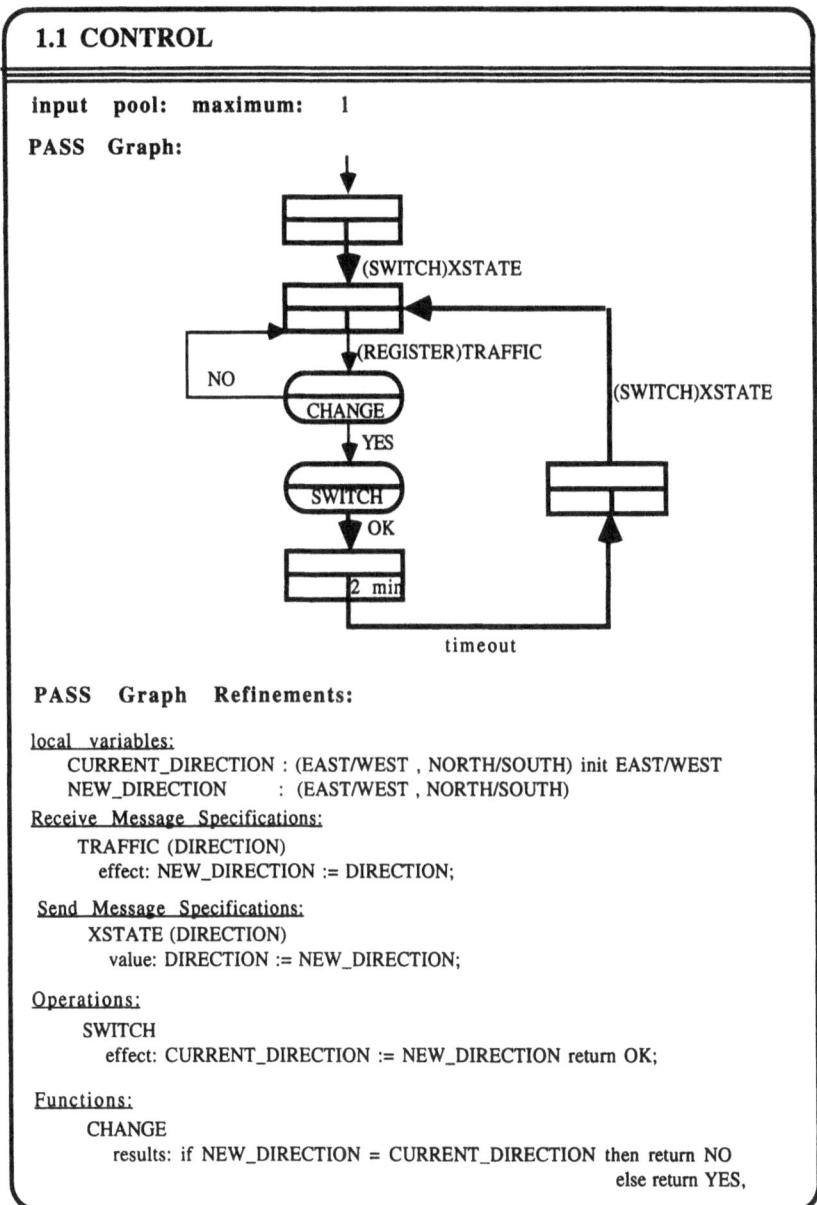

Figure 18.9: PASS Specification of Process CONTROL

The process CONTROL determines whether the open direction has to be changed, and informs the process SWITCH which controls the traffic lights. The figure below shows the PASS specification of the process SWITCH.

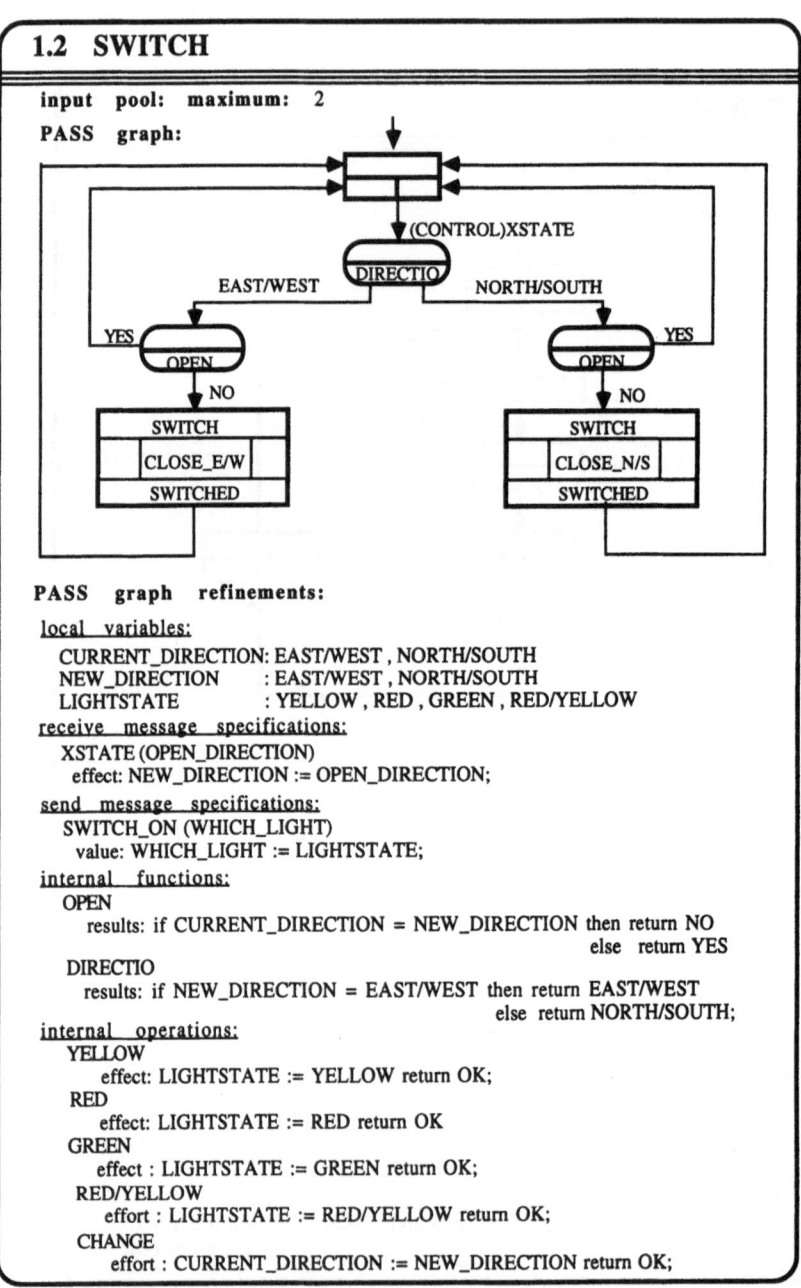

1.2   SWITCH

input   pool: maximum: 2

PASS   graph:

PASS   graph   refinements:

local   variables:
   CURRENT_DIRECTION: EAST/WEST , NORTH/SOUTH
   NEW_DIRECTION   : EAST/WEST , NORTH/SOUTH
   LIGHTSTATE   : YELLOW , RED , GREEN , RED/YELLOW

receive   message   specifications:
   XSTATE (OPEN_DIRECTION)
    effect: NEW_DIRECTION := OPEN_DIRECTION;

send   message   specifications:
   SWITCH_ON (WHICH_LIGHT)
    value: WHICH_LIGHT := LIGHTSTATE;

internal   functions:
   OPEN
    results: if CURRENT_DIRECTION = NEW_DIRECTION then return NO
                                   else   return YES
   DIRECTIO
    results: if NEW_DIRECTION = EAST/WEST then return EAST/WEST
                                else   return NORTH/SOUTH;

internal   operations:
   YELLOW
    effect: LIGHTSTATE := YELLOW return OK;
   RED
    effect: LIGHTSTATE := RED return OK
   GREEN
    effect : LIGHTSTATE := GREEN return OK;
   RED/YELLOW
    effort : LIGHTSTATE := RED/YELLOW return OK;
   CHANGE
    effort : CURRENT_DIRECTION := NEW_DIRECTION return OK;

Figure 18.10: PASS Specification of the Process SWITCH

In the process SWITCH the macros CLOSE_E/W and CLOSE_N/S of type CHANGE are used. These macros define the communication behaviour of the connection to the traffic lights which switches the open direction of the intersection. The figure below shows the specification of this macro type and the declaration of the macros.

macro_type: CHANGE

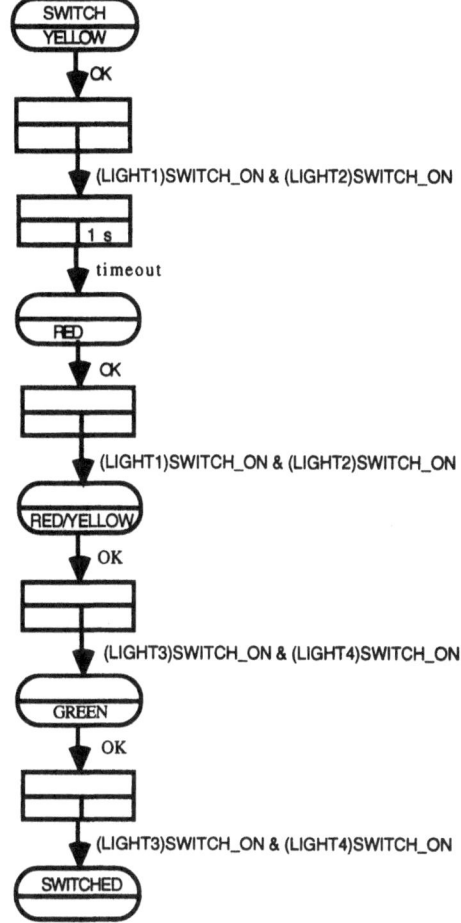

macros:
    declare CLOSE_E/W of type CHANGE where (LIGHT1 = N_LIGHT,
           LIGHT2 = S_LIGHT, LIGHT3 = W_LIGHT, LIGHT4 = E_LIGHT);
    declare CLOSE_N/S of type CHANGE where (LIGHT1 = W_LIGHT,
           LIGHT2 = E_LIGHT, LIGHT3 = N_LIGHT, LIGHT4 = S_LIGHT);

Figure 18.11: Specification of the Macro CHANGE and the Declaration of the Macros CLOSE_E/W and CLOSE_S

18.3 Experience

Up to now PASS has mainly been applied to communication software. Practical experience was gained by implementing the following ISO/OSI communication protocols:
- LLC Type 2 protocol /TSMLA90/
- Transport protocol (OSI layer 4) class 0 /FASCH91/
- Session protocol (OSI layer 5) which was implemented in Pascal /FLCHEF87/
- Presentation protocol (OSI layer 6) which was implemented in Pascal
- Remote operation service element (ROSE, OSI layer 7)
- Association Control service element (ACSE, OSI layer 7)
- Remote database Access (RDA, OSI layer 7)
- Manufacturing Message Service (MMS, MAP protocol)

The implemention of these communication protocols using PASS tools was much easier than traditional coding. The use of PASS Transition Editor PATE (an editor specially designed for use with PASS) helps to avoid incorrect protocol state transition sequences. The plausibility checks in PATE allow the specification to be tested at PASS graph level.

The code generator can be instructed to include a PASS state tracing facility in the program code. This trace records the sequence of PASS states of the protocol automaton. Thus the debugging and maintenance of the implementation is done at an abstract level of PASS and not at the level of the programming language.

PASS has been used to specify several programs for controlling technical processes. Control programs for physical experiments were specified in PASS and implemented in PEARL and hardware /BESO85/.

The control program for a glass tube production line was also specified in PASS and implemented in PEARL. In this case the behaviour of the technical process was also specified and implemented. The implementation of the technical process was used as a test bed for the process control software /BABA85/.

PASS and the use of the tools can be learned very easily. PASS was applied by various people who were not familiar with this technique. PASS tools generate the complete code for the PASS graph and a code frame for PASS graph refinements. The structure of the PASS tools reflects the separation between the main aspects of process description. Thus PASS methodology forces the implementor to create a well structured design.

Control Questions:

1. What is the structure of a communication system described in SAPP?
2. What is the SAPP structure of an OSI based communication system?
3. What is the basic structure of a process control system?
4. How can PASS be used to describe the behaviour of the technical process to be controlled?'

Exercises:

1. Describe the basic structure of your communication system in SAPP.
2. Describe some components of your communication system in PASS.
3. Describe the basic structure of a process control system in your environment in SAPP.
4. Describe the behaviour of some components of this process in PASS.

19 Discussion of SAPP/PASS

This chapter describes how SAPP/PASS fits into the software engineering world discussed in chapters 1 to 9.

19.1 Relationship to Types of Software Life Cycles

SAPP/PASS can be based on the incremental, evolutionary or operational development method. It is also possible to use some combination of them. In the following sections the different aspects of these development methods are discussed in more detail in connection with SAPP/PASS.

19.1.1 Elements of Incremental Software Development

The sequence of decomposition steps suggested in SAPP allows system components to be broken down more or less independently of each other. After decomposing a system into process sets only the most important process sets must be further broken down into processes. These processes are described in PASS and then finally implemented. Other process sets are further decomposed step by step, specified in PASS, and implemented.

Messages between process sets are only exchanged by the corresponding interface processes. The interface processes are the only gates to other processes. In most cases therefore, only the interface processes of already finished processes must be changed, in order to implement the next process set and add it to the existing system. Sometimes it may be necessary to change the interface process and several other processes. In such cases the decomposition of the system should be checked. It could be an indication that the decomposition into process sets has not been properly done. The relationship between processes in different process sets should be as loose as possible. This means that:

1. Messages should be exchanged rarely across process set borders and
2. input pools of interface processes should have many slots for messages from other process sets. Synchronous message exchange across borders between process sets should be avoided.

An interface process represents a process set to its environment. This allows processes to be added to a process set step by step. If changes to the interface process are required then these should be invisible to other process sets. In some cases this can mean that a process set only consists of an interface process. All other processes in the process set can be added later.

The incremental software development method can also be used to develop PASS graph refinements. These can be very complicated. The development of the PASS graph refinements of a process can be a separate project, e.g. the PASS graph refinement can contain a data base system. It can be developed according the incremental software life cycle.

19.1.2 Elements of Evolutionary Software Development

As already mentioned, a system should be decomposed so that the relationships between process sets are very weak. Weak relationships between process sets allow them to be developed more or less independently of each other, as stated earlier. A process set can be decomposed into a number of processes, possibly of different types. Different process structures of a process set should not have much impact on other process sets. This way different process structures inside a process set can be tested.

If new facilities have to be added this can mean that new process sets must be added. In the initial system decomposition this could not have been foreseen. Embedding a new process set primarily means changing processes in process sets which will use these new facilities.

Complicated PASS graph refinements can also be developed in an evolutionary manner. This can be necessary when difficult problems or problems that are not completely understood are to be solved.

19.1.3 Elements of Operational Software Development

Process behaviour is specified in PASS in a form in which it can be directly executed. This allows the behaviour of a process to be tested immediately. PASS graphs of processes can be tested without PASS graph refinements.

PASS graph refinements can be specified in any sequential programming technique, depending on the preference of the implementor and the availability of know how or tools. The implementation of PASS graph refinements can be tested independently of the corresponding PASS graph. PASS graph refinements can be added to the PASS graph later and the complete process can then be executed and tested.

The interworking of processes in a process set can be tested independent of other process sets. Only the communication of the interface process with other process sets must be simulated.

19.1.4 Combinations of Software Development Paradigms

Different development methods can be applied in order to develop a system using SAPP/PASS. An incremental or evolutionary approach can be used to decompose a system into process sets. If the incremental method is used, the whole system is broken down into process sets.

Different types of software life cycles can be chosen to develop process sets. Instead of decomposing the complete system, only an initial subset of the intended system is broken down into process sets. Different types of software life cycle can then be used to implement the process sets. Once the problems of implementing a process set are well known even the conventional life cycle can be chosen as the development procedure.

As already mentioned above the development of PASS graph refinements can follow any software development method.

SAPP/PASS allows the use of different software life cycles at different stages of the development. A suitable method for the particular problem can be selected.

19.2 Reuse of Software

The development of software is very expensive. In order to reduce the cost of development, software which is already available should be used in other projects. Today almost no software is developed from scratch. Software that is to be reused has to be embedded into the system to be developed. This should be supported by a development method. SAPP/PASS allows the reuse of already available software in the following areas:
- in process sets
- in shared objects
- in processes

Reuse of software in process sets:
Software that is already available consists of one or several processes. This software must be integrated into a system. The available software can be considered as processes of a process set. This process set is also represented to other process sets by an interface process. The interface process connects the reused software to the rest of the system and hides the specialties of the reused software.

Reuse of software in shared objects:
Software that is lready available can be integrated into shared objects. Very common examples of the reuse of software in shared objects are file systems and data base systems. The following figure shows an exmple of the use of a data base system inside a shared object.

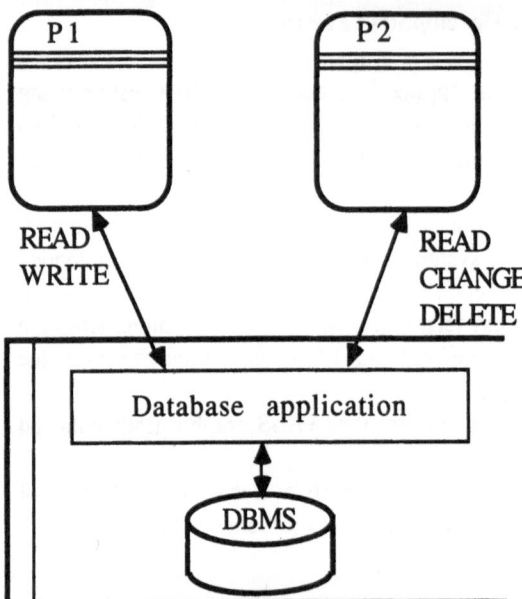

Figure 19.1: Example of the Reuse of Software

In the above example the implementation of the operations READ, WRITE, CHANGE, DELETE is based on a database management system (DBMS). These operations are used by the processes P1 and P2.

When specifying a shared object based on existing software, the description of its facilities will become part of the specification of the shared object.

Reuse of software in processes:
Software that is already available can be used in PASS graph refinements. This is done in the same way as shared objects. A statistics package is an example of software used in PASS graph refinements.

19.3 SAPP Descriptions of Systems

In SAPP more or less the same concepts as in structured analysis are used for requirements specification. The main difference is that the parts of the system identified are considered as single processes or sets of processes. This means that SAPP includes control flow aspects. Processes are asynchronous. SAPP considers a program system as a structure of elements. Such a structure has several levels. Each group of elements is highly independent of the others. The elements of the structure cooperate to reach the common goal.

Structured analysis differs in that it does not make any assumptions about the execution sequences. Each system part identified in structured analysis is only considered as a data transformation.

In SAPP the same ways are used to specify the interaction with the system environment.

The similarity between SAPP and structured analysis SA allows a smooth transformation from one to the other. This means that developers who are used to SA do not need to learn a totally new technology.

19.4 PASS Specifications of Processes

In principle PASS defines only a structure for describing processes. Processes communicate and use local and shared objects. PASS allows the integration of different types of communication and synchronisation. This flexibility allows a developer to use the method that fits the problem best. It is not useful to discuss the advantages and disadvantages of synchronous and asynchronous message exchange or message exchange versus remote procedure call.

Methods at different levels of abstraction can be used to describe the behaviour of a process. It depends mainly on the state of the project and the personal taste of the developer. We suggested a state transition model. This is in accordance with our personal taste because it is similar to a control flow diagram which is known to nearly every programmer. But we have shown that other methods can also be used.

Object-oriented programming and concurrency is a very tricky issue. It has been said that object oriented-programming and concurrency are fundamentally incompatible. Others say that there are problems but they can resolved. Nevertheless there is ongoing discussion. At least until a final solution is found existing concepts for concurrent programming and object-oriented programming concepts can be used in an orthogonal way. Object-oriented techniques can be used in order to define the objects used by a process. The processes or subjects use objects.

19.5 Project Management

The clear structure of SAPP/PASS specifications allows the identification of corresponding development activities which have to be planned. This shows that the life cycle and the methods used influence project management.

In SAPP/PASS, software systems are considered teams of processes which work together to reach a common goal. The development teams are organised in the same way. The teams developing a software system communicate and synchronise with each other during the development process as the subsystems and processes do later in the running system. The structure of the development team reflects the structure of the system to be developed. If that team structure is very complicated then the program structure is complicated and there is a high possibility that something is not being done correctly. If there are communication and synchronisation problems in the development team then this can be an early sign of problems in the structure of the program under development.

19.6 Tools

Several tool concepts have been developed for the different development activities. We have shown that different theoretical concepts can be used as a basis for tools. The different tools developed for different development activities are only loosely coupled. This allows tools to be developed independently of each other. A SAPP tool is more or less independent of PASS tools. The PASS tools must only know that a SAPP tool produces SAPP objects – systems, subsystems, process sets, etc. There are the inputs of a PASS tool set. A PASS tool set may consist of tools for specifying input pools, behaviour description and refinements. A tool for the development of refinements must only know which message types are sent and received and which internal functions and operations are executed.

The structure of PASS allows the use of more or less independent tools.

19.7 Subject Oriented Programming

Object-oriented development methods are currently focused on sequential programs and are centered around data structures with related operations. Objects are mainly passive. They are used by the main program.

There are attempts to incorporate process concepts into the object- oriented programming method. Processes are considered as a special object class.

In SAPP/PASS we use a different approach. We bring together concurrent processes and objects as basic concepts. Processes can be seen as active subjects which use passive objects. For this type of programming we use the term Subject/Object-Oriented development (SOOD).

The basic assumption of subject/object-oriented programming is that the reality which has to be mapped into software. consists of two basic types of components. These components can be active or passive. Active components are called subjects and passive components are called objects.

Objects in subject-oriented programming are passive objects in the usual sense of object-oriented programming.

Subjects communicate with each other and use objects. Communication between subjects means that they exchange information. One subject can send information to another subject. The sending subject can either wait till the receiver 'listens' to it (sychronous message exchange) or the sender sends its information independent of whether the receiver 'listens' to the sender (asynchronous message exchange).

The receiver can wait for information or can react immediately by sending information to other subjects or invoking operations of private or shared objects; it can store that information for later reactions, or can ignore the information received. The information exchanged in a single communication action is called a message.

The use of an object by a subject means the invocation and execution of operations, i.e. methods of an object. Subjects use objects like people use cars. The object 'car' offers several operations, – accelerate, switch light on, etc. – but the possible operations of the car are executed by the subject 'driver'. The subject (or active component), 'traffic light' tells the subject 'car driver' to 'please stop' by switching on a red light. Normally the subject 'car' can either stop or can ignore the message. A subject can ignore messages from other subjects but an object has no influence which of its operations are executed at which time. Objects are passive.

Each subject uses one or several objects exclusively. These objects are called private objects. All objects exclusively used by one subject are called the private property of this subject. Objects which are used by several subjects are called shared objects. Shared objects used by a group of subjects are called the common property of this group of subjects. All subjects of a system form a society. All shared objects are the property of the society.

The following figure shows a society of subjects and the objects they use.

Figure 19.2: Subjects with their Objects

The figure shows the subjects Smith and Taylor. Subject Smith and Taylor communicate with each other. Subject Taylor tells subject Smith that he should close his window. Subject Smith receives the message and executes the appropriate operation. The window is a private object of subject Smith. Subject Smith says 'Thank You' to subject Taylor.

Characteristics of subjects:
Subjects are active. They exchange information and envoke operations in certain sequences. The exchange of information can have several properties. The sender can wait until the receiver has accepted the message or the receiver can wait until it receives a message from the sender This is called synchronous information exchange. Another possibility is that a subject has either an unlimited or limited information store. All messages are deposited in this information store until the appropriate subject decides to accept a message. This is called asynchronous information exchange. In certain states subjects do not even realise that another subject has sent them certain information instead of accepting or storing the information. The subject does not listen to the information sent. This is called impolite information exchange. The type of information exchange can depend on the receiver, sender, type of information, and the states of the sender and receiver. The specification of the type of information exchange for each subject is called the synchronisation characteristics of the subject.

A subject can accept information directly or from its information store and can react to this information. The reaction can be to invoke operations, to wait for other information, or to send information to other subjects. The specification of the possible sequences in which these actions are executed by a subject is called characteristic behaviour.

Control Questions:

1. Which SAPP/PASS elements support incremental program development?
2. How does SAPP/PASS support evolutionary software development?
3. How does SAPP/PASS support operational-oriented software life cycles?
4. How does SAPP/PASS allow the combination of different software development cycles?
5. How does SAPP/PASS support the reuse of software?
6. How does SAPP/PASS allow the integration of existing software into a new designed system?
7. What are the differences between SA and PASS?
8. What are the main components of a PASS specification?
9. In which ways is it possible to integrate object-oriented methods into PASS specifications?
10. What is the basic WBS for SAPP/PASS-oriented software development projects?
11. Show the relationship between the structure of SAPP/PASS specifications and a related tool set.
12. What is the philosphy of subject/object-oriented program development?

Exercises:

1. Assess the SEE you use in your professional environment.
2. Compare your programs with the subject/object-oriented philosophy.

Literature

/ADBRCH82/   Adrion W. R., Branstad M. A., Cherniavsky J.C.: Validation, Verification, and Testing of Computer Software. ACM Computing Surveys, June 1982, also contained in Chow T. S. Software Quality Assurance. IEEE Computer Society, New York 1985

/AGRES86a/   Agresti W. W.: The Conventional Life Cycle Model: Its Evolution and Assumptions, in Agresti W. W. (Ed.) New Paradigms for Software Development. IEEE Computer Society Press, 1986

/AGRES86b/   Agresti W. W.: What are the new Paradigms?, in Agresti W. W. (Ed.) New Paradigms for Software Development. IEEE Computer Society Press, 1986

/AGRES86c/   Agresti W. W.: Framework for a Flexible Development Process, in Agresti W. W. (Ed.) New Paradigms for Software Development. IEEE Computer Society Press, 1986

/AHUL77/   Aho A., Ullmann J.: Principles of Compiler Design. Addison Wesely, 1977

/ALF77/   Alford M. W.: A Requirements Engineering Methodology for Real Time Processing Requirements. IEEE Trans. Software Engineering, January 1977

/ALF85a/   Alford M. W.: SREM at the Age of Eight: The Distributed Computing Design System. IEEE Computer, April 1985

/ALF85b/   Alford M. W. et. al (Ed.): Distributed Systems, Methods and Tools for Specification. Lecture Notes in Computer Science 190, Springer Verlag, Heidelberg 1985

/AND89/   Andres C.: Ein graphentheoretischer Ansatz zur rechengestützten parallelen Komposition von Prozessen für verteilte Echtzeitsysteme. Doctoral Thesis at the University of Erlangen, 1989

/ANSC83/   Andrews G. R., Schneider F. B.: Concepts and Notations for Concurrent Programming. ACM Computing Surveys, March 1983

/AVIZ76/   Avizienis A.: Fault Tolerant Systems. IEEE Transactions on Computing, December 1976

/AXFO89/   Axford T.: Concurrent Programming. Wiley, Series in Parallel Computing, Chichester 1989

/BABA85/   Baacke C., Barthels V.: Steuerung eines Glasformungsprozesses mit Hilfe eines Mikrorechnes M68000. Internal Report of the Computing Center of the University of Erlangen, 1985

/BACC83/   Balzer R., Cheatham T. E. , Green, C.: Software Technology in the 90's : Using a new Paradigm. IEEE Computer, November 1983

/BAKK86/   de Bakker, J. W. et. al (Ed.): Current Trends in Concurrency. Lecture Notes in Computer Science 224, Springer Verlag, Heidelberg 1986

/BALZ81/   Balzer R.: Transformational Implementation: An Example. IEEE Transactions on Software Engineering, January 1981

/BALZ82/   Balzert H.: Die Entwicklung von Software Systemen. Bibliographisches Institut, Mannheim 1982

/BALZ89/   Balzert H. (Ed.): CASE Systeme und Werkzeuge. Bibliographisches Institut, Mannheim 1989

/BARR86/   Barringer H.: A Survey of Verification Techniques for Parallel Programs. Lecture Notes in Computer Sience No. 191, Springer Verlag, Heidelberg 1986

/BARS87/   Barstow D.: Artificial Intelligence and Software Engineering. Proc. of the 9th International Conference on Software Engineering, Montery 1987. IEEE Computer Society Press, Washington 1987

/BATU75/   Basili V. R., Turner A. J.: Iterative Enhancement: A Practical Technique for SoftwarDevelopment. IEEE Transactions on Software Engineering, December 1975

/BAUER82/   Bauer F. L.: From Specifications to Machine Code: Program Construction from Formal Reasoning. IEEE, Proceedings of the 6th International Conference on Software Engineering 1982, pp 84-91
also contained in
Agresti W. W. (Ed.): New Paradigms for Software Development. IEEE Computer Society Press, 1986

/BAWE88/   Barth G., Welsch C.: Objektorientierte Programmierung. Informationstechnik it, June 1988

/BENA85/   Bennis W., Nanus B.: Leaders. Harper & Row, New York 1985

/BENN87/   Bennett J. K.: The Design and Implementation of Distributed Smalltalk. OOPSLA'87 Proceedings Special Issue of SIGPLAN Notices, October 1987

/BERG81/   Bergland G. D.: A Guided Tour of Program Design Methodologies Computer, October 1981
Also contained in
Oman P. W., Lewis T. G. (Ed): Milestones in Software Engineering. IEEE Press, Washington 1990

/BESO85/   Besold R.: Ein universelles Ueberwachungs- und Automatisierungssystem fuer kern- und teilchenphysikalische Experimente. (A General Purpose Control System for Nuclear Experiments). Doctoral Thesis, University of Erlangen, 1985

/BHJL86/   Black A., Hutchinson N., Jul E., Levy H.: Object Structure in the Emerald System. OOPSALA '87 Proceedings. Special Issue of SIGPLAN Notices, November 1986

/BHJLC87/   Black A., Hutchinson N., Jul E., Levy H., Carter L.: Didtribution and Abstract Types in Emerald. IEEE Transactions on Software Engineering, January 1984

/BHLP91/   Bolognesi T., Hagsand O., Latella D., Pehrson B.: The Definition of Graphical G-LOTOS Editor Using the Meta-Tool LOGGIE. Computer Networks and ISDN Systems 22, North Holland 1991

/BOCH83/   Bochmann G. von Concepts for Distributed Systems Design. Springer Verlag, Heidelberg 1983

/BOEHM76/   Boehm B. W.: Software Engineering. IEEE Transactions on Computers, December 1976

/BOEHM84/   Boehm B. W.: Software Engineering Economics. IEEE Transactions on Software Engineering, January 1984
also contained in /THAY88/

/BOEHM88/   Boehm B. W.: A Spiral Model of Software Development and Enhancement. IEEE Computer, May 1988

/BOOCH86/   Booch G.: Object Oriented Development. IEEE Transactions on Software Engineering, February 1986

/BOOCH91/   Booch G.: Object Oriented Design. The Benjamin/Cummings Publishing Company Inc., Redwood City, 1991

/BRO75/   Brooks F. P.: The Mythical Man-Month. Addison-Wesley, 1975

/BRO87/   Brooks F. P.: No Silver Bullet, Essence and Accidents of Software Engineering. IEEE Computer, April 1987

/BSTA88/   Bal H.E. , Steiner J. G., Tannenbaum A.S.: Programming Languages for Distributed Systems. ACM Computing Surveys, 1988

/BUCK79/   Buckley F.: A Standard for Software Quality Assurance. IEEE Computer, April 1979
also contained in

Chow T. S.: Software Quality Assurance. IEEE Computer Society, New York 1985

/CAHA74/ Campbell R. H., Habermann A. H.: The Specification of Process Synchronisation by Path Expressions. Lecture Notes in Computer Sience Vol 16, Springer Verlag, Berlin 1974

/CAM86/ Cameron J. R.: An Overview of JSD. IEEE Transactions of Software Engineering, February 1986

/CAM89/ Cameron J. R.: JSP & JSD: The Jackson Approach to Software Development. IEEE Computer Society Press, Washington 1989

/CAMA83/ Carey T. T. , Mason R. E. A.: Information System Prototyping: Techniques, Tools and Methodologies INFOR, August 1983
also contained in
Agresti W. W. (Ed.): New Paradigms for Software Development. IEEE Computer Society Press, 1986

/CAMC78/ Cavano J. P., McCall J. A.: A Framework for the Measurement of Software Quality. The Proceedings of the ACM Software Quality Assurance Workshop, November 1978
also contained in
Chow T. S.: Software Quality Assurance. IEEE Computer Society, New York 1985

/CHAR86/ Charette R. N.: Software Engineering Environments. McGraw Hill, New York 1986

/CHEN76/ Chen P. P.: The Entity Relationship Model – Towards a Unifying View of Data ACM Transactions on Data Base Systems, March 1976

/CHIK89/ Chikofski E. J.: Computer Aided Software Engineering (CASE). IEEE Computer Society Press, New York 1989

/CHNO92/ Chen M., Norman R. J.: A Framework for Integrated CASE. IEEE Software, March 1992

/CHYU91/ Cheung T.-Y., Yucheng Y.: An Executor for Graphical LOTOS, in Quemada J et al. (Ed.), Formal Description Techniques III.Elsevier Sience Publishers (North Holland, Amsterdam 1991

/CLLM89/ Chari V., Lenotre J.-F., Lumbroso L., Mariani E.: An Estelle Simulator/Debugger Tool (edb), in M. Diaz et. al. (Ed.), The formal description Technique Estelle Elsevier Science Publishers B.V., 1989

/CLM89/ Chari V., Lenotre J.-F., Mariani E.: The Estelle Translater, in M. Diaz et.al. (Ed.), The formal description Technique Estelle. Elsevier Science Publishers B.V., 1989

/CLME81/ Clocksin W. F., Mellish C. S.: Programming in PROLOG. Springer Verlag, Heidelberg 1981

/CODO88/ Couloris G. F. , Dollimore J.: Distributed Systems, Concepts and Design. Addison-Wesley, Workingham, England 1988

/CONN85/ Connor D.: Information System Specification & Design Road Map. Prentice-Hall International Editions, Englewood Cliffs 1985

/CORI85/ Cori K. A.: Fundamentals of Master Scheduling for the Project Manager. Project Management Journal, June 1985
also contained in /THAY88/

/DALY79/ Daly E. B.: Organizing for Successful Software Development Datamation, December 1979
also contained in /THAY88/

/DEFH87/ Dart S. A., Ellison R. J., Feiler P.H., Habermann A. N.: Software development Environments IEEE Computer, November 1987

/DEHO66/ Dennis J. B., van Horn E. C.: Programming Semantics for Multiprogrammed Computations. Communication of the ACM, March 1966

/DELI87/ DeMarco T., Lister T.: Peopleware: Productive Projects and Teams. Dorset House Publishing, New York 1979

/DEMAR79/   DeMarco T.: Structured Analysis and System Specification. Prentice Hall, Englewood Cliffs, 1979

/DEMAR82/   DeMarco T.: Controlling Software Projects – Management, Measurement & Estimation. Yourdan/Prentice Hall, Englewood Cliffs, 1979

/DEUT88/   Deutsch M. S.: Software Quality Engineering. Prentice Hall, Englewood Cliffs 1988

/DIGIT90/   Digital Equipment Corporation. The Digital Cohesion Environment for CASE. Maynard, 1990

/DIGIT91/   Digital Equipment Corporation. The NAS Handbook. Maynard, 1990

/DIJK65/   Dijkstra E.W.: Solution of a Problem in Concurrent Programming. Communications of the ACM, September 1965

/DIJK68a/   Dijkstra E. W.: Cooperating Sequential Processes, in F. Genuys (Ed.) Programming Languages. Academic Press, New York 1968

/DIJK68b/   Dijkstra E. W.: GOTO Statement Considered Harmful, Communications of the ACM, March 1968

/DLSA78/   DeMillo R.A., Lipton R.J., Sayward F.G.: Hints on Test Data Selection: Help for the Practicing Programmer. IEEE Computer, April 1978
also contained in
Chow T. S.: Software Quality Assurance. IEEE Computer Society, New York 1985

/DROB86/   Drobnik O.: Softwaretechnologie für Kommunikationstechnik. Informationstechnik it, Heft 1, 1986

/DUNP91/   Dunphy E.: The UNIX Industry. QED Technical Publishing Group, Boston 1991

/EKEL91/   Ek A., Ellsberger J.: TA-2: A Prototype Analysing Dynamic SDL Properties, in Quemada J et al. (Ed.), Formal Description Techniques III. Elsevier Sience Publishers (North Holland, Amsterdam 1991

/ENGLEH88/   Engelbart D., Lehtman H.: Working Together. BYTE, December 1988

/ENSL78/   Enslow P. H.: What is a Distributed System. Computer, January 1978

/ESTELLE/   International Standard Organization, Information Processing Systems – Open System Interconnection- ESTELLE – AFormal Description Technique based on an extended state transition model. ISO Draft Proposal 9074

/EVD89/   Eijk P. H. van, Vissers C.A., Diaz M. (Ed.): The formal Description Technique LOTOS. North Holland, Amsterdam 1989

/FAIR78/   Fairly R.: Tutorial: Static Analysis and Dynamic Testing of Computer Software. IEEE Computer, April 1978
also contained in
Chow T. S.: Software Quality Assurance. IEEE Computer Society, New York 1985

/FAIR85/   Fairly R.: Software Engineering Concepts. McGraw-Hill, New York 1985

/FAPA88/   Falk S. R., Parnas D. L.: On Synchronisation in Hard-Real-Time Systems. Comm.ACM, March 1988

/FASCH91/   Farber M., Schütt T.: High Speed Protocol Implementations: An Experience with PASS. IEEE Workshop on the Archtecture and Implementation of High Performance Communication Subsystems, Tucson, February 17–19, 1992

/FEDER86/   Feder C.: Ein Interpretierer fuer PASS-Spezifikationen basierend auf einen Graphersetzungssystem. (An Interpreter for PASS Specifications based on an graph replacement System). Diplomarbeit at the University of Erlangen 1986

/FLCHEF87/   Fleischmann A., Chin S. T., Effelsberg W.: Specification and Implementation of an ISO Session Layer. IBM Systems Journal, No.3 1987

/FLHO83/   Fleischmann A., Holleczek P., Klebes G., Kummer, R.: Synchronisation und Kommunikation verteilter Automatisierungsprogramm. (Communication and Synchronisation in Distributed Automation Controll Programs). Angewandte Informatik (Applied Informatics), July 1983

/GASA79/   Gane C. , Sarson T.: Structured Systems Analysis: Tools and Techniques. Prentice Hall International, New York 1979

/GIDD84/   Giddings V. R.: Accomodating incertainty in Software Design. Communications of the ACM, May 1984

/GOEHN81/   Göhner P.: Ingenieurgerechte Spezifikation der Synchronisierung Paralleler Rechenprozesse. Doctoral Thesis, University of Stuttgart, W. Germany

/GOLD86/   Goldberg A. T.: Knowledge Based Programming: A Survey of Program Design and Construction Techniques. IEEE Transactions on Software Engineering, July 1986

/GOMA84/   Gomaa H.: A Software Design Method for Real-Time Systems. Communications of the ACM, September 1984

/GOMA89/   Gomaa H.: A Software Design Method for Distributed Real-Time Applications. The Journal for Systems and Software, September 1989

/GRCA85/   Gracia-Catalin R.: A Taxonomy of Current Isuues in Requirements Engineering. IEEE Computer, April 1985

/GREI89/   Greis H.: Performance Investigations for Communication. Protocool Implementations for Transputer Networks (in German). Master Thesis University of Karlsruhe, April 1989

/GRIES81/   Gries D.: The Science of Programming. Springer Verlag, Berlin 1981

/GUTT79/   Guttag J. V.: Notes on Type Abstraction. Proceedings of Conference on Specifications of reliable Software

/HAIL82/   Hailpern B. T.: Verifying Concurrent Processes Using Temporal Logic. Lecture Notes in Computer Science 129, Springer Verlag, Heidelberg 1982

/HANS73/   Brinch-Hansen P.: Operating System Principles. Prentice Hall, Englewood Cliffs 1973

/HANS78/   Brinch-Hansen P.: Distributed Processes: A Concurrent Programming Concept. Communications of the ACM, November 1978

/HAPI87/   Hatley D. J. , Pirbhai I. A.: Strategies for Real-Time System Specification. Dorset House Publishing, new York 1987

/HEIN88/   Hekmatpour S. , Ince D.: Software Prototyping Formal Methods and VDM. International Computer Series, Addison Wesley, Workingham, England, 1988

/HERG89/   Hergenröder G.: ALLOC – ein wissensbasierter Ansatz zur Lösung des Allokationsproblems von Tasks in verteilten Realzeitsystemen. (ALLOC – a knowledge based approach for solving task allocation problems for distributed Real-Time programs). Mitteilungsblatt des Regionalen Rechenzentrums Erlangen, 1989. Report of the computing Center of the University of Erlangen, Germany 1989

/HEW77/   Hewitt C. E.: Viewing Control Structures as Patterns of Passing Messages. Journal of Artificial Intellegence, Jun. 1977

/HIG79/   Higgins D. A.: Program Design and Construction. Prentice Hall, Englewood Cliffs 1979

/HILL90/   Hill R.: EDI and X.400. Technology Appraisals, Isleworth 1990

/HOARE74/   Hoare C. A. R.: Monitors: An Operating System Structuring Concept. Commun.ACM 17, 10 (October 1974)

/HOARE78/   Hoare C. A. R.: Communicating Sequential Processes. Commun.ACM 21, 8 (August 1978)

/HOARE85/   Hoare C. A. R.: Communicating Sequential Processes. Prentice/Hall International, New Jersey 1985

/ISO7498/   International Standard Organization, Information Processing Systems – Open Systems Interconnection-Basic Reference Model. ISO International Standard 7498

/ISO8326/   International Standard Organization, Information Processing Systems – Open Systems Interconnection- Basic Connection Oriented Session Service Definition ISO International Standard 8326

/ISO8327/   International Standard Organization, Information Processing Systems – Open Systems Interconnection- Basic Connection Oriented Protocol Specification. ISO International Standard 8327

/JACK75/   Jackson M.: Principles of Program Design. Academic Press, London 1975

/JON78   Jones T.C.: Measuring Programming Quality and Productivity. IBM Systems Journal, January 1978
also contained in
Chow T. S.: Software Quality Assurance. IEEE Computer Society, New York 1985

/JON79/   Jones C.: A survey of programming Design and Specification Techniques. IEEE Proceedings, Specifications of Reliable Software
Also contained in
Oman P. W., Lewis T. G. (Ed): Milestones in Software Engineering. IEEE Press, Washington 1990

/JON86/   Jones C.: Programming Productivity. McGraw-Hill, New York 1986

/JORA78/   Jonson O., Ramanathan J.: Recent Directions in Concurrent Programming Languages. IBM Research Report RC 8378, Yorktown Heights, 1978

/KEFR81/   Kerola P., Freeman P.: A Comparison of Life Cycles Models Proceedings of the 5nd International Conference of Software Engineering. San Diego: Institute of Electrical and Electronics Engineers 1981, IEEE Cat. No. 81CH1627-9

/KELL76/   Keller R. M.: Formal Verification of Parallel Programs. Comm. ACM 19,7 (July 1976)

/KERA82/   Keramidis S.: Eine Methode zur Spezifikation und korrekten Implementierung von asynchronen Systemen. Arbeitsberichte des IMMD, Univ. Erlangen 1982

/KRUMM89/   Krumm H.: Funktionelle Analyse von Kommunikationsprotokollen (Functionel Analysis of Communication Protocols). Habilitation Thesis, University of Karlsruhe, 1989

/LAMP83/   Lamport L.: Specifying Concurrent Program Modules. ACM Transactions on Programming Languages and Systems, Vol. 5 , No. 2 , April 1983

/LANTZ/   Lantz K. E.: The Prototyping Methodology. Prentice Hall, Englewood Cliffs, New Jersey

/LAUB84/   Lauber R. J.: Software for Industrial Process Control. IEEE Computer, February 1984

/LEH80/   Lehman M. M.: Programs, Life Cycles and Laws of Software Evolution. Proc. IEEE September 1980

/LEOM90/   Lewis T. G., Oman P. W.: The Challenge of Software Development. IEEE Software, November 1990

/LIBE86/   Liskov B. H., Berzins V.: An Appraisel of Program Specifications, in N. Gehani, A. D. McGettric (Ed.) Software Specification Techniques. Addison Wesley Publishing 1986

/LIEB87   Lieberman H.: Concurrent Object Oriented Programming in Act 1, contained in /YOTO87/

/LIE89/   Lieberknecht G.: Design and Implementation of a PASS Test Environment (in German) Master Thesis, Fachhochschule of Karlsruhe, April 1989

/LIHO89/   Liu L. C., Horowitz E.: A Formal Model for Software Project Mnagement. IEEE Transactions on Software Engineering, October 1989

/LINN86/   Linn R. J.: The Features and Facilities of ESTELLE, in M. Diaz (Ed.) Protocol Specification, Testing and Verification, V. North Holland Publishing, Amsterdam 1986

/LISKOV79/   Liskov B. , Herliby M. , Gilbert L.: Limitations of Synchronous Communication with Static Process Structure in Languages for Distributed Computing. MIT Programming Methodology Group Memo 41-1, 1985

/LISKOV85/   Liskov B.: The Argus Language and System, in M. W. Alford et. al. (Ed.), Distributed Systems. Lecture Notes in Computer Sience, No. 190. Springer Verlag, Heidelberg 1985

/LOTOS/   International Standard Organization, Information Processing Systems – Open Systems Interconnection- LOTOS - A Formal Description Technique based on the temporal ordering of observation behavior. ISO Draft Proposal 8807

/MABU87/   Marco A. , Buxton J.: The Craft of Software Engineering. Addison Wesley, International Computer Sience Series, Workingham, England 1987

/MAKRSL89/   Maggee J., Kramer J., Sloman M.: Constructing Distributed Systems in Conic. IEEE Transactions in Software Engineering, June 1989

/MAWO84/   Manna Z. , Wolker P.: Sythesis of Communicating Processes from Temporal Logic Specifications. ACM Transactions on Programming Languages and Systems, January 1984, Vol. 6 , No. 1

/MCCLU89a/   McClure C.: CASE is Software Automation. Prentice Hall, Englewood Cliffs, New Jersey, 1989

/MCCLU89b/   McClure C.: The CASE Experience. Byte, April 1989

/MCJA80/   McCracken , Jackson M. A.: A Minority Dissenting Position, in Cotterman W. W. (Ed.), Systems Analysis and Design - A Foundation for the 1980's
              also contained in
              Agresti W. W. (Ed.) New Paradigms for Software Development. IEEE Computer Society Press, 1986

/MILN80/   Milner R.: A Calculus of Communicating Systems. Lecture Notes in Computer Science 92, Springer Verlag, Heidelberg 1980

/MMNR90/   Mercurio V.J., Meyers B.F., Nisbet A.M., Radin G.: AD/Cycle Strategy and Architecture. IBM Systems Journal, No. 2, 1990

/MOR82/   Moret, B.: Decision Trees and Diagrams. ACM Computing Surveys, December 1982

/MSKFH89/   Mühlhäuser M., Schill A., Kienhöfer J., Frank H., Heuser L.: A Software Engineering Environment for Distributed Applications, in L. Mezzalira, S. Winter (Ed.), Design Tools for the 90's. North Holland Publishing Company, Amsterdam 1989

/MUEHL86/   Mühlhäuser M.: Entwicklungsunterstützung für anwendungsorientierte verteilte Programme. Doctoral Thesis, University of Karlsruhe 1986

/MUSC92/   Mühlhäuser M., Schill A.: Software Engineering für verteilte Anwendungen. Springer Verlag, Heidelberg 1992

/NAGL79/   Nagl M.: Graph-Grammatiken – Theorie, Anwendungen, Implementierung. (Graph Grammars – Theory, Applications, Implementations). Vieweg Verlag, Braunschweig, 1979

/NAUR69/   Naur P., Randell B. (Ed.): Software Engineering: A Report on a Conference sponsored by the NATO Science Committee, NATO 1969

/NAUR85/   Naur P.: Intuition in Software Development, in H. Ehrig et. al. (Ed.) Formal Methods and Software Development. Springer Verlag, Lecture notes in Computer Science No. 186, Heidelberg 1985

/NEHM84/   Nehmer J.: Systemarchitektur von Betriebssystemen. Informatik Spektrum, April 1984

/NEHM85/   Nehmer J.: Softwaretechnik für verteilte Systeme. Springer Verlag, Heidelberg 1985

/NEHM87/   Nehmer J.: Key Concepts of the INCAS Multicomputer Project. IEEE Transactions on Software Engineering, August 1987

/NEHM88a/   Nehmer J.: private Communication

/NEHM88b/   Nehmer J.: Entwurfskonzepte für verteilte Systeme – Eine kritische Bestandsaufnahme. GI Jahrestagung 1988, Informatik Fachberichte. Springer Verlag, Heidelberg 1988

/NHMWR87/   Nehmer J., Haban D., Mattern F., Wybranietz D., Rombach D.: Key Concepts of the INCAS Multicomputer Project. IEEE Transactions on Software Engineering, August 1987

/NIERS87/   Nierstrasz O. M.: Active Objects in Hyprid. OOPSLA'87 Proceedings. Special Issue of SIGPLAN Notices, October 1987

/NIST91/   National Institut of Standards and Technology. Reference Model for Framework
              of Software Engineering Environments. Draft Version 1.5, Gaitherburgh 1991

/NMMF87/   Neumeier-Mackert I., Mackert L., Fleischmann A.: A Knowledge-based Protocol
              Engineering Environment Technical Report of the IBM European Networking
              Center, No 43.8704, 1987

/OMLE90/   Oman P. W., Lewis T. G. (Ed): Milestones in Software Engineering. IEEE Press,
              Washington 1990

/ORR77/   Orr K. T.: Structured Systems Development. Yourdan Press, New York 1977

/ORR81/   Orr K. T.: Structured Requirements Definition. Ken Orr & Associates, Inc.
              Topeka, KS, 1981

/OSF92/   Open Systems Foundation. OSF DCE 1.0, Introduction to DCE. Cambridge USA,
              March 1992

/PACL85/   Parnas D. L., Clements P. C.: A Rational Design Process: How and Why to Fake it
              in H. Ehrig et. al. (Ed.) Formal Methods and Software Development. Springer
              Verlag, Lecture Notes in Computer Science No. 186, Heidelberg, 1985

/PAMO86/   Partsch H., Möller B.: Konstruktion korrekter Programme durch Transformation
              Informatik Spektrum, August 1987

/PARN72/   Parnas D. L.: On the Criteria to be used in Decomposing Systems into Modules.
              Communications of the ACM, December 1972

/PAST83/   Partsch H., Steinbrüggen R.: Program Transformation Systems. ACM Computing
              Surveys, Septemebr 1983
              also contained in
              Agresti W. W. (Ed.) New Paradigms for Software Development. IEEE Computer
              Society Press, 1986

/PEARL81/   Programmiersprache PEARL (Programming Language PEARL). DIN 66253,
              1981 (DIN = German Standard Organization)

/PETE78/   Peters L. J., Tripp L. L.: A Model of Software Engineering. Proceedings of the 3nd
              International Conference of Software Engineering. New York: Institute of Electri-
              cal and Electronics Engineers 1978, IEEE Cat. No. 78CH1317-7C

/PETE80/   Peters P. L.: Software Representation and Composition Techiques. Proceedings of
              the IEEE, Vol 68, No. 9, September 1980

/PETE81/   Peterson J.-L.: Petri Net Theory and Modelling Systems. Prentice Hall, Engle-
              wood Cliffs 1981

/PETE82/   Peters T. J., Waterman R. H.: In Search of Excellence. Warner Books, New York
              1982

/PETE85/   Peters T. J., Austin N.: In Search of Excellence. Warner Books, New York 1985

/PETE87/   Peters T. J.: Thriving on Chaos. Alfred A. Knopf Inc., 1987

/PETRI62/   Petri C. A.: Kommunikation mit Automaten. Schriften des Instituts für instru-
              mentelle Mathematik, Bonn 1962

/PIAT81/   Piatkowski F.: A Engineering Discipline for Distributed Protocol Systems. Proto-
              col Testing – Towards Proof an INW6/NPL Workshop. National Physical Labora-
              tory, Teddington, U.K., 1981

/PRESS87/   Pressman R. S.: Software Engineering, A Practitioner's Approach. McGraw-Hill
              Book Company, New York 1987

/QMV91/   Quemada J., Manas J., Vazquez E. (Ed.), Formal Description Techniques III.
              Elsevier Sience Publishers (North Holland), Amsterdam 1991

/RALETR78/   Randell B., Lee P. A. , Treleaven P. C.: Reliability Issues in Computing System
              Design. ACM Computing Surveys, June 1978

/RAMA86/   Ramamoorthy C. V., Garg V.,Prakash A.: Programming in the Large. IEEE Trans-
              actions on Software Engineering, July 1986

/RATT90/   Rattray C. (Ed.): Specification and Verification of Concurrent Systems. Work-
              shops in Computing, Springer Verlag, Heidelberg 1990

/REIS82/   Reisig W.: Petrinetze, Eine Einführung. Springer Verlag, Berlin 1982

/RICH83/   Rich E.: Artificial Intelligence. McGraw Hill Series in Artificial Intelligence, New
              York 1983

/RICL89/   Richard J.-L., Claes T.: A Generator of C-Code for Estelle, in M. Diaz et.al. (Ed.), The formal description Technique Estelle. Elsevier Science Publishers B.V., 1989

/ROBS81/   Robson D.: Object-Oriented Software Systems. BYTE, August 1981

/ROGE86/   Rogers B.: The IBM Way. Harper & Row, New York 1986

/ROSS77/   Ross D., Schoman K.: Structured Analysis for Requirements Definition. IEEE Transactions on Software Engineering, January 1977

/ROYCE70/   Royce W., W.: Managing the Development of Large Software Systems: Concepts and Techniques. Proceedings WESCON, August 1970
             also contained in /THAY88/

/RUDIN86/   Rudin H.: Tools for Protocols Driven by Formal Specifications, in Kunig et. al. (Ed.) Embedded Systems. Lecture Notes in Computer Sience No. 284. Springer Verlag, Heidelberg 1986

/SCAN86/   Schneider F. B., Andrews G. R.: Concepts of Concurrent Programming, in J.W. de Bakker et. al. (Ed.) Current Trends in Concurrency. Lecture Notes in Computer Sience No. 224, Springer Verlag, Heidelberg 1986

/SCHA83/   Scharer L.: The Prototyping ALternative. ITT Programming, Vol. 1, No. 1, 1983
             also contained in
             Agresti W. W. (Ed.) New Paradigms for Software Development. IEEE Computer Society Press, 1986

/SCHILL90/   Schill A.: Distributed Application Development: Problems and Solutions. Proceedings, International Networks and Data Communications. Lillehammer, Norway, March 1990

/SCHILL93/   Schill A.: DCE Das OSF Distributed Computing Environment. Springer Verlag, Heidelberg 1993

/SCHN88/   Schneider H. J.: Objektorientierte Strukturierung verteilter Software und statische Typprüfung. Proceedings Prozeßrechensysteme 88, Stuttgart 1988

/SCME82/   Schwartz R. L., Meliar-Smith P. M.: From State Machines to Temporal Logic: Specification Methods for Protocol Standards, in C. Sunshine (Ed.) Protocol Specification, Testing and Verification II. North Holland Publishing, Amsterdam 1982

/SDL/   SDL-Functional Specification and Description Language. CCITT Red Books Volume VI - Fascicle VI.10 and VI.11, 1984

/SDL91/   SDL Bibliography. SDL Newsletter No. 15, November 1991

/SGHM90/   Schill A., Gerteis W., Heuser L., Mühlhäuser M.: DOCASE: An Object Oriented Design Language and Environment for Distributed Application Development. Internal Report, University of Karlsruhe 1990

/SHM89/   Schill A., Heuser L., Mühlhäuser M.: Using the Object Oriented Paradigm for Distributed Application Development. in P.J. Kühn (Ed.), Kommunikation in verteilten Systemen, Informatik Fachberichte, Springer Verlag, Heidelberg 1989

/SHWA89/   Shatz S. M., Wang J-P.: Distributed Software Engineering. IEEE Press, Washington 1989

/SIBL90/   Sidhu D .P., Blumer T. P.: Semi-automatic Implementation of OSI Protocols. Computer Networks and ISDN Systems, January 1990

/SIST91/   Sijelmassi R., Strausser B.: NIST Integrated Tool Set for Estelle, in Quemada J et al. (Ed.), Formal Description Techniques III. Elsevier Sience Publishers, North Holland, Amsterdam 1991

/SLKR87/   Sloman M., Kramer J.: Distributed Systems and Computer Networks. Prentice Hall International, Englewood Cliffs 1987

/SMITH91/   Smith M. F.: Software Prototyping. McGraw-Hill, London 1991

/SSCO89/   Saqui-Sannes P. de, Courtiat J.-P.: ESTIM: The Estelle Simulator Prototype of the Esprit-Sedos Project, in Turner K. (Ed.), Formal Description Techniques, North Holland, Amsterdam 1989

/SSR85/   Scheffer P. A., Stone A. H., Rzepka W. E.: A Case Study of SREM. IEEE Computer, April 1985

/STOTT82/	Stotts P. P. Jr.: A Comparative Survey of Concurrent Programming Languages. SIGPLAN, Vol. 17, No. 10, October 1982
/SWBA82/	Swartout W. , Balzer R.: On the Inevitable Intertwinning of Specification and Implementation. Communications of the ACM, July 1982
/TAST82/	Taylor T. , Standish T. A.: Initial Thoughts on Rapid Prototyping Techniques. ACM, SIGSOFT Software Engineering Notes, December 1982
	also contained in
	Agresti W. W. (Ed.) New Paradigms for Software Development. IEEE Computer Society Press, 1986
/TAUS80/	Tausworthe R. C.: The Work Breakdown Structure in Software Project Management. The Journal of Systems and Software, Vol. 1, 1980, pages 181-186
	also contained in /THAY88/
/THAY88/	Thayer R. H. (Ed.): Software Engineering Project Management. IEEE Computer Society Press, New York 1988
/THDO90/	Thayer R.H., Dorfman M. (Ed.): System and Software Requirements Engineering. IEEE Computer Society Press, Washington 1990
/TISCH89/	Tischer J.: Design and Implementation of a PASS Runtime Environment (in German). Master Thesis, Fachhochschule of Karlsruhe, April 1989
/TSMLA90/	Tanatwy A., Schütt T., Meleis H., LaMaire R., Auerbach R.: High Performance Protocol Implementations: LLC Case Study Proceedings, Second IFIP WG6.1/ WG6.4 International Workshop on Protocols for High-Speed Networks, Palo Alto, November 1990
/TURN89/	Turner K. (Ed.): Formal Description Techniques. Elsevier Sience Publishers (North Holland), Amsterdam 1989
/URB87/	Urbschad K.: Vergleich zweier Implementierungstechniken von OSI Kommunikationsprotokollen (Comparison of two Implementation Techniques of OSI Communication Protocols). Diplomarbeit at the Fachhochschule fuer Technik, Mannheim, 1987
/WALK79/	Walker M.G.: Auditing Software Development Projects: A Control Mechanism for the Digital Systems Development Methodology Proceedings COMPCON, Spring 1978
	also contained in
	Chow T . S.: Software Quality Assurance. IEEE Computer Society, New York 1985
/WAME85/	Ward P. T., Mellor: Structured Development for Real-Time Systems. Prentice Hall, Englewood Cliffs 1985
/WAR74/	Warrier J. P.: Logical Construction of Programs. Van Nostrad Reinhold, 1974
/WAR81/	Warrier J. P.: Logical Construction of Systems. Van Nostrad Reinhold, 1981
/WARD84/	Ward P. T.: Systems Development without Pain - A User's Guide to Modelling Organisational Patterns. Yourdan/Prentice Hall, Englewood Cliffs 1984
/WASS90/	Wasserman A.I.:Tool Integration in Software Engineering Environments in Software Engineering Environments, Eds. Fred Long et. al. Springer Verlag, Berlin 1990
/WEG84/	Wegner P.: Capital Intensive Software Technology, Part 2: Programming in the Large. IEEE Software, July 1984
/WEG87/	Wegner P.: Dimensions of Object Based Language Design. OOPSALA '87 proceedings, ACM 1987
/WEIN71/	Weinberg G. M.: The Psychology of Computer Programming. Van Nostrad Reinhold, New York 1971
/WEKE89/	Weitzel J. R. , Kerschberg L.: Developing Knowledge Based Systems: Reorganizing the System Developing Life cycle. Communication of The ACM, April 1989
/WESE80/	Wesley W. C. , Holloway L. J. , Lan M-T. , Efe K.: Task Allocation in Distributed Data Processing. IEEE Computer, November 1980
/WIRTH71/	Wirth N.: Program Development by Stepwise Refinement. Communications of the ACM, December 1972

/YATS86/   Yau S. S., Tsai J. J.-P.: A Survey of Software Design Techniques. IEEE Transactions on Software Engineering, June 1986

/YOCO79/   Yourdan E., Constantine L. L.: Structured Design: Fundamentals of a Discipline of Computer Programs and System Design. Prentice Hall Inc, Englewood Cliffs, 1979

/YOTO87/   Yonezawa A., Tokoro M. (Ed.): Object-Oriented Concurrent Programming. The MIT Press, Cambridge, Massachusetts 1987

/YOU78/   Yourdan E.: Tructured Walkthroughs. Yourdan Press 1978

/ZAVE81/   Zave P., Yeh R. T.: Executable Requirements for Embedded Systems Proceedings of the 5nd International Conference of Software Engineering San Diego: Institute of Electrical and Electronics Engineers 1981,

/ZAVE82/   Zave P.: An Operational Approach to Requirements Specifications for Embedded Systems. IEEE Transactions on Software Engineering, May 1982

/ZAVE84/   Zave P.: The Operational Versus the Conventional Approach To Software Development. Communications of ACM, February 1984

/ZAVE90/   Zave P.: A Comparison of the Major Approaches of Software Specification and Design
            contained in
            Thayer R. H. , Dorfman M (Ed.): System and Software Requirements Engineering. IEEE Computer Society Press, Washington 1990

/ZILLI87/   Zilli M. V. (Ed.): Mathematical Models for the Semantics of Parallelism. Lecture Notes in Computer Sience, No. 280. Springer Verlag, Heidelberg 1987

/ZOHO88/   Zobel D., Hogenkamp H.: Konzepte der Parallelen Programmierung. Teubner Verlag, Stuttgart 1988

Index